THE KINGDOM IN THE SUN

1130–1194

JOHN JULIUS NORWICH

ff

faber and faber

This edition first published in 2010
by Faber and Faber Ltd
Bloomsbury House, 74–77 Great Russell Street
London WC1B 3DA

Printed by CPI Antony Rowe, Eastbourne

The right of John Julius Norwich to be identified as author of this work
has been asserted in accordance with Section 77 of the
Copyright, Designs and Patents Act 1988

A CIP record for this book is available from the British Library

ISBN 978–0–571–26044–7

For my mother

CONTENTS

CONTENTS

LIST OF ILLUSTRATIONS

ix

LIST OF ILLUSTRATIONS

Acknowledgements: J. Allan Cash, 20, 25. Foto-Marburg, 21 (both).
Burgerbibliothek, Berne, 27, 28, 29, 32. Italian State Tourist Office,
16, 30. Kitzinger, *I Mosaici di Monreale*, 23. Mansell Collection, 2, 5,
6, 7, 8, 9, 10, 11, 12, 18, 19, 22, 24. H. M. Schwarz, *La Sicilia*
(Nuova Italia), 14, 17, 31. C. A. Willemsen and D. Odenthal, *Apulia*,
3, 4. Unacknowledged photographs are the author's own.

Genealogical trees

Maps

The Maps and Genealogical trees are drawn by John Messenger

In Sicily one might find, all within a few miles of each other, the castle of some newly-created baron, an Arab village, an ancient Greek or Roman city and a recent Lombard colony; in one and the same town, together with the native population, there might be one quarter of Saracens or Jews, another of Franks, Amalfitans or Pisans; and among all these various peoples, there would reign that peaceful tranquillity which is born of mutual respect. . . . The bells of a new church, the chanting of the monks in a new abbey, would mingle with the cry of the *muezzin* from the minaret, calling the faithful to prayer. Here was the Latin Mass, modified according to the Gallican liturgy; here, the rites and ceremonies of the Greeks; here, the rules and disciplines of the Mosaic Law. The streets, squares and markets revealed a marvellous variety of costume; the turbans of the orientals, the white robes of the Arabs, the iron mail of the Norman knights; differences of habits, inclinations, celebrations, practices, appearances: infinite and continuous contrasts, which yet came together in harmony.

I. LA LUMIA,
History of Sicily under William the Good, 1867

INTRODUCTION

JUST over sixty years ago, in the preface to his own history of the Norman Kingdom of Sicily, M. Ferdinand Chalandon—a writer, heaven knows, not normally given to excessive dramatisation—noted that an unhappy fate seemed to hang over all would-be historians who tackled the subject; naming no less than three who, as he delicately put it, had 'prematurely disappeared' before their work was completed. In 1963, to a writer embarking on his first full-scale literary venture with an already distinct sensation of having bitten off more than he could chew, it was hardly an encouraging reminder; and there have been many moments in the past seven years when the end of my labours did indeed seem impossibly remote. It is therefore with more surprise than anything else that I now find that I have come to the end of my story.

This second volume of the Hauteville saga is self-contained, in the sense that it presumes the reader either not to have read its predecessor or, if he has, to have forgotten it. It does, however, take up the tale where *The Normans in the South* left off—at King Roger's coronation on Christmas Day 1130 in Palermo Cathedral—and carries it through to that other, blacker Christmas when the most coruscating crown of Europe was laid, by an English archbishop, on the head of one of the most loathsome of German Emperors. The sixty-four short years that separated those two events—less of a span than we have the right to expect for ourselves—constituted the whole lifetime of the Kingdom; they also provided the island with its golden age when, for the first and only time in history, the three great racial and religious traditions of the Mediterranean littoral fused under the southern sun and crystallised into that flashing, endlessly-faceted jewel that was the culture of Norman Sicily.

It is—or at least it should be—above all else the surviving monuments of this culture that draw us to Sicily today; monuments which miraculously translate the Hautevilles' political achievement into visual terms and in which Western European, Byzantine and Islamic styles and techniques effortlessly coalesce in settings of such magical

opulence that the beholder is left dazzled and incredulous. I have
therefore done my best to make this book not only an account of
people and events but also a guide to these monuments. The most
important of them I have described in detail, not in a separate and
indigestible chapter but at suitable points in the course of the narrative, so as to relate them as directly as possible to their founders or to
the circumstances surrounding their construction. The rest, graded
according to the time-honoured star system and furnished with page
references where appropriate, I have relegated to a list in the
appendix. This, I like to think, records every item of Norman work
worthy of the name still surviving in Sicily; it is certainly the most
comprehensive one yet to appear in this country.

But the history of Roger's Kingdom is something more than a
background to its works of art, however memorable they may be. It
is also one of the tragedies of Europe. Had it lasted, had it succeeded
in preserving those principles of toleration and understanding to
which it owed its existence, had it continued to serve as a focus of
intellectual enlightenment in a blinkered and bigoted age and as the
cultural and scientific clearing-house of three continents, then
ours at least might have been spared much of the suffering that
awaited it in the centuries to come, and Sicily might have been the
happiest, rather than the most ill-starred, of Mediterranean islands.
But it did not last; and this book has had to tell not only of how it
flourished, but also of its failure and its fall.

One further point, which I have already made in the introduction
to *The Normans in the South*, must I think be re-emphasised here: that
this is in no sense a work of scholarship. When I started it I knew no
more than anyone else about Sicily or the Middle Ages; and now
that I have finished I have no plans to write any more about either
subject again. Here, quite simply, is a piece of historical reportage,
written for the general public by one of their own number—one
whose sole qualifications for the task were curiosity and enthusiasm.
I hand over my typescript now with the same hope that I had when I
began: that these emotions may prove infectious, and that others
may grow, as I have grown, to love—and to lament—that sad,
superb, half-forgotten Kingdom, whose glory shone ever more
golden as the sun went down.

ACKNOWLEDGEMENTS

MUCH of Chapter 2 of this book was written during a fortnight in June, 1967, when the outbreak of war in the Middle East left me—largely through my own incompetence—stranded in the British Embassy, Khartoum; and I should like to thank Sir Robert and Lady Fowler for the kindness they showed, at an appallingly difficult time for themselves, to an uninvited, unexpected and virtually unknown guest. More thanks wing off to the Languedoc, where Xan and Daphne Fielding saw me so splendidly through Chapter 16. All the other chapters first saw the light in the London Library, of which I seem by now to have become part of the furniture. To Stanley Gillam, Douglas Matthews and every member of the staff—especially those who have to keep calling me down to the telephone—my gratitude is, as always, boundless.

Dr N. P. Brooks of St Salvator's College, St Andrew's, read the book in typescript, saved me several slips and made many invaluable suggestions. Most of these I have accepted; for the few that I have not, I am every bit as grateful. My friend John Parker of the University of York, besides making the substantial indirect contribution listed in the bibliography, also answered several queries about the Orthodox world and solved the Dimitritza problem on p. 342. I also owe a very special debt to Barbarina Daudy, whose astonishing gift of tongues, combined with equally remarkable powers of impromptu translation, saved weeks of my time but cost her untold hours of her own. I can only hope that they and the many others who have given me help and advice at all levels will not feel, on reading the results, that their labours have been altogether in vain.

J. J. N.

PART ONE

MORNING STORMS

I

THE COST OF THE CROWN

How many and what dreadful shocks and tumults resulted from that great clash when the son of Peter Leoni strove to rise up from the north against Innocent of blessed memory. . . . Did not his fall drag down with it a portion of the stars themselves?

John of Salisbury,
Policraticus, VIII, xxiii

On Christmas Day 1130 Roger de Hauteville was crowned King of Sicily in Palermo Cathedral. It was a hundred and thirteen years since the first bands of young Norman adventurers had ridden down into the Italian South—ostensibly in response to an appeal for help made by a Lombard nationalist in the Archangel Michael's cave on Monte Gargano, but effectively in search of fame and fortune; sixty-nine since the army of Roger's uncle Robert Guiscard, Duke of Apulia, had first landed on Sicilian soil. Undeniably, progress had been slow: during the same period William the Conqueror had mopped up England in a matter of weeks. But the country William had had to tackle was a well-ordered, centralised state already deeply penetrated by Norman influences, while Robert and his companions had been faced with anarchy—a South Italy torn apart by the conflicting claims of a Papacy, two Empires, three races and an ever-changing number of principalities, duchies and petty baronies; a Sicily that had languished for two centuries under Saracen domination, where the Greek Christian minority lay helpless as jealous local emirs endlessly squabbled for power.

Bit by bit, the chaos had been resolved. Roger's father Roger I, Great Count of Sicily, had spent the last thirty years of his life welding together the island and its people. With a perception rare for his time, he had seen from the outset that the only hope of success lay in integration. There would be no second-class Sicilians. Everyone, Norman or Italian, Lombard or Greek or Saracen, would have his part to play in the new state. Arabic and Greek, as well as Latin and Norman French, would be official languages. A Greek was appointed Emir of Palermo, a beautiful and resonant title which Roger saw no reason to change; another was given charge of the rapidly growing navy. Control of the exchequer and the mint was placed in the hands of the Saracens. Special Saracen brigades were established in the army, quickly earning a reputation for loyalty and discipline which they were to preserve for well over a century. The mosques remained as crowded as ever they had been, while Christian churches and monasteries, both Latin and Greek—several of them Roger's own foundations—sprang up in increasing numbers throughout the island.

Peace, as always, brought trade. The narrow straits, cleared at last of Saracen pirates, were once again safe for shipping; Palermo and Messina, Catania and Syracuse found themselves thriving *entrepôt* centres on the way to Constantinople and the new Crusader states of the Levant. The result was that by the time the Great Count died in 1101 he had transformed Sicily into a nation, heterogeneous in its races, religions and languages but united in loyalty to its Christian ruler and well on the way to becoming the most brilliant and prosperous state of the Mediterranean, if not of Europe.

Roger II had carried on the work. It suited him perfectly. Born in the South of an Italian mother, educated during his long minority by Greek and Arab tutors, he had grown up in the cosmopolitan atmosphere of tolerance and mutual respect created by his father, and he instinctively understood the complex system of checks and balances on which the internal stability of his country depended. There was little of the Norman knight about him. He possessed none of the warlike attributes which had brought glory to his father and his uncles, and in a single generation had made the name of an obscure Norman baron famous throughout the continent. But of all those Hauteville brothers only one, his father, had developed into a statesman. The rest—even Robert Guiscard himself, for all his genius —were fighters and men of action to the end. Roger II was different.

4

He disliked war and, apart from a couple of ill-starred expeditions during his youth in which he did not personally participate, had avoided it whenever possible. In appearance a southerner, in temperament an oriental, he had inherited from his Norman forbears nothing but their energy and their ambition, which he combined with a gift for diplomacy entirely his own; and it was these qualities, far more than his prowess on the battlefield, that had enabled him at last to acquire for himself the duchies of Apulia and Calabria and so to reunite the South in a single dominion for the first time since the Guiscard's day.

On a bridge crossing the Sabato river outside the walls of Benevento, soon after sunrise on 22 August 1128, Roger was invested by Pope Honorius II with his triple dukedom; and rose from his knees one of the most powerful of European rulers. He had only one more objective to attain before he could treat as an equal with his fellow-princes abroad and impose his authority on his new South Italian vassals. That objective was a crown; and two years later he got it. Pope Honorius's death early in 1130 led to a dispute over the papal succession, as a result of which two opposing candidates were simultaneously elected to the throne of St Peter. The story of these two elections has already been told[1] and there is no need to repeat it here in detail; suffice it to say that both were highly irregular and that now, as then, it is hard to decide which of the protagonists had the stronger claim. The first, however, who had taken the name of Innocent II, soon had virtually the whole continent behind him; his rival, Anacletus II Pierleoni, holding Rome but little else, turned—like so many of his predecessors in moments of crisis—to the Normans; and so the bargain was struck. Roger promised Anacletus his support; in return, and under papal suzerainty, he became King —of the third largest kingdom in Europe.

The arrangement was, in the short term, even more beneficial to Anacletus than it was to Roger. He should have been in a strong enough position. Uncanonical as his election was, it was no more so than that of his rival, and it certainly reflected the majority view in the Curia; in any free vote by all the cardinals Anacletus would have

---

[1] *The Normans in the South*, ch. 23, pp. 323–6.

been an easy victor. Even as things were, he had been acclaimed by twenty-one of them. His piety was generally admitted, his energy and ability unquestioned. Rome was still overwhelmingly loyal to him. Why was it, then, that only four months after the wretched Innocent had been forced to flee the city, Anacletus should in his turn have found the ground falling away beneath his feet?

He himself, perhaps, was partly to blame. Although he has undergone so much subsequent vilification that it is now almost impossible to form a clear picture of his character, it is beyond doubt that he was eaten by ambition and totally unscrupulous in the attainment of his ends. For all his reformist background, he had not hesitated to make use of his family's immense wealth to buy support among the aristocracy and people of Rome. There is no reason to believe that he was more corrupt than the majority of his colleagues, but rumours of his bribes had been assiduously spread by his enemies, who supported them with lurid accounts of his spoliation of Church property once Rome was in his power; and they found a ready audience among those in Northern Italy and abroad whose ears were not temporarily deafened by the jingle of Pierleoni gold. He was also handicapped— paradoxically enough—by his tenure of the Holy City, which held him down in the Lateran while Innocent progressed through Europe whipping up support. Yet these were all secondary considerations. There was one other factor which weighed the scales against Anacletus more heavily than all the others put together, and which was ultimately to prove the destruction of all his ambitions and his hopes. That factor was St Bernard of Clairvaux.

St Bernard was now forty years old and far and away the most powerful spiritual force in Europe. To an objective twentieth-century observer, safely out of range of that astonishing personal magnetism with which he effortlessly dominated all those with whom he came in contact, he is not an attractive figure. Tall and haggard, his features clouded by the constant pain that resulted from a lifetime of exaggerated physical austerities, he was consumed by a blazing religious zeal that left him no room for tolerance or moderation. His public life had begun in 1115 when the Abbot of Cîteaux, the Englishman Stephen Harding, had effectively released him from monastic discipline by sending him off to found a daughter

6

house at Clairvaux in Champagne; from that moment on, almost despite himself, his influence spread; and for the last twenty-five years of his life he was constantly on the move, preaching, persuading, arguing, debating, writing innumerable letters and compulsively plunging into the thick of every controversy in which he believed the basic principles of Christianity to be involved.

The papal schism was just such an issue. Bernard declared himself unhesitatingly for Innocent, and from that moment on the die was cast. His reasons, as always, were emotional. Cardinal Aimeri, the papal Chancellor whose intrigues on Innocent's behalf had been directly responsible for the whole dispute, was a close personal friend. Anacletus on the other hand was a product of Cluny, a monastery which Bernard detested on the grounds that it had betrayed its reformist ideals and had succumbed to those very temptations of wealth and worldliness that it had been founded to eradicate. Worse still, he was of Jewish antecedents; as Bernard was later to write to the Emperor Lothair, 'it is to the injury of Christ that the offspring of a Jew should have seized for himself the throne of St Peter'. The question of St Peter's own racial origins does not seem to have occurred to him.

When, in the late summer of 1130, King Louis VI, 'the Fat', of France summoned a Church council at Etampes to advise him which of the two candidates he should support, Bernard was ready to strike. Rightly sensing that any enquiry into the canonicity of the elections themselves might do his cause more harm than good, he stuck firmly to personalities and immediately embarked on a campaign of such vituperation that, in the minds of his audience, a senior and generally respected member of the Sacred College was transformed, almost overnight, into Antichrist. Though no actual record of the proceedings at Etampes has come down to us, one of the abbot's letters dating from this time probably reflects his words accurately enough.

The adherents of Anacletus, he writes, 'have made a covenant with death and a compact with hell. . . . The abomination of desolation is standing in the Holy Place, to gain possession of which he has set fire to the sanctuary of God. He persecutes Innocent and with him all who are innocent. Innocent has fled from his face, for *when the Lion* [a play on the name of Pierleoni] *roars, who shall not be afraid?* He has obeyed the words of the Lord: *When they persecute you in one city, flee unto another.* He has fled, and by the flight that he has endured after the example of the Apostles he has proved himself truly an apostle.'

Nowadays it is hard to believe that this sort of casuistical invective should have been taken seriously, far less that it should have had any lasting effect. Yet Bernard dominated Etampes, and it was thanks to him that the claims of Innocent II received official recognition in France. Henry I of England presented even less difficulty. He too had hesitated at first; Anacletus had been a papal legate at his court and was still a personal friend. Bernard, however, paid him a special visit to discuss the matter and Henry's resistance crumbled. In January 1131 he loaded Innocent with presents and did homage to him in Chartres Cathedral.

There remained the problem of the Empire. Lothair of Supplinburg, King of Germany, was in a difficult position. A strong, proud, stubborn man of sixty, he had begun life as a comparatively inconsequential noble; his election to the monarchy in 1125 had been largely due to the influence of the papal party working closely with Cardinal Aimeri. He should therefore have been favourably disposed towards Innocent. On the other hand Anacletus had recently sent extremely civil letters to himself, his queen, and to the clergy and laity of Germany and Saxony, informing them of how his brother cardinals 'with a wonderful and stupendous unanimity' had raised him to the supreme dignity of the pontificate; and he had followed up the letters by excommunicating Lothair's arch-enemy, Conrad of Hohenstaufen, who was also laying claim to the German throne. Lothair knew that his victory over Conrad could never be assured till he had had himself crowned Emperor in Rome; whatever the claims of the rival Popes he was unwilling to antagonise the one who actually had control of the Holy City. He decided to defer a decision as long as possible, and left Anacletus's letters unanswered.

But he soon found that he could not sit on the fence for long; the situation was developing too fast. Throughout western Europe the Innocentian faction was gathering momentum, and at Etampes it had received yet further impetus. Already by the autumn of 1130 it was strong enough to force Lothair's hand; a council of sixteen German bishops met at Würzburg in October and declared for Innocent; and

8

at the end of March 1131 the latter appeared with full retinue at
Liège to receive the King's homage.

Lothair could not go against his bishops; besides, it was plain that
Innocent was now the generally accepted Pope. Among all the European princes, there remained to Anacletus only one adherent—Roger
of Sicily. This fact alone would have been enough to lose him any
imperial support that he might otherwise have enjoyed; for by what
right could any Pope, legitimate or otherwise, crown some Norman
upstart King over territories which properly belonged to the
Empire? Since Roger's coronation there could have been no more
serious doubts in Lothair's mind: Innocent it would have to be. And
yet—perhaps as much to save his face as for any other reason—he
still tried to impose one condition: that the right of investiture of
bishops with ring and crozier, lost to the Empire nine years previously, were now restored to himself and his successors.

He had reckoned without the Abbot of Clairvaux. Bernard had
accompanied Innocent to Liège; this was just the sort of crisis in
which he excelled. Leaping from his seat, he subjected the King to a
merciless castigation before the entire assembly, calling upon him
then and there to renounce his pretensions and pay unconditional
homage to his rightful Pope. As always, his words—or, more probably, the force of his personality behind them—had their effect. This
was Lothair's first encounter with Bernard; it is unlikely that he had
ever been spoken to in such a way before. He was not lacking in
moral fibre, but this time he seems instinctively to have realised that
his position was no longer tenable. He gave in. Before the Council
broke up he had made his formal submission to Innocent, and had
reinforced it with an undertaking that the Pope probably found even
more valuable—to lead him, at the head of an imperial German army,
to Rome.

Already at the time of his coronation Roger must have been aware
of the pressures that were building up against Anacletus and—since
he had now irrevocably thrown in his lot with the anti-Pope—
against himself. He had taken a gamble and he knew it. His crown
might indeed have been a political necessity, but he had paid for it
by bringing down upon himself the wrath of half a continent. To

9

some extent this was unavoidable; the appearance of a new power, strong and ambitious, is rarely welcome on the international scene, and Roger had after all set himself up over a land still claimed by both the Western and the Byzantine Empires. It was unfortunate, nevertheless, that at this of all moments he should have had to antagonise not just the temporal forces of Europe but the spiritual as well—particularly when they were represented by such men as Bernard of Clairvaux and Abbot Peter of Cluny. In those first months after the election he would surely have been able to strike a similar bargain with either of the two papal pretenders; how much brighter the future would have looked if it had been Innocent, rather than Anacletus, who had appealed to him for help. As matters stood, Roger must have had an uncomfortable feeling that he had backed the wrong horse.

But Empire and Church, threatening as they might appear, were not the only enemies of the new king. Others, just as dangerous, were considerably nearer to hand. There were the barons, who had already constituted the principal obstacle to order and unity in the peninsula for over a hundred years—since before the Hautevilles were even thought of—and there were the towns. Only in Calabria, where no urban conglomerations of any size or importance existed, were the townsfolk content to accept royal domination. In Campania, the main centres may have been politically less evolved than their northern counterparts where the revival of trade, the loosening of the imperial grip and the beginnings of organised industry had already led to the establishment of those independent mercantile city-states, democratically governed, that were to be so characteristic a feature of later mediaeval Italy; but they too had been ruffled by the breeze of communal self-government, and the variety of forms which this had taken was a significant reflection of the prevailing disunity. In Apulia it was much the same. Bari had become a 'signory', ruled by the nobles of the city under a constitutional prince; Troia had a similar system under its bishop; Molfetta and Trani were communes. None had any wish, if they could avoid it, to be swept up into a disciplined and highly centralised monarchy. It was not long before they were able to make their attitude clear. During his whirlwind progress through the mainland duchies three

years before, Roger had occasionally allowed the towns through
which he passed, in return for their quick submission, to retain
control of their walls and citadels. At the time the arrangement had
served its purpose; but he could no longer afford such concessions.
From now on his authority, if it were to survive at all, would have to
be absolute. In February 1131, he formally requested the citizens of
Amalfi to relinquish the command of their own defences and hand
over to him the keys of their castle.

And they refused. Their argument that the King was riding rough-
shod over the terms on which they had surrendered in 1127 was true
but, so far as Roger was concerned, irrelevant. To him this was an
act of outright defiance, and one which could not be tolerated.
George of Antioch, the young Levantine Greek now on the threshold of his career as the most brilliant of Sicilian admirals, was
despatched with the fleet to blockade the city from the sea and seize
all Amalfitan ships in the roadstead; simultaneously another Greek,
the Emir John, approached with an army from the mountains
behind. Against such might the beleaguered citizens were powerless.
They held out for a time, but when they saw Capri and all the
neighbouring strong-points in Sicilian hands they could only
surrender.

Twenty-five miles away in Naples, Duke Sergius VII had followed
these developments with an anxiety which rapidly gave place to
alarm. At one moment he had considered sending help to Amalfi;
but when he heard the size of the Sicilian force he hastily changed his
mind. And so, as the Abbot of Telese smugly records, the city
'which, since Roman times, had hardly ever been conquered by the
sword now submitted to Roger on the strength of a mere report'.[1]
At last all the territories bestowed on him by Anacletus the previous
September were safely in the hands of the King.

Sailing back to Palermo that summer with three Neapolitan ships
as his escort, Roger was suddenly overtaken by a violent tempest.
After two days, during which it seemed that he and his crews must
perish, he made a vow; if they were spared, then at whatever point
they should be brought safely to shore he would build a cathedral to
Christ the Saviour. The next day—it was the feast of the Transfigura-

[1] Alex. Telese, II, xii.

tion—the wind dropped, and the vessels glided to a quiet anchorage in the bay of Cefalù, under the huge rock that still dominates much of the sea-coast east of Palermo. At one time this rock had sheltered a prosperous little town, the seat of a Greek bishop in Byzantine days; but it had declined in importance during the Saracen occupation and in 1063 it had been sacked and largely destroyed by the Great Count. Now it was for his son to make amends. Stepping ashore, he ordered a chapel to be built near the landing-place in honour of St George, whom he claimed to have seen in a vision during the height of the storm;[1] then he called for measuring-rods and set to work at once to survey a site for his cathedral.

So, at least, runs the legend. Its veracity has been argued by local scholars for a century and more. The sceptics point out that it is attested by none of the local chroniclers—not even by the Abbot of Telese who, besides being Roger's most adulatory biographer, had a particular *penchant* for stories of this kind. The romantics, on the other hand, adduce a contemporary document discovered in the 1880s among the Aragonese archives in Barcelona which, they claim, leaves no further room for doubt.[2] Their case is strong, but not conclusive. All we can know for certain is that on 14 September 1131 Cefalù was once more given a bishop of its own—a Latin one this time—and that already, by that date, the building had begun.

The face of Sicily is changing fast. She is, alas, no more immune than anywhere else in Europe to the attentions of land speculators and property developers, and many are the Arcadian landscapes now ruined by cement-factory or motel. But the island possesses two architectural masterpieces which, viewed from afar as well as in close-up, still have power to catch the breath. The first is the Greek temple of Segesta—the distant prospect of which, however, owes much of its impact to the beauty of the site; one is struck above all by the placing of the building on its eminence, the relation of that

[1] It was not the first time that St George had given moral support to the Normans in moments of crisis; readers of *The Normans in the South* may remember his appearance with Roger's father at the battle of Cerami in 1063.

[2] Rosario Salvo di Pietraganzili, 'La leggenda della tempesta e il voto del Re Ruggiero per la costruzione del Duomo di Cefalù'. In *La Sicilia Artistica ed Archeologica*, vol. II, Palermo, June–July 1888.

eminence to the surrounding hills, the grandeur, the isolation and the silence. This is not to detract from the temple itself; it is superb. But then so are nearly all Greek temples, and one—the fact must be faced—is apt to be very like another.

The second is Cefalù; and Cefalù is unique. Seen first, as it should be, from the coast road to the west,[1] its setting yields nothing to that of Segesta. A gently curving beach fringed with pine and prickly pear leads the eye along to a confusion of roofs, clustered at the far corner of the bay. Above and behind, but still very much a part of the town, rises Roger's cathedral, dominating the houses below as effortlessly as its sisters at Lincoln or Durham. Beyond the cathedral again is the rock that gave the place its name. The ancient Greek inhabitants seem to have seen it as a gigantic head, but it is really more like a pair of great, broad shoulders, four-square and massive, giving the town protection and reassurance. Not so imminent as to be menacing, not so distant as to be incidental, rock merges with town until the two become parts of a single grand design, each complementing the other. And the cathedral forms the link between them.

Such is the first impression. But it is only on arrival in the central piazza that the full splendour of Cefalù is revealed.[2] Now for the second time, but for different reasons, one is astonished by the perfection of its placing. The slope of the rock on which it is built sets it, a little obliquely, on a higher level than the square; it must thus be approached, like the Parthenon, at a slight angle and from below. And, as one approaches, so the realisation grows that here is not just the loveliest Norman exterior in Sicily, but one of the love-liest cathedrals in the world. The façade as we see it, with its twin towers—fraternal rather than identical—and the blind interlaced arcading that runs between them, dates from 1240—a century after Roger's time. By then, that fusion of eastern and western styles so typical of earlier Norman-Sicilian architecture had disappeared; and we are left with a perfect, sunny, southern romanesque, uncluttered but never austere.

So, at least, it seems on the outside. But the great miracle of Cefalù is yet to come. Climb the steps now, pass between two curiously

[1] Plate 1 (top).   [2] Plate 1 (bottom).

13

endearing baroque bishops in stone, cross the inner courtyard to the triple-arched portico—a fifteenth-century accretion, but none the worse for that—and enter the church itself. At first glance it may look a trifle disappointing: the effect of the slender arches—their shape an unmistakable reminder of the proximity of Islam—on the two rows of antique Roman columns is nearly lost under the dead-weight of seventeenth- and eighteenth-century decoration. But soon your eyes forget the sunshine they have left and readjust themselves to the cathedral twilight; they follow the march of the columns towards the sanctuary; from there they are led up, past the high altar and the saints, the angels and the archangels ranged above it; until at last, high in the conch of the great eastern apse, they are met by those of Christ.[1]

He is the Pantocrator, the Ruler of All. His right hand is raised to bless; in his left he carries a book, open at the text beginning 'I am the Light of the World'. It is written in Latin and Greek—and rightly so; for this mosaic, the glory of a Roman church, is itself of the purest Byzantine style and workmanship. Of the master who wrought it we know nothing, except that he was probably summoned by Roger himself from Constantinople and that he was unquestionably a genius. And at Cefalù he produced the most sublime representation of the Pantocrator—perhaps of Christ in any form—in all Christian art. Only one other, at Daphni near Athens, can be said even to rival it; but, near contemporaries though they are, the contrast between the two could hardly be greater. The Christ of Daphni is dark, heavy with menace; the Christ of Cefalù, for all his strength and majesty, has not forgotten that his mission is to redeem. There is nothing soft or syrupy about him; yet the sorrow in his eyes, the openness of his embrace, even the two stray locks of hair blown gently across his forehead, bespeak his mercy and compassion. Byzantine theologians used to insist that religious artists, in their representations of Jesus Christ, should seek to reflect the image of God. It was no small demand; but here, for once, the task has been triumphantly accomplished.

Beneath, his mother stands in prayer. Such is the splendour of her son, the proximity of the four archangels flanking her and the glare

[1] Plate 2.

14

from the window below, that she can easily pass unnoticed: a pity, since if she were standing in isolation amid the gold—as she does, for example, in the apse of Torcello—she too would be hailed as a masterpiece. (The archangels, be it noted, are dressed like Byzantine Emperors, even to the point of carrying the orb and *labarum* of the imperial office.) Further down still are the twelve apostles, less frontal and formalised than so often in eastern iconography, turning a little towards each other as if in conversation. Finally, on each side of the choir, stand two thrones of white marble, studded with Cosmatesque inlays, red and green and gold. One is the bishop's; the other was that of the King.

Here Roger must have sat during his last years, gazing up at the splendour that he had called into being; for an inscription beneath the window records that all these apse mosaics were completed by 1148, six years before his death.[1] He had always conceived of this cathedral as his own personal offering, and had even built himself a palace in the town from which to superintend the building operations.[2] And so it can have come as no surprise to his people when, in April 1145, he designated it as his burial-place, endowing it at the same time with two porphyry sarcophagi—one for his own remains and the other, as he put it, 'for the august memory of my name and the glory of the Church itself'. The sad story of how his wishes were disregarded, so that he now lies not in his own glorious foundation but amid the vacuous pomposities of Palermo Cathedral, will be told later in this book. After eight centuries it would be idle to hope for a change of heart by the authorities; it is hard, nevertheless, to visit Cefalù without putting up a quick, silent prayer that the greatest of the Sicilian kings may one day return to rest in the church which he loved, and where he belongs.

[1] The upper row of mosaics on the walls of the choir, with their inscriptions in Latin instead of Greek, are rather later—presumably the work of local artists in the following century. The same is true of the seraphim on the vaulting above.

[2] Traces of this palace still remain in the so-called *Osterio Magno,* on the corner of the Corso Ruggero and the Via G. Amendola.

2

REVOLT IN THE REGNO

Transalpinati sumus!

Pope Innocent II to the Archbishop of
Ravenna, 16 April 1132

ROGER had weathered one tempest—a fact to which his cathedral at
Cefalù was soon rising in superb testimony. But he knew, even
before the foundations had been laid, that another, greater storm was
gathering fast. Lothair was planning his promised march on Rome,
with the dual purpose of establishing Pope Innocent in the chair of
St Peter and of having himself crowned Emperor. With the Abbot of
Clairvaux, the weight of the western Church and the Kings of
England and France behind him, he would probably succeed; and
what then was to prevent his leading his army on into Sicilian
domains, to rid Europe once and for all of a schismatic Pope and his
only champion?

Once in the South, he would find no lack of support. Even more
than the towns, the vassals of South Italy had always resented their
Hauteville overlords. In the previous century they had been a constant thorn in the flesh of Robert Guiscard, distracting and delaying
him in all his operations. But for their perpetual insurrections he
would never have taken so long to conquer Sicily; he might even
have ended his life as Emperor in Constantinople. Yet Robert had at
least been able to exert some degree of authority; under the son and
grandson who had succeeded him as Dukes of Apulia the last shreds
of that authority were lost and the land had slipped back into chaos.
The vassals were free to do as they wished, to fight and to lay waste,
to rob and to pillage until, as the Abbot of Telese lamented, a peasant
could not even till his own fields in safety.

Cefalù: a distant prospect from the west

Cefalù Cathedral: the west front

Cefalù Cathedral: Christ Pantocrator

One thing only united them—a determination to preserve this freedom and to resist any attempt to reestablish a firm and centralised control. The fact that their suzerain was now no longer a Duke but a King had done nothing to reconcile them to the new order. To be sure, they had no love for the Empire either; but if they had to have a suzerain they liked him to be as far away as possible, and a grizzled old Emperor beyond the Alps was infinitely preferable to a determined and efficient young Hauteville on their doorstep. Almost as soon as the King had returned to Sicily in the summer of 1131 two of the worst of them, Tancred of Conversano and Prince Grimoald of Bari, had stirred up a minor insurrection in Apulia, and by Christmas the port of Brindisi was in their hands.

The King was in no particular hurry to bring them to heel. It was his custom to winter in Sicily whenever possible, and Cefalù was doubtless occupying much of his attention. Besides, he loved his wife and family. Queen Elvira, the daughter of Alfonso VI of Castile, had been married to him for fourteen years. We know sadly little about her except that the marriage was a happy one and that she bore her husband seven children, including the four stalwart sons on whom, during his later years, he was so much to rely. The two eldest of these boys, Roger and Tancred, had made one ceremonial appearance in Italy at Melfi in 1129, when they and their father had received the grudging fealty of the Apulian and Calabrian nobles; but for the most part mother and children remained in Sicily, where during recent summers Roger had had little chance of seeing them.

By March 1132, however, he could no longer delay his return to the mainland. It was not only Apulian rebels who claimed his attention; a graver problem was posed by Anacletus, who met him at Salerno to discuss plans for the future. The anti-Pope was growing worried: in preparation for the imperial coming, his rival Innocent had already appeared in North Italy. There was still no immediate danger; so far as anybody knew, Lothair's army had not yet begun to march. But Rome was already alive with rumours and these, fostered by Anacletus's old enemies the Frangipani, were having an unsettling effect on the populace. To make matters worse, the moon —according to Falco, the chronicler of Benevento—had suddenly

lost its splendour and turned the colour of blood; no one could call
that a good sign. What was needed, Anacletus argued, was a show of
strength—a reminder to the Romans that he was still master in their
city, and that the King of Sicily was behind him. Roger took the
point; two of his leading vassals, Prince Robert of Capua and his
own brother-in-law Rainulf, Count of Alife, were immediately
despatched with two hundred knights to Rome, with instructions to
remain there until further notice.

The gesture, like so many of the King's gestures, was not so
altruistic as it looked. Robert of Capua had fought—though admittedly without much determination—with his fellow-nobles to keep
Roger out of the South Italian dukedoms a few years before. Later,
like the rest, he had capitulated and, in his capacity as leading vassal,
had actually laid the crown on the King's head in Palermo Cathedral.
But he had never become altogether reconciled to the new regime
and Roger was probably glad of the opportunity, in view of the
coming crisis, to send him a safe distance away. The Count of Alife
was an even trickier character. He had betrayed his brother-in-law
more than once before[1] and would undoubtedly do so again if it
suited his book. Moreover, his brother Richard, who held in
fief the city of Avellino, had recently denied the King's suzerainty
and proclaimed himself independent. When Roger had summoned
him to order, his reply had been to put out the eyes and split the
nostrils of the royal messenger. The King had thereupon seized the
disputed territory; but now a further complication ensued. While
Rainulf was away in Rome his wife, Roger's half-sister Matilda,
deserted him and sought refuge at the court, alleging that her
husband's persistent cruelty made any continuation of their married
life impossible.

Roger upheld her action, and when Rainulf—in defiance of his
orders—left Rome to demand the restitution of both his territorial
and his conjugal rights, had replied that though Matilda was of
course free to return to him whenever she liked he had no intention
of forcing her to do so against her will. Meanwhile she and her son
were going back with him to Sicily, and he for his part was obliged
to ask Rainulf for the immediate surrender of the lands she had

[1] *The Normans in the South*, pp. 309–18.

brought with her as her dowry—the Caudine valley and all the castles it contained. On the matter of Avellino he was equally unyielding: Rainulf had never raised an eyebrow when his brother had asserted his independence; by failing to defend the rights of his lawful suzerain he had forfeited all claims to the town. One concession only was Roger prepared to make: if the Count and his followers would like to lay their case formally before him at Salerno, he would listen to anything they might have to say.

Rainulf of Alife had no intention of submitting to such treatment, still less of presenting himself cap in hand at Salerno. Instead he approached Robert of Capua—who had also returned unbidden from Rome—and together the two began to lay their plans.

The Apulian rising was quickly suppressed. After a short siege in May 1132 the inhabitants of Bari surrendered Prince Grimoald and his family to Roger, who packed them off as prisoners to Sicily, while Tancred of Conversano bought his liberty only with a promise—which he never kept—to leave for the Holy Land. The whole campaign was over in a month; it was, however, symptomatic of a deeper discontent throughout the South and, more important still, it created a diversion which kept Roger occupied just at that crucial time when Rainulf and Robert were gathering their forces. If he had moved firmly against them the moment they returned from Rome—and their unauthorised departure from the city would have given him pretext enough—he might have saved himself many of the troubles which awaited him in the next few years. But he missed his opportunity. Sure-footed as he was in the conduct of Sicilian affairs, he had still not caught the measure of his vassals on the mainland. Not for the first time, he had underestimated them. He had wounded his brother-in-law in his pride but not in his effective strength, and had succeeded only in turning a potential opponent into a real one. The Count of Alife was now aggrieved and angry—and dangerous, since he could count on the support of the Prince of Capua, still the strongest military force in South Italy after the King.

Robert of Capua had never been particularly distinguished in the past for his moral courage; but rebellion was in the wind, and Lothair and the imperial army could not be long delayed. Besides, was he not

Rainulf's liege-lord? How could he hope to maintain his status as a
feudal prince if he lost the confidence of his vassals? With all the
energy of which he was capable he threw himself into preparations
for a new, nation-wide revolt. By the late spring of 1132 he and
Rainulf could boast three thousand knights and perhaps ten times
that number of foot-soldiers under arms. And most of the South
Italian barons were behind them.

The strength of the opposition took the King by surprise. He had
just put down one rising; the last thing he wanted was to find himself
faced with another—this time of far more formidable proportions—
just when he needed all his energies to deal with the danger from the
north. It was his habit never to do battle if he could avoid it; some
accommodation might still be possible. In mid-July he sent messengers to the rebels proposing talks. It was no use. The two leaders
were adamant. They had been wronged, and there could be no
question of negotiations until their wrongs were redressed.

Both armies were by this time gathered near Benevento, and for
good reason. Benevento was papal territory. Ever since its citizens
had expelled their ruling princes and put themselves under the protection of Pope Leo IX some eighty years before, they had remained
loyal subjects of the Holy See, and they now constituted the principal
bastion of papal power in South Italy. It was outside the walls of
Benevento that Pope Honorius had invested Roger with his dukedom in 1128, and it was from its pontifical palace that Anacletus, two
years later, had granted him the crown, pledging him also the city's
assistance in time of war. In the present situation this was a significant
commitment; but could Roger count on it now?

At first it seemed as if he could. A certain Cardinal Crescentius,
Rector of Benevento in Anacletus's name, together with the local
Archbishop and a group of the leading citizens, came out to assure
the King of their good will; and on hearing from him that he pro-
posed in return to renounce several financial claims on the city, they
seem to have had no hesitation in promising him active military help.
It was a disastrous mistake; and it lost them, and Roger, the city.
During their absence, Robert's agents had been busy; rumours were
spreading fast that Crescentius and his friends had sold out to the
King of Sicily, and when the terms of the agreement were revealed

the Beneventans were horrified. What was the use of being a papal city if they were going to be swept up in internecine squabbles like everyone else? At a general gathering of the entire populace, they made their position clear:

We cannot ally ourselves in this wise with the King, nor can we accept to puff and sweat and exhaust ourselves on long marches with Sicilians and Calabrians and Apulians, all under the blazing sun; for our lines are cast in quiet places, and we were never accustomed to such perilous ways of life.

There is something disarming about such a protestation, but it may not have been quite so naïve as it seems. The citizens of Benevento must surely have known perfectly well that the eyes of Pope Innocent and King Lothair were upon them. When the great confrontation should occur between Pope and anti-Pope, they were still more anxious than everyone else in the South to end up on the winning side. Gentle and peace-loving as they claimed to be, their reception of Crescentius was such that the Cardinal fled back to Roger, having narrowly escaped with his life; meanwhile the wretched Archbishop locked himself, terrified, in the Cathedral.

For the rebels it was a triumph. Prince Robert now had no difficulty in securing promises of friendly neutrality, with free right of passage for his troops through Beneventan territory; and the Archbishop emerged, quaking, from his refuge to witness the solemn swearing of a new treaty between Capua and Benevento—saving always, he was careful to point out, the city's loyalty to the Pope. Just which Pope he had in mind, he did not make altogether clear; his flock seem to have thought it wiser not to ask.

For Roger the loss of Benevento to his enemies came as a severe blow. How serious it might prove in the long term was still an open question, but its immediate effect was to put his own forces in danger. They were dependent on the Beneventans for food and other supplies; and now, suddenly, the good will on which they relied had turned to open hostility. Moreover the Prince of Capua, secure in the knowledge of local support, might at any moment decide to attack. Once again Roger instinctively recoiled, as he nearly always did, from a direct confrontation. He ordered instead that every section of the army should keep a close watch on his standard and be ready to follow it, in any direction, as soon as it moved.

Shortly after nightfall the signal was given, and under cover of darkness the Sicilian army retreated across the mountains to the south. Although technically the manœuvre might have been described as a strategic withdrawal, its circumstances and speed were distinctly suggestive of flight—for dawn broke to find the royalist forces at the foot of Mt Atripalda, just outside Avellino. Twenty miles at night over mountain paths was no small achievement for an army, but the march was not yet over; the King, so Falco tells us, had been revolving thoughts of vengeance in his mind as he rode and was determined to regain the initiative. Thus, instead of making for his mainland capital at Salerno, he swung off to his right towards Nocera—Prince Robert's chief stronghold after Capua itself. A sudden attack might take the town by surprise; and it would with any luck be several days before the insurgents, who would assume that he had returned to Salerno, discovered where he had gone. Once they found out, they would be sure to hasten to the defence of Nocera, taking the quickest—though not the most direct—route via the coastal plain and the valley running between Vesuvius and the Apennine *massif*; but this would mean a crossing of the wide lower reaches of the river Sarno, where there existed only one bridge—an old wooden construction at Scafati, a mile or two away to the west on the road to Pompeii. If this bridge were destroyed, several more days at least would be gained. A party of sappers was despatched forthwith; their work was quickly done and they returned to find the siege of Nocera under way.

It was a brave and imaginative plan, one of which Roger I or Robert Guiscard would have approved. It deserved to work, and it very nearly did. But the rebel forces moved faster than expected. Only five days after the start of the siege, they had completed a makeshift bridge and were encamped opposite the King on the broad plain to the north of the city—Robert of Capua with a thousand knights on the left, Rainulf on the right with another fifteen hundred, split into three separate divisions. Of these, two hundred and fifty were sent up to the walls to divert part of the besieging force; the remainder made ready for battle.

The date was Sunday, 24 July. Roger was reluctant no longer. He had raised the siege of Nocera as soon as he heard of the enemy's crossing of the Sarno and had made his own dispositions. The first wave of the assault force was already drawn up on the field; now, at the King's command, they lowered their lances, spurred their horses to a gallop, and charged. Prince Robert's line crumbled under their impact; the Capuan infantry in the rear, seeing the horsemen bearing down upon them, panicked and fled towards the river. The bridge, so recently and so hastily erected, proved inadequate for their numbers and their speed; hundreds plunged into the water and were drowned.

A second charge of royalists followed with similar effect; but now the Count of Alife, with five hundred of his own knights behind him, swept in from the flank and fell on the attackers. Momentarily they wavered; and before they had time to reform, this onslaught was succeeded by another, and then by yet another as Rainulf's right and left followed his centre—descending on the enemy, as Falco puts it, like a lion that has not eaten for three days.

The tide was turned. Roger, himself now in the thick of the battle, seized a lance and galloped backwards and forwards through his reeling ranks, calling upon them to rally once again around their King. He was too late. His army was in full retreat, and he had no choice but to follow. That same evening he rode into Salerno, blood-stained and exhausted; four knights only were with him. Of the rest some seven hundred, with twenty loyal barons, had been taken prisoner. The others lay dead on the field or, like the bulk of the infantry, had been cut down as they ran. The spoils were immense. Falco admits that he has not the power to describe 'the abundance of gold and of silver, the rich golden vessels, the infinite variety of clothing for men and caparisons for horses, the cuirasses and other accoutrements' that were seized; while Henry, Bishop of St Agatha, who as a staunch champion of Pope Innocent had followed Robert to Nocera, records that the victors found, among the royal archives, the very Bull by which Anacletus had granted Roger his kingdom.[1]

[1] See *J.B.R.G.*, vol. V, *Monumenta Bambergensia*, p. 444.

It was Roger's first major battle, and it had been a disaster. His losses were enormous, his prestige in Italy dangerously shaken. As the news spread across the peninsula the flame of rebellion spread with it, and more and more towns rallied to the Capuan standard. In Benevento a torch-light procession visited all the principal shrines of the city to render thanks, and arrangements were made to receive a representative of Pope Innocent as Rector in place of the unfortunate Crescentius. In Bari, the population rose up again and massacred several of Roger's Saracen guard; at Montepeloso Tancred of Conversano promptly abandoned his crusading preparations and rejoined the revolt. Meanwhile reports were trickling through from Germany that King Lothair had at last got his army together and was even now marching south across the Alps.

And yet, as the King of Sicily set to work at Salerno to rebuild his shattered forces and to strengthen his fleet for the challenges ahead —his command of the sea being now more vital to him than ever— he is said to have impressed all those around him with his cheerfulness and confidence. To some extent this may have been assumed; but not, perhaps, entirely. Heretofore he had always avoided pitched battles. Diplomacy, bribery, prevarication, attrition, siege tactics— at various stages of his career he had used any or all of these rather than meet his enemy in the open field. The withdrawal from Benevento had been a case in point; many of his men would doubtless have preferred to stay and fight rather than make a shameful retreat under cover of darkness, as demoralising as it was undignified; but the long ride through the mountains had given the King plenty of time to search his soul. If he were to still the murmurings of his army and, perhaps, of his own conscience, it had been imperative for him to prove himself worthy of his race and his name. At last, he had gone some way towards doing so. His generalship may have been faulty, the day a disaster; but he had finally discovered, at the age of thirty-six, that when the call to battle came he did not lack courage.

The reports from the north were well-founded. It was nearly a year and a half since Lothair had promised to escort Pope Innocent to Rome. Unrest in Germany had delayed his departure and still prevented him from raising an army on the scale for which he had hoped. He now decided that the key to his domestic problems lay in the earliest possible acquisition of the imperial crown and the prestige it conferred; and so, in August 1132, with his queen Richenza of Nordheim and a force that amounted to little more than an armed escort, he set off over the mountains and into Lombardy.

It proved a disagreeable journey. As the Lombard cities grew every year stronger, richer and more independent, so their resentment of imperial claims increased. The reception which they therefore accorded to this latest claimant varied between coldness and out-and-out hostility—to which was added, when they saw the size of his following, more than a touch of derision. Lothair had to pick his way with care, passing only through those towns in which his unpopularity was least evident and trusting that Innocent, who had already been several months in Italy, would have succeeded in drumming up sufficient local support to enable him at least to enter Rome in style.

He found the Pope waiting for him near Piacenza. Innocent's appeals had not gone entirely unanswered; the imperial army on the last stage of the journey promised to be about two thousand strong. It was still a disappointing figure, but it was no longer shameful. What was principally lacking now was sea support. Pisa and Genoa in particular, the two great maritime republics of the north-west on whose assistance the Pope had relied, could at that moment see no further than the islands of Corsica and Sardinia, over which they had long been squabbling; without their help the imperial forces would stand little chance in the face of a concerted attack. But meanwhile the autumn rains were beginning, the roads rapidly turning to mud; and Lothair decided to postpone his coronation till the following spring. By then, perhaps, the warring cities might be persuaded to settle their differences for the common good.

The fact that they did so was largely due to the Abbot of Clairvaux. He appeared in Italy soon after Christmas; by March he and Innocent together had alternately hectored and flattered the Pisans and Genoese into a truce, and in the following month they were back again at Lothair's camp, ready for the advance on Rome. For a show of strength, the army that now reassembled itself was still sadly unimpressive; but imperial agents reported that Roger was still occupied with his own problems and that there was consequently no fear of serious opposition on the way to the Holy City.

The church of S. Agnese fuori le Mura still stands today, its aspect essentially the same as in the seventh century when it was built; and in front of it, on 30 April 1133, the Emperor-to-be drew up his army for its final entry. For some days already Rome had been in turmoil. Pisan and Genoese ships had sailed up the Tiber and were now lying threateningly under the walls; and their presence, aided by exaggerated rumours of the size of the oncoming German host, had induced many Romans—including the Prefect himself—to make a hurried change of allegiance. Much of the city thus lay open to Lothair and Innocent. They were received at the gates by the Frangipani and Corsi nobles and their minions—who had never wavered in their opposition to Anacletus—and led in triumph to their respective palaces: the King and Queen to Otto III's old imperial residence on the Aventine, the Pope to the Lateran.

But the right bank of the Tiber, with the Castel S. Angelo and St Peter's itself, the traditional setting for imperial coronations, still remained firmly in the hands of Anacletus; and Anacletus was not prepared to give in. Lothair, conscious of his own weakness, proposed negotiations, but the anti-Pope's reply remained the same as it had always been—let the whole question of the disputed election be reopened before an international ecclesiastical tribunal. If such a tribunal, properly constituted, were to declare against him, he would accept its decision. Till then he would stay in Rome where he belonged. Left to himself, Lothair would probably have been ready to accept this suggestion. Anything in his view would have been better than a continued schism in the Papacy; rival Popes might well lead to rival Emperors, and in such an event his own position might be far from secure. But by now he had been joined in Rome by Bernard; and with Bernard at his side there could be no question of compromise. If Anacletus could not be brought to his knees, he must be ignored. And so it was not at St Peter's but at the Lateran that Innocent was reinstalled on the papal throne and there, on 4 June, with as much ceremony and circumstance as he could command, that he crowned Lothair Emperor of the West, and Richenza his Empress.

For the second time in half a century one putative Pope had performed an imperial coronation while another had sat a mile or two away, impotent and fuming. After the previous occasion Gregory VII had been saved only by the arrival, not a moment too soon, of Robert Guiscard at the head of some thirty thousand troops. Anacletus knew that he could expect nothing from that quarter; the King of Sicily, though still his loyal champion, was otherwise engaged. Fortunately, rescue was unnecessary. Powerless the anti-Pope may have been, but he was not in any physical danger. No imperial attack on Trastevere—the right bank—would be possible without control of the two bridges spanning the river at the Tiber Island; and all approaches to these were effectively dominated by the old Theatre of Marcellus, now the principal fortress of the Pierleoni. In the circumstances, the Emperor had neither the strength nor the inclination to take the offensive. Now that his immediate aims were achieved he thought only of returning to Germany as soon as possible. Within a few days of the coronation he and his army were gone; and the Pisan and Genoese ships had slipped back down the river to the open sea.

To Pope Innocent, Lothair's departure was nothing short of calamitous. At once his remaining supporters in the city began to fall away. Only the Frangipani remained loyal; but they could not hold Rome unaided. By July the agents of Anacletus had everywhere resumed their activity, and the gold was beginning to flow freely once again from the inexhaustible Pierleoni coffers. In August poor Innocent found himself forced once again into exile. He slipped unobtrusively from his diocese—just as he had three years before—and made his way, by slow stages, to Pisa and to safety.

Innocent was not the only one to feel betrayed. For the rebels in South Italy too, the news that the Emperor, so long awaited, had now come and gone without lifting a finger to help them must have dashed what slender hopes of victory they had left. Already the last few months had been disastrous. The year 1133 had started well enough with the revolt spreading, under the leadership of Tancred

of Conversano, to every corner of Apulia. Even Melfi, the first
capital of the Hautevilles, even Venosa, where four of the greatest—
including Robert Guiscard himself—lay buried, had declared against
their King. But, with the other towns that followed their example,
they soon had reason to regret their faithlessness. With the first signs
of spring Roger had crossed from Sicily at the head of a new army—
and a radically different one. In the past when he had been anxious to
win the sympathy and support of the South Italian vassals, he had
found that a following wholly or even predominantly composed of
Muslims was apt to do his prestige more harm than good; he had
therefore used his Saracens sparingly, as little more than a stiffening
for his regular troops. Such scruples bothered him no longer. He
was desperate, and the Saracens had proved themselves among the
loyalest of his subjects, immune alike from subversion by the
Norman baronage and excommunication by the Pope. The army
that he now landed on Italian soil was in essence a Muslim army, the
only remaining way of bringing his Christian vassals to heel.

This altered composition of his fighting force seems to reflect a
parallel change in the character of Roger himself. Whichever we read
of the two chroniclers who have left us detailed accounts of the
ensuing campaign—Falco, the notary of Benevento who hated him
or, at the other end of the scale, the sycophantic Alexander of Telese
—we are conscious of a new facet of his character, merciless and
vengeful. He had always been a master of diplomacy and statecraft,
and would remain one till the end of his life; but the events of the
past two years had taught him that there are situations where such
methods are no longer of any avail; and the battle of Nocera, disastrous though it had been in every other way, had convinced him
of his ability to deal with them. No longer, when the occasion
demanded it, would he shy away from the shedding of blood.

And so, in the spring and summer of 1133, the Sicilian Saracens
fell on rebellious Apulia. Starting with Venosa—for by first assuring
himself of the mountain towns of the centre he hoped to cut off
Tancred and his rebels from their Capuan allies in the west—the
King swept down eastward and southward to the sea, leaving a trail
of desolation behind him. None who resisted were spared; many
were burnt alive—according, at least, to Falco, who calls God to

witness that 'such cruelty to Christian people had never before been known'. Corato, Barletta, Minervino, Matera and other rebel strongholds all fell in their turn, until at last Roger drew up his Saracens before Montepeloso, where Tancred had dug himself in and was awaiting the inevitable siege. With him, notes the Abbot of Telese, were forty knights sent to him by Rainulf of Alife, under the command of a certain Roger of Plenco[1]—'a most courageous soldier but extremely hostile to the King'.

The walls of Montepeloso were no match for the Sicilian siege engines; and after little more than a fortnight, 'with all their trumpets sounding forth and their voices raised in a great shout to heaven', the Saracens burst into the town. Some of the defenders, 'disguised in the vilest garments, lest they should be taken for knights', managed to make their escape, but their leaders were not so lucky. Falco's pen seems to tremble in his hand as he writes:

Then Tancred and the unfortunate Roger [of Plenco] flung down their arms and sought refuge among the darkest and most obscure alleys of the town; but they were sought out, and discovered, and led into the presence of Roger the King. Oh the sorrow, the horror, the weeping! Oh reader, how great would have been your own anguish of heart, had you been present! For the King decreed that Roger should forthwith be hanged by the neck, and that Tancred himself, with his own hand, should pull on the rope. Oh, what crime unspeakable! Tancred, despite his grief, could not but obey the King's command. The whole army was stricken with horror, and called upon God in Heaven to wreak His vengeance upon so great a tyrant and so cruel a man. Next the King ordered that the valiant Tancred should be held a prisoner; we have heard that he was later led captive to Sicily. And then, without further delay, the whole town of Montepeloso, its monasteries and all its citizens, both men and women, with their little ones, were given over to fire and the sword.

After the fall of Montepeloso, Apulian resistance was effectively broken; but Roger's fury was still not assuaged. Now that he had decided to show the mailed fist, he was determined that the lesson should not be lost on any of his subjects. Henceforth, by each and every one, the price of rebellion should be clearly understood. Trani

---

[1] Falco calls him Roger de Pleuto.

he left a burnt-out shell; at Troia, where a municipal delegation was
sent tremblingly out to greet him, he had the five principal magistrates executed on the spot and then razed the city to the ground,
dispersing its survivors around the neighbouring villages. Melfi
suffered a similar fate; Ascoli fared very little better. At last on 16
October, having destroyed the defences of every important town in
Apulia, the King and his Saracens returned to Salerno; on the 19th
they took ship for Sicily.

Roger might have no more to fear from Apulia, but there still
remained his two Campanian vassals to be brought to heel. Robert of
Capua and Rainulf of Alife had hastened to Rome at the first news of
Lothair's arrival and had dutifully attended his coronation, doubtless
expecting that once the attendant formalities were over he and his
army—such as it was—would march south with them against the
King of Sicily. They should have stayed where they were; the speed
and suddenness of Roger's counter-attack caught them unprepared,
separated from their followers at the time they were most needed.
Rainulf had returned with all haste, but he seems to have made no
serious attempt—unless we include the forty knights under the
luckless Roger of Plenco—to stem the tide of the King's advance.
Prince Robert was more cautious and more sensible. The events of
the previous summer had taught him that, with the forces at present
available, not even an overwhelming victory like Nocera could
prove decisive in the long term. Roger's power could never be
broken without outside assistance, and if that were not forthcoming
from the Emperor, then it must be sought elsewhere. Accordingly,
in the last week of June, he had left Rome for Pisa; and there, after
protracted negotiations, he managed to conclude an agreement by
which, in return for three thousand pounds of silver, one hundred
Pisan and Genoese vessels would be put at his disposal in March of
the following year.

With a fleet of this magnitude sailing against him, Roger's command of the sea would have been seriously imperilled. His enemies
might well have risked a full-scale offensive against Messina to block
the straits, or even a direct attack on Palermo itself. But he showed
no particular concern. In the early spring of 1134 he was back again

on the mainland, determined to settle affairs in Italy once and for all.
Sweeping up through rebel territory, he met with scarcely any
opposition. Reports of his treatment of the Apulian towns in the
previous year had long been current in Campania, where the local
populations had taken the point, just as he had intended that they
should. Wherever his army passed, resistance seemed to crumble;
meanwhile the lords of Capua and Alife, strengthened by a thousand
Pisan soldiers but still awaiting the bulk of their promised reinforcements from the northern sea-republics, remained on the defensive.
Now it was their turn to avoid pitched battles. One after another
their castles fell. Even Nocera, scene of Roger's deepest humiliation
barely two years before, surrendered as soon as it became clear that
Rainulf's attempts to relieve it had failed. The King, as merciful this
year as he had been implacable in 1133, took no reprisals; the soldiers
of the garrison, once they had sworn an oath of loyalty, were allowed
to disperse freely to their homes.

Spring turned to summer, and still the Pisan and Genoese fleets
failed to appear. Their presence now was vital, less for strategic
reasons than because nothing else could hope to restore the insurgents' morale. Finally a desperate Prince Robert took ship to Pisa,
ostensibly to make a last appeal for help but also, one suspects, to
save his skin; and Rainulf was left alone to face the oncoming army.
The Count of Alife, for all his faults, had never lacked courage.
Seeing that a confrontation with his brother-in-law could no longer
be avoided, he now mustered all his men in preparation for a final
onslaught. But he was too late. The Sicilian agents that Roger had
managed to infiltrate into the neighbourhood were open-handed
and persuasive; such of the local knights and barons as had remained
at his side now suddenly began to fall away. Rainulf was beaten and
he knew it. He sent messengers to Roger announcing his unconditional surrender and flung himself on the King's mercy.

Towards the end of June the two met at the village of Lauro, near
Avellino. As the Abbot of Telese describes it, it must have been an
affecting scene:

Falling on his knees before the King, he [Rainulf] first tried to kiss
his feet; but the King raised him up with his own hand and made as
if to kiss him in his turn. The Count stopped him, begging him first

31

to cast all anger from him. And the King replied with all his heart, It is cast. Further, said the Count, I ask that thou shouldst henceforth esteem me as I had been thy slave. And the King answered, This will I do. Then the Count spoke once more: Let God himself, he said, be witness of those things which have been spoken between thee and me. Amen, said the King. And at once the King kissed him, and the two were seen to stand for a long time embraced, so that certain of those that were present were seen to be shedding tears for very joy.

Roger was plainly in a very different mood from that in which he had dealt with Tancred of Conversano and the Apulian rebels the year before; and in token of reconciliation he restored to Rainulf his wife and son—the causes, willing or not, of so much of the trouble. They seem to have been happy enough to return home—an indication that Countess Matilda's erstwhile desertion of her husband may have been less straightforward than at first appeared. There were limits, however, to the King's forgiveness. Those lands which had been part of his sister's original dowry remained confiscate; and Rainulf was further required to surrender all the territory he had won since the outbreak of hostilities.

The last enemy was Robert of Capua. He was still, so far as anyone knew, remonstrating with the Pisans for having let him down; and it was at Pisa that a royal messenger now sped to him with Roger's terms: if the Prince returned to Capua before the middle of August and made his submission, he would be confirmed in his possessions, saving only those which the King had captured in the recent fighting. Alternatively, if he preferred to remain absent, his son could be installed on the Capuan throne, with Roger himself acting as Regent on his behalf until the boy became of age. If, however, Robert were to continue in rebellion, his lands would be seized; his principality itself would forfeit its separate identity and revert to the direct control of the Kingdom of Sicily. He could take his choice. Receiving no answer, the King made his formal entry into Capua.

It was, the Abbot of Telese tells us, a great and prosperous city, defended not only by its walls and towers but also by the broad Volturno winding around its base, with scores of little floating water-mills moored along the banks. Now, however, it offered no defence; the King was welcomed in the cathedral with honour and—

if we can accept the Abbot's word for it—with rejoicing. Afterwards he received Duke Sergius of Naples, a faintly ambivalent character in this story, who had always resented Roger's South Italian claims and had made no secret of his sympathy for the insurgents, but who had yet somehow managed to hold himself and his city aloof from any actual fighting. With Capua in the King's hands, Sergius found that he too had no longer any alternative but to come to terms. He too knelt before Roger, and swore him fealty and homage.

The revolt, it seemed, was over. A week or two previously the citizens of Benevento, after yet another internal upheaval, had thrown out Pope Innocent's representatives and declared once again for Anacletus and the King; at last, for the first time in three years, all South Italy was quiet. In each of those three years the autumn had been well advanced before Roger had been able to return home to his family in Palermo; in 1134 he felt free to leave by the end of July.

But if Roger appeared to have solved his problems, for the historian there is still one that remains unanswered. What happened to the reinforcements promised to the rebels by the great maritime city-republics of the north? Negotiations had been completed, prices arranged, dates fixed. The final agreement had been signed at Pisa, in the presence of Pope Innocent himself, the previous February and had been ratified by the rebel barons a week or two later. The hundred ships contracted for, fully manned, were to have arrived in March. Had they done so, the course of events in the summer of 1134 would have taken a very different turn. But they never appeared. What prevented them?

Two of St Bernard's letters, written in 1134 to the Pisans and Genoese respectively, provide us, perhaps, with a significant clue. To the Pisans,[1] characteristically using the Almighty himself as his mouthpiece, Bernard wrote:

He has said to Innocent his anointed, Here let my dwelling be, and I shall bless it. . . . With my support the Pisans shall stand firm under the attacks of the Sicilian tyrant, not shaken by threats, enticed by bribes or hoodwinked by cunning.

To the Genoese,[2] he made himself clearer:

[1] Letter 130.   [2] Letter 129.

I have heard that you have received messengers from Count [*sic*] Roger of Sicily, but I do not know what they brought or with what they returned. To tell the truth, in the words of the poet, *Timeo Danaos et dona ferentes.*[1] If you should find that anyone amongst you has been so depraved as to have held out his hand for filthy lucre, take prompt cognisance of the matter and judge him as an enemy of your good name and as a traitor.

Did the King of Sicily, in the early spring of 1134, bribe the Pisans and the Genoese—and possibly the Venetians as well—to break their commitments and deliberately to delay the help they had promised to Robert of Capua? We shall never be certain. We do know, however, that Sicily, with her unrivalled trading position and financial efficiency, was rich—richer for her size than any other state on the Mediterranean with the possible exception of Venice; and we know too that Roger was a consummate if tortuous diplomatist who always preferred buying off his enemies to fighting them and had long experience in the arts of corruption. St Bernard's suspicions of him may not have been charitable; but it is to be doubted whether they were very far wrong.

[1] I fear the Greeks when they come with gifts. Virgil, *Aeneid,* II, 49.

3

THE IMPERIAL INVASION

So gerieten si an raise
In das lant ʒe Pulle;
Daʒ was der vursten wille.
Der vurste hieʒ da Ruocher,
Den vertraip der chunich Liuther
In Siciliam.

So they embarked on a journey
Into the land of Apulia.
This was the Prince's will.
The Prince's name was Roger
Whom King Lothair pursued
To Sicily.

Lothair's *Kaiserchronik*, 11, 17084–89

THE King who sailed back to Palermo in the high summer of 1134 must have been a happy man. Peace and order had been restored to South Italy, and now reigned throughout his kingdom. Though he had not yet managed to prove himself a general worthy of his Hauteville forbears, his courage on the battlefield was no longer in doubt. He was respected in Italy, by friend and foe alike, as he had never been before. The Emperor of Germany had returned across the Alps rather than take up arms against him; the Pope whom he, alone of all the princes of Europe, continued to uphold was still firmly established in Rome. He had done his work well.

But Roger's troubles were not yet over. Soon after his return to Sicily he fell dangerously ill. He recovered, but only to see his wife in her turn struck down, probably by the same infection. The Greek and Arab doctors of Palermo were among the best in the world, and at Salerno the King had at his disposal the foremost medical school of Europe; but their efforts were in vain. Some time during the first week of February 1135, Queen Elvira died. She remains a shadowy figure, this Spanish princess who married Roger—in circumstances unknown to us—when he was twenty-two and shared his life for the next eighteen years. Unlike his mother Adelaide, she seems never to have involved herself in affairs of state; and she certainly never accompanied her husband on his campaigns in the manner of his aunt, the redoubtable and unforgettable Sichelgaita of Salerno. Alexander of Telese notes that she was renowned for her piety and charitable works, but there is no record of any monastic foundations or churches endowed by her; the abbot's words should probably be taken as being little more than the perfunctory tribute expected from friendly chroniclers on the death of a royal personage. The most moving testimony to her remains her husband's reaction to her death. He was broken-hearted. Now he retired with his grief, seeing no one but a few members of his court and *curia* until, as Alexander puts it, not only his subjects far away but even those who lived close to him believed that he had followed his wife to the grave.

Knowledge of his recent illness lent additional strength to this belief, and word of Roger's death spread quickly to the mainland. There could, at such a time, have been no more dangerous rumour. The King's eldest son was barely seventeen, untried in war or statecraft. In the hearts of Rainulf of Alife and of all the erstwhile rebels hope surged anew; they resolved to strike at once. The Pisans, after months of browbeating from Innocent, Bernard and Robert of Capua, no longer malingered, and on 24 April—thirteen months late—their promised fleet, carrying eight thousand men led by Robert himself, dropped anchor in the port of Naples, where Duke Sergius, effortlessly changing sides once again, gave it a warm welcome. News of its arrival decided the waverers. Within days Campania had reverted to its old chaos.

The history of Italy during the Middle Ages—and indeed beyond—is shot through with accounts of inconclusive wars; of tides of battle ebbing and flowing, up the peninsula and then down again, of cities besieged and captured, relieved and recovered, in a dreary struggle that never seems to end. To the historian they are tedious enough; to others they can be insufferable. Readers of this book will therefore be spared the minutiae of the campaigns that were necessary before Roger succeeded once again in establishing his authority.[1] Suffice it here to say that the insurgents soon had

[1] Any who yearn for further information can find it, in relentless detail down to the last beleaguered citadel, in the pages of Chalandon.

cause to regret their precipitate action. For the first six weeks, assisted by continuing rumours of the King's death and the absence of any counter-indications from Palermo, they were able to make some minor advances; but Roger's mainland governors and the various garrisons under their command kept a firm grip on the country and blocked any real progress. Then, on 5 June, the Sicilian fleet appeared off Salerno.

It was not just the renewed threat to the tranquillity of his mainland dominions that had roused Roger from the torpor into which his wife's death had sunk him; it was anger. He had never been a choleric man by nature, and even now he seems to have felt no deep resentment against the Prince of Capua. Although by ignoring his call for surrender the previous year Robert had remained a declared rebel, although as a sworn vassal of the King he had violated his oath of fealty, at least he had not compounded his offence by swearing a new oath only a few months before taking up arms again. But with the Count of Alife and the Duke of Naples it was different. Within the past year these two had knelt before Roger, placed their hands in his and pledged their allegiance. Rainulf indeed had gone even further, taking advantage of his kinship with a display of mawkish sentimentality which it must have been nauseating to recall. This was treason at its blackest and most shameless; and it would not be forgiven.

We should remember, in fairness to the Count of Alife, that he may have genuinely believed the stories of the King's death. Brother-in-law or not, however, he knew that he could expect no further mercy. He must play for time. Pope Innocent from his Pisan exile was maintaining the pressure on the northern sea-republics—especially on Genoa, whose men and ships, also promised for 1134, had still not arrived; while beyond the Alps the Abbot of Clairvaux was thundering from every pulpit against the schismatic Pope in Rome and his creature-King, vowing that he would never rest until he had launched a new Crusade against them. Even now, if the rebels could hold out long enough, they might still be saved. With his four hundred remaining followers, Rainulf hurried to Naples. Robert of Capua, ignoring the King's offers of a separate peace, accompanied him; and Duke Sergius, more fearful than

37

either, received them with alacrity and began to prepare his city
for a siege.

To the average observer of the South Italian scene in 1135,
possibly even to King Roger himself, the events of that summer
must have seemed merely a continuation of the struggle for power
which had been continuing almost uninterruptedly for the past eight
years. In fact, from the moment that the King's three principal
Campanian adversaries barricaded themselves in Naples, the whole
complexion of that struggle was changed. Hitherto it had been
fundamentally an internal, domestic issue, a trial of strength between
a King and his vassals. The fact that that King was largely responsible for the continued existence of an Anti-Pope in Rome, and thus
for a schism which threw the whole foundation of European
political and religious stability into jeopardy, was incidental. No
foreign state had actually taken up arms against Roger—unless we
count a body of unpunctual and remarkably ineffective Pisan
mercenaries—and when Lothair himself had made his long-awaited
descent into Italy he had been able to see no further than his own
coronation.

The retreat to Naples marks the point at which the leadership of
the opposition to Roger passes out of the hands of his vassals and
on to the international plane. Pope Innocent and Bernard had long
since accepted that Anacletus could never be dislodged from Rome
while the King of Sicily remained able to protect him. Clearly,
Roger must be eliminated; equally clearly, the Emperor was the
man for the job. And St Bernard made sure that Lothair knew it.
Towards the end of 1135 we find him writing to the Emperor:

It ill becomes me to exhort men to battle; yet I say to you in all conscience that it is the duty of the champion of the Church to protect
her against the madness of schismatics. It is for Caesar to uphold
his rightful crown against the machinations of the Sicilian tyrant. For
just as it is to the injury of Christ that the offspring of a Jew should
have seized for himself the throne of St Peter, so does any man who
sets himself up as King in Sicily offend against the Emperor.

At about the same time a similar exhortation, though made for
very different reasons, reached Lothair from a less expected quarter.

In Constantinople the Emperor John II Comnenus had been watching developments in South Italy with concern. The Apulian seaports—themselves until less than a century earlier part of the Byzantine theme of Langobardia, to which the Eastern Empire had never renounced its claim—were only some sixty or seventy miles from the imperial territories across the Adriatic; and the rich cities of Dalmatia constituted a temptation to a little gentle freebooting which, in recent years, Sicilian sea-captains had not always been able to resist. Other raids, on the North African coast, had indicated that the King of Sicily would not long be content to remain within his present frontiers and, if not checked, might soon be in a position to close the central Mediterranean at will. There was also some uncertainty about the Principality of Antioch, founded by Roger's cousin Bohemund during the First Crusade. Bohemund's son, Bohemund II, had been killed in battle early in 1130 leaving no male heir, and the King of Sicily had made formal claim to the succession. His South Italian responsibilities had so far prevented him from pursuing it actively; but he could be counted on to revert to the matter as soon as he had the chance, and the last thing the Emperor wanted was to find a Sicilian army digging itself in along his southern frontier. It looked, in short, as if Roger might soon prove himself a thorn in Byzantine flesh every bit as sharp as Robert Guiscard had been half a century before, and John was determined to stop him. In 1135 he sent ambassadors to Lothair with promises of generous financial backing for a campaign to crush the King of Sicily once and for all.

On its way to Germany the Byzantine mission appears to have stopped in Venice to enlist the support of the Republic. Venetian merchants had also been suffering at the hands of Sicilian privateers; already they estimated their losses at forty thousand talents. The Doge was therefore only too glad to help, and promised a Venetian fleet whenever necessary. Meanwhile Venetian envoys joined the Byzantines to give additional strength to the Greek appeal.

They found that Lothair needed little persuading. The situation in Germany had improved over the past two years—thanks largely to the new prestige conferred upon him by the imperial crown—and his Hohenstaufen enemies had been forced into submission. This

39

time he would have no difficulty in raising a respectable army. With it he would be able to reassert his authority in Lombardy and then, entering his South Italian dominions for the first time, mete out to the Hauteville upstart the punishment he deserved. After that he foresaw little trouble from Anacletus. The anti-Pope's last remaining northern stronghold, Milan, had gone over to Innocent in June, and the schism was now confined to the Sicilian Kingdom and to Rome itself. Once Roger were out of the way Anacletus would be left without a single ally and would be obliged to yield. It would be a fitting climax to Lothair's reign. He sent the Bishop of Havelberg off to Constantinople to carry his compliments to John and to inform him that he intended to march against Roger the following year. Then, with something akin to relish, the old Emperor declared a special tax on all Church property—to defray his own share of the costs of the expedition—and began to prepare his army.

For Roger, 1135 had been a bad year. His own illness, his wife's death, the resurgence of trouble in Italy just when law and order seemed to have been re-established—it was enough to make any man want to turn his face to the wall. But the year had at least ended more satisfactorily than it had begun; and the three ring-leaders of the revolt, Robert, Rainulf and Sergius, by taking refuge with such unseemly haste behind the walls of Naples, had virtually admitted their inability to carry on the struggle without assistance from outside.

And yet, while there was still hope of this assistance, they refused to surrender. By now Robert of Capua too had lost his last chance of reconciliation. The King's patience was exhausted. A short time before, he had created his eldest son, Roger, Duke of Apulia and his second, Tancred, Prince of Bari, thus dispossessing the rebellious Prince Grimoald. That autumn he invested his third son, Alfonso, with the Principality of Capua in Robert's stead—a ceremony which was shortly afterwards followed by Alfonso's solemn enthronement in Capua Cathedral. The boys were still mere fledglings, Duke Roger only seventeen and Tancred a year or two younger, while Alfonso was barely adolescent. But all three were old enough to play their part in their father's grand design, and in

40

this design there was no longer a place for powerful vassals outside his own family. At the end of 1135, for the first time, every principal South Italian fief was in Hauteville hands.

All through that winter Naples held out. By the spring of 1136 there was serious famine. Falco records that many of the inhabitants, young and old alike, men and women, collapsed and died in the streets. And yet, he adds proudly, the Duke and his followers remained firm, 'preferring to die of hunger than to bare their necks to the power of an evil King'. Fortunately for them, Roger's blockade was never entirely effective; though the besiegers had cut off all access by land, the Sicilian navy never managed to achieve similar success in the sea approaches, with the result that both Robert and Sergius were able on separate occasions to slip away to Pisa for essential supplies. Even so, it is unlikely that Naples could have maintained its morale much longer had not Robert also made a hurried journey to Lothair's court at Speyer and returned, laden with imperial honours, to reveal that the Emperor was already well advanced with his preparations for the relief expedition.

Similar reports had already reached Roger, whose agents had left him with no delusions as to just how strong the imperial army would be. And so he too began to make his preparations, basing them on the assumption that the enemy force would be vastly superior in numbers to anything that he himself could muster. A Sicilian victory through force of arms would be out of the question; he would have to put his faith in guile.

It was high summer before Lothair's army was finally gathered at Würzburg. We have been left no very clear indications of its size, but a list of all the great imperial vassals who were present shows that it must have been on a very different scale from the sad little company that had set off with Lothair to Rome in 1132. In the forefront were Duke Henry the Proud of Bavaria, the Emperor's son-in-law, and Conrad of Hohenstaufen, the old enemy and rival who had now made his submission and whom Lothair had confirmed in the possession of all his lands and honours in return for a promise to participate in the coming campaign. There followed an imposing array of lesser nobles and their retinues, of *Markgrafen* and *Pfalzgrafen*, *Landgrafen* and *Burggrafen* from all over the Empire, together with an ecclesiastical contingent which included no less than five archbishops, fourteen bishops and an abbot. By the third week of August they were ready to start; and on about the 21st, with Lothair and his Empress at its head, the huge army lumbered off southward towards the Brenner.

The Emperor was no more popular with the Lombard towns than he had been four years earlier, but this time the size of his following commanded respect. Inevitably there were occasions when his men had to draw their swords; but nowhere was progress seriously delayed. Near Cremona his army was swelled by a Milanese detachment; there too he found Robert of Capua waiting for him. Early in February 1137 he reached Bologna, where he split the army into two. He himself proposed to continue through Ravenna to Ancona, and thence to follow the Adriatic coast into Apulia; meanwhile the Duke of Bavaria, with three thousand knights and perhaps twelve thousand infantry, was to press down through Tuscany and the Papal State, if possible re-establishing Innocent in Rome and assuring himself of the monastery of Monte Cassino, before meeting his father-in-law at Bari for Whitsun.

When, in the year 529, St Benedict had chosen a high hill-crest commanding the road between Rome and Naples as the site for the first and greatest of his foundations, he had inadvertently endowed the abbey with a strategic importance which its occupants, over the next fifteen centuries, would more than once have cause to regret. Later, as Monte Cassino grew in power and prestige, its geographical eminence took second place to its political; but for the Normans, ever since their earliest days in the peninsula, the monastery had always represented, both politically and militarily, one of the principal keys to the South. For Roger II, indeed, it was something more—a vital fortress, almost a buffer-state of its own, guarding the frontier which separated his kingdom from papal territory.

The monastery, for its part, had never found its position as a frontier fortress a particularly easy one. When in doubt, however, it had learnt to cast in its lot with the Normans. Thus it had been careful to remain on good terms with Roger's mainland viceroys, and though there had been a brief crisis a few months before when

its loyalty had fallen—probably unjustifiably—under suspicion, the
new abbot, Rainald, whom it had then been forced to elect was a
staunch supporter of the King. When Henry of Bavaria arrived at
the foot of the hill towards the middle of April, it was to find the
surrounding countryside deliberately laid waste and the gates of
the monastery barred against him. Henry had already had a rough
passage through Tuscany. Pisa and certain other towns which had
always remained loyal to Innocent gave him what help they could;
but Florence and Lucca had been subdued only after a stout
resistance, and Henry was still occupied with Grosseto when, at
the beginning of March, Innocent—probably accompanied by St
Bernard—rode out from Pisa to join him.

From the outset Prince and Pontiff seem to have disliked each
other intensely. Henry was if anything a stronger and more unyielding character than his father-in-law. As Prince of the Empire,
with every expectation of succeeding to the throne on Lothair's
death, he was determined to make no concessions that he might
later have cause to regret; as a general with a job to do; and he had
no intention of taking orders from the Pope or from anyone else.
Matters first came to a head after the capture of Viterbo; an indemnity of three thousand talents—roughly equivalent to some
two thousand pounds of silver—was promptly claimed by Innocent
on the grounds that the town lay within the papal frontiers, but was
retained by Henry as part of the legitimate spoils of war. Then the
Duke decided to by-pass Rome. It was, he maintained, more sensible
to crush Roger first and allow Anacletus to collapse through lack
of support than to waste time and energy in forcibly expelling him
from St Peter's. The logic of this argument was unanswerable and
Innocent accepted it; it meant, none the less, a further indefinite
extension of his exile—to say nothing of the prospect of a long, hot
Apulian summer trailing around in the wake of an imperial army—
and it cannot have improved the Pope's temper.

And now, to crown it all, came the trouble at Monte Cassino, with
the very fountain-head of western monasticism arrogantly defying
not just the imperial army but Innocent himself. Eleven days Henry
waited, blocking all access to the monastery and vaguely hoping for
some sign that it might be prepared to make terms. But none came.

Its store-houses were well stocked with food, its garrison strong and in good heart; its position, in any case, made it virtually impregnable. The Duke, meanwhile, who had undertaken to join Lothair in Apulia by the end of May, had no time to waste. Swallowing his pride, he sent another messenger up the hill with an offer to negotiate.

Though Abbot Rainald's sympathies lay with Roger his first loyalty was to his monastery, his primary objective to get rid of Henry and his army as soon as possible. When the Duke offered, therefore, to leave Monte Cassino untouched and to confirm him as its abbot, in return only for a small recognisance in gold and an undertaking to fly the imperial banner from the citadel, he readily accepted. Innocent had already excommunicated the monastery for its Anacletan sympathies. His immediate reaction to this new agreement, by which the most venerable religious foundation in Europe—and one, moreover, situated on the very border of the Papal State—was left in the hands of an unrepentant champion of Anacletus and under the imperial rather than the papal colours, is not recorded in any of the chronicles. Perhaps it is just as well.[1]

As Duke Henry led his troops south across the Garigliano he may have congratulated himself on a technical victory, but he cannot have cherished any delusions about its real significance. The imperial flag flying over the monastery might temporarily affect Roger's prestige in the area, but in the absence of a garrison there was nothing to stop its being hauled down the moment the German army had disappeared from sight. At Capua, however, the next stage of his journey, better things awaited him. Immediately on his arrival the two local barons whom Roger had appointed to defend the city transferred their allegiance and opened the gates; and Prince Robert, who had accompanied the army from Cremona onwards, was replaced

[1] According to the *Kaiserchronik*, a long and rambling piece of Bavarian doggerel composed around 1150, the abbey was actually taken by a party of Henry's men, who gained admission by disguising themselves as pilgrims, hiding their swords beneath their robes. But this story, in one form or another, is almost *de rigueur* in mediaeval accounts of monastic sieges—see *The Normans in the South*, pp. 77–8. The only surprising thing is that Bernhardi, the punctilious (if tendentious) biographer of Lothair, should have taken it seriously. (*Lothar von Supplinburg*, pp. 700–1.)

on his old throne. The citizens accepted him willingly enough. The majority had always felt him to be their rightful lord, with a stronger and more ancient claim on their loyalties than the King of Sicily could ever boast; and the remainder, seeing him supported by so large a force, bowed to the inevitable. Robert, it is true, had to pay Henry four thousand talents not to turn his men loose on the city; but at such a price he must have considered his restoration cheap indeed.

Now it was the turn of Benevento. This time the populace stood firm, but were unwise enough to launch what they hoped would be a surprise attack on the imperial camp. It proved a disaster. They fled back to the city; the pursuers passed through the gates on the heels of the pursued; and the following morning—it was Sunday, 23 May—the Beneventans too made their submission, merely stipulating that their city should remain inviolate and that the erstwhile supporters of Anacletus should not be made to suffer. Their conditions were agreed; only Cardinal Crescentius, the Anacletan Rector who had already suffered one expulsion five years before, was seized by an old enemy and delivered over to Innocent, who condemned him to live out the rest of his days in the obscurity of a monastic cell.

Cheered by its successes—though possibly a little disappointed at having been once again cheated of a good day's pillage—Henry's army threaded its way over the mountains into Apulia, joining up with Lothair at Bari just in time to participate in the Whit Sunday thanksgiving. The Emperor indeed had a lot to be thankful for. His progress down the peninsula had been smoother than his son-in-law's. Ravenna had welcomed him. Ancona had resisted but had paid the price. Lothair's savage treatment of it had served as a warning to others and brought out many of the local barons to offer him homage and often material assistance. This pattern had continued as he marched south. The towns tended to be hostile, though after the fate of Ancona they generally managed to commute their hostility into a policy of sullen acceptance; but in the country districts most barons had rallied willingly enough.

Once over the Apulian frontier, the Emperor met with no resistance till he reached the spur of Monte Gargano. There Robert

Guiscard's old castle of Monte Sant' Angelo held out for three days against Conrad of Hohenstaufen and submitted only when Lothair arrived with the main army from Siponto and managed to take it by storm.[1] The anonymous Saxon Annalist, who gives us much the most detailed account of the whole campaign, tells us that Lothair then descended into the cave-shrine, where the whole Norman epic had begun, and 'humbly adored the blessed Archangel Michael'. His humility does not, however, seem to have inhibited him from stripping the shrine of its treasure—the gold and silver, precious stones and vestments presented by Duke Simon of Dalmatia some years before. Nor did it improve his treatment of those who opposed him and later fell into his hands. Mutilations, dismemberments and nose-slittings were the rule; and such was the terror he inspired that, on his return journey through the same region, whole populations were to flee at his approach.

Fortunately for the Apulians he was in a hurry, anxious not to waste time over protracted sieges while he still had only half his army with him. Towns like Troia or Barletta that put up a strong or spirited resistance he simply ignored: they could wait till after his son-in-law had arrived. At Trani, however, it was a different story. No sooner had he reached the town than its inhabitants rose up against the Sicilian garrison—it was probably composed for the most part of Saracens, who were seldom popular in Italy—and destroyed the citadel. A Sicilian relief fleet of thirty-three ships was scattered. The way was clear to Bari.

It was, therefore, a joyful and triumphant German congregation which assembled in the church of St Nicholas at Bari on Whit Sunday, 30 May 1137, to hear a High Mass of Thanksgiving read by the Pope himself.[2] So blessed was the hour that, according to the Saxon Annalist, a great golden crown was seen during the service, slowly descending from heaven over the church; above it

---

[1] Its ruins still stand today, and very impressive they are.

[2] Plate 3. This glorious church with its two great western towers, one Lombard, the other semi-oriental, was built to house the remains of St Nicholas of Myra—later metamorphosed into Father Christmas—after they reached Bari in rather dubious circumstances on 9 May 1087. The upper gallery has now been converted into a little museum. It contains, among other things, the huge crown and the enamel portrait of the saint with Roger II, mentioned on p. 98n.

hovered a dove, while from it there swung a smoking censer bearing two lighted candles. This ungainly manifestation seems to have
been a little premature, since the Sicilian garrison in the citadel was
still holding out; it was another month before it finally surrendered.
But in general the Emperor felt he had cause for satisfaction.
Between them, he and Duke Henry had made the imperial strength
felt over most of South Italy; they had come together, their armies
virtually intact, at the appointed time and place; and though they
had on several occasions compromised with the opposition when
time was pressing they had still not met with a single defeat. The
Sicilian on the other hand—they never called him King—had suffered
disaster after disaster. His vassals, including members of his own
family, had turned against him; so had several of his towns. Garrisons had capitulated without a struggle, a valuable fleet had been
put to flight. His arch-enemy Robert of Capua was restored to
power and in firm possession of all his domains. And not once
since the campaign began had he dared to show his face. Roger, it
appeared, was not only a usurper; he was a coward as well.

So must Lothair have reasoned; and yet the situation was not as
simple as that. If Roger remained in Sicily, making no effort to halt
the imperial advance, it was because he knew that the Emperor was
too strong for him; and that he must consequently stick more
closely than ever to his old principle and avoid open engagements.
He had only one element on his side, but that a vital one—the
element of time. Lothair might advance as far as he liked, even up
to the straits of Messina—where Roger was confident of being able
to hold him; but sooner or later he would be driven back, as so
many invading armies had been driven back before, by sickness, the
relentless summer heat of Apulia, or the need to reach the Alps
before the first snowfalls of the winter made them impassable. There
remained a theoretical possibility that the old Emperor might decide
to winter in Italy and continue the campaign the following year; but
it seemed unlikely. His army would be pressing him to return and
he himself would be reluctant to stay too long away from the seat
of his power. Certainly no previous imperial expedition had risked
a second season. And past experience showed that although such
expeditions could have a considerable effect in the short term, the

47

results they achieved seldom lasted for very long after they left. For the time being the only sensible course was to encourage the invaders to extend and exhaust themselves to the limit.

There might also be something to be gained, even at this late stage, by diplomacy. Politically, most of Roger's troubles were due to the fact that his two most powerful enemies, the Emperor and the Pope, were allied against him. If he could only separate them, some settlement might yet be reached. And so—according to the Saxon Annalist—he sent messengers to Lothair with a peace offer; if the Emperor would call a halt and recognise him as King, he for his part would split the Kingdom into two. He would continue to reign in Sicily, but his mainland dominion he would pass to his son, who would hold it forthwith as an imperial fief. In addition he would pay Lothair a substantial war indemnity and send him another son as a hostage.

The proposal was typical of Roger. It sounded reasonable and imaginative, and it would have confirmed the imperial claim on South Italy—which the Normans had tended to forget in the ninety years since Drogo de Hauteville had received his investiture from the Emperor Henry III.[1] In practice it might have meant rather less; Roger had already given his sons mainland fiefs and clearly hoped to leave more and more of the administration in the peninsula to them. The technical suzerainty of the Empire—which in theory existed already—was in any case of little practical value once the Emperor was safely back the other side of the Alps. It would, however, have been a genuine political concession; Roger's offer of his son as hostage would have been a guarantee of his sincerity; and Lothair, had he had only his own interests to consider, would have been well advised to accept an arrangement which, though admittedly less than he hoped to achieve, favoured the Empire and was above all workable.

Unfortunately there were papal interests also at stake; and Pope Innocent was interested in one thing only—the removal, immediately and for ever, of Anacletus from Rome. This was the crucial issue, and Roger's apparent silence on it poses an intriguing problem. Did he really believe that he could draw Lothair into a separate

[1] *The Normans in the South*, p. 74.

Bari: the church of St Nicholas

Troia: the Cathedral

peace, and so persuade him to march back to Germany without taking any direct action against the anti-Pope? Or, for the sake of such a peace, was he by now prepared to leave Anacletus to his fate, and awaiting only some later stage in negotiations before overtly saying so? Neither of these possibilities seems likely. Roger was too realistic a statesman to have made the former mistake, too clear-headed an ally to have contemplated the second. But there is a third explanation, which accords far more closely with what we know of his character and with subsequent events. It is that he had no real intention of coming to terms with the Emperor at all—that his purpose was simply to beguile Lothair with as tempting an offer as could safely be made and which only considerations of the papacy would prevent his accepting, thus putting the greatest possible strain on relations between him and the Pope.

And these relations were deteriorating fast. Innocent was not normally a difficult man. Though he came from an ancient and noble family of Rome—the Papareschi—contemporaries like Bishop Arnulf of Lisieux speak of his robust simplicity and the quiet modesty of his manner. He never raised his voice which, we are told, was gentle and pleasant. His private life was without blemish. Before he became Pope he had no enemies, and even afterwards no one was ever able to level any serious accusations against him. Yet behind this rather colourless exterior lay a fundamental stubborn-ness which, particularly when he had St Bernard at his elbow, made him incapable of compromise. He was determined to be reinstated in Rome before he died, but he was already nearly seventy and time was growing short. Meanwhile the imperial army, during the best part of a year in Italy, had consistently ignored or overridden him. While it wore itself out on cheap triumphs in the remotest corners of the peninsula, he was as far from the throne of St Peter as ever.

We can imagine the Pope speaking, quietly but forcibly, on these lines to Lothair when they met at Bari; and his words doubtless lent additional colour to the stories the Emperor had already heard from his son-in-law about Innocent's attitude at Viterbo, Monte Cassino and elsewhere. But these political and personal differences were themselves only reflections of a more ominous discontent, now making itself felt throughout the camp. The coolness which had long existed between the German army and the papal retinue was developing into open hostility. To some extent this may have been due to a natural antipathy between Teuton and Latin, or between men of the sword and men of the spirit; but there were other, more immediate causes. The climate of Bari is damp and enervating, its summers merciless; malaria was a constant scourge; and the month that the imperial troops were forced to spend besieging the citadel—the longest period that they had stayed in one place since the previous winter—had lost them both their momentum and their morale. Suddenly they seem to have woken up to the pointlessness and inconclusiveness of a campaign against an enemy who refused to come out and fight. If they were ever to force Roger into battle it would mean marching another several hundred miles in almost the opposite direction, passing through barbarous and increasingly hostile country and undertaking a sea crossing which, though short, would in the circumstances be both complicated and dangerous. It would also mean at least another year—and they had been away ten months already—separated from their homes and families. And for what? Just so that a bunch of haughty, endlessly complaining Italians could install themselves in Rome, another two hundred miles away and once again in a different direction, where it was quite obvious that they were not wanted and where there was a perfectly acceptable Pope already.

If Lothair ever in fact intended to march on through Calabria to Sicily—and it is far from certain that he did—this new mood in his army soon dissuaded him. Feudal law laid down precise time limits for the military service due from a vassal to his liege-lord, and not even the Emperor could force his men to go far beyond these limits against their will. After the capitulation of the Bari garrison—whose tenacity he punished by hanging a number of them from gibbets all round the city and flinging the rest into the sea—he decided against any further advance down the coast. Retracing his steps as far as Trani, he turned sharply inland. Perhaps the air of the Apennines would cool his army's temper.

It did nothing of the sort. Nor even, a few days later, did the satisfaction of capturing Melfi, the earliest Hauteville stronghold in Italy, and massacring three hundred of its defenders. By now the imperial camp had been thoroughly permeated by Roger's agents, who were working on the growing disaffection and backing up their arguments with liberal dispensations of Sicilian gold; and they actually succeeded, while the army was still at Melfi, in provoking some of the soldiers to take up arms against the Pope and his Cardinals with the intention of murdering them in cold blood. Lothair heard of the attack just in time; he called for his horse, galloped to the papal tents and somehow managed to restore order before any serious harm had been done. But it was an angry and resentful cavalcade that trailed off once more through the mountains.

At Lagopesole the Emperor called a halt. For a fortnight his army rested while, in the presence of Abbot Rainald and a delegation from Monte Cassino, the whole status of the abbey, including its relations with both Empire and Papacy, was subjected to exhaustive investigation. A full account of what took place—even if we were able to sift truth from falsehood in the distressingly unreliable chronicle of the monastic librarian, Peter the Deacon—need not detain us here; but the conclusions were clear enough. Rainald and his brethren were made to promise 'obedience to Pope Innocent and all his successors canonically elected', and to 'renounce and anathematise all schism and heresy', with particular condemnation for 'the son of Peter Leone, and Roger of Sicily, and all who follow them'. Only then were they received, barefoot, by Innocent and accepted back, with the kiss of peace, into the Church's bosom.

Lothair himself, who had strong feelings about the monastery's imperial status, may have been rather less satisfied than Innocent over the outcome of the Monte Cassino affair. But he could not risk an open breach with the Pope and probably wanted to make some amends for the incident at Melfi. Besides, news had just reached him of far more immediate interest. A Pisan fleet a hundred strong had appeared off the Campanian coast; Ischia, Sorrento and Amalfi had all made their submission. The Pisans had then tried to relieve Naples but, finding the Sicilian blockade too strong for them, had headed south and were now attacking Salerno, Roger's mainland capital. Eager to give the Pisans every support—and also, one suspects, to be properly represented on the spot in the event of any further quick victories—the Emperor hurriedly despatched Duke Henry, with Rainulf of Alife and a thousand knights, to Salerno. They arrived to find the city already under siege by Robert of Capua, with whose help they had no difficulty in sealing it off completely from the landward side. Meanwhile the Pisans, having commandeered the whole Amalfitan fleet of some three hundred vessels, had been joined by a further eighty from Genoa. Their Sicilian opponents, with only some forty ships in the harbour of Salerno, were hopelessly outnumbered. The siege of Naples, which had now been dragging on for two years, was lifted in order to liberate all available fighting men and ships for the defence of the capital; but against a combined force of such proportions the defenders had little hope and they knew it.

Even now, with his Italian kingdom overrun and its very capital threatened, Roger himself made no move. His attitude, craven as it must have appeared, was in fact the only one possible. To have sailed out from Palermo at the head of a new army of Saracens would have been the action of a hero, but hardly that of a statesman; it would have invited a defeat from which, even if he had survived, he could never have recovered. And so he stayed in Sicily, leaving the defence of Salerno to his local governor—an Englishman, Robert of Selby.

This Robert was the first of a long line of his compatriots who, as the century wore on, were to travel south to take service with the Kings of Sicily. We know nothing of his early life; but in the years since his arrival he had clearly gone a long way towards earning the reputation he was to enjoy ten years later, when a contemporary English historian, John of Hexham, was to describe him as 'the most influential of the King's friends, a man of great wealth and loaded with honours'. He had been appointed governor in Campania only a few months before, and he now proved himself worthy of the King's trust. Salerno, throughout that disastrous summer, had remained unflinchingly loyal to its sovereign. Its garrison of four hundred knights was strong and in good heart; soldiers and citizens together were ready to defend themselves, and for three weeks they fought fiercely and with courage.

Then, on 8 August, the rest of the imperial army appeared over
the mountains to the east, the Emperor himself riding at its head.
Lothair had originally intended to leave the siege to his son-in-
law; but the summer was creeping on, and the unexpected force of
the city's resistance had caused him to change his mind. Events
proved him right. To the Salernitans, his arrival meant two things;
first, that in the face of such reinforcements they themselves could
no longer hope to hold out until the winter, when they had counted
on the Germans to withdraw; and second, that by a quick surrender
to Lothair and a simultaneous request for imperial protection they
might yet escape being sacked and pillaged by the Pisans. These
views, eminently sensible as they were, were fully shared by Robert
of Selby. Summoning the elders of the city, he told them so. He
himself, representing the King over the entire province, could of
course have no part in any capitulation; it would be a matter for
Salerno only. Nevertheless, his advice to them was to lose no time
in sending a deputation to the imperial camp to seek peace and
protection.

The next day it was all over. Lothair, surprised, delighted and
doubtless gratified by this new proof of his prestige, imposed
unusually mild terms. In return for a war indemnity, the lives and
property of all Salernitans were guaranteed; even the four hundred
knights of the garrison were given their freedom. Meanwhile Robert
of Selby, with a small picked force, had withdrawn to the high
citadel above the city—that same so-called *castello normanno* that
had witnessed the stand of Salerno's last independent prince against
Robert Guiscard sixty years before and whose ruins can still be
seen—where he intended to keep the Sicilian banners flying until
the King himself should relieve him. When that moment came, he
would at least find his mainland capital still standing.

The arrangement, in fact, was welcomed by all the parties concerned—except one. The Pisans were furious. Not only had they
looked forward to rich plunder from a captured Salerno; they had
also been relying on this opportunity to annihilate one of their
principal trading competitors for years, perhaps decades, to come.
To the Emperor they had been an indispensable ally, without whom
the city would never have been won; to the Pope they had provided

a refuge for much of the past seven years; and in return they had received nothing. If that was all imperial alliances meant, they would have no more of them. If the Emperor could make a separate peace with his enemies, so could they. One of their ships sped off to Sicily to make terms with Roger; the others turned sulkily home.

Pope Innocent was later to have some moderate success in calming the Pisans down; but to Lothair their defection was of no importance. His campaign was over. He was probably none too sure himself just how much lasting good he had achieved. He had certainly failed to crush the King of Sicily as completely as he had hoped; on the other hand he had equally certainly dealt him a blow from which he must have seemed unlikely to recover. Everything now depended on the arrangements that could be made to govern South Italy and fill the vacuum of power once the imperial army had gone. There were three possible candidates for the Dukedom of Apulia—Sergius of Naples, Robert of Capua and Rainulf of Alife. Sergius and Robert were already powerful princes, and he had no wish to strengthen them still further. The Count of Alife, on the other hand, despite—or perhaps because of—his kinship with Roger, had more reason to fear him than either of the others. Two-faced and slippery as he had shown himself to be on occasions, wherever his own interests were concerned he was brave and determined. Furthermore—though Lothair may not have been consciously aware of the fact—he possessed an insidious, persuasive charm which had in the past won over even Roger himself and to which, more recently, the gruff old Emperor had fallen an easy victim. And so Lothair had made up his mind. Only Rainulf, he had decided, could be trusted to hold the dukedom safe for the Empire. His investiture would be the last official ceremony of the Italian expedition, and would set the seal on the campaign.

But who would perform it? The moment the question arose, the old imperial-papal rivalry flared up again as fiercely as ever. It was no good Lothair protesting that the first Apulian investiture, that of Drogo de Hauteville, had been by the Emperor Henry III ninety years before; Innocent quietly pointed out that Robert Guiscard owed his title to Pope Nicholas II. At last a compromise was reached—a tripartite ceremony, at which Rainulf received his symbolic lance at the hands of Emperor and Pope together, Lothair holding the shaft and Innocent the point. Henry of Bavaria, who had long chafed at what he considered the spineless attitude of his father-in-law towards papal pretensions, was outraged; and many of the German knights agreed with him. But Lothair cared little. He had saved his honour; that was enough. He was old and tired, and he wanted to go home.

As August drew to its close, he started on his way. At Capua, disagreeable news awaited him: Abbot Rainald of Monte Cassino, scarcely a month after his oath at Lagopesole, had been in contact with the agents of the King of Sicily. Innocent, with St Bernard's support, had seized on the opportunity to demonstrate his authority over Monte Cassino and had at once appointed, on his own initiative, a commission of two cardinals and Bernard himself to enquire into the canonicity of the abbot's recent election. It was several days before yet another compromise was patched up. On 17 September, before a joint tribunal consisting of both the Emperor and the papal representatives—including St Bernard who, as always, took it upon himself to be principal spokesman—Rainald's election was pronounced uncanonical. The unfortunate abbot had no choice but to lay down ring and staff on the grave of St Benedict; and Wibald, Abbot of Stavelot, a tough Lorrainer who had accompanied the expedition from the start, was 'elected' in his place. We are not told by what means the monks were induced to accept so obvious an imperial nominee; but with the German army encamped at the foot of the hill they probably had little choice in the matter.

Lothair's health was now failing fast; and to all those around him it was plain that his days were numbered. He himself knew it as well as anyone, but he refused to take to his bed; he was a German, and it was in Germany that he wished to die. Rainulf, Robert of Capua and the Campanian vassals accompanied him as far as Aquino, the border of Norman territory. From there, leaving eight hundred of his knights to help the rebels to maintain themselves after his departure, he took the road to Rome; but before reaching the city he turned off towards Palestrina. For him there could no longer be any question of returning the Pope to St Peter's. At the monastery of Farfa he bade him farewell. Henceforth Innocent would have to fight his own battles.

Though he marched with all the speed of which his dispirited, half-disbanded army was capable, it was mid-November before the Emperor reached the foothills of the Alps. His companions implored him to winter there. The sickness was daily increasing its hold on him; it would be folly, they pointed out, to attempt a crossing of the Brenner so late in the year. But the old man knew that he could not afford to wait. With all the determination of the dying he pressed on, and by the end of the month was descending towards the valley of the Inn. But now his last remaining strength deserted him. At the little village of Breitenwang in the Tyrol he stopped at last; he was carried to a poor peasant's hut; and there, on 3 December 1137, at the age of seventy-two, he died.[1]

[1] Passing recently through Breitenwang and enquiring whether there was any memorial to Lothair, I was directed to a fair-sized house on which was fixed a plaque. It read:

> Hier starb am 3. Dezember 1137
> Lothar II
> Deutscher und Römischer Kaiser
> in den Armen seines Schwiegersohnes
> Heinrich des Stolzen.
> In Ehrfurcht gewidmet von
> Frederick R. Sims
> London und Holzgau.

4

RECONCILIATION AND RECOGNITION

Thanks be to God who has given victory to the Church. . . . Our sorrow is turned into joy and our mourning into the music of the lute. . . . The useless branch, the rotten limb has been cut off. The wretch who led Israel into sin has been swallowed up by death and thrown down into the belly of hell. May all those like him suffer the same fate!

St Bernard, on the death of Anacletus
(Letter to Abbot Peter of Cluny)

DURING the twelve years since his accession, Lothair of Supplinburg had proved himself to his German subjects a worthy occupant of the imperial throne. Upright, brave and merciful according to the standards of his time, he had brought back peace to a land riven with civil war; jealous as he was of his imperial prerogatives, he was also a genuinely pious man who had worked hard to heal the schism within the Church; and he left his compatriots happier and more prosperous than he had found them. Once south of the Alps, however, he seemed to lose his touch. Italy to him was a strange and foreign land; its people he mistrusted and misunderstood. Ever unable to make up his mind whether his principal task was to restore the rightful Pope or to crush the King of Sicily, he failed in both; and the indecision produced in him a state of general insecurity which led him to veer between uncharacteristic excesses of cruelty on the one hand and dangerous errors of omission on the other.

Above all, he never realised till it was too late that his show of strength through the mainland dominions of the King of Sicily was nothing but a piece of empty shadow-boxing; and that the only way of bringing Roger under control was by exterminating him altogether. Had he thrown all his strength, at the very outset, into an amphibious attack on Palermo, he might—just possibly— have succeeded; but by the time he learnt this lesson his army was in a state of near mutiny, the Pope was becoming more of an antagonist than an ally, and he himself, worn out by his exertions, the South Italian climate and his own swiftly encroaching disease, was a dying man.

It was less than three months after the imperial party left Monte Cassino that the Empress Richenza closed her husband's eyes in death; yet already by that time Roger had regained control of a large part of his territory. There could be no more conclusive justi- fication of his policy over the past year. He was welcomed at Salerno when he arrived there at the beginning of October; and as he swept up through Campania scarcely a hand was lifted against him—though his newly-arrived Saracen regiments left a trail of death and destruction in their wake. Capua suffered worst. Prince Robert was away in Apulia but his city, if we are to believe Falco, was seized as if by a furious tempest and depopulated by fire and the sword. 'The King,' he goes on, 'commanded that the city should he totally despoiled . . . the churches plundered and stripped of their ornaments, the women and even the nuns brought to dishonour.' Falco, as we know, could not have written objectively if he had tried; but even after allowance is made for his hatred of the Normans it seems clear that Roger was bent once again on making an example of the rebel towns, just as he had after the earlier Apulian insurrec- tion. Benevento he spared out of respect for its papal status; Naples too escaped lightly after Duke Sergius, for the second time in three years, had flung himself at Roger's feet and pledged his allegiance. Few adversaries would have forgiven a twofold treason such as this, but Roger was by nature a merciful man; he may have decided that after so long and arduous a siege the Neapolitans had suffered enough.

Had Sergius learnt his lesson? Would he have proved, in the long run, a faithful vassal at last? There is no telling, for within a month he was dead. In the third week of October he accompanied the King to Apulia where Rainulf, determined to defend his new

Dukedom, was busy forging an army. With the eight hundred German knights left him by Lothair, almost as many again culled from various local militias and with infantry in proportion, this amounted to quite a formidable force; Roger might have been better advised to avoid a head-on confrontation. Perhaps his successes in Campania had made him headstrong; possibly his anxiety to have done with this interminable rebellion may have clouded his judgment. His, however, and not Rainulf's, was the decision to do battle —just outside the village of Rignano, at the south-western edge of Monte Gargano where it drops away two thousand feet to the Apulian plain.[1]

His, too, was the responsibility for the defeat that followed. His young son Roger, whom he had invested with the Duchy of Apulia two years previously and who was now fighting his first major action in an effort to regain it, showed himself a worthy scion of the Hautevilles, charging fearlessly into his adversaries and driving one section right back along the road to Siponto. The King, however, had meanwhile decided to lead a second charge. Just what happened we shall never know, but he was utterly routed. Falco gleefully records—though his account is nowhere corroborated —that King Roger himself was the first to flee. He made straight for Salerno, leaving Sergius, thirty-ninth and last Duke of Naples, dead on the battlefield.

At the time of the disaster of Rignano—30 October 1137—the Emperor Lothair had still five weeks to live. We must hope that news of it reached him before he died; it would have given him comfort. And yet, surprisingly, even Rignano did Roger little lasting harm. A few cities of Campania took advantage of his defeat to claim certain concessions which they might not otherwise have been granted, but all stayed loyal; and a day or two after the King's return to Salerno news was brought to him that Abbot Wibald of Monte Cassino, after just a month and a day in office, had fled in

---

[1] The view from Rignano southward over Apulia long ago earned the village its title of *Balcone delle Puglie*. The mediaeval castle into whose ruins many of the houses have been built is more or less contemporary with the events here described.

terror across the Alps. He had paused, it appeared, only long enough to emphasise to his monks that he was leaving for their sake rather than his own—a protestation which they might have been readier to believe had it not been for the King's well-publicised threats to hang him if he remained. From the safety of Corbie, his next abbacy, Wibald was to keep up a steady flow of invective against Roger for the rest of his life; but he never ventured into Italy again. In his place the monks wisely elected one of their own number, a man of staunch pro-Sicilian and Anacletan sympathies; and thenceforth the great abbey, while preserving its technical independence, became to all intents and purposes a part of the Kingdom.

Back once again in Salerno, Roger was able to take stock of the situation. All in all, he was not dissatisfied. His policy of non-involvement, of allowing the German momentum to burn itself out, had been triumphantly vindicated. The Emperor had come and gone; on his arrival he had seemed to carry all before him, but within two months of his departure there was little left to show for his efforts but an Apulian insurrection—of that old, dreary, endemic kind which Roger, his father and his uncles had all had to deal with countless times over the past century and which could, doubtless, be dealt with again. The Kingdom itself was no longer in peril. The toll in money and lives—apart from the losses at Rignano, which need never have happened—had been minimal. Pope Anacletus was still lording it at St Peter's. Yet again, peaceful statesmanship had carried the day over brute force.

On the debit side, however, there was no denying that Roger's prestige had suffered a grave setback. Many of his less far-sighted adherents had been shocked by his passivity, which they had taken for cowardice; and his showing at Rignano, where he had probably hoped to redeem his reputation, had served only to confirm their suspicions. Moreover, though immediate danger had been averted, the undeniable fact remained that none of Roger's basic problems had been solved. The Sicilian crown was still recognised by no one but Anacletus; Robert and Rainulf, those two inveterate rebels, were still at large; while down at the very bed-rock of all the trouble, the Papacy remained divided.

But this last consideration was less disturbing to Roger than to

his enemies—a fact which explains why, some time at the beginning
of November, the hitherto most redoubtable of all those enemies
came personally to call on the King in Salerno. Like all the other
members of Pope Innocent's entourage, St Bernard of Clairvaux
had had a disagreeable summer. His health had long since been
shattered, and seven months spent trailing round the peninsula in
the imperial wake had left him in a state bordering on collapse. He
and Lothair had never liked each other. It was he, far more than the
mild-mannered Innocent, who had been disgusted by the proprie-
torial attitude shown by both the Emperor and Duke Henry towards
South Italy—which even the 'Sicilian tyrant' knew was a papal fief;
and it was he, almost certainly, who had persuaded and encouraged
his master to stand firm—at Lagopesole, Monte Cassino and elsewhere—against imperial pretensions.

When Emperor and Pope had finally parted company at Farfa,
Bernard had hoped to return to Clairvaux for rest. Instead, they had
sent him back to Apulia in the hopes that his prestige might succeed
where their force had failed and that he might be able to bring
Roger to terms. With a reluctance that he did nothing to conceal,
he had turned back, and had actually been present at Rignano, where
he had met Roger for the first time and had tried, unsuccessfully, to
dissuade him from doing battle.[1] After the débâcle, however,
Bernard rightly counted on finding the King in a more amenable
mood. Roger had no desire to perpetuate the schism. His support of
Anacletus, having originally won him his throne, had very nearly
lost it for him again. The situation was very different from what it
had been seven years ago. At that time it had seemed likely that
Anacletus might win an all-out victory; now it was plain that he
could hope for nothing more than to retain the opprobrious title
of anti-Pope, while living for the rest of his life a virtual prisoner
in the Vatican. For as long as Roger continued to support him in
his pigheadedness the Emperor would continue to encourage the
South Italian rebels; and peace would never return to the land.
Naturally the King, to whom the disloyalty of his own vassals was
so constant a preoccupation, felt reluctant to betray his own
suzerain; but there might be other possibilities besides betrayal. At

[1] *Vita Prima*, II, vii.

all events Bernard's visit provided a welcome opportunity for him to pause in the fighting and to talk instead. He badly needed a little time for recovery, and he knew that as a diplomatist he was more than a match for any of his adversaries. He gave the abbot a cordial welcome and readily agreed to look into the whole question of the Papacy again.

His proposal was that the rival Popes should each send three representatives to Salerno to plead their case; and Bernard accepted it. Poor Anacletus must have been horrified at this sign of vacillation on the part of his only ally, but he could hardly refuse. His choice fell on his papal chancellor, Peter of Pisa, and two of his Cardinals, Matthew and Gregory. Innocent also sent his chancellor— that same Cardinal Aimeri who had been largely responsible for the schism in the first place—together with Cardinals Guido of Castello and Gerard of Bologna, later respectively to become Popes Celestine II and Lucius II. The six arrived in Salerno at the end of November.

It was inevitable that Bernard, though technically not even a member of Innocent's delegation, should have done most of the talking. Once again, as at Etampes, he seems to have deliberately ignored the only legitimate subject for discussion—the canonicity of the original elections. This time, however, he did not fall back on invective; the Anacletans present could have defended their master too well and Roger would have been antagonised. Instead, he based his case on strength of numbers. Innocent enjoyed more present support than Anacletus; Innocent, therefore, must be the rightful Pope. It was a shaky thesis by any standards, but such was the fervour with which it was developed that its deficiencies in logic were largely overlooked.

The robe of Christ, which at the time of the Passion neither heathen nor Jew dared to tear, Peter Leoni now rends asunder. There is but one Faith, one Lord, one Baptism. At the time of the Flood there was but one ark. In this eight souls were saved, the rest perished. The Church is a kind of ark. . . . Lately another ark has been built, and as there are two, one must of necessity be false and will surely sink beneath the sea. If Peter Leoni's ark comes from God, then will Innocent's ark be destroyed and with it the Church of the East and the West. France and Germany will perish, the Spaniards and the English and the lands of the barbarians, all will be lost in the depths of the Ocean. The monks of Camaldoli, the Carthusians, the Cluniacs, those of Grandmont and Cîteaux and Prémontré and innumerable others, monks and nuns, all must be drowned in one great whirlpool, down into the deep. The hungry ocean will consume bishops, abbots and other princes of the Church, with millstones tied about their necks.

Of the princes of the world only Roger has entered the ark of Peter; with all the others perished, shall he only be saved? Can it be that the religion of the whole world should perish, and the ambition of Peter Leoni, whose life is so plain to us, should gain for him the Kingdom of Heaven?[1]

As always, the abbot's rhetoric had its effect. It is given to few advocates, in the course of legal proceedings, to win over opposing counsel; and yet, as Bernard rounded off his tirade, it was not the King but Peter of Pisa who advanced towards him to confess his past errors and implore pardon. This public defection of his own chancellor dealt Anacletus a blow only fractionally less severe than if he had been denounced by the King himself; and as the Abbot of Clairvaux stretched out his hand towards the apostate and led him gently but triumphantly away, there can have been few present at the tribunal who did not believe Pope Innocent's cause as good as won.

Roger, by contrast, was unmoved. The longer he could delay his decision, the better; besides, it was not his practice to make concessions without gaining some commensurate advantage in return. Anacletus was, after all, the only authority for his kingship; this would have to be confirmed by Innocent before there could be any question of a change in his allegiance. So too would his son's title to the Duchy of Apulia, of which Rainulf, as Innocent's appointee, would first have to be formally divested. But a public tribunal was no place for negotiations of this sort. On the ninth day the King gave out that he found the issue too complex for him to be able to decide on the spot. He would need to consult his Curia. He therefore proposed that one cardinal from each side should return to Sicily with him. On Christmas Day he would announce his decision.

Bernard did not accompany Roger to Sicily. Instead he returned to Rome with Peter of Pisa. Probably he suspected by now that his attempts to influence the King had failed. Had he still entertained

[1] *Vita Prima*, II, vii.

any serious hopes, it is hard to believe that he would not have followed up what he had begun and pursued his quarry to Palermo. Certainly it seems to have surprised no one when, as he had promised, Roger announced on Christmas Day that he saw no reason to change his previous opinions. He had upheld Anacletus as the true Pope in the past; he would continue to do so in the future.

If, as seems most likely, Roger's answer was prompted by the refusal of Pope Innocent to accept his conditions, Innocent's own attitude was probably governed by developments in Rome. Anacletus never recovered from the loss of Peter of Pisa. As the tormented year of 1137 drew to its close he appeared to be losing his grip on the city, and from November of that year we find Innocent heading his letters with the word *Romae,* in place of his earlier formula *in territorio Romano.* By now the anti-Pope held little more than St Peter's, the Vatican and the Castel S. Angelo, and it was perhaps just as well for him that, on 25 January 1138, he died.[1] His life, at first so promising, had been a sad one. Throughout the eight years that he had occupied the throne of St Peter to which, rightly or wrongly, he believed himself to be entitled, he had suffered—for the most part in silence—the campaign of invective and abuse that his enemies, led by the Abbot of Clairvaux, had ceaselessly waged against him. This campaign, nurtured down the centuries by Catholic apologists and St Bernard's biographers, still persists; in several modern works of reference the name of Anacletus is either vilified or omitted altogether. He deserved better than this. If his early career was stained with simony, it still remains clearer than that of most other pontiffs of his time. If he must take his share of the blame for splitting the Church in two, Pope Innocent and Chancellor Aimeri must each bear at least as large a part. Had events taken a different turn, or had St Bernard been content to occupy himself with the affairs of his abbey and his Order, then Anacletus, with his wisdom, his genuine piety and his diplomatic experience,

---

[1] Whether the location of his grave was deliberately kept secret by his supporters or whether it was immediately desecrated by those of Innocent we do not know. It has never been found.

might have proved himself an excellent Pope. As things turned out, he maintained an impossibly invidious position with dignity and restraint.

With his death, the schism was effectively at an end. The cardinals who had remained loyal to him did not immediately give up the struggle; in March, possibly with Roger's approval, they elected Cardinal Gregory as his successor under the name of Victor IV.[1] But Gregory's heart was not in it. He had none of the popularity of his predecessor, and the few Romans who at first undertook to give him their support were soon bribed away by Innocent. After a few weeks he could bear the situation no longer. One night in May he slipped out of the Vatican and across the Tiber to St Bernard's lodgings, where he gave himself up; and on 29 May, the Octave of Pentecost, Bernard was able to report to the prior of Clairvaux:

God has given unity to the Church, and peace to the City. . . . The people of Peter Leoni have humbled themselves at the feet of our lord the Pope, and have sworn him faithful homage as his liegemen. So too have those schismatic priests, together with the idol which they set up . . . and there is great gladness among the people.

Neither the death of Anacletus nor the collapse of his faintly ridiculous successor seems to have worried Roger unduly. His continued support for the anti-Pope had not proved the successful bargaining counter for which he had hoped, and the end of the schism certainly cleared the air. Freed now of the commitments that had cast such a blight on the first seven years of his kingship, he saw no point in continuing hostilities with the Holy See. He made public recognition of Innocent as the lawful pontiff, and sent orders to all his subjects to do likewise. Then, his army behind him, he headed for Apulia.

All through the summer and autumn the campaign went on. It must have been a demoralising time for Roger. Once again he swept through the peninsula, sacking and burning wherever he met any

---

[1] We have only Falco's authority for the suggestion that the King was consulted about this election and approved it. Whatever may be thought about the election of Anacletus, no one could defend the legality of Victor's, based as it was on the vote of a mere handful of schismatic cardinals. And by now Roger had everything to gain from ending the split in the Church.

opposition; yet somehow he could not achieve any real break-through. When he returned to Palermo at the end of the year the greater part of Apulia was still in rebel hands. Meanwhile there had been no word of any kind from Rome—nothing to suggest that Innocent was prepared to contemplate a reconciliation; and the following spring, as Roger was preparing for yet another year of struggle, the Pope showed just how far he was from any such idea. At a Lateran Council on 8 April 1139 he pronounced a renewed sentence of excommunication on the King of Sicily, his sons, and all those of his bishops whom Anacletus had consecrated.

But the end of Roger's nine-year calvary was fast approaching; indeed, it was nearer than any of the protagonists knew. The inconclusiveness of the 1138 campaign had suggested that Rainulf would be able to maintain his position indefinitely in Apulia, and the aggressiveness of the Lateran Council indicated that this confidence was shared in Rome. It was misplaced. Within three weeks of the Council he had fallen sick of a fever at Troia; he was bled unsuccessfully; and on 30 April he died. They buried him in Troia Cathedral.

Falco of Benevento has left us a poignant account of the consternation that spread through all rebel-held Apulia at the news of Rainulf's death: of the wailing of virgins and widows, of old men and children, of the tearing of hair, the lacerations of breasts and cheeks. It all sounds rather exaggerated; and yet we cannot avoid the impression that Rainulf was genuinely loved. For all his faithlessness he was an attractive, quixotic figure, with a charm that neither his friends nor his enemies were ever quite able to resist; in his short rule as Duke he seems to have governed wisely and well. He was a brilliant soldier and a brave one—a good deal braver than Roger, whom he twice defeated on the battlefield. A Norman through and through, in the popular imagination of his compatriots he embodied the knightly ideal in a way that his oriental, devious-minded brother-in-law could never hope to emulate. His weakness lay in his statesmanship; he simply did not see that Roger could never be beaten without long-term support, both political and military, from abroad. It was this blindness that led him—in defiance of his solemn oath, and after the King had shown him a rare degree of mercy—into an enterprise that brought misery and suffering to the South and laid it open to acts of cruelty by Roger of the kind which he never committed except when desperate. In short, the harm that Rainulf did his country was incalculable, and the sorrow that attended his death was greater than he deserved.

With Rainulf's death the rebellion was officially at an end. Apart from one or two isolated pockets of resistance which he could deal with at his leisure—notably Bari and the region round Troia and Ariano—only one problem remained. In late June Pope Innocent marched south from Rome with his old ally Robert of Capua. But Innocent could offer no real threat now. The papal army, by all accounts, was not particularly large—a thousand knights at the most— and this time there was every hope that the Pope would be ready to talk. Indeed, soon after the first reports of his approach, two cardinals arrived at the Sicilian camp. His Holiness, they reported, had now reached S. Germano;[1] if Roger would wait upon him there, he would be received in peace.

Taking his son and his army with him, the King rode off over the mountains to S. Germano. For a week the negotiations dragged on. Innocent was apparently quite prepared to recognise the Sicilian crown, but he demanded in return the reinstatement of the Prince of Capua. Roger refused. Again and again over the past seven years he had given Robert the chance to make peace; now his patience was exhausted. When he saw that the Pope on his side was also adamant he resolved to waste no more time talking. Giving out that he had some unfinished business in the Sangro valley, he broke camp and headed away to the north.

As he must have known they would, Innocent and Robert soon reopened hostilities and began beating their way towards Capua, leaving a trail of burning villages and vineyards behind them. Then, at the little town of Galluccio, they suddenly halted. From a high position on their left, the Sicilian army was watching them. Innocent quickly saw the danger and ordered an immediate withdrawal; but he was too late. While his army was still collecting itself, young Duke Roger burst out of an ambush with a thousand knights and swept down into the centre of the papal troops. They broke in disorder.

---

[1] The modern town of Cassino, just below the monastery.

Many were cut down as they fled; countless others were drowned as they tried to cross the Garigliano. Robert of Capua somehow managed to escape, but Pope Innocent was not so lucky. He tried to take refuge, so the legend has it, in the little frescoed chapel of S. Nicola which can still be seen in the church of the Annunziata at Galluccio; but he tried in vain. That evening, 22 July 1139, the Pope and his cardinals, his archives and his treasure, were all in the hands of the King.

Two months before, while Pope Innocent was still assembling his army in Rome, Mount Vesuvius, after nearly a century's quiescence, had burst out in magnificent and terrifying eruption. For a week it had raged, vomiting lava over the neighbouring villages and filling the air with a pervasive reddish dust that darkened the sky over Benevento, Salerno and Capua. No one had doubted that it was a portent, and now at last men knew what it had foretold. The Holy Father himself had been brought low. Here was the greatest humiliation suffered by the Papacy at the hands of the Normans since Duke Humphrey de Hauteville and his brother Robert Guiscard had annihilated the army of Pope Leo IX at Civitate, eighty-six years before.

It was always a mistake for Popes to meet Normans on the battlefield. Just as Leo had had to come to terms with his captors after Civitate, so now Innocent in his turn was forced to bow to the inevitable. At first he refused; the honour and respect with which Roger persisted in treating him seem to have deluded him into believing that he might still be able to impose his own conditions. Only after three days did he finally understand the reality of his situation—and the price of his ransom. On 25 July, at Mignano, Roger was formally confirmed in the Kingdom of Sicily, with the overlordship of all Italy south of the Garigliano. Next, his son Roger was invested with the Duchy of Apulia, and his third son Alfonso with the Principality of Capua. The Pope then said Mass, in the course of which he preached a sermon of enormous length on the subject of peace, and left the church a free man. In the ensuing charter he managed to save a few shreds of the papal honour by presenting the whole thing as being merely a renewal and an extension of Roger's earlier investiture by Honorius II; the King also undertook to pay an annual tribute of six hundred *schifati*.[1] But nothing could disguise the fact that, for the Pope and his party, the treaty of Mignano spelt unconditional surrender.

Writing half a century after these events, the English historian Ralph Niger records in his *Chronica Universalis* that Innocent sealed the treaty by presenting Roger with his mitre; and that the King, having embellished it with gold and precious stones, made it into a crown for himself and his successors. Be that as it may, the two seem to have established a fairly cordial relationship. Together they rode to Benevento, where the Pope was received with such jubilation that, says Falco, it was as if St Peter himself were entering the city; and where, a day or two later in his camp outside the walls, the King received ambassadors from Naples to swear him fidelity and deliver to him the keys of their city.

This submission marked the end of an epoch. For four centuries and more the dukes of Naples had steered their perilous course through the straits and shoals of South Italian politics. Often they had nearly foundered; occasionally even, the Pisans or some other temporary allies had had to take them in tow. Though sailing technically under the Byzantine flag of convenience, they had also in recent years been increasingly obliged to run other colours to the masthead—those of the Western Empire, for example, or even those of the Normans themselves. And yet somehow their ship had always managed to stay afloat. Now it could do so no longer. Naples had suffered three sieges in nine years, and a disastrous famine to boot. Its last duke was dead, the quasi-republican government that had succeeded him an abject failure. The greatness and the glory were gone. When, a few days later, young Duke Roger entered the city to take formal possession in his father's name, he accepted it not as a loyal fief, but as an integral part of the Sicilian Kingdom. The ship had foundered at last.

Only two pockets of resistance remained to be mopped up: the Troia region, where the German rearguard left by Lothair was still

---

[1] 'The *schifatus* was a convex-shaped Byzantine coin worth, in 1269 at any rate, eight *taris* of gold, i.e. somewhat more than a quarter of an ounce of Sicilian gold; i.e. a *schifatus* had about the same value as an English sovereign.' (Mann, *Lives of the Popes in the Early Middle Ages*, vol. IX, p. 65.)

making trouble, and Bari, whither the last few of the rebel barons had retreated to make a final stand. In the first week of August the King appeared below Troia.[1] The town surrendered on his arrival; since the papal capitulation there seemed no point in continuing the struggle and the citizens, encouraged by reports of the mercy that Roger had shown towards the coastal cities of Apulia, invited him to enter in peace. But now the King revealed, for the first time, how deeply he had felt his brother-in-law's treason. He sent back word that he would accept no surrender from the Troians for so long as Rainulf's body was buried within their walls. His message was received with horror in the city, but Troia's spirit was broken. It had no choice but to comply. Four knights, led by one of the most faithful of Rainulf's old supporters, were given the task of breaking open his tomb. The body was dug up in its shroud, dragged on the King's orders through the streets to the citadel and finally cast into an evil-smelling ditch outside the gates. Soon after this lapse Roger seems to have repented of his inhumanity and, at his son's instigation, to have allowed his old enemy a decent reburial; but although he took no further action against Troia he still refused to enter it. In the remaining fifteen years of his life he never went there again.

It was a still vengeful King who now passed grimly on through Trani—to which his son had accorded remarkably generous terms a few months before—to Bari. No city in Apulia had played him false so often, and its continued resistance, despite the surrender of all its neighbours and the generosity with which they had been treated, had destroyed the last remnants of his patience. After a two-month siege, with famine threatening, the defenders were forced to seek terms. Roger, anxious above all to have done with the rebellion and return to Sicily, agreed to their conditions: there was to be no pillage, and prisoners taken on both sides should be returned unharmed. When he found himself within the walls, however, his vindictiveness again got the better of him. One of his knights, newly released from captivity, reported that he had had an eye put out while he was in prison. It was just the pretext Roger was looking

[1] Plate 4.

for. Was this not a breach of the agreement that had been made?
Judges were summoned from Troia and Trani to join those of
Bari in proclaiming the treaty null and void. The rebel Prince,
Jaquintus, was delivered up to the King, together with his principal
counsellors. All were hanged. Ten other leading citizens were
blinded, yet others imprisoned and dispossessed. 'And such was the
fear and trembling in the city,' Falco reports, 'that not a single man
or woman durst venture out into the streets and squares.'

Even on his return to Salerno the King's anger had not entirely
abated. Certain of the Campanian vassals who had been congratulating themselves on having escaped lightly after their part in the
uprising suddenly found their lands and property confiscated. Some
of these too were imprisoned, the majority exiled 'beyond the
mountains'. When, on 5 November, Roger took ship for Sicily, he
left a cowed and chastened baronage behind him.

The year 1139 had been the most triumphant of his reign. It had
seen the death of his arch-enemy Rainulf and the two petty dynasties
of Naples and Bari; and the effective elimination of Robert of Capua
who, though he was to pass the rest of his life intriguing against the
King, was never again to constitute a serious menace to the Sicilian
throne. It had seen the most significant mainland victory for nearly
a century, one which effectively wiped out the shame of Rignano
two years before. It had seen the pacification of the entire South
Italian Kingdom, its utter submission to the King's will, and the
disappearance of the last remnants of the German imperial invaders.
Finally, it had seen the reconciliation between the Kingdom and the
Papacy and the recognition, by the rightful, undisputed Pope, of
the Sicilian monarchy. Roger himself had shown courage, diplomacy,
statesmanship and—at least until just before the end—mercy; and
if in this last virtue he ultimately fell short of his own high standards,
his record remains a good deal better than that of most of his
contemporaries.

'Thus,' concludes Archbishop Romuald of Salerno, 'Roger, most
powerful of Kings, having crushed and destroyed his enemies and
betrayers, returned in glory and triumph to Sicily, and held his
Kingdom in perfect peace and tranquillity.' It sounds like the ending
of a fairy story, and Roger certainly had every cause for satisfaction

as he sailed for home. Yet he cannot have been happy. As his conduct at Troia and Bari had shown, he was sick to the heart. The past
few years had left him with a legacy of bitterness and disillusion
which he would never quite overcome. His generosity had been
too often abused, his trust too often betrayed, the great plans he
cherished for his Kingdom too often set at nought by the selfish
ambitions of the Norman baronage. In Sicily, where there were no
great fiefs, men of three religions and four races were living happily
at peace and in steadily increasing prosperity; in South Italy he had
achieved nothing; his vassals had thwarted him at every turn. He
had begun to hate the peninsula. In future he would leave its affairs
as far as possible to his sons and devote his attention, as he had never
been allowed to devote it in the past, to his island realm.

When, in January 1072, Robert Guiscard and his brother had
battered their way into Saracen Palermo, one of their first decisions
had been to move the administrative centre of the capital. The
Emirs had always ruled from their palace in the district of Al-
Khalesa, down by the sea; but they had also maintained an old castle
on the higher ground a mile and a half to the west, which had been
built some two centuries before to protect the landward approaches.
This castle was cooler, quieter, remoter from all the dirt and hubbub
of the city; it was also more commandingly situated and more easily
defensible in the event of trouble. To the new conquerors that last
point was the vital one; no Norman ever felt truly at ease living
somewhere that he could not adequately defend in an emergency.
Thus the old Saracen fortress, repaired and strengthened, became
the seat of the Norman government and, in due course, the palace
of the Great Count of Sicily.

Over the years, Roger I and his son had put in hand various far-
reaching structural alterations, until little of the original Saracen
fabric was left. By 1140 the building was in essence a Norman
palace; and though much has inevitably been added during the past
eight centuries—*cortiles* and colonnades, loggias and baroque façades,
to say nothing of all the ponderous trappings of the Sicilian
parliament—much, too, still unmistakably proclaims its Norman
origins. The *Torre Pisana*, in particular, at the north end—otherwise

known as the Torre di Santa Ninfa after an early Palermitan virgin whose immoderate admiration of the Christian martyrs led her to follow their example—still stands much as Roger must have known it. Even the copper dome of the local observatory, perched somewhat insensitively on its roof, proves less offensive than one might expect. The crowning of a romanesque tower with a bulbously Islamic cupola is a characteristic tendency of Norman-Sicilian architecture, and the old Palermitan astronomers, whether they recognised the fact or not, were merely continuing the old tradition. It is somehow gratifying to learn that it was from this observatory, on the first evening of the nineteenth century, that they discovered the first and largest of the asteroids and named it Ceres, after the patron goddess of the island.

Yet the *Palazzo Reale*, as it is still called, ultimately captures neither the eye nor the imagination. As an ensemble, it is an architectural hotch-potch which fails to impose any overriding personality; even the *Torre Pisana* seems stilted and uninspired, so that the casual visitor might be forgiven for turning away with a shrug to the more immediately photogenic attractions of S. Giovanni degli Eremiti down the road. Forgiven, but pitied none the less; for in doing so he would unwittingly have deprived himself of one of the greatest excitements that Sicily, and perhaps Europe, has to offer him—his first, unsuspecting discovery of the Palatine Chapel.

As early as 1129, before he became King, Roger had begun to build his own personal chapel on the first floor of his palace, overlooking the inner courtyard. Work on it had been slow, largely because his problems on the mainland allowed him only a few months of each year in which to superintend building operations. But at last, in the spring of 1140, though still unfinished, the chapel was ready to enter service; and on Palm Sunday, 28 April, in the presence of the King and all his leading Sicilian clergy of both the Greek and Latin rites, it was consecrated, dedicated to St Peter, and formally granted the privileges appropriate to its palatine status.

Roger had no more love for Byzantium than had any other member of his family; but both the manner of his upbringing and the oriental atmosphere in which he lived inclined him towards the Byzantine concept of monarchy—a mystically-tinged absolutism in

73

which the monarch, as God's viceroy, lived remote and elevated from his subjects, in a magnificence that reflected his intermediate position between earth and heaven. The art of Norman Sicily, now suddenly bursting into flower, was therefore above all a palace art; and it is fitting that its brightest jewel—*le plus surprenant bijou religieux rêvé par la pensée humaine,* as Maupassant was to describe it[1] seven and a half centuries later—should be the Palatine Chapel at Palermo.[2] It is in this building, with more stunning effect than anywhere else in Sicily, that we see the Siculo-Norman political miracle given visual expression—a seemingly effortless fusion of all that is most brilliant in the Latin, Byzantine and Islamic traditions into a single, harmonious masterpiece.

Its form is in essence that of a western basilica, with a central nave and two side aisles separated from it by rows of antique granite columns, all with richly gilded Corinthian capitals, drawing the eye along to the five steps that lead up to the choir. Western too, though whispering of the South, are the richly ornamented pavements and the coruscating Cosmatesque inlays of the steps, balustrades and lower walls—to say nothing of that immense ambo, proudest of pulpits, studded with gold and malachite and porphyry and flanked by a gigantic Paschal candlestick, a fifteen-foot high bestiary in white marble.[3]

But if we look up now to the mosaics with which the whole chapel glows gold, we are once again brought face to face with Byzantium. Some, alas, of these mosaics, notably those in the upper part of the north wall of the transept, have disappeared; others have been drastically—and in one or two cases disastrously—restored over the centuries. Occasionally, as in the lower half of the central apse and the two side apses, we are confronted with eighteenth-century

---

[1] *La Vie Errante,* Paris, 1890.　　　[2] Plate 5.

[3] Plate 6. This candlestick was almost certainly presented to the chapel by Archbishop Hugh of Palermo when he crowned Roger's son William co-ruler with his father at Easter, 1151. Carved on it, among the angelic supporters of the crucified Christ and roughly at eye-level, a single human figure emerges rather improbably from a palm frond. This figure, wearing a mitre and showing a disturbing resemblance to Mr Punch, was long believed to be a portrait of Roger himself; but since it also bears the papal *pallium,* to which the King was not entitled, it is more likely to represent the donor. (Schramm, *Herrschaftszeichen und Staatssymbolik,* vol. I, p. 80.)

monstrosities which a more enlightened administration would long ago have swept away. The best, however—Christ Pantocrator gazing in benediction from the dome, the circle of angels garlanding him with their wings, the evangelists studious in their squinches— all these are the finest, purest Byzantine, of which any church in Constantinople would have been proud. Over the choir nearly all bear Greek inscriptions, sure testimony of their date and workmanship; by contrast the Virgin in the northern transept,[1] the scenes from the Old Testament in the nave and those from the lives of St Peter and St Paul in the side aisles were added by William I some twenty years later, after his father's death. Here and elsewhere the Latin inscriptions, the preference for Latin saints and certain stylistic attempts to break away from the rigid canons of Byzantine iconography suggest that William was employing native artists—presumably Italian pupils of the original Greek masters. Other Italians, in the later thirteenth century, were responsible for the enthroned Christ on the western wall over the royal dais[2] and the two figures of St Gregory and St Sylvester inside the sanctuary arch, unpardonably introduced in the Angevin period to replace an earlier likeness of Roger himself.

These almost antiphonal responses of Latin and Byzantine, set in so lavish a frame, would alone have earned for the Palatine Chapel a unique place among the religious buildings of the world. But for Roger they were still not enough. Two of the great cultural traditions of his country had been dazzlingly reflected in his new creation, but what of the third? What of the Saracens, the most populous group of all his island subjects, whose loyalty had been unwavering—in marked contrast to that of his Norman compatriots—for more than half a century, whose administrative

[1] Seen from below she is inexplicably off-centre—for which the figure of John the Baptist to the upper left seems an awkward attempt to compensate. From the large window in the north wall, however, she appears in the dead centre of the visible wall space. From this it has been deduced that this window—which communicates with the interior of the palace—was used from about 1160 onwards as a royal box. (For this and much other fascinating detective work on Sicilian mosaics, see Demus, *The Mosaics of Norman Sicily*, London, 1950.)

[2] According to an inscription on the wall of the north aisle, this was restored in the fourteenth century.

efficiency was largely responsible for the prosperity of the Kingdom, and whose artisans and craftsmen were renowned through three continents? Should not their genius also be represented? And so the chapel was further embellished with what is, quite literally, its crowning glory, surely the most unexpected covering to any Christian church on earth—a stalactite ceiling of wood, in the classical Islamic style, as fine as anything to be found in Cairo or Damascus, intricately decorated with the earliest datable group of Arabic paintings in existence.

And figurative paintings at that. By the middle of the twelfth century certain schools of Arabic art had been jockeyed—principally by the Persians, who had never shared their scruples—out of their old abhorrence of the human form, and the tolerant atmosphere of Palermo led them to experiment still further. The details of the paintings are difficult to make out from floor level, but a pair of pocket binoculars will reveal, amid a welter of animal and vegetable ornamentation and Kufic inscriptions in praise of the King, countless delightful little scenes of oriental life and mythology. Some people are riding camels, others killing lions, yet others enjoying picnics with their harems; everywhere, it seems, there is a great deal of eating and drinking going on. Dragons and monsters abound; one man—Sinbad perhaps?—is being carried off on the back of a huge four-legged bird straight out of Hieronymus Bosch.

Yet just as it is the ensemble, rather than the individual details, that makes the real impact on the beholder, so must the Palatine Chapel itself be considered not as the sum of its separate elements but as an integrated whole. It is also a work of profound devotion. No other place of worship radiates such incandescent splendour; no other proclaims with such assurance its origin and purpose. This is a chapel built by a king, for kings to worship in. Yet it is still, above all else, a house of God. The royal dais is raised to the level of the choir, but not to that of the sanctuary. Marble-balustraded, backed with inlays in *opus Alexandrinum* culminating in a huge octagon of porphyry to enhalo the head of the enthroned monarch, it stands at the western end, massive in its majesty. But immediately above it is another throne; this is backed not with marble but with gold; and on it is seated the risen Christ. All the brilliance, all the throbbing colour of this wonderful place, the interplay of verd-antique, ox-blood and cipollino, every inch of it burnished by the million glinting tesserae of the walls, create an atmosphere not of ostentation but of mystery, not of royal pride but of man's humility before his maker. Maupassant chose his metaphor well; entering the Palatine Chapel is like walking into a jewel. And, he might have added, it is a jewel from the crown of heaven.

PART TWO

THE NOONDAY KINGDOM

Palermo: the Palatine Chapel from the high altar

Palermo, the Palatine Chapel: ambo and paschal candlestick

5

ROGER THE KING

Ma quando si acquista stati in una provincia disforme di lingua, di costumi e di ordini, qui sono le difficultà, e qui bisogna avere gran fortuna e grande industria a tenerli.

But when territories are acquired in regions where there are differences in language, customs and laws, then great good fortune and much hard work are required to hold them.

Machiavelli, *Il Principe*,
Book III

I⊤ is not only to the historian, with all his advantages of hindsight and detachment, that the year 1140 appears as the watershed of Roger's reign. The King himself seems to have been fully aware that after ten years of bitter struggle—years which had brought him more than his share of disappointments, betrayals and defeats—his first great task was completed. At last his Kingdom was his own. Of those vassals who had resisted his authority, the most formidable were all dead, dispossessed or in exile. Fighting of a somewhat desultory nature would continue for a few more years yet, notably in the Abruzzi and Campania, where a clearly-defined border had yet to be established with the Papal State to the north. But this would be the primary responsibility of his sons, Roger of Apulia and Alfonso of Capua; they were old enough now to look after their own domains. And in any event the overall security of the Kingdom would no longer hang in the balance.

The way was clear, in fact, for the second stage of Roger's grand design. The country was united and pacified; now it must be given a constitution. Eleven years before, at Melfi, he had already imposed a great oath of fealty on the barons and leading churchmen of South

Italy, setting out the broad outlines of both the political and penal systems by which he intended to govern. But 1129 must have seemed a long time ago. Too much had happened since then—too many oaths broken, too many trusts betrayed. It was better to make a fresh start.

Roger spent much of the first six months of 1140 preparing his new legislation in Palermo. Since it was to apply with equal validity in all parts of the Kingdom, he might well have been content to promulgate it from his capital; but he did not do so. It was on the mainland that his vassals were the strongest, and there that they enjoyed the greatest freedom. On them above all he had to impress the binding force of his royal authority, and of the code of laws through which he meant to exert it. In July he took ship back to Salerno and at the end of the month, after a quick tour of his sons' recent acquisitions in the Abruzzi, rode in state through the mountains to Ariano,[1] where his feudatories had been gathering from all parts of the South.

It is only just over a hundred years ago, in 1856, that the two extant versions of the Assizes of Ariano were discovered—one in the archives of Monte Cassino and the other in the Vatican—and that their importance was first properly understood.[2] Infinitely more far-reaching, both in range and effect, than the oaths sworn at Melfi, they constitute a corpus of law which—though many are borrowed directly from Justinian—yet remains unique in the early Middle Ages, covering as it does every aspect of Roger's rule. Two particular features strike one from the outset. First, as befits so heterogeneous a nation, the King makes it clear that the existing laws of all his subject peoples shall continue in force. Except when there is a direct clash with the new royal ordinances, all the Greeks, Arabs, Jews, Lombards and Normans under his rule are to continue to live, as they have always lived, according to the customs of their fathers.

The second feature, which runs like a *Leitmotiv* throughout the

---

[1] Now Ariano Irpino.

[2] Both texts are given in Brandileone, *Il diritto romano nelle legi normanne e sueve del Regno di Sicilia*. The Vatican text is probably identical to that published by Roger at Ariano. That of Monte Cassino seems to be an abridgement, though it also contains certain later additions.

work, is the stress on the absolutism of the monarchy, stemming in its turn from the divinely-held power of the King. The law is the will of God; and the King—who alone may make and unmake it and stands alone as its ultimate interpreter—is therefore not only a judge but a priest. To question his decisions, or others taken in his name, is both a sin—sacrilege—and a crime—treason. And treason, *crimen majestatis,* is punishable by death. It extends over a wide and fearful range. It covers, for example, offences and conspiracies not only against the King's person but against any member of his Curia;[1] it includes cowardice in battle, the arming of mobs, the withholding of support from the armies of the King or his allies. No other nation, no other legal code in mediaeval Europe conceived of it in such sweeping terms. But then no other European state, with one exception, cherished so exalted a theory of Kingship. That exception was Byzantium.

Byzantium—here was the key to Roger's whole political philosophy. The feudal system which prevailed in his mainland dominions belonged to Western Europe; the civil service that he had inherited from his father in Palermo and the Sicilian provinces was based largely on Arabic institutions; but the monarchy itself, as he conceived of it and personally embodied it, was Byzantine through and through. The King of Sicily was not, in the manner of his lesser brethren to the north and west, merely the apex of a feudal pyramid. Before his coronation, like the Emperors of ancient Rome and their successors at Constantinople, he had been careful to secure the agreement and the acclamation of his people; but by the ceremony itself he was imbued with a mysterious, charismatic essence which set him above and apart from common humankind. This remoteness Roger was deliberately to foster throughout his life. His biographer Alexander of Telese writes of how, despite the quickness and brilliance of his conversation, 'he would never, in public or in private, allow himself to become too affable or jovial or intimate, lest people should cease to fear him'. And when, three or four years later, we find him, in the course of diplomatic negotiations with

[1] The *Curia Regis,* from the reign of Roger II onwards, was the principal organ of central government. Its powers were considerably wider than those of a modern cabinet, since it had important judicial responsibilities, especially in matters of civil law.

Constantinople, demanding recognition as an equal of the Emperor
of Byzantium—God's Vice-Regent on earth, Equal of the Apostles—
it comes as no surprise.[1]

If this theory, though it is unmistakably and repeatedly implied
in the legislation, diplomacy and iconography of the Sicilian Kingdom, is never quite set out in so many words it is probably because
of the one overriding practical difficulty which it raised. Just where,
in all this, did the Pope fit in? The question was never satisfactorily
answered—a failure which does much to explain the curious duality
which appears in all Roger's dealings with the Holy See. As a papal
vassal he was prepared to do homage to the Pope as his lawful
suzerain; as a Christian he was ready to show him all the respect
that he considered due; but as King of Sicily, in matters affecting
the Church within his own frontiers, he would brook no interference. His hand was admittedly strengthened by the hereditary
right of the Apostolic Legation which his father had wrested from
Urban II forty-two years before;[2] but, as we shall see, he showed
in ecclesiastical affairs a stubbornness and self-will which went far
beyond anything that Pope Urban or his successors were ever
prepared to contemplate.

Those of the Ariano Assizes which deal specifically with such
affairs tend to stress the King's rôle as protector of the Christian
Church and of the individual rights and privileges of its representatives. Heretics and apostates—from, not to, Christianity—are to be
punished by the loss of civil rights, and there are heavy penalties for
simony. At the same time bishops are excused attendance in the
public courts, and the lower orders of clergy are granted lesser
exemptions according to their rank. All such measures would have
found favour in Rome, but—and this point doubtless provoked a
very different reaction—all could be countermanded by the King,
against whose judgment or decisions there could be no appeal.
And so far as Roger was concerned this power—let the Pope make
no mistake about it—was derived not through any historic grant of

[1] The fact that Roger styled himself *Rex* rather than *Imperator* in no way
weakened this claim. *Rex* was the accepted translation of the Greek *Basileus*; it is
also, incidentally, used to describe the Emperor Nero on a mosaic in the Palatine
Chapel.
[2] *The Normans in the South,* pp. 273–4.

legatine authority; together with the right to the high canonical insignia—mitre and dalmatic, staff and pastoral ring—which the King wore on appropriate religious occasions, it stemmed directly from God Himself.

Similarly strict control was to be exerted over the feudatories. After ten years of defiance and insurrection they were at last quiescent, but they could not be relied upon to remain so indefinitely. What is interesting about Roger's legislative policy towards them, both at Ariano and later, is his attempt to accommodate an essentially western institution into a predominantly Byzantine political scheme. This meant, in the first place, establishing the maximum degree of separation between Throne and vassalage—a task which was further complicated by the fact that many of the Norman baronial families of Apulia had been in Italy for as long or longer than the Hautevilles and still saw no reason why the grandson of an obscure and impoverished knight of the Cotentin should arrogate to himself powers over them which seemed to exceed those of any other western monarch.

Here was another difficulty that was never entirely overcome, though Roger did his best in the years that followed to lessen its effects by renewing the grant of most of the existing fiefs. Thenceforth his vassals would hold their lands not by virtue of capture or early enfeoffment at the time of the first Norman conquest of Italy in the previous century, but by the King's grace and from the date of their new royal charter. Meanwhile the number, and therefore the power, of the knightly caste was further limited by turning it into what amounted to a closed order, almost like a separate civil service. Assize No. XIX, for example, *De Nova Militia,* lays down categorically that no man can be made a knight or retain his existing knighthood unless he comes of an established knightly family. Other ordinances warn all feudal lords and others—including churchmen—who have authority over townsfolk and villagers to treat them with humanity, and never to demand from them more than what is reasonable and just.

Before leaving Ariano the King announced one further innovation—the introduction, for the first time, of a standard coinage for the whole Kingdom. The unit he had selected was to be called the

ducat, named after his Duchy of Apulia, the first of that glinting
stream of gold and silver by which, for the next seven centuries, so
much of the world's wealth was to be measured. The prototypes,
struck in Brindisi, seem to have been of disappointing quality—
magis aereas quam argenteas, Falco cattily remarks;[1] but they provided
a further effective illustration of Roger's theory of Kingship.
Typically Byzantine in form, they bear on one side a likeness of
the King, enthroned, crowned and robed in full Byzantine regalia,
holding in one hand an orb and in the other a long cross with
double traverse. Beside him, his hand also on the cross, stands his
son Duke Roger of Apulia, in military dress. The reverse of the
coin is more significant still. Early Apulian money, minted in the
reign of Duke William, invariably bore on the reverse a portrait of
St Peter, to denote William's vassalage to the Holy See. Now those
days were gone. The new ducats showed not St Peter but Christ
Pantocrator. King Roger, they seemed to say, had no need of an
intermediary.[2]

Some time in the spring of 1140, King Roger sent his friend the
Pope a present of some beams for the roof of St John Lateran—
which, like so much else in twelfth-century Rome, was sadly in
need of repair. If Innocent took this gesture to mean that he would
have no more trouble with the Hautevilles, he was mistaken; it was
only a matter of months before the King's two sons, in the course of

[1] 'More copper than silver.' The first golden ducats do not appear till 1284—
in Venice, where silver ones had been current since 1202.

[2] The contention, doggedly maintained in the eleventh edition of the *Encyclopaedia Britannica*—the most recent edition has dropped the entry altogether—that
the ducat owed its name to the inscription on it *Sit tibi, Christe, datus, quem tu
regis, iste ducatus* (To thee, O Christ, who rulest this Duchy, be it given) is without
foundation. On a small coin there would have been no room for such a legend,
even in an abbreviated form. The only inscription on these earliest ducats, apart
from the letters identifying the two portraits, consists of the letters AN.R.X.—
anno regni decimo, i.e. struck in the tenth year of Roger's reign. They constituted a
further challenge to the Pope, who naturally counted the years of the Sicilian
Kingdom from his own recognition of it at Mignano in 1139. Another coin,
worth a third of a ducat, was simultaneously minted at the *zecca* in Palermo. A
particularly happy example of Sicilian enlightenment, it bears on the obverse a
Latin inscription surrounding a Greek cross, and on the reverse an Arabic one
reading 'struck in the city of Sicily [*sic*] in the year 535'—of the Hegira, i.e.
1140 A.D.

what they described as 'restoring' former Apulian or Capuan lands, were pushing up as far as Ceprano in Campania and the Tronto in the northern Abruzzi and making frequent disturbing inroads into papal territories. But the two brothers, one feels, were only flexing their muscles, occupying their time as energetic young Norman knights had always done and were meant to do. They probably enjoyed irritating the Pope, but they showed no real hostility towards him. Their father meanwhile, though allowing his sons a fairly free rein, seems to have been genuinely anxious to improve relations with the Church and to eradicate as far as possible the unpleasant memories of the past decade.

Although Innocent, still smarting from his defeat at Galluccio, was not to be so easily placated, his principal ally had displayed a quite astonishing capacity for *volte-face*. Already at the Salerno tribunal St Bernard seems to have decided that Roger was not the ogre that he had always made him out to be, and set about revising his previous opinions. It comes as something of a surprise to find the man whose diatribes against the 'Sicilian tyrant' had long been famous through every corner of Europe, beginning in 1139 a letter to his old enemy with the words:

Far and wide the fame of your magnificence has spread over the earth; what limits are there untouched by the glory of your name?[1]

The King, though doubtless secretly amused at the suddenness of the change, was always ready to meet his enemies half-way. Soon after Mignano, when the last obstacle to good relations had been swept aside, he wrote to Bernard suggesting that he might pay a

---

[1] Three years later, Bernard's friend and fellow-abbot Peter the Venerable of Cluny, like him an outspoken enemy of Anacletus—and therefore of Roger himself—throughout the years of schism, was to address to 'the glorious and magnificent King of Sicily' an even more impressive testimonial:

Sicily, Calabria and Apulia, regions which before your time were given over to the Saracens, or to dens of brigands and caves of robbers, have now—thanks to God, who aided you in your task—become the home of peace and the refuge of tranquillity, a peaceful and most happy Kingdom, ruled, as it were, by a second Solomon. Would that parts of poor miserable Tuscany might be joined, with their neighbouring provinces, to your Realm!

Book IV, letter 37

87

personal visit to Sicily to discuss, among other things, a new monastic foundation in the Kingdom. Bernard, still only fifty years old but worn out with exertion, ill-health and his own particular brand of hysterical asceticism, replied with apparently genuine regret that he could not accept Roger's invitation in person; but he at once sent two of his most trusted monks to Palermo to negotiate in his name. They travelled as part of the suite which accompanied Elizabeth, daughter of Count Theobald of Champagne, from France to marry Duke Roger of Apulia in 1140, and arrived in Sicily towards the end of the year. The result was the foundation a short time later of the first Cistercian monastery in the South— almost certainly that of S. Nicola of Filocastro in Calabria.

The site chosen for this monastery may be yet another indication of Roger's policy towards the Church at this time. Though the Cistercians always inclined towards remote and secluded locations for their abbeys, there seems little doubt that St Bernard would have preferred somewhere in Sicily itself—not too far from the capital, where his abbot could keep a watchful eye—and perhaps exert a positive influence—on the ecclesiastical policies of the King. Roger, with the same considerations in mind, would have resisted any such proposals. However sincerely held his religious views, he retained an instinctive mistrust for the large, powerful monasteries of the mainland. Now that he had established a firm control over the Latin Church in Sicily he had no intention of seeing that control weakened by subversion from within. It was typical of him that during his entire reign he should have allowed only one major Latin foundation in Palermo itself—the Benedictine monastery of S. Giovanni degli Eremiti—and that he should have populated it with monks not from obvious sources like Monte Cassino or the great abbey of La Cava outside Salerno but from a small, relatively obscure community of ascetics at Monte Vergine, near Avellino. In taking this step the King made a considerable sacrifice; to have given S. Giovanni, with its superb location next to the royal palace and its huge endowments, to Cistercians or Cluniacs might have seemed a small price to pay for their favour; at once he would have been hailed as one of the most devout and generous monarchs in Christendom. It was a temptation that few Hautevilles—certainly

88

not Robert Guiscard—could have resisted. But Roger was more subtle in his statesmanship. He had suffered too much from the Church of Rome and from St Bernard in particular. This time he was taking no chances.

S. Giovanni degli Eremiti—St John of the Hermits—stands today as little more than an empty shell. Nothing now remains there to suggest that during the most brilliant years of the Norman Kingdom it was the wealthiest and most privileged monastery in all Sicily. It was founded in 1142, and by the charter he granted it six years later Roger decreed that its abbot should serve *ex officio* as chaplain and confessor to the King, with the rank of bishop, and should personally celebrate Mass on all feastdays in the Palatine Chapel. He further laid down that in its cemetery—which still exists in the open court to the south of the church—should be buried all members of the royal family except the Kings themselves and all the senior officials of the court.[1]

The church itself, now deconsecrated, is surprisingly small.[2] It was built on the site of a much earlier mosque, part of which remains to form an extension of the southern transept. But the inside, despite the traces of tile and mosaic and fresco—and even of the stalactite ceiling of the original mosque—holds little interest for the non-expert. The fascination of S. Giovanni is in its exterior. Of all the Norman churches in Sicily it is the most characteristic and the most striking, its five vermilion domes—each standing on a cylindrical drum to give it greater height—bursting out from the surrounding greenery like gigantic pomegranates, in almost audible testimony of the Arab craftsmen who built them. They are not beautiful; but they burn themselves into the memory and remain there, stark and vivid, long after many true masterpieces are forgotten.

A few yards to the north-west there stands a little open cloister,

---

[1] This last decree was never generally observed. Nearly all the royal family were in fact buried in the chapel of St Mary Magdalen next to the old cathedral. When, forty years later, the cathedral was rebuilt the tombs—which included those of Queens Elvira and Beatrice and of four of Roger's sons, Roger, Tancred, Alfonso and Henry—were transferred to another chapel similarly named. This chapel still stands in the courtyard of the *carabinieri* barracks of S. Giacomo. Of the graves themselves, however, there is no longer any trace. (Deér, *The Dynastic Porphyry Tombs of the Norman Period in Sicily*. Cambridge, Mass., 1959.)

[2] Plate 8.

with gently poised arcading supported on pairs of slender columns, built half a century later than the church and in perfect contrast to it. Sitting there on a hot afternoon, looking up now at the soaring austerity of the royal palace, now at the aggressively baroque campanile of S. Giorgio in Kemonia, yet always aware of those bulbous oriental cupolas half-hidden behind the palm-trees, one is reminded for the hundredth time that in Sicily Islam is never far away. And it is, perhaps, in the church and cloister of what was once the leading Christian monastery of the Kingdom that its presence is most keenly felt.

The confrontation at S. Giovanni degli Eremiti between Muslim East and Latin West is so striking that the visitor tends to forget the third essential strand of civilisation that made Norman Sicily what it was. In all Palermo there is no longer a single building whose exterior recalls Byzantium. Despite the number of senior Greek officials in the Curia, despite all the Greek scholars and sages whom Roger attracted to the court in the later years of his reign, the capital itself had never boasted an indigenous Greek population of any size. It was, first and foremost, an Arab city, scarcely touched by Byzantine influences in comparison with those regions in which Greek peoples had lived since the days of antiquity—regions such as the Val Demone in eastern Sicily or parts of Calabria, where to this day a Greek dialect is spoken in some of the remoter villages.

And yet, from the time of the Sicilian conquest up to the point we have now reached in this story, the Greeks had played a vital part in the building of the new nation. First, they had kept the balance between Christian and Muslim on which the whole future of Norman Sicily depended. Roger's father the Great Count had encouraged Latin immigration, both ecclesiastical and secular, as far as he dared, but he could not allow too much too quickly for fear of frightening the Greek and Arab communities and turning them against him. Besides, such immigration brought its own dangers. If it had not been kept under rigid control there would have been nothing to stop swarms of swaggering Norman barons from the mainland pouring into Sicily, demanding to be given fiefs in keeping with their rank and station and gradually reducing the island to that chaos which always seemed to follow in their wake.

Without the Greeks, then, the Christian element during those early days might have been swamped altogether. But they also performed another invaluable function. They neatly counterbalanced the claims of the Latin Church, and provided both Count Roger and his son with a powerful bargaining—if not actually blackmailing —counter in their dealings with Rome. It seems in the highest degree improbable that there was any foundation for the rumours, current at the end of the 1090s, that the Great Count was seriously contemplating a conversion to Orthodoxy; but it is a good deal likelier that Roger II, at various moments in his long quarrel with Pope Innocent, may have considered renouncing the pontifical authority altogether in favour of some kind of loose caesaropapism on the Byzantine model. What is certain is that in 1143 the Greek Archimandrite Nilus Doxopatrius of Palermo dedicated to Roger—with the King's full consent—a 'Treatise on the Patriarchal Thrones', arguing that with the transfer of the imperial capital in A.D. 330 and the recognition of Constantinople as the 'New Rome' by the Council of Chalcedon in 451, the Pope had lost his ecclesiastical primacy, which now properly belonged to the Byzantine Patriarch.

But now, as the twelfth century nears its half-way mark, the situation can be seen to have changed. Sicily, first of all, has grown steadily richer; and as her prosperity has increased, so too has her political stability. In contrast to the endemic confusion of the Italian peninsula, the island has become a paragon of just and enlightened government, peaceable and law-abiding, an amalgam of races and languages which seems to give strength rather than weakness; and, as its reputation grows, more and more churchmen and administrators, scholars and merchants and unashamed adventurers are drawn across the sea from England, France and Italy to settle in what must have seemed to many of them a veritable Eldorado, a Kingdom in the sun. Meanwhile the importance of the Greek community has begun to decline. It is inevitable that it should. With no comparable immigration from abroad to sustain it, it is increasingly outnumbered by the Latin. In the prevailing atmosphere of religious toleration and easy coexistence, its value as a bulwark

against Islam is negligible. Finally, Roger has now established so
firm a control over his Latin Church that he has no longer any need
for a counterbalance.

Not that there was any discrimination against the Greeks. In
view of the mixed feelings with which the Hautevilles had always
regarded the Byzantine Empire—admiration for its institutions and
its art, distrust laced with more than a tinge of jealousy in every
other field—they might have been excused for treating as second-
class citizens a foreign minority whose political and confessional
loyalties were openly divided. But they never did so. Roger and his
successors continued to support their Greek subjects whenever their
support was necessary; they never lost their concern for the welfare
of the Greeks, or of their Church. The great and distinguished line
of Greek admirals continued throughout the century; at least until
the end of Roger's reign the whole fiscal system of Norman Sicily
remained in Greek and Arab hands.[1] It was just that the emphasis
had shifted. Though from the outset subordinated to the Latin
hierarchy, large numbers of Basilian monasteries had sprung up
over the past fifty years, notably S. Maria del Patirion near Rossano
in Calabria[2]—founded by the Regent Adelaide at the beginning of
the century—and its daughter-house, the monastery of the Saviour
at Messina, established some thirty years later. But the Saviour,
soon to be the chief of all the Greek monasteries in Sicily, was also
the last. Henceforth the royal favours would be lavished on the
new Latin houses—S. Giovanni degli Eremiti and, later, Maniace
and Monreale.

Fortunately the way was still wide open for private patronage;
and it is fitting that the sublimest legacy of the Greek Church in all
Sicily, the only one that still possesses a beauty comparable to that
of the Palatine Chapel and the cathedral of Cefalù, should have been

[1] It is noteworthy that, as Miss Evelyn Jamison points out (*Admiral Eugenius
of Sicily*, p. 40), 'No men of Latin culture seem up to this time to have been
employed in positions high or low by the central offices of finance'.

[2] Visitors to Rossano are usually content to inspect the Byzantine church of
S. Marco and the Archbishop's Palace, home of the justly-famed sixth-century
purple codex. They would be well advised to make the short detour to S. Maria,
lying up in the hills on the way to the neighbouring town of Corigliano. The
monastery buildings are in ruins, but the church itself is still there, with a
superb mosaic pavement which alone is worth the visit.

founded, built and endowed by the most brilliant of all the Greeks in the Kingdom's history.

Though the original and rightful name of his church, S. Maria del Ammiraglio, stands as a perpetual monument to its founder, George of Antioch had no need of such memorials to ensure himself a place in history. We first meet him as the gifted young Levantine who, after early service with the Zirid Sultans of Mahdia, transferred his loyalties to Sicily and in 1123 used his perfect Arabic and unrivalled knowledge of the Tunisian coast to score the only victory in Roger's first, ill-fated African expedition.[1] Since then, as commander of the Sicilian navy, he had served his King with distinction on both land and sea, becoming in 1132 the first holder of the proudest title his adopted country had to offer—Emir of Emirs, the high admiral and chief minister of the realm.[2] Despite so distinguished a career, however, his work on the church must not be thought of as the occupation of his declining years, still less of his retirement. In 1143, the year it was endowed, he must have been in his early fifties; within weeks of the endowment he and his fleet were off on another North African adventure, more successful this time; while before he died he was to carry the Sicilian flag to the banks of the Bosphorus itself, returning to Palermo with all the secrets—and many of the leading craftsmen—of the Byzantine silk industry.

But however secure the great admiral may be in his immortality, it still seems a little unfair that the shorter and more usual name for his church should commemorate not him but an infinitely dimmer figure—one Geoffrey de Marturanu, the founder in 1146 of a nearby Benedictine nunnery with which, some three centuries later, George's church was amalgamated. Nor, alas, have the changes been confined to its name. The Martorana—for so, under protest, it must be called from now on—no longer displays any outward sign of its origins. Once, its exterior too was beautiful. On Christmas Day,

[1] *The Normans in the South*, pp. 299–302.
[2] It is perhaps worth recalling in this second volume a point already made in the first, namely that the word *Admiral*, current with minor variations in so many European languages, is derived through Norman Sicily from the Arabic word *Emir*; and in particular from its compound *Emir-al-Bahr*, Ruler of the Sea.

1184, it was visited by the Arab traveller Ibn Jubair on his way back from a pilgrimage to Mecca. He wrote:

We noted a most remarkable façade, which we could not possibly describe and on which we would fain keep silent, since it is the most beautiful work in the world. . . . It has a bell-tower supported on columns of marble, surmounted by a dome resting on further columns. It is one of the most marvellous constructions ever to be seen. May Allah in his mercy and goodness soon honour this building with the sound of the muezzin's call!

Looking at the outside of the Martorana today, one almost wishes that Ibn Jubair's pious supplication had been granted. His co-religionists could hardly have done worse with it than the Christians. The façade itself he would no longer recognise; in sad contrast to that of the adjoining church of S. Cataldo, whose three heavy cupolas unmistakably if somewhat congestedly proclaim it as a Norman building of the mid-twelfth century, this jewel of all Sicilian churches—as opposed to cathedrals or chapels—has been decked out in lugubrious baroque. Only the romanesque bell-tower, domeless since an earthquake in 1726 but still beautifully proportioned, remains to beckon the traveller within.

There, too, all is not as it was. To accommodate the increasing numbers of nuns, a programme of reconstruction and enlargement was undertaken towards the end of the sixteenth century, and all through the seventeenth the grim work went on. The west wall was knocked down, the former atrium and narthex incorporated into the main body of the church. More unforgivable still, the main apse was demolished in 1683 with all its mosaics, to be replaced by a frescoed *capellone*, the hideousness of which all the efforts of nineteenth-century restorers have been powerless to diminish.

Such, then, is the modern Martorana. The eastern extremity is lost, the western bays ought never to have occurred. Miraculously, however, between the two, George's old church has remained, preserving its traditional Byzantine cross-in-square ground-plan and looking still much as it did when it was first consecrated or when, forty-odd years later, it had so alarming an effect on Ibn Jubair:

The walls within are gilded—or rather, they are made from one great piece of gold. There are slabs of coloured marble, the like of which we have never seen, picked out with golden mosaic and surmounted with, as it were, branches of trees in green mosaic. Great suns of gilded glass ranged along the top blaze with a light that dazzled our eyes and caused us such perturbation of the spirit that we implored Allah to preserve us. We learned that the founder, who gave his name to the Church, devoted many quintals of gold to its building, and that he was vizir to the grandfather of this polytheist King.[1]

Like most of those at Cefalù and the best of those in the Palatine Chapel, the mosaics of the Martorana were all the work of a single team of superb artists and craftsmen imported by Roger II from Constantinople and working in Sicily between 1140 and 1155. Unlike either of the other groups, they contain no later additions. All three show a close interrelation; yet each, unbelievably, has a style of its own. Dr Otto Demus, the most eminent living expert on the mosaics of Norman Sicily, has compared them thus:

The mosaicists of Cefalù, confronted with the task of decorating the high commanding apse of a large cathedral, achieved the quiet grandeur which was called for; the artists of the Palatina, who had to decorate a court chapel, expressed themselves in an elaborate and festive style, full of royal splendour, but lacking something of the classic beauty and simplicity of Cefalù. And the workmen who adorned the private foundation of the Admiral adapted themselves to the intimacy of the small church, condensing and simplifying their models and attaining the most perfect charm which can be found in any surviving mediaeval decoration on Italian soil. This quality was not impaired by the fact that they sometimes followed the work of their colleagues in the two royal churches. They gave as it were the quintessence of what was gentle and lovely and intimate in the great art of Comnenian mosaic decoration.[2]

Only the mosaics in the cupola itself strike one as faintly disappointing. Enthroned and depicted at full length, the Pantocrator

[1] Ibn Jubair was writing in the reign of Roger's grandson, William the Good. To devout Muslims all Christians were polytheists. As believers in the Trinity, what else could they be?
[2] *The Mosaics of Norman Sicily.*

has lost much of the majesty that he shows in the Palatine Chapel, to say nothing of Cefalù; and the four archangels beneath him, bending forward in postures which, Dr Demus assures us, are 'without parallel in Byzantine, or indeed in mediaeval art', have bodies so fantastically distorted as to border on the ridiculous. But drop your eyes now to the supporting walls. Look east to the Annunciation, with Gabriel in a slanting swirl of movement, Mary serene with her spindle as the holy dove flutters towards her. Look west to the Presentation in the Temple, the outstretched arms of the infant Saviour on one side and those of St Simeon on the other bridging the entrance to the nave as perfectly as does the great arch they frame. Within its vault, Christ is born and, opposite, the Virgin dies—her soul, like another swaddled child, is carried reverently up by her Son. Lastly, settle in some comfortable corner and look at everything at once while the dark, glowing gold does its work, irradiating the spirit like a soft and gentle fire.

Barely perceptible among that gold, running along the base of the dome beneath the feet of the adoring archangels, you may just discern a narrow wooden frieze. After centuries in darkness, it was only when the restoration work at the end of the last century let the light back into the dome that it was rediscovered and found to bear traces of an inscription—an old Byzantine hymn in honour of the Virgin. Since the Martorana is a Greek church there would be nothing extraordinary about that, but for one fact—the inscription is in Arabic. Why it was translated we shall never know. Perhaps the wooden surround was the work of Arab Christians —Arabs were always the best carpenters—and this was their contribution to the church. But there is another, more intriguing, possibility—that this hymn was the particular favourite of George of Antioch himself, and that he loved it best in the language in which he had heard it first, half a century before, in his Syrian boyhood.

And now, as you leave the original church, running the gauntlet of those simpering cherubs and marzipan madonnas that mark the real dark ages of European religious art, pause for a moment at a western-facing wall on the north side of the nave near the entrance;

and there, in what was probably the narthex of George's building, you will find, glittering wanly in the half-light, his portrait.[1] It is a dedication mosaic, with the admiral, looking old beyond his years and distinctly oriental, prostrating himself before the Virgin. His body has unfortunately been damaged at some period, and the damage compounded by a clumsy restoration which has given him the appearance of a tortoise; but the head is the original work—presumably done from the life—and almost the entire figure of the Virgin has come down to us unscathed. Her right hand is extended towards him, as if to raise him up; and in her left she holds a scroll on which there is written in Greek:

Child, holy Word, do Thou ever preserve from all adversity George, first among the archons, who has raised this my house from its foundations; and grant him the forgiveness of his sins as Thou only, O God, hast power to do.

Across the nave, in the corresponding space on the southern wall, is the Martorana's last and perhaps its greatest treasure—a mosaic portrait of King Roger himself, being symbolically crowned by Christ.[2] There he stands, bending slightly forward, a purely Byzantine figure in his long dalmatic and stole, his crown with jewelled pendants in the manner of Constantinople; even his arms are raised from the elbows in the Greek attitude of prayer. Above his head, great black letters stride across the gold to proclaim him. *POΓEPIOC PHΞ*, they read, *Rogerios Rex*. This uncompromising use of Greek letters for a Latin word is less curious than it might seem; by Roger's time the normal Greek word for king, *basileus,* was so identified with the Byzantine Emperor that it would have been unthinkable in this context. And yet the simple fact of transliteration makes an impact of its own and—particularly after one has spotted the Arabic inscription on an adjacent pillar—seems to diffuse the whole spirit of Norman Sicily.

This, too, is a portrait from the life; indeed, apart from coins and seals which are too small to give much information and are anyway

[1] Plate 9.   [2] Plate 10.

mainly symbolical, it is the only surviving likeness of the King which we can safely assume to be authentic.[1] Without it we should have nothing to go on but the evidence of Archbishop Romuald of Salerno, a man with a genius for uninformative description. He writes merely that Roger was tall, corpulent, with a leonine face—whatever that may mean—and a voice that was *subrauca*; hoarse, perhaps or harsh, or just vaguely disagreeable. The mosaic tells us far more. It shows a dark, swarthy man on the brink of middle age, with a full beard and long thick hair flowing to his shoulders. The face itself might be Greek, or it might be Italian; it even has a faintly Semitic cast about it. Anything less like the traditional idea of a Norman knight could scarcely be imagined.

It is always dangerous to read too much of a character into a portrait, particularly when the sitter is already familiar and the portraitist unknown. Dangerous, but irresistible. And even in something so hieratic and formalised as the Martorana mosaic, there are certain inspired touches, certain infinitesimal adjustments and gradations of the tesserae, that bring King Roger to life again before us. Here, surely, is the southerner and the oriental, the ruler of subtle mind and limitless flexibility whose life is spent playing one faction off against another; the statesman to whom diplomacy, however tortuous, is a more natural weapon than the sword, and gold, however corrupting, a more effective currency than blood. Here is the patron of the sciences, the lover of the arts who could stop in the middle of a desperate campaign to admire the beauty of Alife, stronghold of his arch-enemy. Here, finally, is the intellectual who has thought deeply about the science of government and rules with the head and not the heart; the idealist without delusions; the despot,

---

[1] The only other contemporary portrait to have come down to us—unless we include the figure on the Paschal candlestick in the Palatine Chapel—is on a curious enamel plaque in the church of St Nicholas at Bari. It depicts Roger's coronation by St Nicholas and was probably the origin of the church's one-time claim that he was crowned there and not in Palermo. (His reputed crown, an immense circle of iron and copper more suited to a barrel than a human head, is also displayed there with some pride.) This is not the place to enquire into the origins of the plaque, on which there is an interesting paper by Bertaux which I have listed in the bibliography. The portrait may be from the life, but was more likely copied from another, now lost. The essential physical features appear much the same as on the Martorana mosaic.

by nature just and merciful, who has learned, sadly, that even mercy must sometimes be tempered in the interests of justice.

The Assizes of Ariano set the seal on the Peace. The years before 1140 were the years of storm, when the thunderclouds hung black over the mainland and when Sicily itself, for all its prosperity, was unable altogether to escape their shadow. Afterwards, the sky lightens. It is only in the last fourteen years of Roger's reign that the sun really shines on his Kingdom.

And the Kingdom responds. We have seen how suddenly the art of Norman Sicily, like some rare subtropical orchid after long seasons of germination, at this moment bursts into glory. So, no less spectacularly, does the court of Palermo. Already at the time of his coronation Roger had inherited from his father a civil service, based eclectically on Norman, Greek, Latin and Arab models, which compared favourably with that of any western nation. When he died, he left his successors a governmental machine that was the wonder and envy of Europe. Under the Emir of Emirs and the Curia, two separate land registries—known as divans[1] after their Fatimid prototypes and staffed almost exclusively by Saracens—supervised the gathering of revenues from customs, monopolies and feudal holdings in Sicily and on the mainland. Another branch of the financial administration, the *camera,* was based on the old *fiscus* of the Roman Empire and administered by Greeks; a third followed the model of the Anglo-Norman Exchequer. Provincial government was in the hands of the Chancellors of the Kingdom, the *camerarii,* and below them the local governors—Latin bailiffs, Greek catapans, or Saracen *amil,* selected according to the race and language predominant in their district. To avoid corruption or peculation, the very lowest officials had direct access to the Curia or even, on occasion, to the King himself. Wandering justiciars, magistrates condemned to perpetual circuit, had responsibility for administering the criminal law, with the assistance of varying numbers of *boni homines*—good men and true—both Christian and Muslim, often sitting together in what was in effect the forerunner

[1] From which comes the Italian word *dogana* and, through it, the French *douane.*

of the modern jury. They too had the right to refer appeals to the King when necessary.

The King: always, everywhere, his people were reminded of his presence, his power, his paradoxical combination of accessibility and remoteness. Himself half-way to Heaven, there was no abuse, no miscarriage of justice too insignificant for his attention, if it could not be settled by those empowered to act in his name. However ubiquitous his representatives, however efficient his machine, neither they nor it were ever permitted to come between himself and the day-to-day work of administration, still less to detract from the mystique that surrounded him, that aura of divine majesty on which, he well knew, the cohesion of his Kingdom depended. It was not for nothing that he had been depicted, in the Martorana, as being crowned by Christ himself.

Emirs, seneschals, archons, logothetes, *protonotarii, protonobilissimi*—even the titles of the high palace dignitaries seemed to add to the pervading splendour. Yet it takes more than civil servants, whatever their disguise, to give brilliance to a court; and Roger's court at Palermo was easily the most brilliant of twelfth-century Europe. The King himself was famous for his insatiable intellectual curiosity and his passion for facts. (When, in 1140, he had made his formal entry into Naples, he had astounded the Neapolitans by informing them of the exact length of their land walls—2,363 paces, a figure of which, not perhaps altogether surprisingly, none of them was aware.) With this curiosity went a profound respect for learning, unique among his fellow-princes.[1] By the 1140s he had given a permanent home in Palermo to many of the foremost scholars and scientists, doctors and philosophers, geographers and mathematicians of Europe and the Arab world; and as the years went by he would spend more and more of his time in their company. Outside his immediate family—and he had been many years a widower—it was with them above all that he was able to cast off some of his regality; we are told that whenever any scholar entered the royal presence, Roger would rise from his chair

[1] Henry I of England was admittedly well-educated by the standards of the time—a fact which was considered remarkable enough to earn him the nickname of Beauclerk. But Henry made no effort to form a cultivated court around him, as Roger did.

and move forward to meet him, then take him by the hand and sit him down at his side. During the learned discussions that followed, whether in French, Latin, Greek or Arabic, he seems to have been well able to hold his own.

In mathematics, as in the political sphere, the extent of his learning cannot be described. Nor is there any limit to his knowledge of the sciences, so deeply and wisely has he studied them in every particular. He is responsible for singular innovations and for marvellous inventions, such as no prince has ever before realised.

Those words were written by Abu Abdullah Mohammed al-Edrisi, Roger's close friend and, of all the palace scholars, the one whom he most admired. Edrisi had arrived in Palermo in 1139; he was to remain there during much of his life, for fifteen years heading a commission set up by order of the King to gather geographical information from all quarters, correlate it, record it in orderly form, and so ultimately to produce one compendious work which would contain the sum total of all contemporary knowledge of the physical world. Sicily, standing at the crossroads of three continents, her ports as busy and as cosmopolitan as any in Europe, made an ideal centre from which such a work could be undertaken, and for all those fifteen years scarcely a ship put in at Palermo or Messina, Catania or Syracuse, without those on board being examined as to every place they had ever visited, its climate and its people. Their interrogators in the first instance were most likely to be official agents of the commission; but any traveller who had outstandingly valuable information to impart was liable to find himself conducted forthwith to the royal palace, there to be further cross-questioned by Edrisi or even, on occasion, by Roger himself.

The results of this work, which was completed in January 1154, barely a month before the King's death, were twofold. The first was a huge planisphere of purest silver, weighing no less than four hundred and fifty Roman pounds, on which was engraved 'the configuration of the seven climates with that of the regions, countries, sea-coasts both near and distant, gulfs, seas and watercourses; the location of deserts and of cultivated lands, and their respective distances by normal routes in miles or other known measures; and the designation of ports.' One would give much for this magnificent object to have been preserved; alas, it was to be destroyed during the riots of the following reign, within a few years of its completion.

But the second, and perhaps ultimately the more valuable fruit of Edrisi's labours has come down to us in its entirety. It is a book, properly entitled *The Avocation of a Man Desirous of a Full Knowledge of the Different Countries of the World* but more generally known as *The Book of Roger*; and it is the greatest geographical work of the Middle Ages. On the very first page we read the words:

The earth is round like a sphere, and the waters adhere to it and are maintained on it through natural equilibrium which suffers no variation.

As might be expected, *The Book of Roger* emerges as a combination of hard topographical facts—many of them astonishingly accurate for a work produced three and a half centuries before Columbus— and travellers' tales; but even the latter suggest that they have been subjected to stern critical appraisal. This is, after all, a scientific work, and we are never allowed to forget it; there is no room for tall stories unless they have at least some claim to veracity. But the author, on his side, never loses his sense of wonder, and the book makes fascinating reading.[1] We learn, for example, about the queen of Merida in Spain, who had all her meals floated to her by water, or about the *Chahria* fish of the Black Sea and the unfortunate effect which it has on the local fisherman who catches it in his net.[2] We are told how during the Russian winter the days are so short that there is hardly time to perform all the five obligatory prayers, and how the Norwegians—some of whom are born totally without necks—harvest their corn when it is still green, drying it at their hearths 'since the sun shines very rarely upon them'. Of England we read:

England is set in the Ocean of Darkness. It is a considerable island, whose shape is that of the head of an ostrich, and where there are

[1] There is, so far as I know, no English translation. A French one exists and is listed in the bibliography.
[2] As the French translation puts it, *il entre aussitôt en érection d'une manière inaccoutumée*—whatever that may mean.

flourishing towns, high mountains, great rivers and plains. This country is most fertile; its inhabitants are brave, active and enterprising, but all is in the grip of perpetual winter.

Though Roger's court circle was by no means entirely composed of Arabs like Edrisi, they probably constituted the largest single group; while among the Europeans there were many who had been attracted to Palermo by very reason of its predominantly Arab flavour. There was nothing new in this. Unlike Christianity, Islam had never drawn a distinction between sacred and profane knowledge. During the Dark Ages, when the Church of Rome—following the dire example of Gregory the Great—feared and even actively discouraged secular studies, good Muslims remembered how the Prophet himself had enjoined his Faithful to pursue knowledge all their lives, 'even if the quest led them to China', for 'he who travels in search of learning travels along Allah's path to Paradise'. Muslim civilisation had thus for years been recognised in the West as superior to anything that Christian Europe could boast, especially in the field of mathematics and the physical sciences. Arabic had become the international scientific language *par excellence*. Moreover there were a number of classical works of learning, both Greek and Latin, which had been lost to Christendom through the barbarian invasions or the engulfing tide of Islam and survived only in Arabic translation. By the twelfth century, owing largely to the work of the Sephardic Jews of Spain, some of these were beginning to reappear in western languages; but this did not appreciably diminish the need for any serious student of science to master Arabic for himself.

Yet it was a diabolically difficult language to learn and, in northern Europe at any rate, competent teachers were few. Thus, for half a century and more, men had been travelling to Spain and Sicily, there to unlock, as they hoped, the secrets of the Muslim world—poor clerks, seeking knowledge that would single them out from their fellows and so clear their path to advancement; dreaming alchemists, combing volumes of oriental lore for formulas of the elixir of life or the philosophers' stone; or true scholars like Adelard of Bath, pioneer of Arab studies in England and the greatest name in English science before Robert Grosseteste and Roger Bacon, who came to

Sicily in the first years of the century and was later to restore Euclid's *Elements,* retranslated by him from the Arabic, to the cultural heritage of Europe.

For certain more specialised fields of enquiry these early Arabists continued to gravitate towards Muslim Spain and in particular to the school of Toledo, which had long been the spearhead of the international scientific renaissance. For others, however, Sicily possessed one overwhelming advantage: while culturally still very much part of the Arab world, it also remained in perpetual contact with the Greek East. In the libraries of Palermo, to say nothing of all the Basilian monasteries in the island and in Calabria, scholars could find the Greek originals of works known in Spain only in extracts, or in translations of doubtful accuracy. Nowadays we tend to forget that, until this twelfth-century revival of interest in ancient learning, western Europe was virtually ignorant of Greek: and Roger's Sicily now became the foremost centre of Hellenic studies outside Byzantium itself. But in Byzantium Arabic culture was unknown and mistrusted. Only in Sicily could both civilisations be studied at first hand and employed to explain, complement and cross-fertilise each other. Small wonder, then, that seekers after truth should flock in such numbers to Palermo and that the island should have established itself by mid-century as not only the commercial but also the cultural clearing-house of three continents.

Once again, all this activity was centred on the person of the King. Roger has been accused of being himself uncreative, in contrast to his grandson Frederick II for example, or even to Richard Cœur de Lion, a troubadour poet of considerable ability. It is true that he left no literary compositions of his own; it would have been remarkable if he had, since that marvellous flowering of European vernacular literature that had already begun in Provence had not yet spread further afield. Such poets as flourished in Palermo in his day—and there were many—were nearly all Arabs. Besides, the King's personal preference was for the sciences. Beauty he loved, but splendour too; and one suspects that he did not find it easy in every case to distinguish one from the other. Anyway, he loved knowledge more.

Yet to say that he was not creative is to ignore the fact that without him the unique cultural phenomenon that was twelfth-century Sicily could never have occurred. So diversified a nation needed a guiding hand to give it purpose, to weld its various elements into one. Intellectually as well as politically, Roger provided that hand. In a very real sense, he *was* Sicily. His was the conception, his the incentive; he and only he could have created the favourable climate that was a precondition of all the rest. Enlightened yet always discriminating, he was the first royal patron, focusing the efforts and energies of those around him, never once losing sight of his eternal objective—the greatness and glory of the Kingdom.

6

ENEMIES OF THE REALM

We have captured the fortifications, that is the towers and palaces of the mighty of the City who, together with the Sicilian and the Pope, were preparing to offer resistance to your authority. . . . We pray you therefore to come without delay. . . . The Pope has entrusted his staff and ring, his dalmatic, mitre and sandals to the Sicilian . . . and the Sicilian has given him much money for your hurt and to injure the Roman Empire, which by God's grace is yours.

Letter from Conrad of Hohenstaufen
to the Emperor John II Comnenus[1]

ON 24 September 1143 Pope Innocent II died in Rome. He was buried in the Lateran, in that same porphyry sarcophagus that had once held the remains of the Emperor Hadrian; but after a disastrous fire in the early fourteenth century his remains were moved to the church of S. Maria in Trastevere which he himself had rebuilt just before his death. There, self-immortalised in the great apse mosaic, he stares down at us from the conch, his church clutched in his hands, a strangely wistful expression in his sad, tired eyes.

Innocent's long struggle with Anacletus had cost him dear; in those eight years of wandering he had suffered far more than his rival, comfortably entrenched in Rome. Even his allies had proved a mixed blessing. Lothair, once safely crowned, had shown him scant consideration, Henry the Proud still less. Bernard of Clairvaux had been loyal but, deliberately or not, had seemed bent on stealing his thunder at every opportunity. His final triumph had been made possible only by the death of Anacletus; and almost at once it had

---

[1] Quoted by Otto of Freising in *Gesta Friderici I Imperatoris*, I. Translated by C. C. Mierow.

been turned to dust by the rout at Galluccio. He had accepted this humiliation as gracefully as he could—even going so far as to ascribe it to some working of the divine providence for the restoration of peace—and he had made terms with the Sicilian King; but he had been ill repaid. Within a year Roger—emboldened by the years of schism when he had done what he liked and Anacletus had never dared to take issue with him—was acting more arrogantly than ever, creating new dioceses, appointing new bishops, barring the Pope's envoys from entering the Kingdom without his consent and even refusing to allow Latin churchmen in his dominions to obey papal summonses to Rome. Meanwhile his two sons were for ever nibbling away at the southern frontiers of the Papal State, their father never lifting a finger to stop them.

Yet even this was not all. At the very end of his life poor Innocent found himself faced with even more serious problems nearer home. For a century and longer, the inexorable movement towards republican self-government had been gathering momentum among the towns of Italy. In Rome itself successive Popes and the old aristocracy had done their best to save their city from the general contagion, and for a time they had managed to do so; but the recent schism had weakened their hold. Innocent in particular had never enjoyed general popularity; coming from Trastevere he had always been considered one degree less of a Roman than Anacletus, and he was known to be a good deal less generous. When, therefore, they learned that Innocent had made a separate peace with the enemy, the Romans seized the opportunity to denounce the temporal power of the Pope, revive the ancient Senate on the Capitol, and declare a Republic. Innocent resisted as best he could, but he was an old man—probably well over seventy—and the effort was too much for him. A few weeks later he was dead.

On the second day after his death there was held an election which, although somewhat hurried because of conditions in the capital, was nevertheless the first perfectly undisturbed papal election that Rome had seen for eighty-two years. Unfortunately the new Pope was almost as old as his predecessor and equally unable to cope with the problems he had inherited. Consecrated in the name of Celestine II, he was that same Guido of Castello who with St Bernard

had pleaded Innocent's cause at Salerno six years before; unlike
Bernard, however, he had not been particularly impressed by the
King. The Treaty of Mignano had shocked and horrified him, and
on his accession he refused to ratify it. Roger, in his eyes, would
ever remain a usurper and a tyrant.

It was a foolish stand, and he lived—though only just—to regret it.
Roger's chancellor and effective viceroy on the mainland was still
that same Robert of Selby who had distinguished himself at Salerno
during Lothair's siege. Since then his reputation had grown steadily,
and in various directions. John of Salisbury, the English scholar
and diplomat, writes of his compatriot that he was

an able administrator and, although without any great learning,
extremely shrewd, ready of speech beyond most of the provincials
and in eloquence the equal of any, feared by all because of his influence with the Prince, and respected for the elegance of his life—this
being the more remarkable in those regions since among the Lombards, who are known to be the most frugal, not to say miserly, of
men, he spent prodigiously on sumptuous living and displayed the
magnificence characteristic of his nation; for he was an Englishman. [1]

Misers, all too often, tend to associate extravagant living with
slackness or indolence. It is unlikely, however, that the Lombards
of South Italy ever nurtured so dangerous a delusion in their dealings
with Robert of Selby. Almost as soon as the new Pope's decision
was announced, the papal city of Benevento found itself under
attack by a Sicilian force. The citizens, caught unawares, naturally
protested that the privileges granted them in their royal charter were
being infringed. Robert arrived in the King's name, strode into the
palace and demanded to be shown the document in question. The
Beneventans handed it to him. They never saw it again. Furious,
they sent their archbishop to complain to the Pope; but scarcely
was he outside the city gates than he was taken prisoner. As reports
of these developments trickled back to Rome, the Pope saw that

---

[1] *Policraticus*, VII, ch. 19. John had had personal and, one suspects, embarrassing experience of Robert's hospitality. In a letter written at about this time
to the Abbot of La Celle, he ruefully relates how he was persuaded by the
chancellor to drink with him 'to my own undoing and the detriment of my
health'. (Letter 85.)

he had gone too far. Without any proper army of his own and beset by steadily increasing pressures from the Roman commune, he had no choice but to give in. Soon afterwards, swallowing his pride, he sent Censius Frangipani and Cardinal Octavian of S. Cecilia off to Palermo to discuss terms.

It would be nice to know more about Robert of Selby.[1] The only other story we know about him concerns the efforts of three Campanian churchmen to secure the vacant bishopric of Avella. Each—once again according to John of Salisbury—secretly offered the Chancellor a large sum of money; Robert, apparently nothing loath, bargained hard until he had agreed with each in turn on a splendid price.

A day was appointed for holding the election, solemnly and in due form. But when that day arrived and the archbishops, bishops and many venerable persons had assembled, the chancellor set forth the pretensions of the competitors, described all that had taken place and announced that he was now ready to proceed in accordance with the opinion of the bishops. They condemned all three simoniac competitors; and a poor monk, ignorant of the whole affair, was canonically elected, confirmed and installed. The others were compelled to pay the amounts to which they had bound themselves, down to the very last farthing.[2]

From both these stories it is clear that Robert's administrative methods were as unorthodox as his way of life. He emerges as a far more cheerful and extrovert character than his master, yet the two seem to have had much in common and it is easy to see why the King should have so admired and trusted him. For both, ends counted more than means. Those ends were above all law, order and tranquillity; the peace of the mainland kingdom during these years and the silence of the chroniclers are the best testimonials of how well, thanks largely to Robert of Selby, they were achieved.

The Pope's two representatives, trying to negotiate with Roger in Palermo, were in a weak enough position from the outset. Their

[1] His entry in the *Dictionary of National Biography* must be treated with caution; it is inaccurate in several important respects, particularly where the chronology is concerned.

[2] *Policraticus*, VII, 19.

embarrassment must have been complete when, one day in the middle of March 1144, they arrived in the King's presence to be informed that Pope Celestine was dead and had already been succeeded by Cardinal Gerard of Bologna—henceforth to be known as Lucius II—a moderate man and, it appeared, one of Roger's personal friends.[1] Since their own special powers had expired with Celestine's death, there was no option for them but to muster what dignity they could and to return to Rome; but they took back to Lucius a proposal from the King for an early meeting.

It was held the following June, at Ceprano; and it failed miserably. After a fortnight's abortive negotiations the two sides separated in an atmosphere of disillusion and bitterness. The friendship of which so much had been expected was over. It was the Pope's loss. Had he and his negotiators shown just a little more realism and flexibility, they might have secured a Norman alliance which would have been a match for the commune in Rome. Instead, by bringing upon themselves a new enemy, they were encouraging the old one to make ever more arrogant demands. The 'senators' now began to insist that the Pope surrender all his temporal rights both inside and outside the city and support himself, as the early fathers of the Church had done, on tithes and offerings. Meanwhile, instead of rallying to his assistance, the young Norman princes aided by Robert of Selby had renewed their forays and were penetrating ever deeper into the papal territories.

Within a matter of weeks after leaving Ceprano Lucius was forced

---

[1] There is something of a problem here. Romuald of Salerno tells us of the King's joy at hearing the news, because Lucius was his *compater et amicus*. If, as Chalandon and Bernhardi both maintain—though I can find no contemporary confirmation—this was the same Gerard who had been the pro-Innocentian Rector of Benevento during the schism and subsequently, with his papal predecessor, one of Innocent's delegates to the Salerno tribunal, this friendship would seem a little hard to explain. If we give the word *compater* its usual meaning of godfather, the problem becomes harder still. Mann suggests that the new Pope was in fact godfather to one of Roger's children, but this is equally improbable. Throughout the lifetime of Queen Elvira he seems to have been in Rome or acting as Legate in Germany. Elvira had died in 1135 and the King was not to marry again till 1149; he is hardly likely to have asked a Prince of the Church to stand sponsor to one of his bastards. Conceivably they were fellow-godfathers at some baptism in Salerno, but whose? Duke Roger of Apulia did not marry till 1140.

to sue for peace; and in October—though only after his son Alfonso had been killed in a skirmish—Roger reluctantly agreed to a seven-year truce. But it was too late. As 1144 drew to its close the situation in Rome reached flash-point; fighting between the republicans and the papalists broke out in many parts of the city. In January 1145 we find the Pope writing to Peter of Cluny of how he had been unable to ride from the Lateran to S. Saba on the Aventine for the ordination of the monastery's new abbot. Then, in early February, feeling his back to the wall, he decided to take the offensive. Assisted by his Frangipani allies—to whom he had made over the Circus Maximus as a fortress—he personally led an armed attack on the Capitol. It was a heroic action, but it ended in disaster. A stone flung by one of the defenders struck him on the head; mortally wounded, he was carried by the Frangipani to Gregory the Great's old monastery of St Andrew on the Caelian; and there, on 15 February, he died.

Fifteen years before, almost to the day, Pope Honorius II had breathed his last in that same monastery. His death and the events which followed it had given birth to the Kingdom of Sicily, but they had had dire consequences for Rome. Those consequences, it appeared, were not yet over.

Apart from his unwilling ratification of his sons' truce the previous October, Roger had made no effort to help his old friend—if such Pope Lucius really was—in his distress. At first sight this indifference seems to stand out in unedifying contrast to the attitude of previous Norman leaders—Robert Guiscard, to take but one example, whose memorable march on Rome with twenty thousand followers in 1084 had saved Pope Gregory VII from an equally critical situation, even if he had destroyed a good deal of the city in the process. The Guiscard, however, was answering a call to the aid of his rightful suzerain, from whom he had formally received all his honours and titles at Ceprano four years before. Roger had also gone, at his own request, to Ceprano in the sincere hope—and probably the confident expectation—of a similar investiture. He had asked no more than he had already been granted by Innocent, but he had been rebuffed. He had received nothing at the papal hands, and had done no homage in return. The Pope no longer had any claim on his loyalty.

Besides, Robert Guiscard's spectacular rescue of Gregory from the Castel S. Angelo was more than just his duty as a vassal; it was a political necessity. Had he left the Pope to his fate, he would have also left all the South open to invasion by the Emperor. This time the papal enemy was the Roman populace itself, concerned only with the city and its immediate neighbourhood. The imperial threat, though it still existed, was a good deal less imminent. Lothair's successor, Conrad of Hohenstaufen, had troubles of his own. His election as King of Germany in preference to Henry of Bavaria had set a new spark to the old rivalry between their two houses—that age-long struggle of Welf against Hohenstaufen, Guelph against Ghibelline, that was to stain both Germany and Italy red for centuries to come. Even now, seven years after his accession, Conrad was still hard put to preserve his throne.

Not that Italy had ceased to beckon. An imperial coronation by the Pope could not but strengthen his political position, just as it had strengthened Lothair's before him; and beyond Rome lay Palermo, an even more tempting objective. The thought of that Sicilian bandit, who had now for fifteen years claimed dominion over huge tracts of imperial territory despite repeated efforts to eject him, rankled as much as ever; and Conrad knew perfectly well that the ever-turbulent Welfs would never have been able to maintain their opposition but for the huge subsidies they were receiving from Roger's agents—a fact of which he was doubtless regularly reminded by the bitter little group of South Italian exiles hanging round his court, Robert of Capua, Count Roger of Ariano and Rainulf's brother Richard among them. He had never forgiven Pope Innocent for what he considered a craven betrayal at Mignano, nor St Bernard for having made his own peace with Sicily immediately afterwards; and ever since his accession he had been dreaming of a punitive expedition to the South. It would have to be larger than Lothair's, better organised and better equipped, with a naval force capable of pursuing the war beyond the Straits of Messina if necessary —something, in fact, conceived on a very much grander scale than anything he was capable of mounting by himself, even if his domestic difficulties enabled him to do so. Fortunately he had an ally ready to hand.

St Bernard—from a
stained glass window
now in the National
Germanic Museum,
Nuremberg

Palermo: S. Giovanni degli Eremiti

The Byzantine Empire also had claims on South Italy; indeed, there may have been old men alive in Bari who still dimly remembered those heroic days, nearly a lifetime ago, when in defiance of Robert Guiscard and the massed Norman army their fellow-citizens had held out for nearly three years in their Emperor's name. Ever since, the restoration of the Italian provinces had loomed large in Greek ambitions. We have seen how as early as 1135 the Emperor John Comnenus had offered Lothair financial assistance against the King of Sicily; it seems likely that a considerable proportion of the expenses of the subsequent expedition was paid for in Byzantine gold. That expedition had failed; but John's determination held firm.

Since then the situation had worsened. When Roger's cousin Bohemund II of Antioch had been killed in 1130 he had left as his only child a two-year-old daughter, Constance; and Roger had laid claim to the throne as the senior surviving member of the House of Hauteville. Five years later he had tried to kidnap the little princess's husband-to-be, Raymond of Poitiers, as he passed through South Italy on his way to join his bride; Raymond had managed to escape only by disguising himself, first as a pilgrim and then as steward of a rich merchant. In 1138 the King had even gone so far as to arrest the Patriarch Radulph of Antioch on a journey to Rome. The Patriarch, whose persuasive charm of manner was in no way affected by a pronounced squint, was soon allowed to proceed; and on his return Roger had treated him very differently, giving him a royal welcome in Palermo and even providing him with an escort of Sicilian ships. Particularly in contrast to his outward journey, it all seemed a little overdone; if Roger really were plotting to seize the throne of Antioch the Patriarch would be a most valuable ally. John Comnenus, who had never trusted either of them, grew ever more suspicious.

During the next few years ambassadors shuttled backwards and forwards between Germany and Constantinople as the two Emperors began to make serious plans for an alliance against their common enemy. Then, in the spring of 1143, John went off on a hunting expedition in the mountains of Cilicia and accidentally scratched himself, between the fourth and little fingers of his right hand, with

a poisoned arrow. At first he ignored the wound, but in the following days the infection spread up his whole arm until, in the words
of a contemporary chronicler, it was swollen to the thickness of his
thigh. His doctors advised amputation, but the Emperor had no
faith in them and refused; and a week or so later he died of blood-
poisoning. His youngest son Manuel who succeeded him was at
first rather better-disposed towards the King of Sicily, and even
toyed with the idea of a marriage alliance; but the negotiations came
to nothing, relations between the two grew worse until they were
finally broken off altogether, and the Sicilian envoys ended up in
prison in Constantinople.

Not, perhaps, altogether without relief, Manuel turned back to
the Western Empire. His father had for some time before his death
been considering another imperial marriage—this time of Manuel
himself, with Conrad's sister-in-law Bertha of Sulzbach—and in
1142 had actually had the proposed bride brought, on approval,
to Constantinople. Manuel's initial reaction to this proposal had
been lukewarm, and his first sight of the German princess had done
little to inflame his ardour; soon, in any case, the minor upheavals
that followed his succession and his brief flirtation with Sicily had
caused the idea to be dropped. But at the end of 1144 he began to
have second thoughts. Conrad for his part was positively enthusiastic. Such a marriage, he wrote, would be a pledge of 'a permanent
alliance of constant friendship'; he himself would be a 'friend of the
Emperor's friends and an enemy of his enemies'—he named no
names, but Manuel would have no difficulty in filling in the blank—
and, if there should ever be any slight to Manuel's honour, he would
come in person to his assistance with all the massed strength of the
German state behind him.

And so the arrangements were made. Bertha, who had been living
for the past four years in forgotten obscurity, now re-emerged into
public view, shed her barbarous Frankish name for the more
euphonious Greek one of Irene, and in January 1146 duly married
the Emperor. He should have made her a splendid husband.
Young, gifted, famous for his dark good looks, he possessed a
gaiety and charm that came as a refreshing contrast after the high-
principled austerity of his father. Whether he was in his palace of

Blachernae or one of the hunting-lodges in which he spent so much of his time, any excuse was good enough for a celebration; while the visit of foreign rulers—particularly from the West—was always a signal for prolonged and elaborate festivities. Unlike most of the older generation of Byzantines he had spent his life in constant contact with the Franks of Outremer, and he genuinely admired western institutions. He introduced knightly tournaments to Constantinople and, being a superb horseman, took part in them himself —an activity that must have shocked many of his more old-fashioned subjects. But there was nothing shallow about him. When he was on campaign all his apparent frivolity fell away and he proved himself a brilliant soldier, tireless and determined. 'In war,' wrote Gibbon, 'he seemed ignorant of peace, in peace he appeared incapable of war.' A skilful diplomat, he also had the imagination and sureness of touch of a born statesman. And yet, through it all, he remained the typical Byzantine intellectual who liked nothing better than to immerse himself for hours in theological arguments of the most speculative kind; and his skill as a physician was, as we shall see, soon to be attested by Conrad of Hohenstaufen himself.

But he never liked Bertha much. As the Greek historian Nicetas Choniates explains,

His wife, a princess from Germany, was less concerned with the embellishment of her body than with that of her spirit; rejecting powder and paint, and leaving to vain women all those adornments which are owed to artifice, she sought only that solid beauty which proceeds from the splendour of virtue. This was the reason why the Emperor, who was of extreme youth, had little inclination for her and did not maintain towards her that fidelity which was her due; although he bestowed great honours upon her, a most exalted throne, a numerous retinue and all else that makes for magnificence and induces the respect and veneration of the people. He also entertained a criminal relationship with his niece, which has left a shameful stain upon his reputation.[1]

It was not in vain that King Roger had built up, over the years, the formidable network of foreign observers and agents that had made him easily the best-informed ruler in the western world. From

[1] *History of the Emperor Manuel Comnenus*, I, ii.

Germany and Constantinople—and, in all probability, from several
other places as well—he had been kept constantly posted of all
these developments as they occurred; and he had followed them with
growing concern. He had had difficulties enough with old Lothair;
this time there would be two enemies instead of one, both famous
for their skill and courage in battle and both at the height of their
powers. Conrad was fifty-three—only two years older than himself—
and Manuel not yet out of his twenties. There would also be the
Byzantine navy to contend with, and a possible direct attack on
Sicily itself. In such an eventuality, could he trust his Greek subjects
to stay loyal?

Roger had long been conscious of just such a danger. To avert it
he had for years been sending his massive subsidies to the Welfs in
Germany, knowing that to keep Conrad fully occupied at home was
the best way of discouraging him from any military adventures
abroad; and it was with a similar object in view that he had proposed
a marriage alliance with Byzantium. Both plans had failed. He had no
more diplomatic weapons in his armoury with which he could hope
to deflect the two determined Emperors from their intentions. War
seemed certain; victory, to say the least, improbable.

He could not know, at the dawn of the year 1146, that he had
already been saved twelve months before—saved, paradoxically, by
a disaster to Christendom, and one that would soon bring a second,
yet greater one in its wake. The first of these twin disasters was the
fall of Edessa. The other was to be the Second Crusade.

7

THE SECOND CRUSADE

Now there was in Sicily, among the Muslims of the country, a most learned and wealthy man. The King had much regard for him and showed him great deference, placing him above the priests and monks of his court, so that the Christians of the country accused him of being himself also, in his heart of hearts, a Muslim. One day, when the King was sitting in a belvedere looking out over the sea, a pinnace was seen approaching. Those in the vessel brought news that the Sicilian troops had penetrated into Muslim lands, where they had found much booty and killed several men—in a word, that they had gained great successes. At that moment this Muslim was sitting by the King, and seemed to be asleep; the King said 'Ho, thou! Hast thou not heard what tidings have just been told?' The Muslim replied 'No'. The King repeated, they have told us such and such: 'where was then Mahomet, while these countries and their inhabitants were suffering such treatment?' The Muslim replied, 'He had left them, to be present at the conquest of Edessa. The Faithful have just taken that city.' At these words the Franks who were present began to laugh; but the King said: 'Do not laugh; for, as God is my witness, this man never lies.'

Ibn Al-Athir

IN the first years of the Christian era, King Abgar V of Edessa was stricken with leprosy. Having heard reports of recent miraculous occurrences in Palestine, he wrote a letter to Jesus Christ, asking him to come to Edessa to cure him. Jesus declined, but promised to send one of his disciples to heal the King and preach the Gospel to his subjects. With this reply, according to some authorities, he enclosed a portrait of himself, miraculously imprinted on canvas. Later, as good as his word, he arranged with St Thomas to send Thaddeus, one of the Seventy, who accomplished both parts of his mission to the satisfaction of all concerned.

So runs the legend, as told by Eusebius and others; and, as proof of its veracity, the Saviour's letter, written by his own hand in Syriac on parchment, was long exposed to public veneration in the cathedral of Edessa.[1] We know now that Christianity did not in fact reach the city before the end of the second century; but by the middle of the twelfth Edessa could boast other, better authenticated claims to sanctity. It was the site of the earliest recorded Christian church building; it witnessed the first translation into a foreign language—Syriac again—of the Greek New Testament; and one of its later kings, Abgar IX, was, so far as history can tell, the first royal monarch ever to receive Christian baptism.

In more recent times, again, the County of Edessa was the first to be established of all the crusader states of the Levant. It dated from the year 1098 when Baldwin of Boulogne had left the main army of the First Crusade and struck off to the east to found a principality of his own on the banks of the Euphrates. He had not stayed there long; two years later he had succeeded his brother as King of Jerusalem—where, for a short and painful period towards the end of his life, he was destined to become Roger of Sicily's stepfather.[2] But Edessa had continued as a semi-independent state—under the theoretical suzerainty of Jerusalem—until, after a twenty-five-day siege, it fell, on Christmas Eve 1144, to an Arab army under Imad ed-Din Zengi, Atabeg of Mosul.

The news of its fall horrified all Christendom. To the peoples of western Europe, who had seen the initial successes of the First Crusade as an obvious sign of divine favour, it called in question all their comfortably-held opinions. After less than half a century Cross had once again given way to Crescent. How had it happened? Was it not a manifestation of the wrath of God? Travellers to the east had for some time been returning with reports of a widespread degeneracy among the Franks of Outremer. Could it be that they were no longer deemed worthy to guard the Holy Places against the Infidel under the banner of their Redeemer?

Among the Crusaders themselves, long familiarity with these

[1] Subsequently this letter was to find its way to Constantinople, where it disappeared during the revolution of 1185. See ch. XVIII.
[2] *The Normans in the South*, pp. 286–9.

shrines had made possible a more rational approach. To them Edessa had been a vital buffer state, protecting the principalities of Antioch and Tripoli—and through them the Kingdom of Jerusalem itself—from the Danishmends, the Ortoqids and the other warlike Turkish tribes to the north. Luckily these tribes had always been divided against each other, as had the Arab tribes across the eastern mountains; but Zengi, an ambitious politician as well as a brilliant general, was already beginning to unite them behind him and dreaming only of the day when, as the acknowledged champion of Islam, he would deliver Asia once and for all from the Christian invader.

Whatever the Franks may have thought about their spiritual worth, their military weakness was beyond dispute. The first great wave of crusading enthusiasm, culminating in the jubilant capture of Jerusalem in 1099, was now spent. Immigration from the west had slowed to a trickle; of the pilgrims, many still arrived unarmed according to the ancient tradition, and even for those who came prepared to wield a sword a single summer campaign usually proved more than enough. The only permanent standing army—if such it could be called—was formed by the two military orders of the Hospitallers and the Templars; but they alone could not hope to hold out against a concerted offensive under Zengi. Reinforcements were desperately needed; the Pope must declare a Crusade.

Although Edessa had fallen nearly eight weeks before the death of Pope Lucius, his successor Eugenius III had already been over six months on the throne before he received official notification of the disaster. The special embassy that brought it—together with an urgent appeal for help—found him at Viterbo.[1] Eugenius's pontificate had not had an auspicious beginning. His election, held in safe Frangipani territory immediately on the death of the unfortunate Lucius, had been smooth enough; but when he had tried to proceed from the Lateran to St Peter's for his consecration the commune

---

[1] The embassy was led by Hugh, Bishop of Jabala in Syria. According to the historian Otto of Freising who was with the Pope at the time, Hugh also told of a certain John, 'a king and priest who dwells beyond Persia and Armenia in the uttermost east and, with all his people, is a Christian'. A direct descendant of the Magi, he ruled with an emerald sceptre. Thus the legendary Prester John makes his first entrance into recorded history.

had barred his way, and three days later he had fled the city.

The speed of his flight surprised no one; indeed, the only surprising thing about Eugenius was that he should have been elected in the first place. An ex-monk of Clairvaux and disciple of St Bernard, he was a simple character, gentle and retiring—not at all, men thought, the material of which Popes were made. Even Bernard himself, when he heard the news of the election, did not take it well. One might have expected him to be gratified at the raising of the first Cistercian to the Throne of St Peter; instead, obviously nettled at the elevation of one of his 'children' over his head, he made no secret of his disapproval. In a letter addressed collectively to the entire papal Curia, he wrote:

May God forgive you what you have done! . . . You have made the last first, and lo! his last state is more dangerous than the first. . . . What reason or counsel, when the Supreme Pontiff was dead, made you rush upon a mere rustic, lay hands on him in his refuge, wrest from his hands the axe, pick or hoe, and lift him to a throne?[1]

To Eugenius he was equally outspoken:

Thus does the finger of God raise up the poor out of the dust and lift up the beggar from the dunghill, that he may sit with princes and inherit the throne of glory.[2]

It seems an unfortunate choice of metaphor, and it says much for the new Pope's gentleness and patience that he showed no resentment. But Bernard was after all his spiritual father, and besides, Eugenius was no Urban II; he had neither the drive nor the personality to launch a Crusade single-handed. In any case events in Rome made it impossible for him to cross the Alps and, as he put it, to sound the heavenly trumpet of the Gospel in France. In the months to come he was to need his old master as badly as he had ever needed him in his life.

When Pope Eugenius came to consider the princes of the West, he could see only one suitable candidate for the leadership of the new Crusade. Ideally, the honour should have fallen to the western

[1] Letter 237.   [2] Letter 238.

Emperor, but Conrad—as yet only King of the Romans pending his imperial coronation—was still beset with his own difficulties in Germany. When these were solved, he would be more interested in settling the Italian problem than in oriental adventures. King Stephen of England had had a civil war on his hands for six years already. Roger of Sicily was, for any number of reasons, out of the question. The only possible choice was Louis VII of France.

Louis asked nothing better. He was one of Nature's pilgrims. Though still only twenty-four, he had about him an aura of lugubrious piety which made him look and seem older than his years— and irritated to distraction his beautiful and high-spirited young wife, Eleanor of Aquitaine. He was already under a crusading vow, having assumed it from his elder brother Philip after the latter's death in a riding accident some years before. Moreover, his soul was in anguish. In 1143, during a war with Theobald, Count of Champagne, his army had set fire to the little town of Vitry—now Vitry-en-François—on the Marne; and its inhabitants, more than a thousand men, women and children, had been burnt alive in the church where they had taken refuge. Louis had watched the conflagration, but had been powerless to prevent it. Ever since, the memory of that day had weighed him down. The responsibility he knew to be his; nothing less than a Crusade, with its promise of a plenary indulgence for all sins, could be sufficient atonement.

At Christmas 1145 Louis informed his assembled tenants-in-chief of his determination to take the Cross, and implored them to follow him. Odo of Deuil reports that 'the King blazed and shone with the zeal of his faith and his contempt for earthly pleasures and temporal glories, so that his person was an example more persuasive than any speech could be'. It was not, however, persuasive enough. His vassals' reaction was disappointing. They had their responsibilities at home to consider. Besides, the reports they had heard about life in Outremer suggested that their dissolute compatriots had probably brought the disaster on themselves. Let them work out their own salvation. That hard-headed churchman Abbot Suger of St Denis, former guardian and tutor to the King, also turned his face firmly against the proposal. But Louis had made up his mind. If he himself could not fill the hearts and minds of his vassals with crusading fire, he must find someone who could. He wrote to the Pope, accepting his invitation; then, inevitably, he sent for the Abbot of Clairvaux.

To Bernard, who had always taken a lively interest in the affairs of the Holy Land, here was a cause after his own heart; exhausted as he was, broken in health and by now genuinely longing for retirement in the peace of his abbey, he responded to the call with all that extraordinary fervour that had made him, for over a quarter of a century, the dominant spiritual voice in all Christendom. Willingly he agreed to launch the Crusade in France, and to address the assembly that the King had summoned for the following Easter at Vézelay.

At once the magic of his name began to do its work, and as the appointed day approached men and women from every corner of France poured into the little town. Since there were far too many to be packed into the cathedral, a great wooden platform was hastily erected on the hillside. (It stood until 1789, when it was destroyed by the Revolution.) Here, on Palm Sunday morning, 31 March 1146, Bernard appeared before the multitude for one of the most fateful speeches of his life. His body, writes Odo, was so frail that it seemed already to be touched by death. At his side was the King, already displaying on his breast the cross which the Pope had sent him in token of his decision. Together the two mounted the platform; and Bernard began to speak.

The text of the exhortation which followed has not come down to us; but with Bernard it was the manner of his delivery rather than the words themselves that made the real impact on his hearers. All we know is that his voice rang out across the meadow 'like a celestial organ', and that as he spoke the crowd, silent at first, began to cry out for crosses of their own. Bundles of these, cut in rough cloth, had been already prepared for distribution; when the supply was exhausted, the abbot flung off his own robe and began to tear it into strips to make more. Others followed his example, and he and his helpers were still stitching as night fell.

The new Crusaders included men and women[1] from all walks

[1] The legend of a whole female regiment, with Eleanor herself as its titular head, is surprisingly confirmed by the Byzantine chronicler Nicetas Choniates, who reports the appearance in Constantinople of 'a body of women on horse-back, dressed and armed like men, completely military in appearance and seemingly braver than Amazons'.

of life—among them many of those vassals whom Louis had failed to rouse from their apathy only three months before. All France, it seemed, had been infused with Bernard's spirit; and it was with pardonable pride that—his earlier resentment against Pope Eugenius now forgotten—he could write to him shortly afterwards:

You have commanded, and I have obeyed . . . I have declared and spoken; and now they [the Crusaders] are multiplied, beyond number. Cities and castles are deserted, and seven women together may scarcely find one man to lay hold on, so many widows are there whose husbands are still living.

It was indeed a remarkable achievement. No one else in Europe could have done it. And yet, as events were soon to tell, it were better had it not been done.

His success at Vézelay acted on St Bernard like a tonic. No longer did he contemplate a return to Clairvaux. Instead he swept through Burgundy, Lorraine and Flanders to Germany, preaching the Crusade to packed churches wherever he went. His line of approach, always direct, was at times alarmingly so. In a letter to the German churchmen he wrote:

If the Lord has called little worms like yourselves to the defence of His heritage, do not conclude that His arm has grown shorter or that His hand has lost its power. . . . What is it, if not a most perfect and direct invention of the Almighty, that he should admit murderers, ravishers, adulterers, perjurors and other criminals for his service and for their salvation?

By autumn Germany too was aflame; and even Conrad, who had at first predictably refused to have any part in the Crusade, repented[1] after a Christmas castigation from Bernard and agreed to take the Cross.

Pope Eugenius received this last news with some alarm. Not for

[1] It may be that Conrad's change of heart was accelerated by a miraculous occurrence two days previously when Bernard, entering the cathedral of Speyer on Christmas Day, had prostrated himself three times to the statue of the Virgin, which had promptly returned his greeting.

the first time, the Abbot of Clairvaux had exceeded his brief. His instructions had been to preach the Crusade in France; no one had said anything about Germany. The Germans and the French were bound to squabble—they always did—and their inevitable jockey-ings for position might easily lead to the foundering of the whole enterprise. Besides, the Pope needed Conrad in Italy; how else was he ever to re-establish himself in Rome? But it was too late to change things now. The vows had been taken. Eugenius could hardly start discouraging would-be Crusaders before the movement was even on its way.

In France, meanwhile, Louis VII had flung himself into prepara-tions and had already written to enlist the sympathies of Manuel Comnenus and Roger of Sicily. To Manuel, fond as he was of indivi-dual westerners and the western way of life, the prospect of another full-scale incursion of his Empire by undisciplined Frankish armies was disagreeable in the extreme. He knew the problems that the First Crusade had caused his grandfather fifty years before—the descent on Constantinople by hordes of Latin thugs and barbarians, all of them out for what they could get and expecting to be lodged, fed and often even clothed by the Byzantines at no cost to themselves; the swaggering arrogance of their leaders, refusing to do the Emperor homage for their eastern conquests, which all too often had merely substituted one hostile neighbour for another. Admittedly the Danishmend Turks were giving him a lot of trouble just now; it was even conceivable that the new wave of Crusaders might prove better behaved than their predecessors and even turn out to be a long-term blessing; but he doubted it. His reply to Louis was as lukewarm as it could be made without offence. He would provide food and supplies for the Crusading armies, but everything would have to be paid for. And all the leaders would be asked once again to swear their fealty to him as they passed through his Empire.

Writing to the King of Sicily, Louis found himself in a slightly embarrassing position. He himself had formally recognised Roger in 1140 and had no quarrel with him; but he was fully aware that the two Emperors did not share his benevolence. Nor did the Christian rulers in the East. Not only had Roger already made formal claim to Antioch, even trying to lay hands on its present prince, Raymond of

Poitiers, who—to complicate matters further—was the uncle of young Queen Eleanor of France; there was also the unfortunate fact that, by the terms of his mother's marriage with King Baldwin, the Crown of Jerusalem in default of a direct heir should have passed to him. In the event, this contract was later declared null and void; and Baldwin, once he had spent all Adelaide's money, had shipped her unceremoniously back to Palermo. It was an insult that her son had never forgiven, and relations between Sicily and the Crusader states had remained bad. Louis knew that Roger would never be welcome in Outremer and doubted whether he would even consent to go— except as a conqueror.

On the other hand, Roger was now the acknowledged master of the Mediterranean—a position he had further strengthened during the summer of 1146 when, by the capture of the Libyan city of Tripoli, he had effectively sliced the Middle Sea in two. No longer could any ship hope to sail from one end of it to the other without his consent. If, then, the Second Crusade were to succeed, it was essential that the King of Sicily should remain well-disposed; but it was hoped that he would not embarrass everyone by insisting on active personal participation. On the first point Louis was soon reassured. Roger not only declared himself sympathetic to the Crusade; he offered to provide transportation, supplies and, in addition, a considerable force of fighting men to swell the Crusader ranks. On the second, however, his reply was less satisfactory; in the event of this offer being accepted, he himself or one of his sons would willingly lead a Sicilian army to Palestine.

Like most of the King's diplomatic communications, this reply was deeply disingenuous. Roger was just as opposed to the Second Crusade as his father had been to the First. Many of the most distinguished and influential of his subjects were Muslims, whom he understood and whose language he spoke; he liked them, one suspects, a good deal more than the French or the Germans. Furthermore, as we have seen, he had always hated the Frankish states of the Levant. Tolerance was the corner-stone of his kingdom; why should he now support a movement that preached the exact opposite, in a way that would be bound to arouse resentment among an important section of his own people?

In reality, he can have had no intention of taking the Cross; not, at least, any further than Antioch. To him the Crusade meant two things only—a means of distracting the two Empires from an attack on Sicily and an opportunity of extending his own influence in the East. But both these objectives would be furthered if he could secure the friendship or support of the King of France, and for this a policy of benevolent neutrality towards the Crusade would not be enough. The situation called for at least some degree of controlled enthusiasm, shown in a line of action that could at any moment be turned from its original aim and redirected against the states of Outremer— or even, if need be, against Constantinople itself.

However, when Roger's envoys formally advanced his proposals to a preliminary conference of the Crusaders held at Etampes early in 1147, King Louis politely declined. His ally Conrad was in any case resolved to take the overland route; even had he not been, the Sicilian offer was impractical. Roger's navy, huge as it was, would not have been adequate to carry the whole crusading force. To have accepted it would have meant dividing the army, putting half of it at the mercy of a notoriously untrustworthy monarch who had already attempted to kidnap the Queen's own uncle on a similar voyage, and leaving the other half to negotiate the long passage through Anatolia—the most perilous part of the whole expedition. They were understandable fears, which might well have been justified in the event; and though Louis's rejection of Sicilian help led to Roger's complete withdrawal from all active participation in the Crusade, his decision was probably a wise one.

St Bernard's uncomplimentary letter to the German clergy quoted earlier in this chapter had been, perhaps, more prophetic than he knew. Largely because of the promise of plenary absolution which accompanied all successful crusading journeys, the crusader armies tended to be even more disreputable than most others in the Middle Ages; and the German host that set off, about twenty thousand strong, from Ratisbon at the end of May 1147 seems to have contained more than its fair share of undesirables, ranging from the occasional religious maniac to the usual collection of footloose ne'er-do-wells and fugitives from justice. Hardly had they entered Byzantine territory than they began pillaging the countryside, raping, ravaging and even murdering as the mood took them. Often the leaders themselves set a poor example to those that followed behind; at Adrianople—now Edirne—Conrad's nephew and second-in-command, the young Duke Frederick of Swabia (better known to history by his subsequent nickname of Barbarossa) burnt down a monastery in reprisal for an attack by local brigands, and slaughtered the perfectly innocent monks. Fighting became ever more frequent between the Crusaders and the Byzantine military escort which Manuel had sent out to keep an eye on them, and when in mid-September the army at last drew up outside the walls of Constantinople—Conrad having indignantly refused the Emperor's request to avoid the capital altogether by crossing directly over the Hellespont into Asia—relations between German and Greek could hardly have been worse.

Even before the populations along the route had recovered from the shock, the French army in its turn appeared on the western horizon. It was a rather smaller force than that of the Germans, and on the whole more seemly. Discipline was better, and the presence of many distinguished ladies—including Queen Eleanor herself—accompanying their husbands doubtless exercised a further moderating influence. Yet even their progress was not altogether smooth. The Balkan peasantry by now showed itself frankly hostile—not surprisingly in view of what it had suffered from the Germans scarcely a month before—and asked ridiculous prices for what little food it had left to sell. Mistrust soon became mutual, and led to sharp practices on both sides. Thus, long before they reached Constantinople, the French had begun to feel considerable resentment against Germans and Greeks alike; and when they finally arrived on 4 October they were scandalised to hear that the Emperor Manuel had chosen that moment to conclude a truce with the Turkish enemy.

Although Louis could not have been expected to appreciate the fact, it was a sensible precaution for Manuel to take. The presence of the French and German armies at the very gates of his capital constituted a far more serious immediate danger than the Turks in Asia. The Emperor knew that in both camps there were extreme elements pressing for a combined western attack on Constantinople; and indeed only a few days later St Bernard's cousin Godfrey, Bishop of Langres, with all 'the un-Christian intolerance of a monk of Clairvaux',[1] was formally to propose such a course to the King. Only by deliberately spreading reports of a huge Turkish army massing in Anatolia and implying that if the Franks did not make haste to pass through the hostile territory they might never manage to do so at all did Manuel succeed in saving the situation. Meanwhile he flattered Louis—and kept him occupied—with his usual constant round of banquets and lavish entertainments, while arranging passage for the King and his army over into Asia at the earliest possible moment.

As he bade farewell to his unwelcome guests and watched the ferryboats, laden to the gunwales with men and animals, shuttling across the Bosphorus, the Emperor foresaw better than anyone the dangers that awaited the Franks on the second stage of their journey. He himself had only recently returned from an Anatolian campaign; though his stories of the gathering Turkish hordes had been exaggerated, he had now seen the Crusaders for himself and he must have known that their shambling forces, already as lacking in morale as in discipline, would stand little chance of survival if suddenly attacked by the Seljuk cavalry. He had provided them with provisions and guides; he had warned them about the scarcity of water; and he had advised them not to take the direct route through the hinterland but to keep to the coast, which was still under Byzantine control. He could do no more. If, after all these precautions, the Crusaders still persisted in getting themselves slaughtered, they would have only themselves to blame. He, for his part, would be sorry—but not, perhaps, inconsolable.

It cannot have been more than a few days after bidding them farewell that Manuel received two reports, from two very different

[1] Sir Steven Runciman, *A History of the Crusades*, vol. II, p. 268. The bishop had formerly been prior of Clairvaux—a fact which led him, according to John of Salisbury, to claim special authority on the grounds that Bernard had committed the King to his counsel. His pomposity was, however, regularly punctured by Bishop Arnulf of Lisieux, worldliest of prelates, who maintained that he was just like the wine of Cyprus—sweet to the taste but lethal unless diluted with water. (*Historia Pontificalis*, ch. xxiv.)

quarters. The first, brought by swift messengers from Asia Minor, informed him that the German army had been taken by surprise by the Turks near Dorylaeum and massacred. Conrad himself had escaped, and had returned to join the French at Nicaea, but nine-tenths of his men now lay dead among the wreckage of their camp.

The second report brought the news that the fleet of King Roger of Sicily was at that very moment sailing against his Empire.

One of the perennial difficulties confronting any historian of the Middle Ages is that the chroniclers on whose works he must rely are so seldom of an analytical turn of mind. They usually give the facts —with varying degrees of accuracy—clearly enough. Questions of cause and motivation, however, they tend to ignore; and there is one such question in particular on which we might wish that they had been more explicit. How serious, in fact, was Roger's attack in 1147 on Byzantium?

Some authorities have maintained that it was very serious indeed —that the operation was timed to coincide with the arrival of the French at Constantinople, and that Roger's original plan was that the Sicilians and French together should then combine to overthrow the Emperor and seize his capital. They even suggest that Manuel had foreknowledge of this plan, which would explain his insistence on oaths of fealty before allowing the Franks to approach. It is an intriguing theory; but there seems to be little evidence for it apart from the conduct of the Bishop of Langres—and even he made no mention, so far as we can tell, of Sicilian help. Had Louis accepted Roger's original offer of transport for himself and his army, might he conceivably have been persuaded to join in a concerted attack on Constantinople before passing on to Palestine, just as the Venetians —to their lasting shame—were to persuade the Franks of the Fourth Crusade fifty-seven years later? Surely not. Louis had no real quarrel with the Byzantines; he was vowed to the Crusade, and he would, one suspects, have vehemently resisted any attempt by the King of Sicily to deflect him from his goal.

If Roger's action is to fit logically into the framework of preceding and following events, it must be looked at in a different light. He was a statesman, not an adventurer. Had he still contemplated a combined operation with the French he would surely have taken far more trouble to ensure that they were sympathetic to his idea. In the circumstances, he had no reason to believe that Louis would help him at all; his envoys had had a noticeably cool reception at Etampes the previous spring. If the Sicilian navy had appeared off Constantinople while the French were there, they might well have found the latter allied with the Greeks against them.

In the event, they did not make for the capital at all. Under the command of George of Antioch, they sailed in the autumn of 1147 from Otranto and headed straight across the Adriatic to Corfu. The island fell without a struggle; Nicetas Choniates tells us that the inhabitants, oppressed by the weight of Byzantine taxation and charmed by the honeyed words of the Greek-Sicilian admiral, welcomed the Normans as deliverers and willingly accepted a garrison of a thousand men.[1] Next, turning southward, the fleet rounded the Peloponnese, leaving further detachments at strategic positions, and sailed up the eastern coast to Euboea. At this point George seems to have decided that he had gone far enough. He turned about, made a quick stab at Athens[2] and then, on reaching the Ionian islands, headed eastward again up the Gulf of Corinth, ravaging the coastal towns as he went. His progress, writes Nicetas, was 'like a sea monster, swallowing everything in its path'.

Of the raiding parties that George sent ashore, one penetrated the hinterland as far as Thebes, centre of the Byzantine silk manufacture. The spoils were considerable. Stocks of rich damasks and bale after bale of brocades were carted back to shore and loaded on to the Sicilian vessels. But the admiral was still not satisfied. A large number of women workers—expert alike in the cultivation of the silkworm and

[1] Otto of Freising maintains that Corfu was taken by the old trick of a bogus funeral procession; but Otto knew little of Byzantine affairs, and variants of the funeral story are too frequent in mediaeval chronicles to encourage much belief. See p. 44n.

[2] The fact that the Norman sack of Athens is mentioned by western chroniclers only has led to some doubt as to whether the city really was raided at this time. The recent American excavations in the Agora have, however, tended to confirm that it was. See K. M. Setton, 'The Archaeology of Mediaeval Athens', in *Essays in Medieval Life and Thought, Presented in Honour of Austin Patterson Evans* (New York, 1955), p. 251.

its exploitation and almost certainly Jewish[1]—were herded to the ships. They too would be welcomed in Palermo. From Thebes the raiders moved on to Corinth, where—although the Corinthians had received advance warning of their arrival and had fled to the higher citadel of Acrocorinth with everything of value that they possessed— a short siege produced the desired result. The city was pillaged, the relics of St Theodore carried off, and George of Antioch sailed back in triumph, via Corfu, to Sicily.

'By this time,' writes Nicetas, 'the Sicilian vessels were so low in the water with the weight of their plunder that they seemed more like merchantmen than the pirate ships they really were.'[2] He spoke no more than the truth. Thebes, Athens and Corinth were the wealthiest cities in Greece. If this were not piracy, then the word had no meaning. But piracy was not all. Just as George's raids along the North African coast were undertaken less for their own sake than to secure control of the Mediterranean narrows, so his first Greek expedition was a calculated thrust against the western extremities of the Byzantine Empire, launched by Roger as a deliberate act of policy and for impeccable strategic reasons. The Second Crusade, he knew, had not permanently saved Sicily from attack by either Empire; it had merely postponed the day, affording him a year or two of grace in which to prepare his defences. By occupying Corfu and other carefully chosen strongpoints on the Greek mainland, he had deprived Byzantium of the principal bridgehead from which to launch an offensive against South Italy.

That, surely, was the real purpose of the expedition. But if it could provide certain additional benefits, so much the better. The silk-workers proved just such a bonus. It has sometimes been claimed that they were the nucleus around which the celebrated royal silk-mills of Palermo were built up. This theory does them too much honour—though they may well have introduced certain new techniques. Ever since the time of the Omayyads it had been the practice,

[1] The Hebrew traveller Benjamin of Tudela, who visited Thebes about twenty years after George's raid, reported two thousand Jews in the city. 'They are,' he wrote, 'the most skilled artificers in silk and purple cloth throughout Greece.'

[2] Another report, to the effect that the ships were so weighed down with plunder as to be submerged up to the third bank of oars, indicates the degree of caution necessary when dealing with certain imaginative chroniclers.

in all the principal Islamic kingdoms of the East and the West as well as in Constantinople itself, to maintain a silk workshop in or near the palace for the manufacture of robes and vestments for ceremonial court occasions. Sicily was no exception, and the Palermitan silk industry had thus been a thriving concern since the days of the Arabs—from whose language the *Tiraz*, or royal workshop, took its name.[1] Another long-established Muslim custom, however, required the ladies of the *Tiraz*, when not at their looms, to render other more intimate services to the gentlemen of the Court. This tradition too the Normans, eclectic as ever, had appropriated with enthusiasm; and it was not long before the *Tiraz* became a useful, if slightly transparent, cover for the royal harem. As we read of George of Antioch's seizure of the luckless Thebans it is difficult not to wonder which of their two possible functions he had more in mind.

The news of the Sicilian depredations in Greece stung Manuel to a fury. Whatever he himself might have thought about the Crusade, the fact that a so-called Christian country should have taken deliberate advantage of it to launch an attack on his Empire disgusted him; and the knowledge that the admiral concerned was a renegade Greek can hardly have assuaged his wrath. A hundred years before, Apulia had been a rich province of the Byzantine Empire; now it had become nothing but a nest of pirates, a springboard for unprovoked aggression by his enemy. Here was a situation that could not be tolerated. Roger, 'that dragon, threatening to shoot the flames of his anger higher than the crater of Etna . . . that common enemy of all Christians and illegal occupier of the land of Sicily',[2] must be eliminated from the Mediterranean for ever. The West had tried to do so, and had failed miserably. Now it was the turn of Byzantium. Given adequate help and freedom from other military commitments, Manuel believed that he could succeed. Fortunately the crusading armies had passed on. He himself had already concluded a truce with

[1] The best Norman-Sicilian example still extant is Roger II's superb mantle which is now in the Kunsthistorisches Museum at Vienna. It is of red silk, embroidered in gold with a tremendous design of tigers savaging camels. The Arabic inscription around the border identifies it as a product of the *Tiraz* of Palermo, dating from the 528th year of the Hegira—A.D. 1133.

[2] Imperial Edict of February 1148.

the Turks in the spring of 1147, and this he now confirmed and
extended. It was essential that every soldier and sailor in the Empire
should be free for the grand design that he was planning, a design
that might well prove to be the crowning achievement of his life: the
restoration of all South Italy and Sicily to the Byzantine fold.

The next problem was to find suitable allies. With France and
Germany out of the running, Manuel's thoughts turned to Venice.
The Venetians, as he well knew, had long been worried about the
growth of Sicilian sea power; they had voluntarily joined the delegation which his father had sent to Lothair to discuss an anti-Sicilian
alliance twelve years before. Since then their alarm had increased, and
with good reason. No longer could they control the Mediterranean
as once they had done; and while the bazaars of Palermo, Catania and
Syracuse grew ever busier, so affairs on the Rialto had begun, gently
but ominously, to slacken. If now Roger were to consolidate his hold
on Corfu and the coast of Epirus, he would be in a position to seal
off the Adriatic; and the Venetians might at any moment find themselves under Sicilian blockade.

They bargained a little, of course; no Venetian ever gave anything
for nothing. But in March 1148, in return for increased trading
privileges in Cyprus, Rhodes and Constantinople, Manuel got what
he wanted—the full support of the Venetian fleet for the six months
following. The Emperor meanwhile was working feverishly to
bring his own navy to readiness; his secretary, John Cinnamus,
estimated its strength at five hundred galleys and a thousand transports—a worthy complement to an army of perhaps twenty or
thirty thousand men. As its admiral the Emperor appointed his
brother-in-law, the Grand Duke Stephen Contostephanus; the army
he placed under the Grand Domestic, a Turk named Axuch who had
been taken prisoner as a boy fifty years before and had grown up in
the imperial palace. Manuel himself would be in overall command.

By April the huge expeditionary force was ready to leave. The
ships, refitted and provisioned, lay at anchor in the Marmara; the
army waited for the order to march. Then, suddenly, everything went
wrong. A South Russian tribe, the Polovtsi or Kumans, swept over
the Danube into Byzantine territory; the Venetian fleet was held up
by the sudden death of the Doge; a succession of freak summer

storms disrupted shipping in the eastern Mediterranean. It was autumn before the two navies met in the southern Adriatic and the joint sea blockade of Corfu began. The land attack, meanwhile, was still further delayed. By the time he had dealt with the Polovtsi it was plain to Manuel that the Pindus mountains would be blocked by snow long before he could get his army across them. Settling it in winter quarters in Macedonia he himself rode on to Thessalonica, where an important guest was awaiting him. Conrad of Hohenstaufen had just returned from the Holy Land.

The Second Crusade had been an ignominious fiasco. Conrad, with such of his Germans as remained after the slaughter at Dorylaeum, had marched on with the French as far as Ephesus, where the army had stopped to celebrate Christmas. There he had fallen gravely ill. Leaving his compatriots to continue the journey without him, he had returned to Constantinople to recover, and there he had stayed as a guest in the imperial palace till March 1148, when the Emperor had put Greek ships at his disposal to carry him to Palestine. The French, meanwhile, though they had fared rather better than the Germans, had had an agonising passage through Anatolia, during which they in their turn had suffered heavily at Turkish hands. Although it was largely the fault of Louis himself, who had ignored Manuel's warnings to keep to the coast, he persisted in attributing almost every encounter with the enemy to Byzantine carelessness or treachery or both, and rapidly built up an almost psychopathic resentment against the Greeks. At last in despair he, his household and as much of his cavalry as could be accommodated had taken ship from Attalia, leaving the rest of the army and pilgrims to struggle on by land as best they might. It had been late in the spring before the remnant of the great host that had set out so confidently the previous year dragged itself miserably into Antioch.

And that was only the beginning of the trouble. The mighty Zengi was dead, but his mantle had passed to his still greater son Nur ed-Din, whose stronghold at Aleppo had now become the focus of Muslim opposition to the Franks. Aleppo should thus have been the Crusaders' first objective, and within days of his arrival in Antioch Louis found himself under considerable pressure from

Prince Raymond to mount an immediate attack on the city. He had refused on the grounds that he must first pray at the Holy Sepulchre; whereat Queen Eleanor, whose affection for her husband had not been increased by the dangers and discomforts of the journey from France and whose relations with Raymond were already suspected of going somewhat beyond those normally recommended for a niece and her uncle, had announced her intention of remaining at Antioch and suing for divorce. She and her husband were distant cousins; the question of consanguinity had been conveniently overlooked at the time of their marriage, but if resurrected could still prove embarrassing—and Eleanor knew it.

Louis, who for all his moroseness was not without spirit in moments of crisis, had ignored his wife's protests and dragged her forcibly off to Jerusalem—though not before he had succeeded in so antagonising Raymond that the latter henceforth refused to play any further part in the Crusade. No one doubted that he had carried off the situation with what dignity he could, but the effect on his reputation, particularly at such a moment, had been unfortunate. He and the tight-lipped Eleanor arrived at the Holy City in May, soon after Conrad; they were welcomed with due ceremony by Queen Mélisende and her son Baldwin III, now eighteen; and there they remained until, on 24 June, all the Crusaders were invited to a huge assembly at Acre to discuss their plan of action. It did not take them long to reach a decision: every man and beast available must be immediately mobilised for a concerted attack on Damascus.

Why Damascus was chosen as the first objective we shall never understand. It was now the only important Arab state in all the Levant to continue hostile to Nur ed-Din; as such it could, and should, have been an invaluable ally to the Franks. By attacking it, they drove it against its will into Nur ed-Din's Muslim confederation and, in doing so, made their own destruction sure. They arrived to find the walls of Damascus strong, the defenders determined. On the second day the besieging army, by yet another of those disastrous decisions which characterised the whole Crusade, moved its camp to an area along the eastern section of the walls, devoid alike of shade and water. The Palestinian barons, already at loggerheads over the future of the city when captured, suddenly lost their nerve and began to urge retreat. There were dark rumours of bribery and treason. Louis and Conrad were shocked and disgusted, but soon they too were made to understand the facts of the situation. To continue the siege would mean not only the passing of Damascus into the hands of Nur ed-Din but also, given the universal breakdown of morale, the almost certain annihilation of their whole army. On 28 July, just five days after the opening of the campaign, they ordered withdrawal.

There is no part of the Syrian desert more shattering to the spirit than that dark-grey, featureless expanse of sand and basalt that lies between Damascus and Tiberias. Retreating across it in the height of the Arabian summer, the remorseless sun and scorching desert wind full in their faces, harried incessantly by mounted Arab archers and leaving a stinking trail of dead men and horses in their wake, the Crusaders must have felt despair heavy upon them. This was the end. Their losses, both in material and in human life, had been immense. They had neither the will nor the wherewithal to continue. Worst of all was the shame. Having travelled for the best part of a year, often in conditions of mortal danger, having suffered agonies of thirst, hunger and sickness and the bitterest extremes of heat and cold, this once-glorious army that had purported to enshrine all the ideals of the Christian West had given up the whole thing after just four days' fighting, having regained not one inch of Muslim territory. Here was the ultimate of humiliations—which neither they nor their enemies would forget.

But for Conrad personally there had emerged from the shambles of the Second Crusade one remarkable result, as happy as it was unexpected. He had formed a deep regard and affection for Manuel Comnenus. When he had fallen ill at Ephesus the previous Christmas the Emperor and his wife had themselves sailed down from Constantinople, picked him up and brought him safely back to the capital; and for the next two months Manuel, who prided himself on his medical skill, had tended him with his own hands and nursed him back to health. Conrad's first passage through Constantinople with his army had not left him with the pleasantest of memories; he was all the more touched at the consideration that he was now being shown. The Emperor, with his intelligence, his charm and his German wife—a sister of Conrad's own—was a perfect host; when his patient was cured he had seized the opportunity to arrange a magnificent series of horse-races and entertainments in his honour, and had finally sent him on his way to Palestine in a Byzantine squadron, together with two thousand horses, all fully equipped, from the imperial stable. Conrad, not surprisingly, had been sorry to leave, and had promised to visit Manuel again on his homeward journey.

And so, the ill-starred Crusade safely in the past, the two monarchs met again at Thessalonica, and Manuel bore Conrad away for his second winter in Constantinople. Their friendship remained unaffected after the six months' separation, and Christmas was marked by a further union of the two imperial houses when, with the utmost pomp and the usual elaborate festivities, Manuel's niece Theodora was married to Conrad's brother Henry of Austria.[1] This year, however, there were serious political problems to be discussed, the most pressing of which was Roger of Sicily. The Byzantines were already at war with him; their navy was at that very moment blockading Corfu and their army was prepared to march just as soon as the melting of the snows made it possible to cross the Pindus. Conrad had not yet opened hostilities, but asked nothing better than to do so. Agreement was quickly reached, and in the first days of 1149 the two rulers undertook, by a treaty of formal alliance, to launch a joint attack on the King of Sicily during that year. Only if one of the parties were struck by grave illness or faced with the imminent danger of losing his throne could this commitment be set aside; even then it would not be cancelled but merely postponed. Sensibly in the circumstances, the treaty also enshrined an understanding about the future of Apulia and Calabria after they had been wrested from Roger's grasp. Both Empires had claimed these territories in the past, and both Manuel and Conrad were anxious to avoid a subsequent wrangle in their division of the spoils. The compromise that they reached did them both credit. Both regions would be made over

---

[1] A slight gloom may have been cast over the proceedings by the horror felt by many Byzantines at the fate of a Greek princess being delivered over to the mercy of Frankish barbarians; Sir Steven Runciman (*History of the Crusades*, vol. II) quotes a poem of condolence addressed to her mother in which she is described as being 'immolated to the beast of the West'.

by Conrad to Byzantium as the belated dowry of his sister-in-law
Bertha, now the Empress Irene.

Once future plans had been settled, there was no reason for either
of the new allies to linger in Constantinople. In early February they
parted—Conrad to Germany and preparations for his new Italian
offensive, Manuel back to his army and the siege of Corfu, whence
recent reports had not been encouraging. The Sicilian-held citadel
rose invulnerable on its high crest in the mountainous north of the
island, towering almost perpendicularly above the sea and safely out
of range of Byzantine projectiles. The Greeks, wrote Nicetas, seemed
to be shooting at the very sky itself, while the defenders could
release downpours of arrows and hailstorms of rocks on to those
below. (People wondered, he adds rather disarmingly, how the
Sicilians had taken possession of it so effortlessly the previous year.)
During one of the attacks the Grand Duke Contostephanus was
killed and his place taken by Axuch, who had by this time arrived
with the land army; but the change of leadership had no effect on the
progress of the siege. As the weeks went by it became clear that
Corfu could never be taken by storm. The only hope—barring
treachery from within—would be to starve out the garrison, who
had had a full year in which to provision themselves; and even then
the blockade might at any moment be broken by a Sicilian fleet
arriving with reinforcements and supplies.

It is a commonplace of warfare that a siege can impose just as
great a strain on the morale of the attacking force as on that of the
beleaguered garrison. The coming of spring saw the outbreak of
serious quarrels between the Greek sailors and their Venetian allies.
Axuch did what he could to smooth things over, but failed; and the
climax came when the Venetians occupied a neighbouring islet and
set fire to a number of Byzantine merchantmen anchored offshore.
By some mischance they also managed to gain possession of the
imperial flagship, on which they even went so far as to perform an
elaborate charade, dressing up an Ethiopian slave in the imperial
vestments—Manuel's dark complexion had not gone unnoticed—
and staging a mock coronation on the deck, in full view of the
Greeks. Whether Manuel was present to witness this monstrous
insult against his imperial majesty is not clear; if not, he certainly

arrived soon afterwards. He never forgave the Venetians their conduct; for the moment, however, he needed them. A combination of
patience, tact and his celebrated charm soon restored a slightly
uneasy harmony; the Venetian ships resumed their allotted stations;
and the Emperor assumed direct personal command of the siege.
There would be time enough, later, for revenge.

Much as he longed to forget his disastrous Crusade, King Louis—
unlike Conrad—found himself in no hurry to leave Outremer. The
prospect of Easter in Jerusalem doubtless appealed to his piety; and,
like so many travellers before and since, he may have been reluctant
to exchange the gentle sunshine of a Palestinian winter for the stormy
seas and snowbound roads which lay between himself and his own
kingdom. He knew, too, that his marriage to Eleanor was past
redemption. Once back in Paris he would have to face all the unpleasantness of a divorce and the political repercussions that could
not but follow. On and on he stayed, touring the shrines of the Holy
Land and reflecting on the perfidy of the Greeks, and in particular of
Manuel Comnenus himself, whom he still held responsible for the
calamities of his outward journey. Now he understood. A Christian
in name only, the Emperor was in reality the foremost enemy and
betrayer of Christendom; a secret ally of the infidel, he had opposed
the Crusade from its inception and done everything in his power to
ensure its failure. Its first task should have been to eliminate him—as
Roger of Sicily was very properly attempting to do.

In the spring of 1149, Louis set his face reluctantly for home. This
time he and Eleanor had resolved to travel by sea, but had been
unwise enough to entrust themselves to Sicilian transport—dangerous
craft in which to brave Byzantine waters. Somewhere in the southern
Aegean they encountered a Greek fleet—presumably on its way to
or from Corfu—which turned at once to attack. Louis managed to
escape by hastily running up the French flag; but one of his escort
vessels, containing several followers and nearly all his baggage, was
captured by the Greeks and borne off in triumph to Constantinople.
Queen Eleanor, whose relations with her husband were now such
that she was travelling on a separate vessel, narrowly avoided a
similar fate; she was rescued by Sicilian warships just in time.

Finally, on 29 July 1149, Louis landed in Calabria. There Eleanor joined him, and the pair rode together to Potenza, where Roger was waiting to greet them and where they were to stay as his guests.[1] The two Kings, meeting for the first time, took to each other at once. In the past, as we have seen, their approaches had been inhibited by the dispute of Roger and Raymond of Poitiers, Eleanor's uncle, over the question of Antioch; but since then a new rivalry had arisen—that of Louis and Raymond over the question of Eleanor—and Louis no longer felt constrained. Neither, for that matter, had his recent maritime adventure softened his feelings towards Byzantium; he and Roger may have discovered, during those August days at Potenza, that they had more in common than either had imagined.

After three days their host left them to return to Sicily, and Louis and Eleanor moved on to Tusculum, the nearest town to Rome in which the Pope could safely install himself. Eugenius gave them a suitably royal welcome; politically, for reasons we shall shortly see, he was not particularly encouraging, but for the moment he was less concerned with future military alignments in Europe than with the immediate domestic problems of his guests. A gentle, kind-hearted man, he hated to see people unhappy; and the sight of Louis and Eleanor, oppressed by the double failure of the Crusade and of their marriage, seems to have caused him genuine personal distress. John of Salisbury, who was employed in the Curia at the time, has left us a curiously touching account of the Pope's attempts at a reconciliation:

He commanded, under pain of anathema, that no word should be spoken against their marriage and that it should not be dissolved under any pretext whatever. This ruling plainly delighted the King, for he loved the Queen passionately, in an almost childish way. The Pope made them sleep in the same bed, which he had decked with priceless hangings of his own; and daily during their brief visit he strove by friendly converse to restore the love between them. He heaped gifts upon them; and when the time for their departure came he could not hold back his tears.

[1] Later, in an attempt to bolster Roger's claim to legitimate kingship, the story was put about that Louis had personally re-crowned him during their time together at Potenza. Sheer fabrication though it undoubtedly is, it was to find its way into one of the several interpolations of Romuald of Salerno's chronicle.

Those tears were perhaps made all the more copious by the knowledge that his efforts had been in vain. Had Eugenius known Eleanor
better, he would have seen from the start that her mind was made up
and that neither he nor anyone else could change it. For the time
being, however, she was prepared to keep up appearances, accompanying her husband to Rome where they were cordially received by
the Senate and where Louis prostrated himself as usual at all the
principal shrines; and so back across the Alps to Paris. It was to be
another two and a half years before her marriage was finally dissolved
—St Bernard having persuaded Eugenius to withdraw his early
strictures—on grounds of consanguinity; but she was still young
and only on the threshold of that astonishing career in which, as wife
of one of England's greatest Kings and mother of two of its worst,
she was to influence the course of European history for over half a
century.

The people of Paris received Louis and Eleanor with rejoicing,
and even went so far as to strike medals 'to our unconquered King',
one portraying him in a triumphal chariot with a winged Victory
soaring above, the other illustrating the theme of dead and fugitive
Turks on the banks of the Meander. But they deceived no one.
Elsewhere, men were readier to look facts in the face—though
even then they usually sought to explain or to justify them. Pope
Eugenius, for example, saw in the Crusade a calamity sent by God
as an object-lesson in the transience of terrestrial things. Otto of
Freising points out philosophically that it provided easy opportunities for the acquisition of a martyr's crown. It was left to St Bernard
who, if he did not actually initiate the Crusade, at least gave it its
impetus and its inspiration, to say honestly what he thought. For
him, it was not simply a calamity or even a lesson, but a divine
judgment—one that represented 'so deep an abyss that anyone must
be accounted blessed who is not scandalised thereby'.[1] In passing
this judgment the Almighty had acted, as always, with perfect
justice; but this time, for once, he had left his mercy aside.

In the frantic search for a scapegoat that followed, it was perhaps
inevitable that all fingers save one—Conrad's—should have pointed
to Manuel Comnenus; it was also unfair. The blame for the failure of

[1] *De Consideratione*, II, i.

any military operation can attach only to those directly concerned—
those who plan it and those who carry it out. In the Second Crusade,
both planning and performance were atrocious. From the start the
idea was a bad one. The lasting presence in strength of an alien
power in a distant land is possible only when it is acceptable locally;
when it is not, its days are numbered. If it cannot maintain itself by
its own efforts any attempt at propping it up artificially, especially by
military means, is bound to fail. Having decided to mount the attack,
the leaders of the West made one mistake after another. They co-
ordinated neither their preparations nor their timing; by a mixture
of disingenuousness and sheer political ineptitude they antagonised
their most important ally; they arrived too few in numbers and too
late; initially indecisive, they eventually settled on a misguided line
of action and then lacked the courage to carry it through. They
hesitated, retreated, and collapsed.[1]

[1] It is irrelevant, but irresistible, to compare the planning of the Second
Crusade with that of the Suez affair eight centuries later.

8

CLIMACTERIC

Our hearts and the hearts of almost all Frenchmen are burning with
devotion for you, and love of your peace; all this we feel particularly in
view of the base, lamentable and unheard-of treachery to our pilgrims of
the Greeks and their detestable King. . . . Rise, and help the people of
God to take their vengeance!

Letter to Roger II from
Abbot Peter of Cluny

T HE Crusade had been bad for reputations. Conrad of Hohenstaufen and Louis Capet had been discredited, Manuel Comnenus
had been blamed, Pope Eugenius and St Bernard together had had
to bear the spiritual responsibility. Among the great princes of
Europe in the first rank of power and importance, only Roger of
Sicily had emerged unscathed. And it was Roger who now became
the focal point for all those dissatisfied spirits who called for an
immediate and victorious Third Crusade to wipe out the humiliations
of the Second.

The irony of the situation must have amused him. A Crusader
neither by temperament nor by conviction, he had not scrupled to
take full political advantage of western woolly-mindedness on the last
occasion, and he was quite ready to do so again. For the fate of the
Christians of Outremer he cared not a rap; they deserved all they got.
He himself preferred the Arabs every time. On the other hand,
the Levant tempted him. Was he not the legitimate Prince of
Antioch, perhaps even the rightful King of Jerusalem? More
important still, he had to defend himself against Byzantine attack,
and in such an eventuality opposition would be the best defence.
While Manuel's present unpopularity lasted it would be an easy
matter to turn the weight of any fresh Crusade against him.

Roger therefore willingly accepted his role—improbable as it was
—of avenger of the West, and set to work building up his new
image. That, above all, was why he had travelled to meet the King of
France at Potenza, where he had been assured of Louis's support.
His major difficulty, as always, was with Conrad. To the several
excellent reasons that the King of the Romans already had for hating
him another, perhaps the strongest of all, had now been added—
jealousy. Conrad knew that his reputation had been dealt a severe
blow by the failure of the Crusade; Roger's—unaccountably and
quite unjustifiably—had never been higher. It was the German
Emperor, crowned or not, who remained historically and by divine
right the sword and shield of western Christendom; and Conrad
resented this new usurpation of his imperial prerogatives, as unpardonable in its way as the seizure of South Italy itself.

St Bernard tried hard to change his attitude, but to no avail.
Bernard was a Frenchman, and the French, as far as Conrad was
concerned, were almost as bad as the Sicilians; besides, he had painful
recollections of the last time he had taken Bernard's advice against
his better judgment. Neither was he any more amenable to the arguments of Peter of Cluny or Cardinal Theodwine of Porto, one of the
most influential voices in the Curia. All these ecclesiastical per-
suaders, he knew, were rabidly anti-Byzantine—particularly the
Abbot of Clairvaux, who clearly felt responsible for the Crusade and
was only too anxious to shuffle as much of the blame as possible off
his own shoulders and on to those of the Eastern Emperor. Conrad
saw through them all. But Manuel was his friend, and he trusted
him. The two were in any case bound by a solemn alliance, which he
for his part did not intend to break.

It was not as if Roger had showed the faintest sign of wanting a
reconciliation. On the contrary, he had begun a new intrigue with
Count Welf of Bavaria, brother of Henry the Proud and Conrad's
still-determined rival for the imperial throne. Welf had called in at
Palermo on his way home from the Crusade, and Roger had offered
him still bigger subsidies than before to organise a confederation of
German princes against the Hohenstaufen. This new league threatened to be a formidable one, a menace which might well keep Conrad
occupied in Germany for some time to come. Once again his plans for

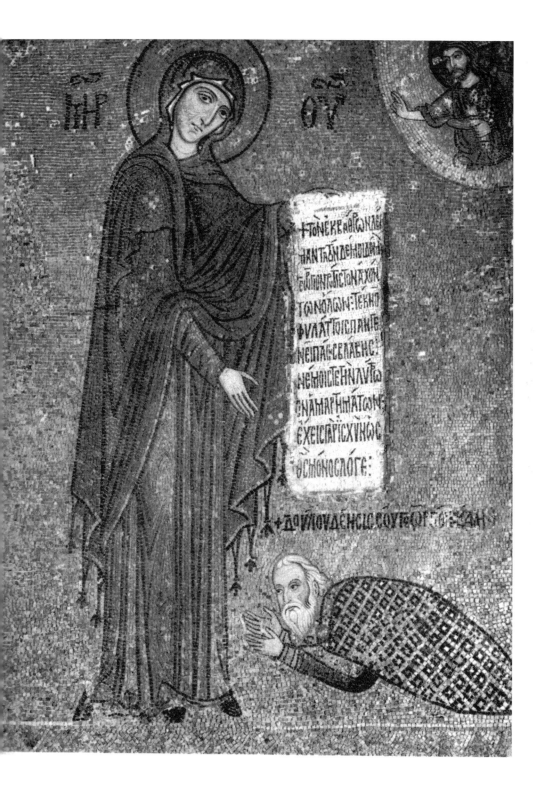

Palermo, the Martorana: George of Antioch before the Virgin

Palermo, the Martorana: King Roger II crowned by Christ

a punitive Italian expedition would have to be postponed—but his determination sooner or later to settle scores with the King of Sicily remained stronger than ever.

For Manuel too the year 1149 ended less auspiciously than it had begun. Some time in the late summer Corfu had fallen to him—probably through treachery, since Nicetas tells us that the garrison commander subsequently entered the imperial service; but before the Emperor could follow up his advantage and cross to Italy news was brought to him of a Serbian insurrection, to which the neighbouring Kingdom of Hungary was giving active military support. At about this time too he must also have heard—with particular irritation—of the most recent exploit of George of Antioch who, after the incident with Louis and Eleanor, had taken a fleet of forty ships right up the Hellespont and over the Marmara to the very walls of Constantinople. Thence, after an unsuccessful attempt at a landing, the Sicilians had sailed some distance up the Bosphorus, pillaging several rich villas along the Asiatic shore, and before departing had even fired a few impudent arrows into the grounds of the Imperial Palace.

Roger's capture of Corfu, temporary as it was, had proved a useful holding operation; and the Balkan rising that followed so conveniently after it meant a further postponement of Manuel's own invasion plans. Looking back, one feels that the sequence of events was almost too convenient; could it be, one wonders, that the King of Sicily had indirectly engineered this as well? The chroniclers preserve a discreet silence—perhaps they were not too sure themselves—but it seems probable enough. Roger, whose cousin Busilla had married King Coloman, had always maintained close ties of friendship with the Hungarian throne. If our suspicions are right, then the year 1149 must mark the highest point of his diplomatic virtuosity. Facing the most formidable military alliance that could be conceived in the Middle Ages, that of the Eastern and the Western Empires acting—as they rarely acted in the six and a half centuries of their joint history—in complete concert one with the other, he succeeded in the space of a few months in immobilising both of them. It was a feat comparable to that of his uncle, who in 1084 had actually had the armies of both Empires retreating before him in different

directions. But Robert Guiscard had had a force of thirty thousand
of his own behind him; Roger had achieved his objective without
calling a single Sicilian soldier to arms.

There was another difference too; whereas the Guiscard had had
the advantage of papal support, towards Roger Pope Eugenius's
attitude remained ambivalent. Naturally he could never forget that
Roger was his immediate neighbour to the south, a perennial thorn
in the papal flesh, always difficult and on occasion dangerous. On the
other hand the King of Sicily now appeared undeniably well-
disposed. At the beginning of 1149 he had offered Eugenius both
military and financial assistance in his struggle against the Roman
commune; and the Pope, seeing the situation in Rome steadily
deteriorating and knowing that he could expect no help from Conrad
who was still away in the East, had accepted. Thus, thanks to a body
of Sicilian troops under Robert of Selby, he had managed to return
to the Lateran by the end of the year. Since then, while he still mistrusted Roger's motives, he saw him as a useful ally whom it would
be foolish to antagonise without good cause.

And so the Pope wavered; and he was still wavering when in the
early summer of 1150 he recived a letter from the King of Sicily with
proposals for a meeting. Roger's purpose is clear. An armed conflict
between himself and the Empires could not, as it seemed to him, be
long delayed. It might be offensive—a new 'Crusade' in which he
would lead the forces of the West against the Infidel, represented in
the first instance by Manuel Comnenus. For this he would find allies
in plenty, though not unless he could first obtain the Pope's blessing.
Alternatively there might be a defensive operation. The delaying
tactics that he was at present employing to keep his two enemies
occupied on home ground could not last for ever. Already Conrad
could claim one major victory over Welf, and Manuel was well on
the way to restoring the situation in the Balkans. Within a year—
perhaps even less—the pair of them might be in a position to launch
their two-pronged invasion of his realm. In such an event he would
have far fewer allies on whom to rely; and papal support would be
still more necessary.

The little town of Ceprano, standing conveniently on the border
between the Kingdom of Sicily and the Papal State, had seen respect-

ability bestowed on Robert Guiscard by his investiture at the hands of Gregory VII seventy years before—a thought which may well have given Roger some encouragement when, in July 1150, he rode there to meet Eugenius; for a similar investiture was now his first and most important objective. To obtain this, the formal recognition by the Pope of his legitimate sovereignty, he was prepared to concede much. Nothing else stood between himself and the leadership of western Europe. His right of appointment of Sicilian bishops, of refusing admission to papal envoys, even the hereditary privilege of the Apostolic Legation would have been reasonable prices to pay for such a reward.

But Ceprano had also witnessed failures. It was, after all, only six years since Roger and Pope Lucius had separated in disappointment and bitterness after the breakdown of other negotiations from which both had stood to gain; and the result of the coming talks with Lucius's successor was no foregone conclusion. The Pope had just been obliged once again to leave Rome; a renewed offer of Sicilian troops might prove a useful sweetener. As against this, Conrad was now back in Germany, collecting his forces, building up his strength, and rapidly living down his recent disgrace. If he were contemplating an early clash, then Eugenius would be unlikely to weaken his hand —and compromise the papal position—by confirming Roger's kingship.

And so it proved. The Pope may already have been under pressure from Conrad; he was certainly being bombarded with letters from Abbot Wibald of Corbie, a sworn enemy of Roger since the latter had expelled him from Monte Cassino and now Conrad's closest ecclesiastical adviser. John of Salisbury, who was probably present at Ceprano, tells us how Roger made every concession he could; 'but neither his prayers nor his gifts were of any avail'.

Although John is careful to note that King and Pontiff parted on relatively amicable terms, this new failure to achieve recognition must have come to Roger as a bitter blow. It could mean one thing only, that Eugenius had decided to throw in his lot with Conrad; and this, in its turn, meant that all his own plans for an offensive coalition against Manuel would have to be abandoned. From the moment the Ceprano talks ended, he gave up any further attempt to influence papal policy. Instead, he returned to Sicily to prepare for the coming storm.

He might almost have been relieved, as his ships sailed for Palermo, had he known that he would never set foot on the Italian mainland again.

His tents weep him, and his palaces; the swords and the lances are for him like women mourners. Hearts, no less than garments, are rent with grief. For the arms of the brave have fallen; valiant souls are filled with dread; and the eloquent seek for words in vain.

Thus had the Arab poet Abu ed-Daw lamented the death, on 2 May 1148, of Duke Roger of Apulia, the King of Sicily's eldest son. How he died we do not know; most probably he fell in some skirmish on the northern frontiers of his dukedom, where he had been intermittently engaged for several years. It was a grievous loss. The young Duke—he was only just thirty when he died—had been a Hauteville in the old tradition, a brilliant fighter and capable administrator, fearless in battle and utterly loyal to his father. More and more in the past decade Roger had tended to leave the affairs of the mainland to him—with Robert of Selby holding, perhaps, a watching brief—and he had shown himself a worthy heir to the Sicilian Crown. And now he was dead, the fifth of Roger's and Queen Elvira's six children to die before his father. Tancred, Prince of Bari, had already been nearly ten years in his grave; Alfonso, Prince of Capua and Duke of Naples, had died in 1144 in his early twenties. Another boy, Henry, had not survived his infancy. One only remained, the King's fourth son, William; he inherited the dukedom on his brother's death, and on Easter Day, 1151, Roger had him consecrated and crowned by the Archbishop of Palermo as co-ruler of the Sicilian Kingdom.

To crown a son in the lifetime of his father was no rare thing in the Middle Ages. The practice was regular in Byzantium, where it had been inherited from the earlier days of the Roman Empire; it was also to be followed in England, some twenty years after William's coronation, when King Henry II crowned his own first-born. Its purpose was to ensure the continuity of the royal line and to guard against the possibility of civil strife resulting from a disputed succession. Roger was still only fifty-five; his father had lived to be seventy. There is no suggestion among the contemporary chronicles that he was ill, though it is possible that he had already felt the onset of the disease that was to kill him three years later. Nor could there be any possible doubt about the claim to the throne of the King's only surviving legitimate son. Roger seems, however, to have been genuinely concerned about the succession; otherwise he would hardly have been likely, after fourteen years as a widower, to contract a second marriage in 1149, to a certain Sibyl of Burgundy; and a third, four years later when Sibyl had died in childbed.

Whatever his reasons, he cannot have thought that the news of William's coronation would be well received by the Pope. Technically speaking, he was within his rights; Archbishop Hugh of Palermo, recently promoted from the archbishopric of Capua, had been granted the *pallium* by the Pope, on the grounds that he was one of those 'who presided over the chief cities of certain nations and were therefore privileged by the Papacy to create princes for their own people'.[1] Eugenius had never meant to imply that this grant included the right to perform royal coronations without prior reference to the Holy See, but the phrasing had been unfortunate; and the fact that he himself had given Roger the opportunity to take such a step can only have added to his irritation. It does not seem to have occurred to him that if the King of Sicily did have some good reason for wishing to ensure his son's succession he could hardly— in the light of Eugenius's refusal to grant the investiture himself— have acted otherwise. As far as he was concerned, Sicily and the *Regno* were papal fiefs, of which no disposition could be made without his authority. This authority had once again been flouted. As John of Salisbury confirms, 'he took the news ill, but oppressed as he was by the evils of the time he could offer no resistance'.

If the Pope had ever been in any doubt as to where his best interests lay, he was in doubt no longer. The two special legates

[1] John of Salisbury, *Historia Pontificalis*, chs. 33–4. The *pallium* is a circular band of white wool, shorn from two lambs blessed on St Agnes' Day in the church of S. Agnese fuori le Mura, and marked with six black crosses. It is worn by the Pope across his shoulders and granted by him to Archbishops and Metropolitans, at their petition, to enable them to perform their special functions.

he now sent to Conrad soon showed themselves to be little more than figures of fun;[1] but one point they made abundantly clear. The Emperor-to-be was awaited with impatience in Italy. When he came, for whatever his purpose, he would have the See of St Peter whole-heartedly behind him.

The future of the Kingdom of Sicily had never looked blacker than it did at the start of the year 1152. Conrad of Hohenstaufen was ready to march; Manuel Comnenus, having restored order within his own Empire, was ready to join him. The Venetians had once again pledged their support. The Pope, after long hesitation, had allied himself on their side. And meanwhile the great anti-imperial coalition by which Roger had set so much store had melted away. Louis of France was still in theory an ally; but the death of Abbot Suger the previous year had robbed him of his confidence and, in a large measure, of his freedom of action. Besides, his divorce from Eleanor, now imminent, was occupying his mind to the virtual exclusion of all else. Two years before, at Flochberg, Welf and his friends had sustained a defeat from which they had never recovered. Hungary and Serbia had, for the moment, no more fight left in them.

But just as a few years earlier Roger had been saved from a similar situation by the Second Crusade, so now fate intervened once more to deliver him. On Friday 15 February 1152 King Conrad died at Bamberg. He was the first Emperor-elect in the two centuries since the restoration of the Empire by Otto the Great not to have been crowned at Rome—a failure which somehow seems to symbolise his whole reign. 'A Seneca in council, a Paris in appearance, a Hector in

[1] John of Salisbury's description of the papal legates is worth a quotation. 'Jordan [of S. Susanna] used his Carthusian Order as a pretext for his meanness. Ever parsimonious, he wore filthy garments and was austere in speech and demeanour; since like will ever attract like, he had been made chamberlain to the Lord Pope. Octavian [of S. Cecilia, the future Anti-Pope Victor IV], though nobler, easier in manner and more generous, was proud and pompous, a syco-phant of the Germans and a seeker after Roman favour—which he never won. And although the Pope had charged them to act in concert, no sooner had they started out than they began to argue as to which was the greater. . . . Quarrel-ling over everything, they soon made the Church a laughing-stock. . . . Thus it was that complainants converged in swarms upon the papal court, for these two disturbed the churches just as men disturb beehives when they seek to extract the honey from the bees.'

battle',[1] great things had been expected of him; but he died with his promise unfulfilled and his country as divided as always; never an Emperor—just a sad, unlucky King. He was buried in Bamberg Cathedral next to the recently-canonised Emperor Henry II—a distant predecessor who had also, long ago, found the Normans too strong for him.

Otto of Freising, Conrad's half-brother, tells us that the presence at his bedside of certain Italian doctors—probably from the medical school of Salerno—gave rise to inevitable mutterings about Sicilian poison; but though Roger must have welcomed this timely removal of his most dangerous enemy there is no reason to suspect that he was in any way involved. Conrad was fifty-nine and had had a hard life; and mediaeval chroniclers are notoriously reluctant to ascribe to natural causes more deaths than are absolutely necessary. Conrad's mind remained unclouded to the end, and his last injunctions to his nephew and successor, Duke Frederick of Swabia, were to continue the struggle which he had begun until the so-called King of Sicily was finally brought to book. Frederick asked nothing better. Encouraged by the Apulian exiles at the court, he even hoped at one moment to keep to Conrad's original schedule and to march against Roger immediately, picking up his imperial crown on the way. As always, however, the succession brought its own problems, and he soon had to accept a further indefinite postponement. Where foreign adventures were concerned, Conrad's death had left him hamstrung just as Suger's had crippled Louis VII a year before. Sicily had been granted another reprieve.

And these deaths were only the beginning. During the next two years Conrad and Suger were to be followed to their graves by nearly all the great figures who had dominated the European stage over the previous decade. On 8 July 1153 Pope Eugenius died suddenly at Tivoli, and was buried in St Peter's. Though never a great Pope, he had during his papacy revealed a firmness of character which few had suspected at the time of his election. Like so many of his predecessors, he had been forced to spend money freely to buy support

[1] This description, by the poet-chronicler Godfrey of Viterbo, is possibly more apt that its author realised. Seneca's position as adviser and confidant of Nero resulted in his suicide; Paris was the lover who ultimately lost; Hector the hero who fled.

among the Romans, yet he personally had always remained incorruptible; his gentleness and unassuming ways had earned him much genuine love and respect of a kind that cannot be bought for gold. Till the day of his death he continued to wear, under his pontifical robes, the coarse white habit of a Cistercian monk; and at his funeral the popular grief was such that, in the words of Bishop Hugh of Ostia, 'one would have believed that he who in death was so honoured on earth was already reigning in Heaven'.[1]

When the news of his death reached Clairvaux, the Abbot himself was failing fast. We have it on Bernard's own authority that by this time he was in constant pain and unable to touch solid food. His hands and feet were swollen with dropsy. Sleep had become impossible. He too seems to have kept his faculties to the end; but on Thursday 20 August, at nine o'clock in the morning, he died at the age of sixty-three. His is a hard character to assess. Modern biographers seem no less susceptible to his magnetism than were his contemporaries; one after another they rhapsodise over his humility, his charity and his general saintliness. For as long as they confine themselves to his spiritual attributes, their encomiums are possibly justified. It is in the political sphere that St Bernard's record becomes, to say the least, questionable. History is full of instances in which ecclesiastics have played valuable and constructive parts in affairs of state; but these men of the Church have nearly always been men of the world as well, realists who have been able to view the great issues of their time with a cool, objective eye. The Abbot of Clairvaux provides a perfect example of what is apt to occur when this condition is not fulfilled. He was that fortunately rare phenomenon, the genuine mystic and ascetic with a compulsion to interfere in politics. His reputation and the sheer force of his personality ensured that he was listened to; his formidable rhetorical gifts and powers of persuasion did the rest.

His weakness was that he was all emotion. He saw the world with the eye of a fanatic, in black and white—the black to be stamped out by any means available, the white to be upheld whatever the price. Scarcely ever in his letters or other writings do we find a trace of

[1] Just over seven centuries later, in 1872, he was to be beatified by Pope Pius IX.

logical argument, still less of political understanding. Such a man, raised to a position of virtually limitless influence and prestige, could only cause havoc; and St Bernard's major interventions in the world political scene were, all too often, disastrous. His incitement of Lothair II against Roger of Sicily ended—as it could only have ended—in débacle and was arguably the cause of the old Emperor's death; his launching of the Second Crusade led to the most shameful Christian humiliation of the Middle Ages. Had he lived it would have surprised no one to find him advocating, as his cousin the Bishop of Langres had already advocated, a punitive expedition against Constantinople of the kind which, when it occurred half a century later, was to deal Eastern Christendom so shattering a blow.

Suger, Conrad, Bernard—one by one, the giants were disappearing from the scene. About this time, too, death robbed Sicily of her High Admiral, George of Antioch. The Emir of Emirs has played, it must be admitted, a somewhat shadowy rôle in this story. We have seen him as a young adventurer, as a patron of the arts who has left as his memorial one of his country's loveliest churches, and finally as an elderly buccaneer of courage and *panache*. As an admiral, however, as the man who was for well over a quarter of a century responsible more than any other for the rise of Roger's naval power throughout the Mediterranean, we have done him less than justice. For this the Sicilian records of the time are partly to blame. There exists only one reliable contemporary chronicle covering the second half of George's lifetime—that of Romuald of Salerno; but the Archbishop, not surprisingly, is more concerned with mainland politics than with naval affairs. We are thus obliged to fall back on Arab writers; and while they have left us splendidly detailed reports of the Admiral's seafaring exploits, even they are able to tell us little enough about the man himself.

Yet George of Antioch was the sole architect of Roger II's North African Empire. His capture of Tripoli in 1146—itself the culmination of some ten or fifteen years of regular raids and minor conquests along the coast—had given his master control of the entire littoral as far as Tunis and had consequently marked a turning-point in Roger's African policy. Before it, Sicilian incursions on African soil had all been more or less piratical; henceforth we see authority established on a permanent basis. This authority was not aimed at political domination: Roger was too much of a realist to see such an objective as either possible or even desirable. He was interested only in the economic and strategic advantages to be gained from a North African Empire. Both were immense. By occupying the chief commercial centres of the coast, he could eliminate middlemen; the King's agents, operating at the head of the great caravan routes to the south, with a virtual monopoly of grain and many other commodities as well, were soon able to control a large proportion of the internal trade of the continent. Strategically the position was simpler still: command of the narrow seas between Sicily and Tunis meant mastery of the central Mediterranean.

Only one local ruler of importance continued in power, Prince Hassan of Mahdia. Twenty-three years earlier, at the age of fourteen, after a crushing defeat of the Sicilian navy at the fortress of ad-Dimas,[1] Hassan had been hailed through the length and breadth of the Arab world as a hero of Islam; since then, however, he had voluntarily recognised Roger as his suzerain and had entered into a treaty of alliance which appeared to be to the mutual benefit of both rulers. This happy state of affairs might well have been allowed to continue indefinitely had not the local governor of Gabes in 1147 rebelled against Hassan and offered the city to Roger on condition that he himself were appointed governor. Roger accepted the offer; Hassan, understandably, objected; and the consequent rupture led, in the summer of 1148, to the despatch of two hundred and fifty Sicilian ships under George of Antioch against the port of Mahdia.

Hassan knew that prolonged resistance was impossible. The country was in the grip of a famine and totally dependent on Sicilian corn; Mahdia could not hope to hold out for more than a month at the outside. Calling his people together, he laid the facts before them. Those who preferred to stay and take their chance with the Sicilians might do so; the remainder, with their wives and children and what possessions they could carry, could follow him into voluntary exile.

---

[1] *The Normans in the South*, pp. 298–302.

It was not till the late afternoon that the Sicilian fleet entered harbour. The few inhabitants who had elected to stay offered no opposition; and the admiral, according to the late twelfth-century historian Ibn al-Athir, found the palace in its normal state. Hassan had taken his crown jewels but had left whole rooms full of other treasures—together, it appears, with a large number of his concubines. 'George put the treasure-rooms under seal; the ladies were all collected in the castle'—after which their fate is unknown.

George's conduct was, as usual, exemplary. After only two hours of pillage—probably the minimum necessary if he were not to find a mutiny on his hands—order in Mahdia was restored. Local citizens were appointed as governors and magistrates; care was taken that no religious susceptibilities were offended; all the fugitives were invited back to the city—beasts of burden were even sent out to help them with their belongings—and offered food and money on their return. The usual *geziah* or poll-tax was insisted upon, but was deliberately kept low. Only poor Hassan seems to have suffered, though not at Sicilian hands; he was ill-advised enough to seek refuge with his cousin, who promptly confined him to an island off the coast where he languished for the next four years. His subjects, however, including the populations of Sfax and Soussa which hastily surrendered in their turn, soon settled down under their new masters; so that five and a half centuries later the North African historian Ibn Abi-Dinar was able to write:

This enemy of Allah restored both the cities of Zawila[1] and Mahdia; he advanced capital for the merchants, did good to the poor, confided the administration of justice to a *qadi* acceptable to the people, and ordered well the government of those cities . . . . Roger consolidated his dominion over the greater part of that region; levied taxes with gentleness and temperance; reconciled the hearts of the people; and governed with justice and humanity.

When George of Antioch died in the year 546 of the Hegira—that is in 1151 or 1152—'beset', so Ibn al-Athir informs us, 'with many diseases, among them piles and the stone', he left three memorials: the church of the Martorana, his beautiful seven-arched bridge over

---

[1] The principal commercial suburb of Mahdia.

the Oreto, and the African Empire. The first two still remain;[1] the third was to last little more than a decade. It was with George that it reached its apogee; perishable as it proved, he left it one of the brightest jewels in the crown of Sicily.

The old admiral's work was completed; yet he died too soon. Had he been spared for another three years he would have survived his master; and the King's subsequent reputation would have escaped its saddest, most baffling and—almost certainly—its most un-deserved stain.

The life of King Roger of Sicily ends, as it began, in obscurity. Of his death we know little, save the day it occurred—26 February 1154. As to its cause, Ibn al-Athir speaks of an angina; while from Hugo Falcandus—perhaps the greatest of all the chroniclers of Norman Sicily—who begins his history with the new reign, we have only a single sentence intriguingly ascribing the King's death to 'exhaustion from his immense labours, and the onset of a premature senility through his addiction to the pleasures of the flesh, which he pursued to a point beyond that which physical health requires'. His last two years seem to have been tranquil enough. From both the Eastern and the Western Empires the immediate danger to the Kingdom had been averted, at least temporarily; his son William, already crowned, had assumed some, if not all, of the burdens of state; and Archbishop Romuald of Salerno finds so little to report between the deaths of Conrad and Eugenius and that of Roger him-self, that he falls back on a description of the King's country palaces.

In order that none of the joys of land or water should be lacking to him, he caused a great sanctuary for birds and beasts to be built at a place called Favara,[2] which was full of caves and dells; its waters he

---

[1] The Oreto has now been diverted, and George's bridge now spans nothing but mountains of refuse from a nearby gypsy encampment; but it is still known as the Ponte dell' Ammiraglio. On 27 May 1860 it was the scene of the first clash between the Neapolitan forces and Garibaldi's Thousand.

[2] The word comes from the Arabic *Buheira*, meaning a lake. The Favara—also called Maredolce—is a sad place today. The great lake that used to encompass it has dried up, and there are only traces left of the wide courtyard, surrounded with arcades in the oriental style, which was the chief feature of the palace. Just one small wing remains, containing what is left of the chapel, crumbling among the lemon-groves.

stocked with every kind of fish from divers regions; nearby he built
a beautiful palace. And certain hills and forests around Palermo he
likewise enclosed with walls, and there he made the Parco—a
pleasant and delightful spot, shaded with various trees and abound-
ing with deer and goats and wild boar. And here also he raised a
palace, to which the water was led in underground pipes from springs
whence it flowed ever sweet and clear. And thus the King, being a
wise and prudent man, took his pleasure from these places according
to the season. In the winter and in Lent he would reside at the
Favara, by reason of the great quantity of fish that were to be had
there; while in the heat of the summer he would find solace at the
Parco where, with a little hunting, he would relieve his mind from
the cares and worries of state.

So, at least, runs the Archbishop's account in the earliest extant
version of his work. Other, later manuscripts, however, include
before the last two sentences a long and sinister interpolation, utterly
different both in style and subject from Romuald's bucolic idyll.
This tells the story of Roger's treatment of his admiral, Philip of
Mahdia. It is not a pleasant episode, and it raises far more questions
than it answers; but since it constitutes almost the only clue we have
to the internal state of the realm in the twilight of the King's life, it
is worth looking at in some detail. We must make of it what we can.

The story as it appears in this curious passage runs, very briefly, as
fellows. George of Antioch had been succeeded as Admiral by a
certain eunuch, Philip of Mahdia, who had risen through long service
in the Curia to be one of Roger's ablest and most trusted ministers.
In the summer of 1153 he was despatched with a fleet to Bône on the
North African coast, whose ruler had appealed to Roger for aid
against an Almohad invasion from the west. Philip captured the city
without difficulty, treated it much as his predecessor would have
done, and returned triumphantly to Palermo. There, after a hero's
welcome, he suddenly found himself thrown into prison on
charges of having secretly embraced Islam. Arraigned before the
Curia, he initially protested his innocence but finally admitted his
guilt. The King then made a tearful speech, pointing out that while
he would willingly have pardoned the friend whom he loved any
crime committed against his own person, this was an offence against
God and could consequently not be forgiven; whereupon the

'counts, justiciars, barons and judges' pronounced sentence of death. Philip was tied to the hoofs of a wild horse and dragged to the palace square, where he was burnt alive.

The manifest improbability of this account, coupled with the fact of its being so obviously a later interpolation in Romuald's manuscript, might almost justify our dismissing it as a complete fabrication. Roger had grown up with Arabs; he spoke their language; he had trusted them, even more than most of his fellow-Normans, all his life. Many of the highest offices in the central government were Muslim-staffed. Both the army and the navy relied on Saracen strength. Commercial prosperity was assured by Arab merchants, treasury and mint were under the control of Arab administrators. Arabic was an official language of the state. Just as his father had turned his back on the First Crusade, so Roger had refrained from playing any active part in the Second. Was it conceivable that he should now publicly impeach his Admiral on religious grounds, opening the way to almost certain confessional strife from which his country might never recover?

Unfortunately, this strange tale cannot be ignored; for it appears, in a slightly different version, in two independent Arab sources—Ibn al-Athir, writing towards the close of the century, and Ibn Khaldun some two hundred years later. These two chroniclers both adduce a second explanation for Philip's fate—the clemency he is alleged to have shown to certain respected citizens of Bône whom he had allowed, with their families, to leave the city after its capture. This reason is plainly no more convincing than the first. Not only does it contradict the version in Romuald's history, which specifically states that Philip returned after his expedition *cum triumpho et gloria*; but it also suggests that he was punished for a policy which, as we have seen, was almost invariably followed in all Roger's North African conquests. Ibn al-Athir even mentions that the citizens concerned were 'virtuous and learned men', a fact which would make Roger's conduct even more inexplicable since we know from several writers, including Ibn al-Athir himself, that Arab intellectuals were his favourite companions.

If, then, we are to accept that the story has some basis of fact, we must look for some other explanation. It must be remembered that

Philip was not simply a Muslim; if, as his name implies, he was of
Greek origin— the fact that he was surnamed 'of Mahdia' is no more
indicative of his race than were the words 'of Antioch' in the name
of his predecessor—it follows that he was also an apostate; and the
Sicilian Kingdom, for all its tolerance, had always discouraged
apostasy. We know, for example, that members of Count Roger's
Saracen regiments were forbidden to receive Christian baptism,[1] and
conversions in the other direction were even less popular. In
isolation, such a conversion could hardly have been sufficient cause
for the vicious treatment that Philip received; but it has been
inferred that, in his last years, Roger may have fallen victim—like
many other rulers before and since—to some form of religious
persecution mania, which might have led him to take violent or
unreasoning measures of this kind. The most thorough modern
biography[2] suggests that he simply gave in to the Latin clergy, which
is known at this time to have been working to diminish Greek
influence in the Curia. But both these theories ignore the fact that
nearly all the Arab writings—and there are many—which testify so
warmly to the King's pro-Muslim sympathies date from after the
incident. We need take only one example, the preface to Edrisi's
Book of Roger, which bears an Arabic date corresponding to mid-
January 1154—a few months after Philip's death and only a few
weeks before the King's. In this Roger is referred to as 'governing
his people with equity and impartiality'; later Edrisi speaks of 'the
beauty of his actions, the elevation of his sentiments, the depth of his
insight, the sweetness of his character and the justice of his spirit'.
Some degree of hyperbole must be permitted to an oriental, writing
of his royal friend and patron; but it is hardly likely that a pious
Muslim could bring himself to use such terms immediately after so
atrocious an *auto da fé.*

The conclusion seems inescapable. If Philip was indeed put to
death for either of the reasons given, it can only have been at a time
when the King was incapacitated. (The possibility of his absence we
can discount. There would almost certainly be a record of it, for one
thing; for another, those responsible would never have dared to

---

[1] *The Normans in the South,* pp. 275–6.
[2] Caspar, *Roger II und die Gründung der Normannisch-Sicilischen Monarchie.*

execute such a sentence on Roger's chief minister without first obtaining the royal assent.) We know that two and a half years earlier Roger, while still only in middle age, had had his son crowned as co-ruler; we know too that within months of Philip's condemnation he was dead. Hugo Falcandus's reference to a ' premature senility' might be quoted in support of this theory; alternatively the King may simply have suffered a series of strokes or heart attacks (Ibn al-Athir's 'angina') which gossiping tongues—and none were more venomous than Hugo's—ascribed to his private excesses. There seems, in any event, to have been a waning of his physical and mental faculties, which may well in the end have rendered him incapable of attending to state affairs.

Once this theory is accepted, the tragedy of Philip of Mahdia becomes credible. There remains the problem of why the inter-polator of Romuald's history should have taken such pains to involve Roger personally; but his story—which, it is worth noting, contains no suggestion of criticism—seems to date from the very end of the century[1] at a time when, as we shall see, it would have been in the interests not only of the Church of Rome but even of the rulers of Sicily themselves to present the greatest of the Norman Kings rather as a stalwart defender of the Christian faith than as an example of enlightened tolerance; and the two Arab writers might well have echoed them.

Yet even Ibn al-Athir himself betrays a certain lack of conviction; for elsewhere in his history we find another passage in which Roger is portrayed in a very different light. After describing the several Arabic innovations which the King introduced into the Sicilian court ceremonial, he concludes: 'Roger treated the Muslims with honour and respect. He was at his ease with them and protected them always, even against the Franks. Therefore they loved him in return.' From an Arab historian, the King could have asked for no finer epitaph; and it is with these words that his case must ultimately rest.

King Roger was buried in Palermo Cathedral. For nine years already a great porphyry sarcophagus had awaited him in his own

[1] U. Epifanio, whose article (see bibliography) is still, after more than sixty years, the fullest and most detailed study of the affair, tentatively puts the inter-polation some half a century later still.

foundation of Cefalù; but during those nine years many things had
changed. Palermo had grown in importance as a metropolitan see;
Cefalù was only a bishopric and, worse still, one that had been
founded by the anti-Pope Anacletus. In the minds of many, and
particularly to the Roman Curia, it continued to symbolise Roger's
long defiance of papal claims and his determination to be master in
his own house. In consequence it was still not recognised in Rome.[1]
For many years to come the canons of Cefalù would indignantly
assert that Palermo had been chosen only as a temporary resting-
place for the King; William, they claimed, had promised that his
father's body would be delivered into their care as soon as the status
of their cathedral had been properly regulated. But this promise, if
indeed it was ever made, was certainly never kept; and the sarcophagus stood empty for sixty years after Roger's death before being
itself transferred to Palermo, there in due course to receive the mortal
remains of his illustrious grandson, the Emperor Frederick II.[2]

Meanwhile a new tomb, also of porphyry, had been prepared in
Palermo for the dead King.[3] The cathedral in which it was erected
has been repeatedly—and disastrously—rebuilt over the centuries,
but the tomb itself still occupies its original place in the south aisle,
where it now stands surrounded by those of his daughter, son-in-
law and grandson. Of the four, his is the least ornate, a simple,
gabled structure whose only decoration is in the twin supports of
white marble, each carved to represent a pair of kneeling youths on
whose shoulders the sarcophagus rests, and in the lovely classicising
canopy, sparkling with Cosmatesque mosaic, which probably dates
from the following century. The tomb has been opened more than
once, to reveal Roger's body still dressed in the royal mantle and
dalmatic, on its head the tiara with pearl pendants such as we see in
the mosaic portrait in the Martorana. It was the King's last gesture
towards Byzantium, the Empire he hated but whose concept of
monarchy he adopted for his own.

The monarchy: this above all was Roger's gift to Sicily. From his
father he had inherited a county; to his son he bequeathed a kingdom

[1] Not until 1166 did Pope Alexander III authorise the formal consecration of
Bishop Boso of Cefalú, and then only as a suffragan to the Archbishop of
Messina.
[2] See p. 390.   [3] Plate 11.

that embraced not just the island itself and a largely desolate tract of Calabria, but the entire Italian peninsula south-east of a line drawn from the mouth of the Tronto to that of the Garigliano—all the land ever conquered by the Normans in the South. Across the sea it stretched to Malta and Gozo, and then beyond to the whole North African coast, with its hinterland, between Bône and Tripoli. On his sword were engraved the words '*Apulus et Calaber, Siculus mihi servit et Afer*'[1]. It was no more than the literal truth.

But Roger's achievements are not to be measured in terms of territory alone. No one knew better than he that if Sicily were to survive as a European power it must develop into something more than a group of widely differing ethnic, linguistic and religious communities. In the prevailing atmosphere of prosperity and success, these communities had cooperated astonishingly well; but who could tell whether they would maintain their solidarity in a crisis? The Norman baronage had proved itself faithless; what of the rest? If, for example, the island itself had to face a full-scale invasion by the Byzantines, would the Greek community stay loyal? If the Almohads, in the name of Islam, were to launch a counter-attack through North Africa and thence press northward to Sicily, could the Muslims of Syracuse, Agrigento and Catania be trusted to resist them?

Until every one of his people could be persuaded to see himself first and foremost as a subject of the King, these dangers would be very real. This task of persuasion and consolidation could only be a slow, delicate process, spread over several generations; but to it Roger had devoted his life. His father, during the first phase of the Norman-Sicilian state, had concentrated on the problem of reconciling the various elements, previously hostile, to a system of cooperation and interdependence; he himself had taken it a stage further, by giving his subjects a new pride—that of belonging to a great and prosperous nation. Of that nation's greatness, the monarchy must be the living, visible symbol. The very existence of so many laws and languages, of such a variety of religions and customs, called for a strong central authority elevated and remote enough to embrace them all. It was this consideration, quite as much as his

[1] 'The Apulian, Calabrian, Sicilian and African all obey my will.' (Radulph de Diceto, *Opuscula*, vol. II, p. 276.)

innate love of magnificence and his oriental cast of mind, that led Roger to surround himself with an almost mystic splendour which far outshone that of any of his fellow-monarchs of the West.

For with him this splendour was never more than a means to an end. The gold and the jewels, the palaces and the parks, the glinting tesserae and the gorgeous brocades, the great silken canopies held above his head—a custom borrowed from the Fatimid caliphs—on ceremonial occasions, all served a specific purpose: to glorify not Roger himself, but his ideal of what a King should be. And though few sovereigns of his day spent more lavishly, none was more conscious of the value of money. Alexander of Telese notes how he would personally go through all his exchequer accounts, how he never spent anything without making a careful record of the sum involved, how he was as scrupulous in the paying of debts as in their collection. Luxury he loved, as much as any Eastern potentate —it is not for nothing that Michele Amari, greatest of Sicilian Arabists, calls him 'a baptised Sultan'—but his Norman blood saved him from the indolence it so often brings in its train. If he enjoyed— as he had every right to enjoy—the pleasures of kingship, he never shirked its responsibilities; and such was his energy that his friend Edrisi could write in awe that 'he accomplished more in his sleep than others did in their waking day.'

He was only fifty-eight at the time of his death. Had he been granted another fifteen years, his country might have found that national identity which he had laboured so hard to create; had his new young queen borne him a son, the Hauteville dynasty might have survived the century and the whole history of South Europe would have been changed. But such speculations, though intriguing, are also pointless. For a few more years yet Norman Sicily, through a remarkable series of military and diplomatic triumphs, was to increase its influence and prestige from London to Constantinople. Two more Emperors were to be humbled, one more Pope brought to his knees. For a few more years yet the cultural brilliance of the Court of Palermo was to continue undimmed and unparalleled in Europe. But already the internal fabric of the state was showing signs of decay; and with the reign of William the Bad the Kingdom, though still golden in its splendour, embarks on its last, sad decline.

PART THREE

THE LENGTHENING SHADOWS

9

THE NEW GENERATION

King William . . . was handsome of aspect and majestic of presence,
corpulent of body, sublime of stature, haughty and greedy for honours;
a conqueror on land and sea; in his Kingdom more feared than loved.
Though he gave much thought to the acquisition of wealth, he dispensed
it with some reluctance. Those who were faithful to him he raised up to
riches and honours; those who betrayed him he would condemn to
torture, or else banish from the Kingdom. Most punctilious in attending
the Holy Office, he held all ecclesiastical persons in the highest respect.

Romuald, Archbishop of Salerno

THE practice of distinguishing reigning monarchs by some characteristic epithet as well as by a bare Roman numeral was never
really popular in England. The Unready, the Confessor, the Conqueror and the Lion-Heart are the only four royal sobriquets in our
history which will unmistakably identify their bearers. In Europe,
however, throughout the Middle Ages and beyond, circlets sparkle
round the heads of Drunkards, Stammerers and Devils, of Philosophers, Navigators and Fowlers; of the Handsome and the Bald, the
Quarrelsome and the Cruel, the Debonair, the Simple and the Fat.
Most intriguing of all, perhaps—though himself uncrowned—was
the father of the Byzantine Emperor Romanus I, universally known
to his contemporaries as Theophylact the Unbearable. And yet, in
the whole limping, simpering, swaggering pageant, two men only
have been called upon to carry through eternity the most starkly
uncompromising label of them all—the Bad. One was King Charles
II of Navarre; the other was King William I of Sicily.

The new King did not altogether deserve his nickname. It was
not even given him till some two hundred years after his death—

and was principally due to two misfortunes which he never managed to overcome. The first was his father, Roger II, by whom he was outshone; the second was the principal chronicler of his reign, who vilifies him at every opportunity. The true identity of the author of the *Historia de Regno Sicilie*, though it remains one of the most perplexing enigmas of the Norman Kingdom, lies beyond the scope of this book;[1] we know him only as Hugo Falcandus, which was almost certainly not his name and was indeed only attached to him four centuries later. All we can say is that he was a writer of sophistication and polish, about whom no less an authority than Edward Gibbon could say that 'his narrative is rapid and perspicuous, his style bold and eloquent, his observation keen. He has studied mankind and feels like a man.' Alas, there were two virtues he did not possess. As a man he lacked charity; as a historian, accuracy. His pages are a grisly succession of plots and counterplots, of intrigues and assassinations and poisonings—a tale compared with which the chronicles of the house of Borgia read like an object-lesson in moral rectitude. He sees evil lurking everywhere. There is scarcely an action to which he does not ascribe some sinister motive, scarcely a character who does not emerge as a fiend incarnate. His most lethal venom of all, however, he keeps for the King.

William's appearance, too, was against him. No contemporary portraits survive, apart from those on coins; but a monkish chronicle[2] of the time writes that he was a huge man, 'whose thick black beard lent him a savage and terrible aspect and filled many people with fear'. His physical strength was herculean. He could separate two linked horseshoes with his bare hands; once, we are told, when a fully-laden pack horse stumbled and fell when crossing a bridge, he picked it up unaided and set it on its feet again. Such characteristics must have served him in good stead on the battlefield, where he showed unfailing courage and, to use a cliché of the time, was always to be found where the fighting was thickest; but they can hardly have added to his popularity.

[1] See Notes on the Principal Sources, p. 404.

[2] The *Chronica S. Mariae de Ferraria*, another enigmatic work which, it has been suggested, may be indirectly attributable to the author of Falcandus's history. See Evelyn Jamison, *Admiral Eugenius of Sicily*, pp. 278–97.

If, however, William outstripped his father in physique and
military aptitude, he fell far short of him in political ability. Like all
the Hautevilles before him, Roger II had always had an immense
appetite for work. There was no governmental task to which he
could not—and, at one time or another, did not—turn his hand. His
son was the reverse. Born with three elder brothers between him and
the throne, William had received little of that early training in
politics and statecraft that had given Duke Roger, Tancred and
Alfonso positions of high responsibility while still in their teens. He
had never been groomed for greatness, and when their premature
deaths thrust greatness upon him at the age of thirty, it caught him
unprepared. Lazy and pleasure-loving, he was to devote the greater
part of his time to those occupations with which Roger had only
employed his rare hours of relaxation—discussing art and science
with the intellectuals whom he kept at the court, or dallying with his
women in the palaces which, in the words of one traveller, ringed
Palermo like a necklace—the Favara, the Parco, possibly a summer
pavilion at Mimnermo,[1] and, later, in his own new and splendid palace
of the Zisa. Even more than his father, he was an oriental; the East
had entered into his very soul. Married in early youth to Margaret,
daughter of King Garcia IV Ramirez of Navarre, he appeared after
his succession to take little interest in her or in the four sons she bore
him. His life was more like a sultan's than a king's, and his character
embodied that same combination of sensuality and fatalism that
has stamped so many eastern rulers. He never took a decision if he
could avoid it, never tackled a problem if there was the faintest
chance that, given long enough, it might solve itself. Once goaded
into action, however, he would pursue his objectives with ferocious
energy—if only, notes Chalandon a little unkindly, in order to
return as quickly as possible to more congenial pursuits.

Unlike his father, then, William tended to leave the day-to-day
business of the Kingdom to his ministers, nearly all of them profes-

[1] So, at least, the name appears in the early editions of Falcandus; this, however, is probably a corruption of Minenium, from the original Arabic name of
Al-Menani. The building—what remains of it—is now known as the Palazzo
dell' Uscibene, in the modern village of Altarello. The original structure probably dates back to Saracen times, but the present decoration of sea-shells in
stucco is, it need hardly be said, a comparatively recent addition.

sional clerks and civil servants of the middle class who owed their position and advancement to the King alone and whose loyalty was consequently beyond question. Even in their selection he seems to have given himself the minimum of trouble; with only two exceptions that we know of, he simply confirmed the chief functionaries of his father's reign in their existing ranks and offices.

Of these two exceptions one was an Englishman, Thomas Brown. The son or nephew of a certain William Brown, or Le Brun, a clerk in the service of King Henry I, he had come to Sicily in about 1130 when still little more than a boy—probably in the company and as the *protégé* of Robert of Selby. We first hear of him in 1137, and from that time on his name appears regularly in the official documents that have come down to us.[1] Throughout Roger's reign Thomas seems to have enjoyed his confidence and favour; there is even reason to believe that he personally drafted the foundation charter for the Palatine Chapel in 1140. But on William's accession, for reasons unhappily obscure, he lost his high office and returned to England, where he became King's Almoner under Henry II.[2]

Though we cannot be sure, it seems more than probable that Thomas's abrupt departure from Sicily was in fact occasioned not by the King himself but by his new Emir of Emirs, Maio of Bari— whose elevation, besides being the only other important change effected by William in the ranks of his advisers, proved to be one of the most fateful acts of his entire reign. It came as no surprise. Maio had been at least ten years in the royal service and had already reached the rank of Chancellor when William singled him out to succeed the ill-fated Philip of Mahdia in the Kingdom's supreme administrative post. Son of a prosperous oil merchant and judge in Bari, he had received a thorough classical education in his youth and was well able to hold his own in the rarefied intellectual society

---

[1] It is a sign of Thomas's importance—and illustrative too of the polyglot Sicilian administration—that he should figure in the Latin, Greek and Arabic archives. Thus in 1137 we find Roger II granting a charter to the monks of Monte Vergine *per manum magistri Thome capellani regis*; six years later, μάστρο Θωμᾶ τοῦ Βρόυνου is named as one of the adjudicators of a boundary dispute; while in 1149 he appears in the disguise of قايد برون, Caïd Brun, a member of the royal Diwan with a secretary called Othman.

[2] *Dialogus de Scaccario*, Stubbs, *Select Charters*, Oxford, 1870.

of the court. He was moreover a discerning patron of the arts and sciences and he has even left us with one work of his own, an 'Exposition of the Lord's Prayer', which, if not an achievement of any outstanding individuality, shows that he was admirably grounded in scholastic philosophy as well as in the works of the early Fathers of the Church. But above all Maio was a statesman; and it was he, rather than his master, who was to shape Sicilian policy for the first six years of the new reign. Stern, pitiless, unswerving in the pursuit of policies which he believed to be justified, he never feared unpopularity—indeed, there were occasions when he seemed deliberately to be courting it. In consequence, though he has been harshly dealt with by Hugo Falcandus and others, there can be no doubt of his political acumen. But for him, William would have been lucky to keep his throne more than a matter of months.

For ten years now the country had enjoyed internal peace, but many of the barons, especially in Apulia, were still unreconciled to the Kingdom; and memories of Roger's savage repression were beginning to fade. Others, who had decided to throw in their lot with the King, had gravitated to the capital in the hopes of obtaining power or preferment but had been disappointed. Roger's mistrust of his compatriots had lasted to the end of his life. These semi-literate Norman barons, arrogant, self-seeking, talking no language but their own, were hopelessly unqualified for positions of responsibility in a highly centralised state; and their record as vassals was not such as to encourage the granting to them of any large fiefs on the island. They had therefore been obliged to watch while Greeks, Italians and Saracens—men often of humble birth, and of races which they considered vastly inferior to their own—rose to eminence and distinction; and, as they watched, so their dissatisfaction grew. Roger, after years of struggle, had ultimately earned their grudging respect; but now that his iron hand had gone, the threat of further trouble could not be far distant; and both William and Maio knew it.

To know it, however, was not to yield to pressure. Maio had been trained by Roger; no one saw more clearly the danger of allowing any part of the Sicilian government to fall into the hands of the feudal aristocracy. He excluded them as mercilessly as ever, drawing his staff from men of his own class and background, the prosperous professional bourgeoisie, both Italian and Arab. Greeks he seems to have been less ready to employ in positions of high authority. Being himself an Italian from the largely Greek city of Bari, he may have been prejudiced against them from childhood; but in Sicily, as we have seen, their influence was now on the wane—Maio's own elevation to an office which had hitherto been a Greek preserve is a case in point, and cannot have increased his popularity among the Greeks of Palermo. Besides, relations with Byzantium were steadily worsening; and it is hardly to be wondered at that, in the circumstances, the Chancellor should have given preference elsewhere.

Meanwhile the immigration of able men from western Europe continued to increase, and with it the power of the Latin Church. Even more than the Norman aristocracy, its hierarchy had yielded to the magnetic pull of Palermo; by the time of William's accession, most of the Sicilian bishops and a good many of the incumbents of mainland sees were in semi-permanent residence at court. This absenteeism was later to reach such scandalous proportions as to require papal intervention; but at the time it aroused little comment and Maio, who saw the Church as one of his principal supports against the baronage, seems if anything to have encouraged it. It also brought to the capital a number of highly capable clerics, among them two more Englishmen destined to play vital parts in Sicilian affairs —Richard Palmer, Bishop-elect of Syracuse, and Walter of the Mill, formerly Archdeacon of Cefalù and later Archbishop of Palermo. But it led to the growth in the Sicilian body politic of an increasingly influential ecclesiastical party which could not fail to do the country harm. By its very nature this party was bound to be intolerant alike of Orthodoxy and Islam, impatient of the whole permissive structure on which the Kingdom was based. Already, in its hounding of Philip of Mahdia, it had dealt that structure its first damaging blow; in succeeding years further blows would follow until Norman Sicily itself, its political and philosophical foundations shattered, collapsed in ruins to the ground.

Thus, when William the Bad received his second coronation at the hands of Archbishop Hugh of Palermo on Easter Sunday, 4 April 1154, the formal acclamation of his assembled vassals might have struck a sensitive ear with a slightly hollow ring. But for the moment the vassals, discontented as they might be, could be kept at least partially under control. The immediate danger to the Kingdom came not from them but from its three old enemies: the Western Empire, Byzantium and the Papacy. It was William's misfortune that his reign should have coincided with the reigns of two Emperors of outstanding ability and the pontificates of the two greatest Popes of the twelfth century. It was his good luck that his enemies—who, united, would have been invincible—mistrusted each other even more than they feared and hated him.

To be sure, they had good reason to do so. The young Frederick Barbarossa, now about thirty-two years old, seemed to his German contemporaries the very nonpareil of Teutonic chivalry. Tall and broad-shouldered, attractive rather than handsome, he had eyes that twinkled so brightly under his thick mop of reddish-brown hair that, according to one chronicler who knew him well,[1] he always seemed on the point of laughter. But beneath this easy-going exterior there lurked a will of steel, an utter dedication to a single objective. 'My wish,' he wrote succinctly to the Pope, 'is to restore to the Roman Empire its ancient greatness and splendour.' It was a conception that left no room for compromise, and, in particular, it ruled out the possibility of any real alliance with Constantinople. Since 1148 Manuel Comnenus had made no secret of the fact that he considered South Italy to be Byzantine territory. Conrad, who knew how much he needed Manuel's friendship, had been prepared to agree to a partition, and on his deathbed he had implored his nephew to pursue the same policy; but to the young Barbarossa such an idea was unthinkable. Barely a year after his accession he had signed a treaty with the Pope at Constance, by the terms of which it was agreed that Byzantium would be allowed no concessions on Italian territory; if its Emperor were to attempt to seize any by force, he would be expelled. The brief honeymoon between the two Empires was at an end.

To Manuel, Conrad's death therefore meant a good deal more than the loss of a friend and ally. Occurring as it did on the eve of the

---

[1] Acerbus Morena, *podestà* of Lodi, who with his father Otto was one of the first lay historians of North Italy.

great campaign that was to restore to Constantinople its long-lost
Italian provinces, it also spelt a serious political reverse—just how
serious, Frederick's behaviour was soon to show. But though Manuel
quickly saw that he could no longer expect any help from the Western
Empire, he was unaware of the precise terms of the Treaty of
Constance and still believed in the possibility of some sort of
Italian partition. One thing only was clear—that whatever he was to
regain he would have to fight for. If, as seemed likely, the Germans
marched against William of Sicily, it was essential that a strong
Byzantine force should be present, ready to protect the legitimate
rights of the Eastern Empire. If they did not, then he proposed to
take the initiative on his own. When, therefore, in the early summer of
1154, he received ambassadors from Sicily offering, in return for a
peace treaty, the restitution of all Greek prisoners and all the spoils
from George of Antioch's Theban expedition, he refused outright.
Such an offer could only mean that the new King was afraid of an
imperial invasion; if he was afraid, he was weak; if he was weak, he
would be defeated.

The mutual suspicions that divided the two Empires, together
with their common hatred for the Sicilian Kingdom, were fully
shared by the Papacy. Eugenius's successor, Anastasius IV, was old
and ineffectual, concerned chiefly with his own self-glorification; but
he did not last long, and when, in the last days of 1154, his body was
laid to rest in the gigantic porphyry sarcophagus that had previously
held the remains of the Empress Helena—transferred, on his own
orders, to a modest urn in the Ara Coeli a few months previously [1]—
he was succeeded by a man of very different calibre: Adrian IV, the
only Englishman ever to occupy the Throne of St Peter.

Nicholas Breakspear was born around 1115 at Abbot's Langley in
Hertfordshire, at that time a dependency of the monastery of St
Albans. While still a student he had moved to France, and later—
after a short and not particularly successful period as prior of St
Rufus, near Arles—to Rome. There, thanks to his eloquence, ability and outstanding good looks, he had soon caught the attention
of Pope Eugenius. Fortunately for him, the Pope was a convinced

[1] The sarcophagus is now in the Sala a Croce Greca of the Vatican Museum.
Helena's remains, however, have disappeared without trace.

Anglophile; he once told John of Salisbury that he found the English
admirably fitted to perform any task they turned their hand to, and
thus to be preferred to all other races—except, he added, when
frivolity got the better of them. Frivolity, however, does not seem
to have been one of Nicholas's failings. Early in 1152 he was sent as
Papal Legate to Norway, there to reorganise the Church throughout Scandinavia. Two years later he was back again in Rome, his
mission accomplished with such distinction that, on Anastasius's
death the following December, the forceful, energetic Englishman
was unanimously elected to succeed him.

It was a wise choice, for energy and force were desperately
needed. At the time of Adrian's accession Frederick Barbarossa had
already crossed the Alps to his first Italian campaign. On his arrival
in Rome he would be sure to demand his imperial coronation; but
even if he were to receive it, there was little likelihood that the Pope
would ever be able to trust him as an ally. Indeed, with his known
absolutist views, Frederick was unlikely to prove anything but a constant anxiety to the Holy See. Another, separate invasion was threatened from the Byzantine East. In the South, William I's Sicily might
be going through a critical stage, but was still outwardly as strong
and prosperous as ever. Worst of all was the situation in Rome itself.
Encouraged by the tractability of Eugenius and Anastasius, the
Senate had grown still more arrogant; meanwhile its position had
been further reinforced, and the Pope's own spiritual authority
dangerously weakened, by the teachings of a monk from Lombardy
whose influence, skilfully built up over the past decade, had by now
made him the virtual master of Rome.

His name was Arnold of Brescia. In his youth he had studied in the
Schools of Paris—probably under Abelard at Notre Dame—where
he had been thoroughly imbued with the principles of the new
scholasticism, essentially a movement away from the old mystical
approach to spiritual matters, and towards a spirit of logical,
rationalistic enquiry. To the mediaeval Papacy, radical ideas of this
sort would have seemed quite subversive enough; but Arnold
combined with them a still more unwelcome feature—a passionate
hatred for the temporal power of the Church. For him the State was,
and must always be, supreme; the civil law, based on the laws of

175

Ancient Rome, must prevail over the canon; the Pope, for his part, should divest himself of all worldly pomp, renounce his powers and privileges, and revert to the poverty and simplicity of the early Fathers. Only thus could the Church re-establish contact with the humble masses among its flock. As John of Salisbury wrote:

Arnold himself was frequently to be heard on the Capitol and in various assemblies of the people. He had already publicly denounced the Cardinals, maintaining that their College, beset as it was with pride, avarice, hypocrisy and shame, was not the Church of God but a house of commerce and a den of thieves, men who took the place of the scribes and Pharisees among Christian peoples. Even the Pope himself was other than what he professed; rather than an apostolic shepherd of souls, he was a man of blood who maintained his authority by fire and the sword, a tormenter of churches and oppressor of the innocent, whose only actions were for the gratification of his lust and for the emptying of other men's coffers in order that his own might be filled. . . . There could be no toleration of one who sought only to impose a yoke of servitude on Rome, seat of Empire, fountain of liberty and mistress of the world.[1]

Naturally, the Papacy had fought back. Naturally, too, it had used the Abbot of Clairvaux—to whose unquestioning, unwavering faith Arnold's views were anathema—as its champion. In consequence, as early as 1140 Arnold had been condemned, together with his old master Abelard, at the Council of Sens and had been expelled from France. By 1146, however, he was back in Rome; and the Roman Senate, fired by his blazing piety and recognising in his ideas the spiritual counterpart of its own republican aspirations, had welcomed him with open arms.

Pope Eugenius, another ascetic, possibly out of some secret sympathy for Arnold, had allowed him to return to the capital; and Anastasius, *vieillard pacifique et conciliant* as Chalandon describes him, had turned a deaf ear to his thunderings. But Adrian was of a different stamp. When, on his accession, he found himself confined by Arnold's supporters to St Peter's and the Leonine City, he had at first merely ordered the agitator to leave Rome; but when, predictably, Arnold took no notice and instead allowed his followers to attack and

[1] John of Salisbury, *Historia Pontificalis.*

Palermo Cathedral: tomb of Roger II

Frederick Barbarossa—from a twelfth-century Bavarian MS.

grievously wound the venerable Cardinal Guido of S. Pudenziana as he was walking down the Via Sacra on his way to the Vatican, the Pope played his trump card. For the first time in the history of Christendom, Rome itself was laid under an interdict.

It was an act of breath-taking courage. A foreigner, who had been Pope for only a few weeks, knew the city and its increasingly xenophobic inhabitants hardly at all and was able to rely on little or no popular support, had dared by a single decree to close all the churches of Rome. Exceptions were made for the baptism of infants and the absolution of the dying; otherwise all ceremonies and sacraments were alike forbidden. No masses could be said, no marriages solemnised; dead bodies might not even be buried in consecrated ground. In the Middle Ages, when religion still constituted an integral part of every man's life, the effect of such a moral blockade was immeasurable. Besides, Easter was approaching. The prospect of the greatest feast of the Christian year passing uncelebrated was bleak enough; without the annual influx of pilgrims, one of the principal sources of the city's revenue, it was bleaker still. For a little while the Romans held out; but by the Wednesday of Holy Week they could bear it no longer and marched on the Capitol. The Senators saw that they were beaten. Arnold and his followers were expelled; the interdict was lifted; the church bells pealed out their message; and on Sunday, as he had always intended to do, Pope Adrian IV celebrated Easter at the Lateran.

Frederick Barbarossa, meanwhile, kept the feast at Pavia, where on the same day he was crowned with the traditional Iron Crown of Lombardy. Like more than one Emperor before him, he had been astonished at the intensity of republican feeling in the cities and towns of North Italy, by their determination to cast off the old feudal obligations in favour of civic independence and communal self-government; and he had considered it his duty—at the cost of some delay to his original plans—to give a further demonstration of imperial strength. Milan, the perennial focus of revolt, was too strong for him, but her ally Tortona had looked an easy victim. The little town had made a herioc stand against the combined forces of the Empire, Pavia and Montferrat; but when, after two months' siege, the wells ran dry and the inhabitants were parched into surrender, they had paid dearly for their heroism. Though their lives were spared, their city had been razed until not one stone was left on another.

After Easter, however, Frederick delayed no longer. His descent through Tuscany was so fast that to the Roman Curia it seemed positively threatening. The fate of Tortona was by now common knowledge throughout Italy; Henry IV's treatment of Gregory VII seventy years before had not been forgotten; and several of the older cardinals could still remember how, in 1111, Henry V had laid hands upon Pope Paschal II in St Peter's itself and held him two months a prisoner until he capitulated. In all the recent reports now circulating about the new King of the Romans, there was nothing to suggest that he would not be fully capable of similar conduct. No wonder the Curia began to feel alarm.

Hurriedly, Adrian sent two of his cardinals north to the imperial camp. They found it at S. Quirico near Siena, and were cordially received. Then, as an earnest of his goodwill, they asked Frederick for help in laying hands on Arnold of Brescia who, after wandering for some weeks round the Campagna, had at last taken refuge with some local barons. Frederick readily agreed; he detested Arnold's radical views almost as much as the Pope himself and welcomed this new opportunity to show his power. Sending a body of troops to the castle in question, he had one of the barons seized and held as a hostage until Arnold himself should be delivered. The fugitive was immediately given up to the papal authorities; and the cardinals, reassured, applied themselves to their next task— to make arrangements for the first, critical interview between Pope and King.

The meeting was fixed for 9 June at Campo Grasso, near Sutri. It began auspiciously enough with Adrian, followed by his bishops and cardinals and escorted by a great company of German barons sent forward by Frederick to greet him, riding in solemn procession to the imperial camp. But now trouble began. At this point, according to custom, the King should have advanced to lead in the Pope's horse by the bridle and to hold the stirrup while its rider dismounted; he did not do so. For a moment Adrian seemed to hesitate. Then, dismounting by himself, he walked slowly across to the throne which had been prepared for him and sat down. Now at last Frederick stepped forward, kissed the Pope's feet and rose to receive the traditional kiss of peace in return; but this time it was Adrian who held back. The King, he pointed out, had denied him a service which, in reverence for the apostles Peter and Paul, his predecessors had always rendered to the Supreme Pontiff. Until this omission was rectified, there could be no kiss of peace.

Frederick objected that it was no part of his duty to act as a papal groom; and all that day and the next the dispute continued. Adrian would not be shaken. He knew that what appeared on the surface to be a minor point of protocol concealed in reality something infinitely more important—a public act of defiance that struck at the very root of the relationship between Empire and Papacy. Against this knowledge explanations and arguments were of no avail. Suddenly and surprisingly, Frederick gave in. He ordered his camp to be moved a little further south, to the neighbourhood of the town of Monterosi; and there, on the morning of 11 June, the events of two days before were restaged. The King advanced to meet the Pope, led in his horse by the bridle for the distance, we are told, of a stone's throw; then, firmly holding the stirrup, he helped him to dismount. Once again Adrian settled himself on the throne that awaited him; the kiss of peace was duly bestowed; and conversations began.

Adrian and Frederick would never entirely trust one another; but the incident had somehow increased their mutual respect and the ensuing discussions seem to have been amicable enough. The terms agreed at Constance were confirmed. Neither party would enter into separate negotiations with William, Manuel or the Roman Senate. Frederick for his part would defend all legitimate papal interests, while Adrian in return would excommunicate all enemies of the Empire who, after three warnings, persisted in their opposition. Reassured of each other's intentions, the two rode on together towards Rome.

From the side of the Papacy there was now no longer any objection to the imperial coronation.[1] This ceremony, on the other hand, had

[1] One chronicler (Helmold, *Chronica Slavorum*) maintains that Frederick had sent ambassadors from Tuscany to Adrian with a formal request for the

not been performed since the establishment of the Roman Commune; how would Rome itself now greet its Emperor-to-be? It was an open question, and Frederick's recent move against Arnold of Brescia had made it more problematical still. But he and Adrian were not kept long in suspense. While they were still some distance from the city they were met by a deputation sent out by the Senate to greet them and to make clear the conditions on which they would be received.

Bishop Otto of Freising, probably an eyewitness, has left us what appears to be a verbatim record of what took place. The dialogue began with a long set speech by the leader of the Roman deputation. Though not by any means hostile, it was bombastic and patronising; it suggested that Rome alone had made Frederick's Empire what it was and that consequently the new Emperor would do well to consider his moral obligations to the city—obligations which apparently included making a sworn guarantee of its future liberty and an *ex gratia* payment of five thousand pounds of gold.

The spokesman was still in full spate when Frederick interrupted him. Speaking, as Otto neatly puts it, 'without preparation but not unprepared'[1], and with 'his usual modest charm of expression', he pointed out that all Rome's ancient glory and traditions had now passed, with the Empire itself, to Germany. He had come not to receive gifts from the Romans but to claim what was rightfully his. Naturally, he would defend Rome as necessary; but he saw no need for formal guarantees and had no intention of giving any. As for gifts of money, he would bestow them as and where he pleased.

Frederick's quiet assurance took the ambassadors off their guard. In reply to enquiries whether they had anything more to say, they could only stammer that they must return to the capital for instructions; with that, they took their leave. As soon as they were gone, Pope and King held an urgent consultation. Adrian, with his experience of the Roman Senate, had no doubt that trouble was to be

coronation; and that they had received the following reply: 'Let him first regain for St Peter the land of Apulia, which William the Sicilian holds by force; then let him come and be crowned by us.' It seems improbable. Adrian was not likely to dispute imperial claims to Apulia at such a time; and he certainly did not insist on this condition at the subsequent negotiations.

[1] *Ex inproviso non inprovise.*

expected. He advised the immediate despatch of a body of troops, to be accompanied by Cardinal Octavian of Monticelli, to occupy the Leonine City[1] by night and hold it against all adversaries. Even with this precaution, he pointed out, the danger would not be entirely averted. If they wanted to avoid trouble, he and Frederick would have to move quickly.

The date was Friday, 17 June. Such was the urgency of the situation that the two agreed not even to wait for the following Sunday as they would normally have done. Instead, at dawn on Saturday, Frederick rode down from Monte Mario and entered the Leonine City, which his troops had already surrounded, by the Golden Gate near St Peter's. The Pope, who had arrived an hour or two previously, was awaiting him on the steps of the basilica. They entered it together, a throng of German knights following behind. Adrian himself celebrated Mass; and there, over the tomb of the Apostle, he hurriedly girded the sword of St Peter to Frederick's side and laid the imperial crown on his head.

Cardinal Boso Breakspear, Adrian's nephew and biographer, tells us that at this point the German knights thronging St Peter's raised so deafening a cheer that it seemed as though a very thunderbolt had fallen from heaven; but there was no time for any further celebration. As soon as the ceremony was done the Emperor, with the imperial crown still on his head, rode back to his camp outside the walls, his huge retinue following on foot. The Pope meanwhile took refuge in the Vatican to await developments.

It was still only nine o'clock in the morning; and the Senate was assembling on the Capitol to decide how best to prevent the coronation when the news arrived that it had already taken place. Furious to find that they had been outwitted and outmanœuvred, they sprang to arms; soon a huge mob was pressing across the Ponte S. Angelo into the Leonine City while another, having crossed the river further downstream at the island, advanced northwards through Trastevere. The day was growing hotter. The Germans, tired by their forced march through the night and the excitement of the past few hours,

[1] This comprised that part of Rome on the right bank of the Tiber, including the Vatican, St Peter's and the Castel Sant' Angelo, which was fortified by Pope Leo IV in the ninth century, immediately after the sack of the city by the Saracens.

wanted to relax—to sleep and to celebrate. Instead, they received the
order to prepare at once for battle. Had not their Emperor sworn,
that very morning and before them all, to defend the Church of
Christ? Already its safety was threatened. For the second time that
day Frederick entered Rome, but he wore his coronation robes no
longer. This time he had his armour on.

All afternoon and evening the battle raged between the Emperor
of the Romans and his subjects; night had fallen before the imperial
troops had driven the last of the insurgents back across the bridges.
Losses had been heavy on both sides. For the German casualties we
have no reliable figures; but Otto of Freising reports that among the
Romans almost a thousand were slain or drowned in the Tiber,
and another six hundred taken captive. As for the wounded, he had
given up trying to count them. The Senate had paid a high price for
its arrogance.

And yet, if the Romans had revealed themselves as poor diplo-
mats, they had at least proved brave fighters; and it must be admitted that they had good grounds for resentment. Previous
Emperors arriving for their consecration had been accustomed to
show the city and its institutions at least some marks of respect—
swearing obedience to its laws and submitting themselves to the
votes and acclamations of its people. Frederick had done none of
these things. He had ignored the Romans entirely—and he had done
so at a moment in their history when their Commune had given them
a new sense of civic pride, a new awareness of their past greatness and
the splendour of their heritage. To argue that they had treated him
with singular tactlessness and thus to a large extent brought their
punishment on themselves was neither here nor there; Frederick's
initial treatment of Pope Adrian at Sutri hardly suggested that even
in other circumstances he would have been much more amenable.

The Emperor too had bought his crown dearly. His victory had
not even gained him entrance into the ancient city, for the sun rose
the next morning to show all the Tiber bridges blocked and the
gates of the city barricaded. Neither he nor his army was prepared
for a siege; the heat of the Italian summer, which for a century and a
half had consistently undermined the morale of successive invading
armies, was once again beginning to take its toll with outbreaks of

malaria and dysentery among his men. As Otto feelingly describes it, 'all the air round about became heavy with the mists that rose from the swamps nearby and from the caverns and ruined places about the City: an atmosphere deadly and noxious for mortals to breathe.' The only sensible course was to withdraw, and—since the Vatican was clearly no longer safe for the Papacy—to take Pope and Curia with him. On 19 June he struck camp again and led his army up into the Sabine Hills. A month later he was heading back towards Germany, leaving Adrian powerless at Tivoli.

Although the Pope had been careful, after his first meeting, to allow no open breach with the Emperor, he had good reason to feel resentful. At considerable risk to his own safety he had performed the coronation required of him; he had received little in return. Since leaving Rome he had done his utmost to persuade Frederick to keep to his original plan and march without further ado against William of Sicily; but, though Frederick personally would have been willing enough, his ailing German barons would have none of it. Promises were readily given to return in the near future, when a healthier and more numerous imperial force would bring Romans and Sicilians alike to heel; meanwhile the Pope was left, isolated and in exile, to get on as best he could.

The story of the coronation of Frederick Barbarossa is almost told, but not quite; for, apart from the Emperor who was crowned and the Pope who crowned him, there is a third character who, although he was not even present in Rome on that dreadful day, influenced the course of events as much as either of them. Arnold of Brescia was one of the first of those astonishing popular leaders whom Italy has thrown up at intervals all through her history—fanatics of genius who, by the sheer magic of their personalities, gain absolute and unquestioned domination over their fellow-men. Sometimes, as with Arnold himself or with Savonarola three hundred years later, this domination has a spiritual basis; sometimes, as with Cola di Rienzo, it is inspired by a historic sense of mission; occasionally, as Mussolini showed, it can be political through and through. One characteristic, however, these men have all had in common. All have failed, and have paid for their failure with their lives.

No record exists to tell us exactly when or where Arnold suffered his execution. We know only the manner in which he met his death. Condemned by a spiritual tribunal on charges of heresy and rebellion, he remained firm to the end and walked calmly to the scaffold without a trace of fear; as he knelt to make his last confession, we read that the executioners themselves could not restrain their tears. They hanged him none the less; then they cut him down and burned the body. Finally, in order to ensure that no relics should be left for veneration by the people, they threw the ashes into the Tiber.

For a martyr, misguided or not, there could be no greater honour.

10

THE GREEK OFFENSIVE

The Emperor Manuel often held that it was an easy matter for him to win
over the peoples of the East by gifts of money or by force of arms, but
that over those of the West he could never count on gaining a similar
advantage; for they are formidable in numbers, indomitable in pride,
cruel in character, rich in possessions and inspired by an inveterate
hatred for the Empire.

Nicetas Choniates, History of Manuel Comnenus, VII, i

OF the many German armies which, in the past century and a half,
had marched down into South Italy to restore imperial power in the
peninsula, none had ever remained there more than a few months.
The Emperors who led them had soon discovered that even if this
enervating, pestiferous land were technically theirs, they for their
part could never belong to it. Here they would always be strangers,
and unwelcome strangers at that; and their men, toiling along in their
heavy homespun under a torrid Apulian sky, sickened by the unaccustomed food and plagued, even more than they knew, by the
clouds of insects that whined incessantly about their heads, felt
much the same. Nearly all, both the leaders and the led, longed for
the day when they would once again be able to see a firm mountain
barrier rising between themselves and the scene of their sufferings.

Frederick Barbarossa was an exception. He would have been
genuinely glad to remain in the South and deal with William of
Sicily if he could only have carried his knights with him; but they
were resolved to return at once to Germany, and he knew that he
must not impose his will too far. This enforced withdrawal saddened
and frustrated him; and it can have been little consolation that when
he reached Ancona—after the largely gratuitous destruction of

Spoleto on the way—he was met by three emissaries from Constantinople, led by the erstwhile governor of Thessalonica, Michael Palaeologus, bringing him rich presents from their master and promising him considerable subsidies if he would change his mind. Frederick kept them waiting some time for his answer; even at this late stage it was worth making one last attempt to inject a little of his own spirit into his followers. But the German barons had had enough; and after a few days the Emperor was obliged to admit to the Greeks that there was nothing he could do.

Palaeologus and his companions were not unduly upset by the news. Strategically it might have been useful to have the German army fighting their battles for them; diplomatically, however, the situation would be very much simpler without the involvement of the Western Empire, particularly as there was by now no shortage of other, more manageable allies closer to hand—King William's rebellious Apulian vassals. They too had put their trust in Frederick and had been disappointed by his hasty departure; but they felt no special ties of loyalty to him any more than to anyone else. Now that he had let them down, they were perfectly ready to accept subsidies and support from Constantinople instead.

All that year, Apulian resistance to the new King of Sicily had been stiffening. This can partly be attributed to the expectation of Frederick Barbarossa's appearance on the scene in what was hoped to be fire and wrath; but much of it was also due to the spirit and determination of a new leader—Robert de Bassonville, Count of Loritello. Robert was the very prototype of the dissatisfied Norman aristocrat. As first cousin of the King—he was the son of Roger II's sister Judith—he considered himself exceptionally qualified for high office; Hugo Falcandus even suggests, with his usual malice, that Roger had considered making him his successor instead of William. Thus he viciously resented the pre-eminence of Maio and the Emir's continued discrimination against the landed nobility. The gift of the distant County of Loritello, which William had bestowed on him at the time of his own accession, had done nothing to mollify him; almost at once, he had begun stirring up discontent among the neighbouring barons. William for his part cherished no delusions about Robert's loyalty. Already in the early spring of 1155, on his first visit to Salerno as King, he had refused to receive him into his presence; and on his return to Sicily soon after Easter he had sent instructions to his Viceroy, Asclettin, to have the Count of Loritello arrested forthwith. Robert, however, had escaped to the Abruzzi, where he had spent the summer gathering his forces—and where he now heard, for the first time, of Michael Palaeologus's arrival in the peninsula.

The two met at Viesti, and at once agreed to join forces. Each was able to provide just what the other lacked. Palaeologus had a fleet of ten ships, seemingly limitless funds and the power to call when necessary on further reinforcements from across the Adriatic. Robert could claim the support of the majority of the local barons, together with the effective control of a considerable length of coast—a vital requirement if the Byzantine lines of communication were to be adequately maintained. By contrast, the royalist army under Asclettin was far away beyond the Apennines—powerless to oppose any swift, surprise strike in northern Apulia.

And so, in the late summer of 1155, Robert of Loritello and Michael Palaeologus struck. Their first attack was directed against Bari. Until its capture by Robert Guiscard in 1071, this city had been the capital of Byzantine Italy and the last Greek stronghold in the penin-sula. The majority of its citizens, being Greek, resented the govern-ment of Palermo—particularly since Roger had withdrawn several of their ancient privileges after the last Apulian rising—and looked gratefully towards any opportunity of breaking free from it. A group of them opened the gates to the attackers; and though the Sicilian garrison fought bravely from the old citadel and the church of St Nicholas, they were soon obliged to surrender and to watch while the Bariots fell on the citadel—by now the symbol of Sicilian domination—and despite Palaeologus's efforts to stop them, razed it to the ground.

News of the fall of Bari, coupled with a sudden spate of rumours of King William's death—he was indeed seriously ill—shattered the morale of the coastal towns. Trani yielded in its turn; then, despite the heroic efforts of its commander, Count Richard of Andria, the neighbouring port of Giovinazzo. Further south, resistance was still fierce; William of Tyre reports that when the Patriarch of

Jerusalem arrived that autumn in Otranto on his way to visit the Pope, he found the entire region in such turmoil that he was forced to re-embark and make his way by sea up the coast as far as Ancona. But the Greeks and the rebels together continued to gain ground everywhere until, as the winter rains began, the whole of Apulia seemed on the point of collapse.

Now at last, at the beginning of September, Asclettin's royalist army, consisting of some two thousand knights and an unknown but apparently considerable force of infantry, appeared in the field. On their arrival they were joined by Richard of Andria with those of his men who had remained loyal, but the opposition was too strong for them. Hardly had they reached the coast before they found themselves surrounded at Barletta. In a desperate effort to increase his strength, Count Richard broke through the cordon with a body of knights and made a dash for his own territory of Andria, hotly pursued by Robert of Loritello and John Ducas, Michael Palaeologus's principal lieutenant. They caught up with him just as he arrived before the walls. Rather than face a siege, for which he knew that his town was unprepared, Richard turned and gave battle on the spot. At one moment it looked as if he might carry the day; the Greeks' line was broken, and they and their allies retired in disorder. Sheltering, however, behind the long walls of stones which were (and still are) a feature of the region, they managed to reform and return to the charge; and before long the royalists were in full retreat. Count Richard himself, unhorsed by a blow from a flying stone, was finished off by a priest of Trani who, we are told, ripped him open and tore out his entrails. Seeing their lord lying dead, the population of Andria surrendered to Ducas.

The first pitched battle of the new revolt had ended in disaster. For those still loyal to King William, the future looked grim.

From Tivoli first and later from Tusculum, Pope Adrian had followed these developments with satisfaction. Though he had no love for the Greeks, he greatly preferred them to the Sicilians; and it delighted him to see his arch-enemy William, having escaped the vengeance of Barbarossa, finally receiving his deserts. Barely three months before, riding south with Frederick from Sutri to Rome, the

Pope had forsworn any separate diplomatic negotiations with Byzantium, but times had changed; now that the Emperor had defaulted on his own undertakings, Adrian felt once again free to act in whatever way he saw fit. When, therefore, he received a letter from Michael Palaeologus offering him military help against the King of Sicily together with a subsidy of five thousand gold pounds in return for the grant of three coastal towns in Apulia he was interested. He replied that he himself already had troops at his disposal and that he was ready forthwith to embark on the campaign as an ally. On 29 September 1155 he marched south.

It may seem surprising, just a century after the great schism between the Eastern and Western Churches, to find the Emperor of Byzantium putting himself forward as the patron and protector of the Pope of Rome, and the Pope accepting his overtures. It was in fact a policy which had been inaugurated, on the Byzantine side, by John Comnenus as early as 1141; Manuel was merely continuing it and, seeing circumstances so favourable, increasing the pressure. Adrian doubtless recognised in the South Italian situation the opening up of an opportunity that might never recur. He was encouraged, too, by the exiled Apulian vassals who, faced with the possibility of regaining their old fiefs, joyfully agreed to recognise the Pope as their lawful suzerain in return for his support. Already on 9 October, at S. Germano, Prince Robert of Capua, Count Andrew of Rupe Canina and several other Norman barons were reinvested with their hereditary possessions, and before the end of the year all Campania and most of Northern Apulia was in Byzantine or papalist hands.

Michael Palaeologus, mopping up the few pockets of resistance that remained, could congratulate himself on a success greater than he could have dared to hope. In barely six months he had restored Greek power in the peninsula to a point almost equal to that of a hundred and fifty years previously, before the Normans set about the deliberate destruction of the Byzantine theme of Langobardia and seized it for themselves. News had recently been brought to him that his Emperor, encouraged by such rapid progress, was sending out a full-scale expeditionary force to consolidate the position. At this rate it might not be long before all South Italy acknowledged the dominion of Constantinople. William of Sicily would be crushed, his odious Kingdom liquidated. Pope Adrian, seeing the Greeks succeed where the Germans had failed, would be persuaded of the superiority of Byzantine armies and would adjust his policies accordingly; and the great dream of the Comneni—the reunification of the Roman Empire under the aegis of Constantinople—might be realised at last.

Over-confidence is always dangerous; but few impartial observers at the end of 1155 would have held out much hope for the future of the Sicilian monarchy. On the mainland the King's enemies were in control everywhere except in Calabria; and Calabria probably remained loyal only because it had not yet been attacked. It would never be able to resist a determined Byzantine onslaught; if it fell, the rebels and their Greek allies would be only a mile or two from Sicily itself.

And there, on the island, the situation was now equally menacing. From September to Christmas the King lay in Palermo, desperately ill; Maio of Bari, assisted by Archbishop Hugh of Palermo, assumed complete control of the Kingdom. The Emir of Emirs had never been popular, and succeeding reports of one defeat after another on the mainland gave his enemies among the Norman nobility the very opportunity they needed to stir up unrest. He, they murmured, and he alone was responsible for this collapse. It would never have occurred if the Emirate had been bestowed on one of their own number. To have entrusted the supreme executive power in the realm to a Lombard tradesman's son was an act of unpardonable folly. Such a man was bound to be ignored by the proud barons of the peninsula. Even now, with the Sicilian state falling in ruins about his head, he seemed to have no real understanding of the gravity of the situation. He had sent no military reinforcements to Asclettin; he did not even appear worried.

There was only one thing to be done. Maio must be removed. And if his removal should also entail the removal of William himself, then so much the better. The King was already ill; perhaps, with a little help from the right quarter, he might never recover—in which case it would be a relatively easy matter to put the blame on the Emir, the only one of his ministers with unrestricted access to the royal bedchamber. William had already showed himself unfit to govern; how much more satisfactory it would be if the crown were to pass to his three-year-old son. The rightful ruling class could then come into its own, and the Norman barons would regain the power—and the perquisites—to which their birth entitled them.

But the Emir of Emirs kept his nerve. Not even Falcandus, who detested him, can hold back a word of grudging admiration for the way in which, whatever the crisis, he remained cool and unruffled, his face never betraying any sign of his real emotions. This steady refusal to panic—merely to remain, thanks to his spies, always a jump ahead of any plots that might be hatched against him—saved him more than once during that winter. In the twilight world of intrigue and conspiracy, he seems to have been still quietly confident of being able to hold his own. And, before long, his enemies began to agree with him. By the first weeks of 1156 they abandoned their earlier tactics, and adopted instead those which had proved so successful to their fellow-vassals in Apulia. Withdrawing to Butera in the far south of the island, a group of barons under a certain Bartholomew of Garsiliato came out in open rebellion.

At first sight it did not seem a very serious uprising. The insurgents were few in number, their stronghold remote. Nevertheless, this was the first time since the original conquest nearly a century before that a group of Christian vassals on the island of Sicily itself had declared themselves publicly against their ruler; and Maio saw that the time had come for action. Experience on the mainland had shown just how rapidly such revolts could spread. The local population around Butera was largely Arab, and Muslim loyalties must be preserved at all costs. Moreover it looked as if the King, now almost recovered, would have some hard campaigning to do in Italy during the months to come. If so, it was essential that he should have his hands free.

William was still tired after his illness; and he had inherited in full measure his father's preference for diplomatic negotiation over armed force. Remaining himself in Palermo, he therefore sent an emissary to Butera in the person of Everard, Count of Squillace, to treat with the rebels and to ask them why they had taken so drastic a step. Within a few days Everard returned with the answer. They had acted, they claimed, not in defiance of their King but only against the Emir, who with his henchman the Archbishop was plotting to assassinate William and seize the throne for himself. All they asked was that the King should recognise the dangers that threatened him and rid himself of his evil counsellors before it was too late. They themselves would then lay down their arms and come to Palermo to implore his pardon.

William may have been lethargic, but he was not a fool; and he trusted Maio a great deal more than any Norman baron. He took no action, sent no acknowledgement to the rebels' message, and waited for their next move. He did not have to wait long. Towards the end of March, riots broke out in Palermo itself. That they were inspired and financed by the rebels was beyond a doubt; though the anger of the rioters was principally directed against Maio and Archbishop Hugh, there were also loud calls for the release from prison of Simon of Policastro, a young Count who had until recently been Asclettin's right-hand man in Campania but who had since been incarcerated by Maio without trial, on charges of suspected treason.

The appearance of the mob outside his royal palace roused William from his apathy. It was at last borne in on him that there could be no more peace, no more privacy, till the problem was settled. Now that his mind was made up, he moved quickly. To assuage the rioters, he gave orders for the immediate release of Simon of Policastro; then, with Maio at his side but accompanied also by Simon himself as mediator—for he still hoped to avoid bloodshed if possible—he led his army at top speed to Butera.

Perched on a high pinnacle of rock between two steep valleys, Butera was a perfect natural stronghold; and the insurgents were initially resolved to fight hard in its defence. That they did not do so was largely due to the generosity of William's terms and the persuasiveness of Count Simon. He convinced them that the King had no intention of dismissing his counsellors, in whom he had implicit trust, and one of whom was accompanying him at that moment; nevertheless he was disposed, in the circumstances, to show leniency to those who had taken up arms against him. Let them surrender at once; their lives and property would be spared, their liberty preserved; their only punishment would be exile from the Kingdom at the King's pleasure. The rebels accepted the offer. Butera was surrendered, and Sicily was at peace again.

'King William was a man,' wrote Hugo Falcandus, 'who found it hard ever to leave his palace; but once he was obliged to go forth, then—however disinclined to action he had been in the past—he would fling himself, not so much with courage as in a headstrong, even foolhardy spirit, in the face of all dangers.' As ever, Hugo's malice shows through; but it is still possible to detect some faint tinge of admiration in his words, as well as their underlying truth. Now that William had finally embarked on campaign and could look back on one victory already behind him, he had no intention of calling a halt. His health was restored, his blood was up. Spring had come, and spring was the season for campaigning. He was ready to tackle the mainland.

Army and navy met at Messina; this was to be a combined operation, in which the Greeks and their allies were to be attacked simultaneously from land and sea. To Messina also was summoned Asclettin, to explain his lamentable showing over the past months. Asclettin seems to have been an uninspired and somewhat colourless commander (not surprisingly, his previous post having been that of Archdeacon of Catania) and it may well be that other, more serious, charges had been laid against him. Certainly, at Messina, not a single voice was raised in his defence—not even that of Maio, whose creature he was and who had raised him to the Chancellorship in defiance of the King's own wishes. But whether traitor, coward or scapegoat, his goods were confiscated and he himself was cast into prison—where, several years later, he died.

William's treatment of Asclettin epitomised his whole attitude to the coming campaign. This would be in no sense a continuation, however intensified, of last year's pathetic performance. It would be a new operation, offensive rather than defensive, freshly conceived and planned; a blow struck by the combined military and naval power of the Sicilian Kingdom at the enemy's weakest point—the heel of Apulia. In the last days of April, the army crossed to the mainland and set off through Calabria, while the fleet sailed down through the straits and then turned north-east towards Brindisi.

For three weeks already Brindisi had been under siege. The Byzantines, relying as always on bribes and treachery, had managed to gain entrance to the outer town; but the royalist garrison in the citadel was putting up a determined resistance to them and their progress in Apulia had come, at least temporarily, to a stop. It was only the last of several reverses they had suffered in recent months. First, thanks to the increasing arrogance of Michael Palaeologus, they had gradually lost the confidence and goodwill of the Norman rebels until Robert of Loritello had ridden off in disgust. Then Palaeologus himself had died, after a short illness, in Bari. For all his overbearing ways he had been a brilliant leader in the field, and his death had been another blow to his countrymen. His successor John Ducas had eventually got the army moving again and had even achieved a reconciliation with the Count of Loritello; but the old confidence between the allies was never quite restored, the momentum of 1155 never quite regained.

And now news was brought to the Byzantine headquarters that the Sicilians were advancing in formidable numbers and strength, led by King William himself. Once again, the Greeks saw their fellow-fighters begin to fall away. The mercenaries chose, as mercenaries will, the moment of supreme crisis to demand impossible increases in their pay; meeting with a refusal, they disappeared *en masse*. Robert of Loritello deserted for the second time, followed by his own men and most of his compatriots. Ducas, left only with the few troops that he and Palaeologus had brought with them, plus those which had trickled over the Adriatic at various times during the past eight or nine months, found himself impossibly outnumbered.

It was the Sicilian fleet that arrived first, and for another day or two he was able to hold his own. The entrance to Brindisi harbour is by a narrow channel, barely a hundred yards across. Twelve centuries before, Julius Caesar had blocked it to Pompey's ships; and now Ducas, by placing the four vessels at his command in line abreast across its mouth and stationing well-armed detachments of footsoldiers along each bank, followed similar tactics. But when a day or two later William's army appeared to the west, Byzantine hopes were at an end. Attacked simultaneously from the land, the sea and the inner citadel, Ducas could not hope to hold the walls; he and his men were caught, in Cinnamus's words, as in a net.

The battle that followed was short and bloody; the Greek defeat was total. The Sicilian navy had occupied the little islands that circled the harbour entrance and effectively prevented any possibility of escape by sea. Ducas and the other Greek survivors were taken captive. On that one day, 28 May 1156, all that the Byzantines had achieved in Italy over the past year was wiped out as completely as if they had never come.

William treated his Greek prisoners according to the recognised canons of war; but to his own rebellious subjects he was pitiless. This was another lesson he had learnt from his father. Treason, particularly in Apulia where it was endemic, remained the one crime that could not be forgiven. Of those erstwhile insurgents who fell into his hands, only the luckiest were imprisoned. The rest were hanged, blinded or tied about with heavy weights and cast into the sea. It was the first time since his accession that the King had shown himself in Apulia, and he was resolved that the Apulians should not forget it. From Brindisi he moved to Bari. Less than a year before, the Bariots had readily thrown in their lot with the Byzantines; now they too were to pay the price for their disloyalty. Slowly they filed from their homes, to prostrate themselves at the feet of their ruler and to implore his mercy; but their prayers were unavailing. William merely pointed to the pile of rubble where until recently the citadel had stood. 'Just as you had no pity on my house,' he said, 'so now I shall have no pity on yours.' He gave them two clear days in which to salvage their belongings; on the third day Bari was destroyed. Only the Cathedral, the great church of St Nicholas and a few smaller religious buildings were left standing.

'And so it came about that of the mighty capital of Apulia, celebrated for its glory, powerful in its wealth, proud of the nobility of its citizens and admired for the beauty of its architecture by all who saw it, there now lies nothing but a heap of stones.' Thus Hugo Falcandus salutes, a trifle pompously, the city that was a city no more. The Jewish traveller Benjamin of Tudela, writing of it a year or two later, was more succinct: 'From Trani it is a day's journey to Bari, that great city which King William of Sicily destroyed. In consequence of its destruction, neither Jews nor Christians now dwell therein.'

It was the same old lesson—a lesson that the history of South Italy alone should have made self-evident, yet one that the princes of mediaeval Europe seemed to find impossible to absorb: that in distant lands, wherever there existed an organised native opposition, a temporary force could never achieve permanent conquest. Whirlwind campaigns were easy, especially when backed by bribes and generous subsidies to the local malcontents; the difficulties arose when it became necessary to consolidate and maintain the advantage gained. For such a purpose no amount of gold was of any avail. The Normans had succeeded in establishing themselves only because they had arrived as mercenaries, and remained as settlers; even then, the task had taken them the best part of a century. When they embarked on foreign adventures—such as the two invasions of the Byzantine Empire by Robert Guiscard and Bohemund—even they were doomed to failure. In North Africa, admittedly, they fared a little better—though the days of the North African Empire were numbered. But where South Italy was concerned there was no exception to the old rule. Its truth had been demonstrated, unpleasantly, to five of the eight men who had occupied the imperial throne of the West during the past century and a half—most recently to Lothair and Frederick Barbarossa himself. Now it was the turn of the Eastern Empire, and Manuel Comnenus.

But the Greeks and the Bariots were not the only sufferers. As William marched his exultant army westward across the Apennines, his approach caused a general panic among those vassals who had recently returned, in the wake of Pope Adrian, from exile. Some fled back precipitately to the papal court; others like the Count of Loritello escaped to the Abruzzi, where they might be able to carry on a sporadic guerrilla warfare for some time to come. Their leader, however, Prince Robert of Capua, was less fortunate. He too fled, hoping to reach the Papal State; but just as he was crossing the Garigliano into safety he was seized by Count Richard of Aquila and delivered up to the King. By this treachery—for he was one of the Prince of Capua's own vassals and had long been his companion in exile—Count Richard managed to save his own skin. Robert, on the other hand, was sent in chains to Palermo, where his eyes were put out by command of the King.

He was lucky to have escaped with his life—a life which for thirty years he had devoted to subversion and revolt. The chief vassal of the Kingdom, who, in one of his rare bursts of loyalty, had laid the royal crown on the head of Roger II more than a quarter of a century before, the richest and most powerful prince in the *Regno* after the King himself, he might have been the mainstay of the monarchy. He, if anyone, could have brought to the peninsula the stability and peace it so badly needed. But he chose the other course. Twice he had been forced to capitulate; twice he had been offered the King's pardon. It was enough. If the days of the last Prince of Capua ended in darkness, he had only himself to blame.

One lonely figure remained to face the coming storm. All Pope Adrian's allies were gone. Frederick Barbarossa was back in Germany; Michael Palaeologus was dead and his army annihilated; the Norman barons were either in prison or in hiding. Adrian himself, unable to return to Rome since Frederick's coronation, had spent the winter with his court at Benevento. Now, as the Sicilian army drew near, he sent most of his Cardinals away to Campania—mainly for their greater safety but also, perhaps, for another reason. He knew now that he would have to come to terms with William. Die-hard cardinals had wrecked too many potential agreements in the past; if he were to save anything from the disaster, he would need the utmost freedom to negotiate.

As soon as the vanguard of the Sicilian army appeared over the hills, the Pope sent forth his Chancellor, Roland of Siena, with two other cardinals who had remained at Benevento, to greet the King and bid him, in the name of St Peter, to cease from further hostilities.[1] They were received with due courtesy, and formal talks began. The going was not easy. The Sicilian negotiators, led

[1] William of Tyre suggests—and Chalandon, surprisingly, accepts his word without question—that the Sicilians were forced to lay siege to Benevento and starve the Pope out before he would have any dealings with them. For Adrian, anxious now to obtain the best terms he could, such a course would have been ridiculous; and William of Tyre is in any case contradicted by Boso, who was in the city at the time.

by Maio, Archbishop Hugh and Romuald of Salerno, were in a position of strength and drove a hard bargain, but the papal side fought every inch of the way. It was not until 18 June that agreement was finally reached.

The original manuscript of the Treaty of Benevento still exists in the Vatican Secret Archive. It was drawn up by one of Maio's *protégés*, a bright young notary called Matthew of Ajello,[1] and the prevailing mood of victorious exaltation, bordering even on truculence, shows through every line of his neat, crabbed handwriting. The King, we read, 'having defeated and put to flight those enemies, Greek and barbarian, who had infiltrated, not by strength but by treachery, into his Kingdom', had consented to abase himself before the Pope merely in order not to appear ungrateful before the Almighty, from whom he expected continued cooperation in the future. The political terms of the agreement are then set out in detail. William had obtained from the Pope everything he wanted—more than had ever been granted to his father or grandfather. His kingship was recognised not only over Sicily, Apulia, Calabria and the former Principality of Capua, together with Naples, Salerno, Amalfi and all that pertained to them; it was also now formally extended, for the first time, to that whole region of the northern Abruzzi and the Marches which King Roger's elder sons had claimed and fought for during the previous decade. An annual tribute was agreed for all these lands, amounting to the six hundred *schifati* in respect of Apulia and Calabria which had already been settled by Roger and Pope Innocent at Mignano seventeen years before, plus another four hundred for the new territories to the north.

In mainland ecclesiastical affairs William was prepared to be rather more accommodating. Henceforth all disputes within the Church might be submitted to Rome for arbitration; the Pope's consent would be sought for all transfers; he would have free right of consecration and might send legates at will into the *Regno* so long as they did not impose too heavy a burden on the local churches. But where Sicily was concerned, nearly all the King's traditional privileges were preserved. Adrian was obliged to confirm the Apostolic

---

[1] I use the name by which he is generally known. In fact he was from Salerno; Ajello was the county later bestowed on his son by King Tancred.

Legateship, renouncing the right to send special envoys or to hear appeals. He might summon Sicilian clerics to Rome, but they could not obey without first obtaining the King's permission. Ecclesiastical elections were subject to a similar control. Theoretically they were the responsibility of the clergy, proceeding by secret ballot; but they too could be vetoed by the King if the chosen candidate did not meet with his approval.

The instrument by which the Pope accepted these conditions was drafted in equally flowery terms. It is addressed to

William, glorious King of Sicily and dearest son in Christ, most brilliant in wealth and achievement among all the Kings and eminent men of the age, the glory of whose name is borne to the uttermost limits of the earth by the firmness of your justice, the peace which you have restored to your subjects, and the fear which your great deeds have instilled into the hearts of all the enemies of Christ's name.

Even when allowance is made for the traditional literary hyperbole of the time, it is hard to imagine Adrian putting his signature to such a document without a wince of humiliation. He had been Pope only eighteen months, but already he had learnt the bitterness of desertion, betrayal and exile; and even his shoulders were beginning to bow. He appears now in a very different light from that in which we saw him when he placed Rome under an interdict or pitted his will against that of Frederick Barbarossa just twelve short months before.

It was in the church of S. Marciano, on the banks of the river Calore just outside Benevento, that William received at the papal hands the three pennoned lances by which he was invested with his chief dominions—the Kingdom of Sicily first, next the Duchy of Apulia and finally the Principality of Capua. The investitures were sealed by the Kiss of Peace; then, after bestowing appropriate gifts of gold, silver and precious silks on the Pope and all his retinue, he rode back by slow stages through Naples[1] to Salerno. In July he

---

[1] When he ordered the building of the Castel Capuano (now the Law Courts) and, by enlarging a small island just off the shore, laid the foundation for the future Castel dell'Ovo.

took ship for Sicily, where the ringleaders of the insurrection who had fallen into his hands were now awaiting sentence. One of the captives, Count Geoffrey of Montescaglioso, who had played a prominent part in both the Sicilian and the Apulian revolts, was blinded; many more were imprisoned, including the King's two young nephews William and Tancred, sons of Duke Roger of Apulia; others, if we are to believe Falcandus, were cast into pits full of vipers, while wives and daughters were sent to the harems or forced into prostitution. But there were rewards, too, for those who had given loyal service—in particular Maio's brother Stephen and his Sicilian brother-in-law Simon, the royal seneschal, who were both appointed master captains of Apulia. With his two closest relatives in positions of such authority, the Emir of Emirs thus became more powerful than ever; while William for his part had demonstrated, in a manner that could not possibly be misunderstood, his continuing trust in his chief minister and his contempt for the opinions of those who dared to set themselves up against him.

Later, he would have cause to regret this arrogance. For the moment, however, he was determined to enjoy his triumph, and the humiliation of his enemies, to the full. Not without reason had he caused to be inscribed, around the royal cypher with which the Treaty of Benevento was sealed, the words which his grandfather, the Great Count, had had engraved on his sword in 1063, after the battle of Cerami:

DEXTERA DOMINI FECIT VIRTUTEM;
DEXTERA DOMINI EXALTAVIT ME.[1]

[1] The right hand of God gave me courage;
The right hand of God raised me up.

II

REALIGNMENTS

For I call on the Lord Adrian to witness than no one is more miserable than the Roman Pontiff, nor is any condition more wretched than his. . . . He maintains that the papal throne is studded with thorns, that his mantle bristles with needles so sharp that it oppresses and weighs down the broadest shoulders . . . and that had he not feared to go against the will of God he would never have left his native England.

John of Salisbury, Policraticus, VIII, xxiii

THE news of the Apulian *débâcle* was received with horror in Constantinople. The unfortunate Ducas, unable to defend himself from his Palermo prison, made a convenient scapegoat; but though it was he who took much of the blame the ultimate responsibility was clearly the Emperor's, and Manuel was determined to recover his honour. This recovery was made even more necessary the following summer, when a Sicilian fleet of a hundred and sixty-four ships, commanded by Maio's brother Stephen—now promoted Admiral— and carrying nearly ten thousand men, swooped down on the prosperous island of Euboea, sacking and pillaging all the villages and towns along its coasts. From there they sailed on to Almira on the Gulf of Volos, which received similar treatment; and then, if we are to believe Nicetas Choniates, sped up the Hellespont and through the Marmara to Constantinople—where a hail of silver-tipped arrows was loosed upon the imperial palace of Blachernae.[1]

[1] This story bears such a resemblance to that of George of Antioch's similar raid in 1149 that several scholars have suggested that Nicetas is confusing the two. He may be; but surely there is no reason why Stephen should not have been tempted to repeat his predecessor's famous exploit, nor why his sailors should not have felt equally quiver-happy under the palace walls. An odder feature of

And so, some time during the summer of 1157, Manuel Comnenus sent a new emissary to Italy—Alexis, the brilliant young son
of his Grand Domestic, Axuch. His ostensible orders were much the
same as those given to Michael Palaeologus—to make contact with
such rebel barons as were still at liberty, hire mercenaries for a new
campaign along the coast, and generally stir up as much disaffection
and discord as he could. But he had also been entrusted by his
Emperor with a second task; to establish secret contact with Maio and
discuss terms for a peace. Until that peace was concluded there could
be no cessation of hostilities; the fiercer the fighting, the more favourable to Constantinople William's conditions were likely to be. For
a year already, however, it had been growing ever clearer to Manuel
Comnenus that the time had come for a radical change in his foreign
policy. He now knew that he could never hope to reconquer Apulia by
force of arms. His best hope lay in close ties with the Pope, and in
trying to play him off against Barbarossa; and since the Treaty of
Benevento this must inevitably involve some accommodation with
the King of Sicily.

Alexis discharged both parts of his mission with equal success.
Within a few months of his arrival he had Robert of Loritello again
ravaging Sicilian territory in the north and Andrew of Rupecanina
driving down through the Capuan lands and seriously threatening
Monte Cassino beneath which, in January 1158, he even defeated a
royalist army in pitched battle. Meanwhile, although his support
for these operations debarred him from undertaking peace talks in
person, he was able to call on the services of the two most distinguished of the Greeks who were still held captive in Palermo, John
Ducas and Alexius Bryennius; and through their mediation, some
time in the early spring, a secret agreement was concluded. Alexis,
having fooled his Apulian supporters into thinking that he was
going to fetch more men and supplies, left them in the lurch and

this second account, and one which no other commentator seems to have raised,
is the reference by name to Blachernae. This palace stood at the north-west
corner of the city; to have reached it, the Sicilians would have had either to
launch a land expedition of several miles along the well-defended land walls, or
to sail right up the Golden Horn and then scale a steep hill. Here Nicetas surely
nods; their target is much more likely to have been the old palace of the Emperors
on the Marmara, near Seraglio Point.

slipped off to Constantinople; William, though still understandably suspicious of Byzantine motives, sent off a diplomatic mission to Manuel[1] and returned all his Greek prisoners—except the indispensable ladies from the *Tiraz*; and the Counts of Loritello and Rupecanina, suddenly bereft of funds, had no course but to abandon their new conquests and to ride off in search of another champion.

They found one in Frederick Barbarossa.

*   *   *   *   *

Frederick's relations with the Eastern Empire had deteriorated sharply during the last three years. He had always mistrusted the Greeks; and reports of the Apulian campaign, which he saw as a typically underhand attempt on their part to slip in as soon as his back was turned with the object of snatching away territories which were rightfully his, had alarmed and infuriated him. To add insult to injury, they had set up their headquarters at Ancona, a city which lay under direct imperial control; and had even had the audacity, if reports were true, to forge letters purporting to issue from his chancery, in order to obtain the submission of certain strategic towns. His initial reaction was to break off all relations with Manuel. When, in June 1156, an embassy arrived from Constantinople to discuss his projected marriage to a Byzantine princess (he had divorced his first wife, in somewhat discreditable circumstances, three years before) he refused even to receive it—marrying instead, after the shortest possible preliminaries, the rich and exceedingly attractive Beatrice of Upper Burgundy. Later, when he heard of the Greek defeat at Brindisi, he had relented to the point of resuming formal contacts with his brother-Emperor; but the damage was done and both of them knew it.

Frederick was equally angry with the Pope. Had not Adrian given him a personal undertaking not to enter into any private

---

[1] At the head of this mission went William's sometime tutor and close friend, Henry Aristippus. He returned with a valuable present from the Emperor to the King—a Greek manuscript of Ptolemy's *Almagest*. This tremendous work, a synthesis of all the discoveries and conclusions of Greek astronomers since the science was born, was hitherto known in the West, if at all, only through Arabic translations.

communications with either the Eastern Emperor or the King of Sicily? Was it not a fact, none the less, that he was in constant correspondence with the one, while with the other he had actually signed a treaty of peace and friendship—a treaty, moreover, by which he not only recognised William's claim to a spurious crown but, in ecclesiastical affairs, allowed him privileges more far-reaching even than those enjoyed by the Emperor himself? By what right, in any case, did Adrian so graciously confer imperial territories on others? Did the Empire count for nothing in his eyes? Was there no limit to papal arrogance?

It was not long before his worst suspicions were confirmed. In October 1157 he held an imperial Diet at Besançon. The location had been carefully selected; Besançon was the capital of Upper Burgundy—later to be known as the Franche-Comté—and he was anxious that no effort should be spared to impress his wife's family and his own newly-acquired subjects with the power and magnificence of his Empire. Ambassadors converged on the town from all sides, from France and Italy, from Spain and England—and, of course, from the Pope. The effect of all Frederick's careful arrangements was, however, slightly spoilt when, in the presence of the assembled company, the papal legates read out the letter they had brought with them from their master. Instead of the customary greetings and congratulations that everyone had expected, the Pope had chosen this of all moments to deliver himself of a strongly-worded complaint. It appeared that some time previously the aged Archbishop of Lund, while travelling through imperial territory, had been set upon by bandits, robbed of all he possessed and held to ransom. Such an outrage was in itself serious enough; but, the Pope went on, it was further aggravated by the fact that although the Emperor had already been furnished with full details of all that had occurred, he appeared as yet to have taken no steps to bring to justice those responsible. Turning to more general topics, Adrian began recalling his past favours to the Emperor—reminding him in particular of his coronation at papal hands and adding, more than a little patronisingly, that he hoped at some future date to bestow still further benefices upon him.

Whether the Pope was deliberately intending to assert his feudal overlordship over the Emperor we shall never know. Unfortunately, however, the two words he used, *conferre* and *beneficia,* were both technical terms used in describing the grant of a fief by a suzerain to his vassal. This was more than Frederick could bear. If the letter implied, as it appeared to imply, that he held the Holy Roman Empire by courtesy of the Pope in the same way as any petty baron might hold a few fields in the Campagna, there could be no further dealings between them. The assembled German princes shared his indignation; and when Cardinal Roland, the papal chancellor, blandly replied by enquiring from whom Frederick did hold the Empire if not from the Pope, there was general uproar. Otto of Wittelsbach, Count Palatine of Bavaria, rushed forward, his hand on his sword; only the rapid intervention of the Emperor himself prevented an incident compared with which the misfortunes of the Archbishop of Lund would have seemed trivial indeed. When Adrian heard what had happened he wrote Frederick another letter, this time in rather more soothing terms, protesting that his words had been misinterpreted; and the Emperor accepted his explanation. It is unlikely that he really believed it, but he had no wish for an open breach with the Papacy at a moment when he was about to launch the greatest military operation he had yet undertaken—the subjugation of Lombardy.

The *bagarre* at Besançon, as anyone could have seen, was merely a symptom of a far deeper rift between Pope and Emperor—one which no amount of diplomatic drafting could ever hope to bridge. The days when it had been realistic to speak of the two swords of Christendom were gone—gone since Gregory VII and Henry IV had hurled depositions and anathemas at each other nearly a hundred years before. Never since that time had their respective successors been able to look upon themselves as two different sides of the same coin. Each must now claim the supremacy, and defend it as necessary against the other. When this involved the confrontation of characters as strong as those of Adrian and Frederick, flash-point could never be far off. Yet the root of the trouble lay less in their personalities than in the institutions they represented. While the two of them lived, relations between them—exacerbated by a host of petty slights both real and imagined—became even more strained; but it was only after their deaths that the conflict was to emerge into open war.

If, however, Frederick had put the doctrine of the two swords behind him, there was another eleventh-century concept of Empire which he still stubbornly refused to outgrow. During his first passage through North Italy on the way to his coronation he had been appalled by the spirit of independence and freedom among the Lombard towns, their blatant republicanism and their lack of any respect for his authority. Pressed for time and impatient for the imperial crown, he had delayed there only long enough to make his presence felt and to leave the smoking ruins of Tortona as a mark of his displeasure. Since then he had had plenty of opportunities, notably in Rome itself, to gauge the strength of Italian communal feeling; but he still could not—or would not—understand. For him the Lombards were insubordinate; that was all there was to it. In July 1158, accompanied by the King of Bohemia and a huge army, he crossed the Alps to teach them a lesson.

There is, fortunately, no need for us to follow in any detail the fortunes of Frederick Barbarossa in Lombardy. A few of the towns had remained loyal to him and showed it; a few seized the opportunity offered by the presence of the imperial forces to turn them against their enemies or commercial rivals; others bowed, reed-like, before the storm with every intention of springing up again the moment it was past; one or two even fought magnificently back. But for us the interest of the campaign lies not in the conduct of the individual towns so much as in its effect on that latest and most unexpected newcomer to the Italian scene—the Sicilian-Papal entente.

The Treaty of Benevento proved to be of immeasurably greater significance than either William or Adrian could have known at the time. For the Papacy it inaugurated a new political approach to European problems—one which it was to follow to its own considerable advantage for the next twenty years. Adrian himself, though for some time afterwards he remained strangely hesitant as if unable to adjust to the new pattern, was at last brought to accept what he must always have suspected—that the Emperor was not so much a friend with whom he might occasionally quarrel as an enemy with whom, somehow, he had to live. His concordat with William gave him a powerful new ally and enabled him to adopt a firmer attitude in his dealings with Frederick than could ever otherwise have been possible—as the Besançon letter bears witness. It was a tendency that Maio and William were quick to encourage.

In papal circles, so radical a change in policy was bound to meet with opposition at first. Many leading members of the Curia— those, presumably, whom Adrian sent away to Campania before beginning the negotiations—still clung to their imperialist, anti-Sicilian opinions; and the news of the terms agreed had apparently caused almost as much consternation in the Sacred College as in the imperial court. Gradually, however, in the months that followed, opinion swung round in William's favour. There were several reasons. Barbarossa's arrogance was one, as shown at Besançon and confirmed by several other incidents before and since. Besides, the Sicilian alliance was now a *fait accompli*; it was useless to oppose it any longer. William, for his part, seemed sincere enough. On the Pope's recommendation, he had made his peace with Constantinople. He was rich, he was powerful; and, as several of Their Eminences could—if they wished—have testified, he was also generous.

And now, as Frederick Barbarossa set out to sack and ravage the Lombard cities, a great wave of revulsion against the Empire swept down through Italy. With it, too, there was an element of terror. When the Emperor had finished with Lombardy, what was to prevent him from continuing to Tuscany, Umbria, even to Rome itself? Soon, too, Frederick's victims began to appear—the widows and fatherless children, the refugees from the burning towns and devastated villages, the exiled mayors and magistrates; and, inevitably, the conspirators. All were looking, in their separate ways, for a centre of resistance, for some strong power able to focus their aspirations and ideals; liberty against domination, republicanism against imperialism, Italian against Teuton. And in the alliance forged between an English Pope and a Norman King they found it.

Throughout 1158, Maio had been working to strengthen support

for Sicily within the papal Curia—with the invaluable help of
Cardinal Roland, Adrian's Chancellor and most trusted associate,
who had been the chief architect and was now one of the principal
protagonists of the Norman alliance. Together they did their work
well. In the spring of 1159 there occurred the first great counter-
thrust against Frederick that can be directly ascribed to papal-
Sicilian instigation. Milan suddenly threw off the imperial authority,
and for the next three years the Milanese stoutly defied all the
Emperor's efforts to bring them to heel. The following August,
representatives of Milan, Crema, Piacenza and Brescia met the Pope
at Anagni, a little town situated conveniently near the frontier of
the *Regno*. And there, in the presence of envoys from King William—
Maio may easily have been there himself—was sworn the initial
pact that was to become the nucleus of the great Lombard League.
The towns promised that they would have no dealings with the
common enemy without papal consent, while the Pope undertook
to excommunicate the Emperor after the usual period of forty days.
Finally it was agreed by the assembled cardinals that on Adrian's
death his successor should be elected only from those present at
the conference.

Perhaps it was obvious already that the Pope had not long to live.
While still at Anagni he was stricken by a sudden angina, from
which he never recovered. He died in the evening of 1 September
1159. His body was taken to Rome, and was laid in the undistinguished third-century sarcophagus in which it still rests and which
can still be seen in the crypt of St Peter's. During the course of the
demolition of the old basilica in 1607 it was opened; the body of
the only English Pope was found entire, dressed in a chasuble of
dark-coloured silk. It was described by the archaeologist Grimaldi
as being that of 'an undersized man, wearing Turkish slippers on
his feet and, on his hand, a ring with a large emerald'.

Adrian's pontificate is hard to assess. To hail him as the greatest
Pope since Urban II is not to say very much; he certainly towers
above the string of mediocrities who occupied the throne of St
Peter during the first half of the century, just as he himself is overshadowed by his magnificent successor. Yet it remains difficult to
see how Gregorovius could have written that his nature was always

Palermo: S. Cataldo (tower of the Martorana at left)

Palermo, S. Cataldo: interior

SS. Trinità di Délia, near Castelvetrano

Palermo, Royal Palace: the Pisan Tower

'as firm and as unyielding as the granite of his tomb'. In the early days it certainly seemed so; but his complete *volte-face* after Benevento, however ultimately beneficial to papal interests, was imposed upon him by force of circumstances, and from that time on he seems to have lost much of the incisiveness that marked his early career. He left the Papacy stronger and more generally respected than he found it, but much of this success was due to its identification with the Lombard League—for which, in turn, he had the diplomacy of Maio of Bari and the wise statesmanship of Cardinal Roland to thank. And he failed utterly to subdue the Roman Senate.

He was Pope for less than five years; but those years were hard and vital for the Papacy, and the strain told on him. Before long his health had begun to fail, and with it his morale. He confided to his compatriot John of Salisbury, who knew him well, that the burden of the Papacy had now become greater than he could bear, and that he often wished that he had never left England. He died, as many Popes had died before him, an embittered exile; and when death came to him, he welcomed it as a friend.

Thus, in the three years separating the Treaty of Benevento from the death of Pope Adrian IV, a curious change occurs in the relative position of King William of Sicily on the European stage. The King himself remains at the still centre of this change. His Sicilian policies, framed and executed by Maio of Bari, continued constant, based as they were on the twin principles of friendship with the Papacy and opposition to the Western Empire. Never did he have any quarrel with the city-states or towns of North Italy, except when they had been bribed or otherwise cajoled into collaboration with his enemies. But, all around him, alignments were shifting. The Papacy, brought to its knees at Benevento, rediscovered a fact that its history over the past hundred years should have made self-evident—that its only hope of survival as a potent political force lay in close alliance with Norman Sicily; Frederick Barbarossa, impressed despite himself by the speed and completeness of William's victories over the Byzantines in Apulia and looking on him with undiminished hatred but new respect, decided on the indefinite postponement of his own punitive expedition into the *Regno*; and, as the supreme paradox, the Lombard towns began to see in the Sicilian monarchy—entrenched in feudalism and more absolutist by far than the Western Empire or any other state of Western Europe— the stalwart defender of their republican ideals, hailing its King as a champion of civic liberty almost before the dust had settled on the ruins of Bari.

But while William and Maio worked for the downfall of one Empire, they were themselves in the process of losing another. North Africa was rapidly slipping away. The rot had begun in the winter of 1155–56, when Sicilian fortunes were at their lowest. At that time the Greeks were sweeping unchecked through Apulia. The Prince of Capua and his followers were seizing back their old patrimonies in Campania and elsewhere. In Sicily itself another band of insurgents was defying the central government from the heights of Butera. Meanwhile there was, living quietly in the capital, an old Sheikh from North Africa named Abu al-Hassan al-Furriani. Some years before, he had been appointed by King Roger as governor of his own city of Sfax, but being already advanced in years he had soon retired in favour of his son, Omar, in pledge of whose good conduct he had himself gone as a voluntary hostage to Palermo. Now, seeing the Kingdom menaced on three fronts and rightly surmising that it could not possibly fight back on a fourth, he wrote secretly to his son proposing an immediate uprising against the Sicilians. He was fully aware, he said, that he himself would probably pay for it with his life, but that was of no great moment; he was an old man, and for such a cause he would be happy to die.

Omar did as he was bid. On 25 February 1156 the native population of Sfax rose up and massacred every Christian in the city. William, hearing the news, at once sent over an ambassador to demand the governor's surrender; if he did not give himself up immediately, his father's life would be forfeit. On his arrival, however, the ambassador was stopped at the gates; and the next morning he was met by a long funeral procession following a coffin. With it came a message from Omar. It read: 'He who is being buried today is my father. I remain in my palace to mourn his death. Do with him as you will.' The ambassador returned to Palermo to report, and old

Abu al-Hassan, praising Allah with his last breath, was led to the gallows on the banks of the Oreto and hanged.[1]

But the collapse of William's North African Empire had begun. The islands of Djerba and Kerkenna followed where Sfax had led, and some time during the year 553 of the Hegira—between 2 February 1158 and 22 January 1159—the signal was given for revolt in Tripoli itself. By the middle of 1159 only Mahdia, with its suburb of Zawila, was left in Sicilian hands. Thither had flocked all William's remaining Christian subjects in Africa, arriving in such numbers that a new Archbishop had to be installed to minister to them all. His ministry was short-lived. Already three years previously the local Muslims had made one attempt to take over the city, failing only because of the opportune arrival of a Sicilian fleet; now the Almohads themselves appeared in strength under their leader Abd al-Moumen firmly resolved to eradicate the last traces of Christian domination from the continent. Mahdia was ringed by land and sea, and on 20 July the siege began.

For the first few weeks, morale in the beleaguered city remained high. There was a garrison of three thousand men, provisions were plentiful and no one doubted that a fleet would soon be on its way from Palermo with relief. Sure enough, on 8 September there it was—no less than a hundred and sixty Sicilian vessels, hastily recalled from a raiding expedition to the Balearics, under the command—surprisingly, in the circumstances—of King William's chief eunuch, a converted Muslim from Djerba who had been baptised in the name of Peter. The situation appeared to be saved; Abd al-Moumen, horrified at the size of the navy now bearing down upon him, even ordered sixty of his own ships to be beached so that, if the forthcoming battle went against him, he and his men should at least have some means of escape.

He need not have worried. Hardly, it seems, had battle been joined outside the harbour mouth when Peter's flagship suddenly turned about and made with all speed for the open sea; and the others followed. The Almohads, taking full advantage of their good

---

[1] This story is told by no less than three of the principal Arab sources for Norman Sicily—Ibn al-Athir, At-Tigani and Ibn Khaldun, the last two writing as late as the fourteenth century. The heroism of the two Al-Furriani was not, it seems, quickly forgotten.

fortune, set off in pursuit and captured seven or eight of the Sicilian vessels before returning jubilantly to port.

What had happened? Hugo Falcandus, who can always be trusted to interpret everyone's actions in the unkindest possible light, has no doubts on the matter. Peter, he points out, was, 'like all the eunuchs of the palace, only in name and dress a Christian, and a Saracen at heart'. It followed that his retreat must have been due not to incapacity or cowardice, but to treachery pure and simple. The other chroniclers are more charitable; they make no suggestion of any betrayal, and at-Tigani even quotes an eye-witness account by a certain Ibn Saddad, according to whom the Sicilian fleet had been scattered by a gale and was attacked by the Muslims before it had time to reform. This, or some similar catastrophe, seems to have been the true explanation; for nowhere do we find any record of disciplinary action taken against Peter on his return to Palermo. On the contrary, he had a long and distinguished political career before him. Clearly he was no George of Antioch; but there is no evidence, apart from Falcandus's unsupported testimony, that he acted with dishonour.

The same, alas, cannot be said for the Sicilian government. The garrison held out bravely for another six months, confidently awaiting another relief expedition; none came. At last, when supplies were running so low that the men had begun eating their horses, they sent Abd al-Moumen an offer. Let him allow one or two of their number to go to Palermo and ascertain, once and for all, whether any further help could be expected; if the answer was negative, the garrison commander would surrender the city forthwith. The request was granted. The emissaries left, and soon afterwards returned with the sad and, to the Christian community of Mahdia, almost unbelievable news: in Palermo, North Africa was already considered lost. It had quite simply been written off. On 11 January 1160 Mahdia surrendered. The garrison were given safe conduct, with arms and baggage, back to Sicily.

Falcandus, it is hardly necessary to add, suggests that the Almohad leader was in contact with the palace eunuchs in Palermo and already knew in advance of William's decision. This theory, like so many others from the same pen, can probably be discounted; but there remains another more important and more intriguing question. Why did William and Maio let North Africa go so easily? In their European policy they had proved—once the King had shaken off his initial inertia—vigorous, energetic and imaginative. How could they now watch, impassively, while the North African Empire crumbled before their eyes? It was not, after all, only during the siege of Mahdia that this apathy had come upon them; there indeed they had made at least some attempt to fight back. But what of Sfax and Djerba, of Kerkenna and Tripoli? In none of these places had there been more than a token resistance, if that. In 1156, admittedly, the Sicilian forces were fully extended on other, more important fronts; but by 1160 there were no enemies to occupy them elsewhere, and still there was no sign of any counter-offensive—any move, even, military or diplomatic—to regain their former possessions. What held them back?

These questions also occurred to William's subjects at home, many of whom lost no time in blaming Maio for the loss of the overseas empire; and the Emir of Emirs became more unpopular than ever. But in fact, when we look back over these years, his apparently feeble attitude is shown in its proper light and becomes comprehensible. He was playing for higher stakes. By now the pattern of Italian politics had become infinitely more complex and more challenging than in the days of Roger II and George of Antioch, when the African territories had been conquered. Suddenly there had appeared a chance of gaining the moral leadership of all Italy in its emerging struggle against German imperial power; and moral leadership today could mean political leadership tomorrow.

To achieve it, however, Sicily must have freedom of action. With two Empires, a Papacy and an endless number of independent and semi-independent city-states to deal with, to say nothing of an endemic revolutionary situation within her own borders, she could not afford to indulge in enterprises and adventures outside her logical sphere of influence. And, as Maio was intelligent enough to understand, North Africa was well outside. To recover it would mean not just the despatch of an expeditionary force, the siege and capture of a city or two. It would mean the forcible subjection of a whole people and the breaking of a great power—for the Almohads, with an Empire which already extended from the Atlantic to the frontiers of Egypt and from Andalusia to the southern limits of the Sahara, could have held their own against virtually any European army or armies that might have been thrown into the field against them.

The old principle still held good—expeditionary forces could make conquests, but they could not hold them. The fact had been proved time and time again; to it, Sicily owed her continued existence as a nation. Those who forgot it paid dearly for their forgetfulness. Maio of Bari had no intention of falling into the same error himself.

12

MURDER

This Maio was a very monster; indeed, it would be impossible to find vermin more loathsome, more pernicious or more damaging to the Kingdom. His character was capable of any baseness, and his eloquence was equal to his character. Great was his facility for pretence or dissimulation at will. He was, in addition, much given to debauchery, for ever seeking to bring noble matrons and virgins to his bed; the more unstained their virtue, the more ardently did he strive to possess them.

Hugo Falcandus

WILLIAM had slipped back into his old ways. It might have been expected that his crushing defeat of the Byzantines, and the three ensuing years of intense diplomatic activity during which his star rose higher and higher in the European firmament, would have given him a taste for politics, or at least have tempted him to prove himself as gifted a statesman as he had a general. They did neither. No sooner had he returned to Sicily in July 1156 and passed sentence on those who had taken up arms against him than he once more abandoned himself to a life of pleasure. The old attractions of palace and park, of bower and bedchamber, were too strong. For the next six years he never once visited the mainland, seldom even setting foot outside Palermo and its immediate neighbourhood. The handling of state affairs, both domestic and foreign, he placed as before in the capable hands of Maio of Bari.

Maio's power was now at its zenith. Not only was this Apulian merchant's son the effective ruler of the Kingdom; he was rapidly becoming, thanks to the success of his foreign policies, one of the most influential statesmen in Europe.[1] The baronial party, both on the mainland and in Sicily, resented him more than ever. More than ever they found themselves outcasts, obliged to stand impotently by while the government of the Kingdom became, as they saw it, the exclusive preserve of two separate groups, the one detested, the other despised: first, the Emir's family and henchmen, men like Stephen and Simon, the Master Captains in Apulia; like Archbishop Hugh of Palermo, or like the young Salernitan notary Matthew of Ajello who had drafted the Treaty of Benevento and was obviously being groomed by Maio as his eventual successor; second, the palace eunuchs—almost all of them, like that Peter who had cut such a sorry figure against the Almohad fleet, being baptised Saracens and thus politically as well as physically suspect in the eyes of their enemies.

It was small wonder, in such conditions, that the air of Palermo was heavy with rumours. Men whispered that the Emir was scheming to seize the crown for himself—indeed that he had already appropriated several items of the regalia, which he had been showing off to his friends. He had had no difficulty in laying his hands on such treasures; they were passed to him by the Queen, whose infatuation for him was well known. Others made even more scandalous assertions—that he had revived his plans to do away with the King, and that he had already bribed the Pope, through the agency of Matthew of Ajello, to give him his blessing as William's successor.

Where rumours were so rife, conspiracies were bound to follow. In Palermo, Maio's ubiquitous agents and informers were usually able to nip them in the bud; but the mainland provided would-be plotters with opportunities in plenty and here, some time towards the end of 1159, a group of dissatisfied nobles evolved a scheme to

[1] He was also beginning to build the church of S. Cataldo, immediately west of the Martorana (Plate 13). With its three high cupolas and honeycomb windows, this church looks, from the outside, as Islamic as S. Giovanni degli Eremiti. Like S. Giovanni, too, its interior is now stripped of all decoration—though the floor and the altar are both original and quietly remarkable in their way (Plate 14). S. Cataldo is, incidentally—with the possible exception of the lovely little SS. Trinità di Delia just outside Castelvetrano—the last Norman Sicilian church in which the Arabic influence is apparent (Plate 15). Henceforth every new Latin church to be built also looked like one.

rid Sicily for ever of the Emir and his whole hated clan. Surprisingly, this group seems not to have included William's own two principal enemies to date; Robert of Loritello and Andrew of Rupecanina were certainly in sympathy with their aims, but preferred to devote their energies to more active warfare along the northern borders of the *Regno*. The leaders of the present conspiracy were, on the whole, less notable figures—barons of the second rank like Richard of Aquila, Roger of Acerra and Bohemund of Tarsia, Count of Manopello. Among them, however, one name stands out, a name we shall meet on several occasions in the story of the coming years—Gilbert, Queen Margaret's cousin, who had recently arrived at court and been sent almost at once to South Italy with the title of Count of Gravina.

Unlike most of the previous conspiracies that had so plagued the peninsula for a century and more, this one had as its object not insurrection but murder. Maio of Bari was to be assassinated. But by whom? There could be no possibility of entrusting the task to hired killers; the Emir was too important, his spies too well-informed. The blow must be struck by one of the parties to the plot, one who knew Maio and could approach him easily, without arousing his suspicions. Thus the choice fell on a young aristocrat, Matthew Bonnellus.

Though Bonnellus bore no title and was therefore not, strictly speaking, a member of the nobility, he came from one of the oldest Norman families in the South. He was brave, he was handsome and, with his vast estates on both sides of the straits of Messina, he was also extremely rich. It had thus been no surprise to anyone when Maio—who, for all his mistrust of the aristocracy, was like everyone in those days something of a snob and who certainly knew a good *parti* when he saw one—had given him preferment at the court and had singled him out as a prospective son-in-law. Shortly afterwards, reports of baronial unrest had arrived from Calabria; and Bonnellus, who had important family connections in the region, had been the obvious emissary to send on a mission of diplomatic pacification. It was, arguably, the greatest mistake of Maio's career. Loving the young man, as Falcandus puts it, like his own son, he seems to have seriously overestimated his intelligence and his fundamental reliability. Once on the mainland, Bonnellus proved unable to resist the pressures which were put on him, notably those exerted by the ravishingly beautiful Countess Clementia of Catanzaro. Within days he too was on the side of the conspirators, sworn to destroy his benefactor; in return for which service he was promised the hand in marriage not of a little Bariot *bourgeoise* but of Clementia herself, the richest and most influential heiress in Calabria.[1]

One of the dangers of being a dictator—as Maio by now effectively was—is that it becomes progressively harder to believe unpalatable truths. Repeated warnings from his brother Stephen had no effect on him. At last he was presented with incontrovertible evidence of the plot, complete with the names of all the principal conspirators with Matthew Bonnellus at the head of the list; but even then the arrival of a single letter from Matthew, announcing that his mission had been successfully completed and asking, as a reward, that his longed-for marriage to Maio's daughter should be brought forward in date, was enough to soothe away all the latter's fears. Reassured, he flung himself into arrangements for the wedding; while his intended son-in-law, now back in Palermo, quietly busied himself with a very different set of plans.

On St Martin's Eve, 10 November 1160, he was ready. And, writes Falcandus,

... as the sun went down and the twilight began to fall, you might have seen the whole city alive with vague and sudden rumours, with the citizens moving about hither and thither in groups, anxiously enquiring of each other what was that about to happen that was causing such consternation. Others, with their heads bowed but their ears ever alert for news, were meeting together in the squares and the piazzas, all expressing contradictory opinions. Most of them seemed to think that the King was coming that night, at

[1] At this point in the story, Chalandon falls victim to one of his mercifully rare flights of romantic imagination. He suggests that Matthew Bonnellus's mission to Calabria was arranged by Maio in order to put a stop to the love affair he was already having with the Countess Clementia—whom he describes as the natural daughter of Roger II—in Palermo. As his authority for this story he cites Falcandus; but Falcandus says no such thing. It is in fact highly improbable that Matthew ever met Clementia in Palermo, since she lived permanently in Calabria. Neither is there any reason to doubt her being the perfectly legitimate daughter of Count Raymond of Catanzaro.

Maio's instigation, to the Archbishop's palace, and that there, in that very street, he was to be slain.

They were wrong only in the choice of victim; it was not William but his Emir of Emirs who was calling on Archbishop Hugh that night, and who would not live to see the morning. Whether Hugh was himself an accomplice we cannot tell; Falcandus of course maintains that he was. In any case, soon after Maio's arrival, Matthew Bonnellus silently stationed his men along the Via Coperta, which connected the Archbishop's palace with the Emir's own house. He himself took up a position near the Porta S. Agata, where the street suddenly narrowed before splitting into three. There, in the shadows, he settled down to wait.

At length the palace doors opened and Maio emerged. He was deep in conversation with the Archbishop of Messina and followed by a small escort. Still unconscious of the enemies that surrounded them, they began to move down the Via Coperta; but before they had reached the Porta S. Agata they were accosted by two frightened figures—the notary Matthew of Ajello and the chamberlain Adenulf, who had somehow discovered what was afoot and had hastened to warn their master of the danger. Maio stopped in his tracks and gave orders that Bonnellus should be brought to him at once; but he was too late. The assassin, hearing his name called, leaped from his hiding-place and flung himself forward with drawn sword.

It was all over quite quickly. Maio did his best to defend himself, but his escort had already melted away. He was surrounded and struck down; and his attackers disappeared into the night. Matthew the notary, who had already risked his life to avert the ambush, was also caught in the *mêlée*; gravely wounded, he just managed to scramble away to safety. Meanwhile the body of Sicily's last Emir of Emirs, slashed and lacerated by a dozen sword-thrusts, lay lifeless against the wall where it had fallen.

But not for long. Hearing the tumult, the inhabitants of the nearby houses had hurried to the scene, and within minutes the news was all over Palermo. From every corner of the city men poured into the Via Coperta. Some, according to Falcandus, refused to believe that the blood-soaked corpse at their feet could be that of the great and formidable Emir under whose iron rule they had suffered for nearly seven years; but the majority knew that there could be no mistake and made no effort to conceal their joy. They hurled the body into the centre of the street, kicked it, spat on it; the hair and beard they tore out in handfuls. At last, tiring of the sport, they paused; but they did not disperse. After the violence and brutality of the past hour, what had begun as a curious, faintly apprehensive crowd had been transformed into a wild, vindictive mob. It clamoured for more blood, more destruction. Suddenly it turned and surged away down the street, leaving the former object of its wrath an obscene and shapeless bundle in the dust.

Away in his private apartments on the first floor of the royal palace, the King had heard the shouting, and had soon afterwards received from his Master of the Horse a detailed account of what had happened. As always in a real crisis, William had acted quickly and decisively—so quickly, indeed, that when the mob reached Maio's house they found it already protected by a detachment of the royal guard, the Emir's wife and family having been escorted to the palace for their safety. Other detachments had been sent out to patrol every quarter of the city; it was essential that the rioters should not get out of hand before the King had decided on his future course of action.

But what should this course be? William needed no Emir of Emirs to tell him that his position was both delicate and dangerous. Not only, as he himself put it, had he lost his right hand; he was threatened with the loss of his neck. He was aware that the great mass of his subjects, Muslim and Christian, proletariat as well as aristocracy, had hated Maio and were firmly on the side of Matthew Bonnellus; he knew too just how empty were many of their protestations of loyalty to himself. If he were to yield to his distracted Queen's entreaties by taking firm action against Maio's murderers, he might unleash a general uprising which he would be unable to quell. Regretfully, he saw that he had no choice but to come to terms with the assassins. One day, when his position was more assured, he would punish them as they deserved. For the moment he must hide his anger, dissemble as best he could, and welcome them as his deliverers.

The following morning, 11 November, the King summoned to his presence his old friend and former tutor Henry, Archdeacon of Catania—usually known as Henry Aristippus—and appointed him head of an interim administration. Almost certainly a Norman by birth despite his Greek nickname, Henry was above all a scholar and a scientist. The range of his interests can be judged from the works he translated into his beautiful Latin—two Platonic dialogues, the *Meno* and the *Phaedo*, the fourth book of Aristotle's *Meteorologica*, the *Lives of the Philosophers* by Diogenes Laertius and the *Opuscula* of St Gregory Nazianzen. In addition he was an enthusiastic astronomer and, thanks to the proximity of Mt Etna, an intrepid vulcanologist. He was hard-working and utterly trustworthy; but he was neither an administrator nor a statesman. William seems to have chosen him as much for his gentle, conciliatory character and his knowledge of languages as for any other reason. He deliberately refrained from investing him with Maio's titles—Aristippus became neither Emir of Emirs nor even Chancellor—but he did give his old tutor two lieutenants to help him in his task. One was Count Sylvester of Marsico, a middle-aged aristocrat distantly related to the royal family. His appointment was obviously intended as a sop to Bonnellus and his friends—of whom, though the King could not have known it, Sylvester may even have been an accomplice.[1] The other was considerably more important: Richard Palmer, Bishop-elect of Syracuse, that learned and almost obsessively ambitious Englishman who was destined to remain for the next thirty years one of the leading figures of the political and religious hierarchy of Sicily.

Although two members of this triumvirate had been on friendly terms with Maio in the past they also accepted the necessity of reaching some sort of accommodation with Bonnellus, whose responsibility for the murder was now common knowledge. The

[1] One of his first actions on Maio's death was to secure the Emir's property in Palermo for himself—including the church of S. Cataldo, in which his daughter Matilda is buried.

first policy that they adopted, politically expedient as it may have been, therefore redounds to the credit of none of them, and still less to that of William himself—the deliberate and systematic blackening of the Emir's character to the point where his assassin could be shown as the saviour of the country. To his wife and children, already kept in the palace for their protection, the official attitude changed. Gradually they came to realise that they were no longer in care, but in custody. Maio's son was arrested and imprisoned, as was also his chief eunuch; under torture, the two were said to have revealed a whole series of embezzlements and extortions. The worst of those rumours that had so long been circulating were now, it seemed, confirmed.

Once the ground had been suitably prepared William could no longer put off the grant of his royal pardon. Immediately after the murder Matthew Bonnellus had fled with his friends to his castle of Caccamo;[1] thither now arrived royal emissaries, to assure him that the King wished him well, and that he might return without danger to the capital. Though it is unlikely that Bonnellus ever trusted William an inch, recent events had left him in no doubt of his own personal popularity. He accepted the King's invitation. A few days before, he and his men had fled from Palermo at full gallop, under cover of darkness. Now they rode back in triumph. And so, reports Falcandus,

as Bonnellus entered the city, a great crowd swarmed out to greet him, numbering as many men as women; and they accompanied him with immense rejoicing to the gates of the palace. There he was welcomed graciously by the King, and once more received back fully into the royal favour. . . . Thus, by this celebrated deed, he won the love and admiration of the nobility and the common people alike. . . . Meanwhile in Sicily, and especially in Palermo, all the people claimed with one accord that if any man should attempt to do him harm, he should be adjudged a public enemy; and that they would even take up arms against the King himself if he should ever try to exact a penalty for the Emir's death.

[1] This castle, rebuilt and restored but undeniably impressive, still stands on the western slopes of Mt Calogero some seven miles from Termini Imerese. Within, visitors are still shown the Salone della Congiura, in which Bonnellus and his fellow conspirators are said to have held their councils.

Even when we allow for Falcandus's exaggeration, it is clear that as 1161 opened Matthew Bonnellus had become one of the most powerful figures in the Kingdom. But that wave of popularity that had carried him so superbly forward on its crest was soon to break. William, increasingly irritated by the young man's arrogance and encouraged by the Queen to assert his strength and authority, began to recover his nerve. Dissimulation never came easily to him. His true feelings towards the murderer of his friend and counsellor grew daily more evident. Then, one day, he demanded of Bonnellus the payment of duty on his dead father's estate amounting to sixty thousand *taris*—a debt that Maio had deliberately overlooked for the sake of his prospective son-in-law.

The debt was paid: but the incident was a warning. Bonnellus did not underestimate the Queen's influence over her husband; nor that of the palace eunuchs, all creatures of Maio, whom he knew to be urging the King to avenge their old master. He had seen sinister figures loitering around the gates of his house in Palermo, he knew that palace agents were watching him and following his every movement; and he could not escape the conclusion that his life was in danger.

Ever since the Emir's death, Matthew had been under pressure from his associates to move against the King; but he had always held back. To deliver Sicily from a detested tyrant was one thing; to lay hand's on the Lord's anointed was quite another, and he was far from certain of how William's subjects would react. Such a move might lose him all the popularity, and with it all the power, that he was now enjoying. Slowly, however, he began to see that his counsellors had been right. The King, too, must go.

Yet even now Matthew shrank from the idea of regicide. The important thing was to remove William from the seat of power. Once he were safely out of the way there would be plenty of time to decide what to do with him. And as long as he suffered no violence and his little son Roger were enthroned in his stead, royalist opinion should be manageable. Moreover there were at present in Palermo two men of undoubted Hauteville blood who had never concealed their dislike of the King and who could be relied upon to give open support to his removal. The first was his half-brother Simon, Roger II's illegitimate son, who had borne him an understandable grudge ever since William had refused to allow him to keep the Principality of Taranto, with which Roger had invested him in 1148, on the grounds that it was too important a fief to go to a bastard. The second was his nephew Count Tancred of Lecce, natural son of Duke Roger, who in consequence of the part he had played in the Apulian revolt, had spent the last five years in the palace dungeons.

It was perhaps the thought of Tancred that suggested to the conspirators the basic idea for their plot. To seize the person of the King was no easy task. He seldom appeared in public; of his two principal residences, the Favara was set in the middle of a lake, while the royal palace in Palermo was still in essence the Norman fortress that the two Rogers had made it. Furthermore its exterior was patrolled by a special guard, three hundred strong, commanded by a castellan known for his absolute incorruptibility and loyalty to his sovereign. Beneath the south-west corner of that same building, however, was the political prison, which the upheavals of the recent years and the repressive policies of Maio of Bari had kept filled to capacity. If all its inmates could be simultaneously released they might, as it were, storm the building from within.

Fortunately for Bonnellus and his friends, the palace official directly responsible for the safety of the prisoners proved open to persuasion; sweetened by an enormous bribe and, doubtless, the promise of advancement to some position of higher authority under the new regime, he readily agreed not only to liberate them at a pre-arranged signal but also to supply them with arms. The prisoners were alerted, and their duties explained to them. When all had been arranged, Matthew rode off to another of his castles, at Mistretta, away in the Nébrodi mountains some miles to the south-east of Cefalù. Here, it seems, he proposed to hold William till the King's ultimate fate could be decided; he now set about preparing it for its royal prisoner and putting its defences in readiness to withstand an attack. He told his associates that he would be back in Palermo shortly, and in any case well before the day appointed for the *coup*; on no account were they to take any action until his return.

Had he been a little older and wiser, he would have known that in any military or paramilitary operation one of the first duties of a leader, particularly during the crucial period immediately before the action, is to keep contact at all times with his men. Away at Mistretta there was no means of reaching him in an emergency; and now, suddenly, an emergency arose. The scheme was indiscreetly revealed to a local knight who proved loyal to the King; from that moment on, the plotters were no longer safe. There was no time to be lost waiting for Bonnellus; the only hope lay in putting their plan into operation at once, before they were themselves arrested.

On the morning of 9 March 1161, at about the third hour after sunrise, the signal was given. The dungeons were flung open, the prisoners snatched the weapons that had been laid out ready for them and hurried to let in the conspirators by the side door where they were waiting. Then, led by the princes Simon and Tancred who knew the palace well, they ran to the large room in the Pisan Tower where they knew the King would be holding his regular morning conference with Henry Aristippus. William was taken utterly by surprise. Seeing that flight was impossible, he dived for the window and began shouting for help; but hardly had the first cry left his lips when he was seized bodily and dragged away. Two of the plotters, William of Lesina and Robert of Bova, the first described by Falcandus as 'a most atrocious man'—*vir atrocissimus*—the second 'famous for his cruelty', now advanced threateningly upon him with drawn swords; only the intervention of a third, Richard of Mandra, saved his life. Meanwhile another group made straight for the Queen's apartments and arrested Margaret and her two sons.

As soon as the royal family had been safely secured, the pillage began. The palace was a veritable treasure-house, and the intruders went through it like locusts. The collections of gold and jewels so lovingly amassed by Roger and William over the past forty years were ransacked. Nothing portable was left behind. The precious pots and vases, with everything else that could do duty as a container, were filled with coins from the coffers and carried off, as were all the royal and ecclesiastical vestments from the *Tiraz*. Saddest of all perhaps, Edrisi's great silver planisphere, despite its immense weight, disappeared never to be seen again. A fire was lit in the courtyard, and nearly all the government records, including the entire registry of fiefs and the services due for them, were hurled on to the flames. Meanwhile all those eunuchs who could not make good their escape were put to the sword; the harem—left undefended—was broken into, its inmates dragged screaming away or violated on the spot.

The massacre of the eunuchs introduced a new and sinister element into the situation. The aristocratic party had long objected to what it considered the disproportionate influence of Muslims at the court, and the initial success of the *coup* seems to have released a pent-up hatred of the whole Islamic community. Suddenly, no Saracen was safe. Even those working innocently in the *diwan*, the mint and other public offices had to flee for their lives; several of the Muslim artists and sages whom William, like his father, accommodated permanently in the palace—among them one of the most distinguished Arabic poets of his day, Yahya ibn at-Tifashi— were hunted down and killed; while down in the lower part of the city a Christian mob descended on the bazaar, forcing all the Arab merchants and shopkeepers, who since the African defeats of 1159– 60 had been forbidden by law to carry arms, to retreat to the specifically Muslim quarter of the town where the narrow streets gave them the protection they needed.

By now a still larger crowd had gathered in the great square before the palace. Swept by conflicting and contradictory rumours, its prevailing mood was still one of bewilderment. The King was dead; he was alive; he was a prisoner; he was free; it was a Saracen plot to seize power; it was a Christian one to purge the government of Muslim influence. Within the building, however, the ringleaders knew that this atmosphere of uncertainty could not last. Sooner or later, popular feeling must crystallise; and on the form it eventually took the success of the entire *coup* would depend. It was not enough to curry the favour of the mob by flinging an occasional handful of coins out of the palace windows. The time had come for a public declaration of policy and intent. It was therefore announced that William's eldest son Roger had formally succeeded his father on the Sicilian throne, and that he would be crowned in the Cathedral within a very few days—just as soon, in fact, as Matthew Bonnellus returned to Palermo. Meanwhile the little boy, now nine years old, was mounted on a horse and solemnly paraded through the streets of the capital, and the people were invited to acclaim their new King.

Their reaction does not seem to have been enthusiastic; and when the procession was repeated on the following morning, an acute observer might have noticed that even those accompanying the young prince were looking a trifle uncomfortable. Before long the whole city knew why. The conspirators, their ranks now swollen by a number of senior government and church officials who had since pledged their support, were themselves in open conflict. A growing body of opinion was now turning against the idea of a child king, and was favouring instead the succession of Simon, Roger's bastard son.

For the moment there was deadlock, and the leaders of the revolt decided to leave the issue open until the return of Bonnellus. It was a fatal mistake. Any political *coup*, if it is to succeed, must be swift and certain. Momentum is everything. The people must be presented with a *fait accompli*; there can be no half-way pauses and changes of direction. Thus a second vital rule was broken, and King William's throne was saved. The royalists seized the opportunity to regroup themselves; their agents went to work in the streets and taverns, spreading rumours unfavourable to Bonnellus and his party and everywhere finding ready listeners. The conduct of the insurgents and in particular the sack of the palace had had a deplorable effect. All respectable citizens had been revolted by the bloodshed and the violence, and shocked by the indiscriminate looting of riches which might one day be needed for the defence of the Kingdom. Little by little public opinion began to harden; sympathy grew for the captive King; and the conspirators suddenly awoke to find all Sicily united against them.

Their last hope lay in Matthew Bonnellus. By his absence he had avoided any direct responsibility for what had occurred; if he could be brought back quickly enough, the magic of his name and prestige might yet save the day. Two of the leaders rode off at top speed to Mistretta to fetch him. They were too late. Scarcely had they left Palermo when a group of high ecclesiastics, whose loyalty to the King had never wavered, took an initiative of their own. They were led by the Archbishops Romuald of Salerno and Robert of Messina,

Bishop Tristan of Mazara and Richard Palmer, the Bishop-elect of
Syracuse. None of them had been particular friends of Maio, but
they had no wish to see their own considerable influence at court
destroyed by the aristocrats. They also genuinely deplored the offer
of violence to an anointed King. On Saturday 11 March they called
on the people of Palermo to storm the palace and rescue their
sovereign; and the people responded.

The rebels soon saw that against such numbers resistance was
hopeless. To gain time, they tried to negotiate, pointing out that
Bonnellus would soon return and that once he resumed control all
the present misunderstandings would be resolved. It was no use.
The name had lost its magic. Meanwhile those defending the walls
reported that they could not hold out much longer; if the building
were taken by storm, it would be a miracle if any of them escaped
with their lives. They were beaten. Running to the captive King, they
fell on their knees before him and implored his pardon.

William was saved—in theory; but he was not yet out of danger.
Physically he remained in the power of his enemies, to whom he was
an invaluable hostage. They were desperate, and if they thought they
had nothing to lose they might yet carry him with them to destruction. Walking slowly to a window of the Pisan Tower[1], he showed
himself to the crowd gathered below. Immediately a great cry went
up, a demand for the palace gates to be opened and vengeance taken
on the traitors; but William raised his hand for silence. His subjects,
he said, had given him more than adequate proof of their loyalty and
affection. He would ask them now simply to lay down their arms and
to disperse quietly to their homes, allowing free egress from the
palace to all those still within, to whom he had granted his royal
pardon. The crowd obediently withdrew; the rebels slipped out and
fled back to Caccamo.

Only after they had gone did Romuald and his fellow-churchmen
enter the King's chamber. From the window, shortly before, William
had spoken bravely and well; but they found him now in a state of

[1] Plate 16. Falcandus claims that it was from the neighbouring Gioaria that
William addressed the throng, in which case he almost certainly spoke from the
window of what is now known as the *Sala di Ruggero*. (See pp. 241–2.) But
Romuald of Salerno, who was an eye-witness, is categorical on the subject,
and we must accept his word.

near-collapse, sobbing uncontrollably. After the events of the past three days, such emotion would in any case have been easy enough to understand; but the real tragedy, they now learned, had occurred at the moment of his salvation. During the last assault on the palace his little son and heir Roger, who had been in the room with him, had been struck in the eye by a stray arrow, and now lay dying. This final shock had been too much; William's spirit was broken.[1] With difficulty the bishops persuaded him to descend to the great hall beneath, where a numerous delegation of his subjects, heedless of his earlier injunction, was waiting to congratulate him on his escape. He appeared before them but still could not trust himself to speak. All he could do was stammer a few words into the ear of Richard Palmer—'a man of great learning and eloquence' as Falcandus reminds us—who relayed them in the King's name to the assembled company. It was a strangely humble speech, in which William admitted his past wrongs, acknowledged that his recent sufferings were not undeserved and promised to revoke certain recent decrees which had caused resentment. As an earnest of his good intentions, the local customs dues levied on all foodstuffs brought into the city were abolished from that moment.

Whether this last idea was the King's or Palmer's, it suited the occasion perfectly. William was cheered to the echo. Henceforth, at least in Palermo, his position was re-established, his popularity assured.

But, though the rebellion had failed, the rebels were still free and under arms; and from the castle of Caccamo to which they had retreated there came no word of surrender. Militarily, the King remained vulnerable. He had no forces in the capital except the three hundred men of the palace garrison; they had been singularly ineffectual during the past few days and were no longer to be relied upon. He therefore summoned the bulk of the army and the fleet from Messina; meanwhile, playing for time, he sent an ostensibly friendly

[1] Falcandus, leaping at the chance of pinning a new atrocity on to his old enemy, admits the arrow wound but suggests that little Roger was in fact kicked to death by his father, in a rage at what he considered to be the boy's earlier disloyalty: a suggestion so improbable that one wonders whether it could ever have been taken seriously.

message to Matthew Bonnellus, now himself back at Caccamo, asking why he was giving asylum to enemies of the Crown.

Matthew's reply was an interesting one. He began by assuring the King that he was himself quite unconnected with the last uprising. It was true, however, that the insurgents were his friends and colleagues; how then could he possibly refuse them shelter? They had done what they did out of sheer despair, only because there was no other way of obtaining redress for the wrongs that they, with all other members of the nobility, were obliged to suffer. To cite but one example, they could no longer even marry off their daughters without prior permission of the Curia; and this permission was often so long in coming that many a lady had to wait for a husband till she was long past child-bearing age, while others were condemned to perpetual virginity.[1] In short, there could be no reconciliation between King and aristocracy until William agreed to restore the old customs and usages introduced by Robert Guiscard and Roger I in the preceding century.

Once again Matthew had miscalculated. This was no time for arrogance. His reply infuriated the King. If, William protested, the nobles had first laid down their arms and then come to him as suppliants, he would have listened sympathetically to their grievances; as it was, he would willingly sacrifice his kingdom or even face death itself rather than give in to threats. Negotiations were immediately broken off; he had nothing more to say.

The rebels had badly overplayed their hand. Bonnellus saw that his only hope was to strike again—and to strike quickly, before the expected reinforcements could arrive from Messina. Suddenly and without warning he and his men swooped down from Caccamo to a point near Favara, only a mile or two from Palermo itself, and from there spread out to occupy all the approach roads to the capital. It was a bold and well-executed plan. The Palermitans, taken by surprise and without adequate provisions or defences, began to panic; and if Matthew had pressed his advantage home and marched straight into the city this second attempt might well have proved

---

[1] This grievance was prompted by something more than paternal compassion; Bonnellus apparently forbore to add the real reason for the nobles' indignation— the fact that if they died childless their estates reverted to the Crown.

successful. Instead, at the critical moment, he hesitated. As he did so the first ships from Messina appeared in the harbour; soldiers were hurriedly disembarked and posted in key positions; other loyal detachments arrived from the interior of the island to join them; and the rebels, now hopelessly outnumbered, retreated once again to Caccamo.

This time they were ready to talk reasonably; and the terms which William was prepared to offer proved more generous than any of them had a right to expect. There were no executions, no imprisonments. Most of the leaders elected to go into exile, including Simon, Tancred and William of the Principate—another distant cousin of the King—to whom passage was offered in Sicilian ships as far as Terracina. Several were sent on forced pilgrimages to Jerusalem. Richard of Mandra on the other hand—who, on that first fateful morning, had shielded his sovereign's body with his own—received a free pardon. As for Matthew Bonnellus, the driving force behind three *coups* within six months, he too was granted a pardon and summoned back to the court, where William once again received him with every show of friendliness and favour.

Why, at such a moment, did the King show himself so astonishingly merciful? Only five years before, after an insurrection no whit more serious than that which was just over, he had embarked on an orgy of hanging, drowning and blinding, filling his prisons with those lucky enough to escape anything worse, leaving the smouldering ruins of what had once been Bari as an example of the fate which awaited any city in his dominion that dared set itself up against him. How can it be that, after three days of terror from which he had narrowly escaped with his life, we find him pronouncing no more fearful sentences than those of comfortable exile, and receiving back with open arms the traitor who had come nearer than any other in the Kingdom's history to toppling the Sicilian throne?

The first, short answer is that although the insurgents had failed in both their attempts to seize power, they had still not surrendered. The fortress of Caccamo was commandingly situated and strongly defended, and if Matthew had resolved to stand firm it might well have held out for a year or more. Just what effect this would have had on the general morale in Palermo is hard to assess, but the terror caused by the recent blockade suggested that it might be serious; and William could not risk any more major disturbances in the capital. Only by the total cessation of hostilities and the speedy dislodging of his enemy from Caccamo could tranquillity be restored. But Matthew would not surrender unless he were sure of a pardon. In such a case it would hardly be possible to make an example of his followers.

It was lucky for William that the young man was as conceited as he was foolish. Otherwise he could never have been persuaded, as he apparently was, that his prestige was still such as to make him at once indispensable and invulnerable. But when at last he swallowed the bait and stood, truculent as ever, once more before his sovereign, William must have known that Matthew Bonnellus was finished. Victim of his own vanity, he would never make trouble again. He was to enjoy a few more weeks of liberty, swaggering about Palermo and boasting of his power over the King; but when, towards the end of April, new revolts broke out in central Sicily and on the mainland, William decided to have done with him once and for all.

The arrest itself presented no problems. Matthew was simply summoned to the palace. Despite several secret warnings he still believed his position unshakable, and obeyed without hesitation. Once there, he was seized by the guards and hustled away to what Falcandus is at pains to describe as a particularly revolting dungeon —not, this time, in the palace itself (William never made the same mistake twice) but in the adjacent fortress, usually known by its Arabic name of al-Halka, the Ring.

The civil disturbances that followed seem to have been little more than a formality. Since his return to Palermo Matthew had worked hard to keep his image bright, and on hearing of his capture his agents in the town lost no time in mobilising support for a popular demonstration. But the citizens' hearts were not in it. They were tired of unrest and upheaval, and were discouraged almost before they began. Both the palace and the Halka had been put under close guard; a rather desultory attempt to burn down the gates was easily frustrated; and, writes Falcandus,

seeing that they could achieve nothing, the people . . . suffered a sudden change of heart—preferring, as is characteristic of the Sicilians, to bow to the needs of the moment rather than to maintain any constant faith. And as many as had formerly cried out for the liberation of Bonnellus now took pains to make it clear that they had never been among those who sought his friendship.

Among the King's supporters only one casualty is recorded—Adenulf, the royal chamberlain, who was set upon and stabbed to death by one of Bonnellus's knights. The rebel side, however, was less fortunate; William's mood of clemency was past. Few of those who now fell into his hands escaped death or mutilation. And Matthew himself, blinded and hamstrung, was left to languish in his dungeon cell—in which, not long afterwards, he died.

13

THE END OF A REIGN

Civis obit, inquit, multum majoribus impar
Nosse modum juris, sed in hoc tamen utilis aevo.
Gone is a citizen [he said] who though no peer
Of those who disciplined the state of yore . . .
Yet in this age irreverent of law
Has played a noble part.

[Tr. E. Ridley]

From Cato's funeral oration on Pompey, as given by Lucan, *Pharsalia*,
Book IX; quoted, according to Hugo Falcandus, by the Bishop-elect of
Syracuse on the death of William I.

THE revolts in the Sicilian heartland and in Apulia were serious but
short-lived. In the former, the danger lay not so much in any direct
threat to the safety of the King as in the ominously confessional turn
which events had taken. The two nobles primarily responsible,
Tancred of Lecce and Roger Sclavo, had left Caccamo just in time
and withdrawn to the south of the island, taking Piazza[1] and
Butera and deliberately stirring up the local Lombard[2] communities

[1] Now more generally known as Piazza Armerina—a name derived from the
fortified camp—*castrum armorum*—built by the Great Count Roger I on the
nearby Piano Armerino. As a town it is now best known for the ruins of a third-
century imperial Roman villa, the so-called *Villa del Casale*, probably destroyed
by William in 1161 and rediscovered only in quite recent years. The floor-
mosaics of this palace have justly made it one of the most popular tourist attractions of all Sicily. Visitors to Piazza should not, however, overlook the lovely
little priory of S. Andrea, a mile or two away to the north. It was built in 1096 by
Simon, Count of Butera, cousin of Roger II through his mother Adelaide and
probably—though Chalandon does not accept this—the natural father of Roger
Sclavo.

[2] The past half-century had seen an enormous growth in the Lombard colonies
originally introduced into Sicily by Roger I. Apart from Piazza and Butera, their
principal centres were Randazzo, Nicosia, Capizzi, Aidone and Maniace. La
Lumia, writing just a century ago, noted that the inhabitants of these areas still
spoke a dialect more akin to those of North Italy than to normal Sicilian.

against the Muslim peasantry. The terror spread as far as Catania and Syracuse. In many areas the Saracens escaped massacre only by disguising themselves as Christians and taking flight; even when order had been re-established, few returned to their former homes.

On the mainland, too, the pot was back on the boil. Robert of Loritello, never inactive for long, had driven down into the Basilicata—the instep of Italy—as far as Taranto and Oriolo; Andrew of Rupecanina was raising a similar revolt in Campania; Salerno, disloyal for the first time, had joined the insurgents; and now even Calabria, in the past the most reliable of all the King's dominions, had been aroused by the Countess Clementia—perhaps in revenge for William's treatment of her lover—and was taking up arms against him. Only a few barons in the entire peninsula had remained loyal—men like Bohemund of Manopello and the Queen's cousin Gilbert of Gravina who, despite their complicity in the plot against Maio, had recently been restored to favour.

But however desperate things might become on the mainland, Sicilian problems must be dealt with first; William could only appeal to Gilbert to hold the situation there as best he could with such forces as were already available, while he himself marched against Tancred and Roger Sclavo. By the end of April he was in the field. Piazza, after a few weeks' siege, was sacked and levelled to the ground. Butera, his next objective, presented a more formidable challenge. The rebels, hoping that the troubles beyond the straits might at any moment force the King to raise the siege, fought with determination—even consulting astrologers to determine the most favourable occasions for sorties and counter-attacks. Since William was able, through his own astrologers, to predict the precise moments they would choose and make his dispositions accordingly, this method seems to have done more harm than good; nevertheless, winter was already closing in before shortage of food, combined with growing discontent on the part of the civilian population, persuaded them to surrender the town in return for their own safe conduct into exile. William accepted their terms and let them go; but on the town that had betrayed him twice in five years he had no pity. By Christmas the proud pinnacle where once Butera had stood bore nothing but a heap of smouldering ruins.

After a pause in Palermo to keep the feast and to prepare for the coming campaign, the King crossed to the mainland early the follow-following March. As he pressed up through Calabria, the Countess Clementia and her family had retreated to their fortress of Taverna, up in the mountains due north of Catanzaro. They too fought hard, releasing quantitites of heavy barrels studded with spikes which trundled down the steep escarpments into the ranks of the besiegers, causing heavy and hideous casualties; but William's second assault was successful. The Countess's two uncles were executed; she and her mother were taken prisoner and sent back to an unknown fate in Palermo.

Henceforth, as on his previous campaign, the opposition seemed to disintegrate at William's approach. He himself showed no mercy. When his Great Chamberlain, the eunuch Johar, was caught in the act of absconding with the royal seals, he had him drowned on the spot. At Taranto, which capitulated after the shortest of struggles, he hanged all the supporters of Robert of Loritello that he could find—though Robert himself had already fled to join Frederick Barbarossa in Lombardy. Up through Apulia, across the mountains into Campania, everywhere it was the same story—quick surrenders followed by hangings, blindings and mutilations, occasionally commuted to the payment by a whole town or district of 'redemption money'—a compulsory imposition which, though it frequently ruined those upon whom it fell for many years to come, did much to replenish the King's own ransacked treasury.

Some time in the summer he reached Salerno. Many of the elders of the city who had identified themselves with the revolt had disappeared; but the remainder came out to greet their King with every protestation of affection and loyalty. William would not listen; he refused point-blank even to enter the city. His betrayal by his own capital was the ultimate treason, and it demanded the ultimate penalty. And indeed Salerno would undoubtedly have suffered the same fate as Bari half a dozen years before had it not been for the intervention of two powerful protectors. The first was its patron saint, St Matthew, who according to Archbishop Romuald suddenly sent out of a clear and cloudless noonday sky a tempest of such fury as to uproot the tents of the entire army, including William's own, in their camp outside the walls. Thus, it seems, was the King persuaded of the divine displeasure that he would incur if any harm came to the city. The second advocate was the saint's namesake and a native son of Salerno, Matthew the Notary, who persuaded Sylvester of Marsico and Richard Palmer to intercede on behalf of his birthplace.

The combined efforts of the two Matthews had their effect. William contented himself with ordering a purge of all unreliable elements and hanging all those who were found guilty of conspiring against him. Salerno was saved.

But though the immediate danger was over, the damage done could never be entirely repaired. When, in the late summer of 1162, William returned to Sicily, it was to find the island tormented and terrorised by confessional hatreds on a scale unprecedented in its history. He had left it in a hurry, knowing full well that many of those who had taken part in the Sicilian uprisings had not yet been brought to justice; and he had entrusted the task of tracking them down, together with the government of Palermo itself, to one of the palace Caïds,[1] a baptised eunuch called Martin. It had been a disastrous choice. Martin had narrowly escaped with his life when the rebels had stormed the palace in the previous year; his brother had been killed in the massacre that followed; and ever since that day he had nurtured a deep loathing for all Christians. Thus, on William's departure for the mainland the previous March, a veritable reign of terror had begun. Everywhere, those who had at any time plotted or even spoken against the King or his ministers were hunted down, and many an old score between Muslim and Christian must have been settled by a timely denunciation to the public investigators. Those on whom suspicion fell were subjected to various forms of trial by ordeal which, since survival was usually equated with guilt, could be relied upon to eliminate all undesirables, however tenuous the case against them. The local authorities, ordered to institute purges in all areas under their control, were too frightened to disobey. Redemption money was levied even in those towns and districts which had

---

[1] Caïd, the Arabic word for master or leader, was the title given to the Muslim or originally Muslim administrative officials of the palace. In the Latin chronicles it usually takes the form of *gaitus* or *gaytus*.

never wavered in their loyalty. Thus order was restored and the state coffers refilled—but at a heavy price. The respect which, despite every upheaval, the bulk of the local populations had felt for the central government was hereafter tinged with a new, unhealthy fear; and the harmony which the two Rogers had worked so hard to create between their Christian and their Muslim subjects was destroyed for ever.

Among the victims was Henry Aristippus. Falcandus claims that he had been party to the last plot and had forfeited any hope of a pardon by abducting certain ladies of the harem for his own delectation; considering Henry's age and record, it is hard to say which of the two charges is the more improbable. There is another, far simpler explanation for his downfall. He was a gentle scholar, suddenly swept up into a world of plot and counter-plot, of court intrigue at its most violent and vicious. His position in such a world was bound to make him enemies; and when it was time for those enemies to overthrow him they did so without a qualm, using weapons he did not understand and against which he had no defence. And so William's oldest friend and staunchest supporter shared the same fate as his bitterest and most unscrupulous adversary; like Matthew Bonnellus, Henry Aristippus ended his career in a dungeon cell, and never knew freedom again.

The crisis was past. In the space of a single year William had suffered the loss of his most trusted counsellor, murdered in a public street; of his own son and heir, shot by an insurgent's arrow before his very eyes; of much of his country's wealth and nearly all his personal possessions; and, not least, of his reputation and his self-respect. He had survived two major attempts to dethrone him— one of which had very nearly succeeded and had resulted in his being held a captive, with his family, in hourly expectation of death—only to find both his island and his mainland Kingdom in a state of open revolt. Here, surely, was the ultimate vindication of Maio's policies, however unpopular they may have been; one short year after the Emir's death, Sicily must have seemed on the point of disintegration. Yet only one more year had sufficed for William to restore his authority, together with a large part of his finances; and by the time he returned to Palermo his grip on his country was firmer and more assured than ever it had been. A few months later, the prisoners in the palace dungeons made one more attempt at a mass escape as in 1161; they failed, and the King closed down the palace prison for ever. With that single exception, his reign was never again troubled with sedition or revolt.

William was still young—a little over forty. He had shown himself to be a man of courage and strength, when these qualities were indispensable. But now that he could afford to relax he once more cut himself off from all the cares of kingship, leaving the government in the hands of a new triumvirate in which Henry Aristippus was replaced by the notary Matthew of Ajello, and old Count Sylvester—who died at about this time—by Caïd Peter, that same slightly colourless eunuch who had made such an indifferent showing at Mahdia but who had now been promoted to the rank of Great Chamberlain of the Palace. Only one member remained unchanged—Richard Palmer, the still unconsecrated Bishop of Syracuse. Together, the three represented a wide cross-section of the King's subjects: the Italian-Lombard bourgeoisie, the Muslim bureaucracy and the Latin Church. Only two groups were pointedly omitted—the Greeks and the Norman aristocracy, who had if anything even less say in the government than before. But the importance of the Greeks was declining fast; and as for the Norman aristocracy, it had only itself to blame.

And so William, 'having given strict orders to his ministers to tell him nothing that might disturb his peace of mind'—as the reader may suspect, we have to rely largely on Falcandus for such knowledge as we have of this period—relapsed once again into his private world of ease and pleasure. But not altogether into idleness; 'for,' writes Romuald of Salerno, 'in those days, King William built near Palermo a palace of considerable height, constructed with superb artifice, which he called the Zisa;[1] and he surrounded it with beautiful fruit-bearing trees and pleasant gardens, and with divers water-courses and fish-pools he rendered it delectable.'

The neighbourhood of the Zisa—out beyond the Porta Nuova to

---

[1] The word comes from the Arabic *aziz*, or magnificent. The earliest versions of Romuald's chronicle wrongly transcribe it as *Lisa*.

the north-west of the city—is now a good deal less salubrious than it
was eight centuries ago; and those centuries have also taken their
toll of the building itself. Recently, however, it has been carefully
restored and it remains, after the Royal Palace, the most splendid of
all the Norman secular buildings left to us. The exterior is, undeniably, somewhat forbidding; in the twelfth century palaces were still
designed to do duty as fortresses should the occasion require, and
William's experiences over the past few years were not such as to
encourage him to make an exception. Though the little square
towers at each end and the gently recessed blind arches do something
to lighten the structure, the general effect at first sight is more
awesome than attractive; and the crenellations along the roof,
cut into the original entablature during the fifteenth or sixteenth
century and making nonsense of the great Arabic inscription that
formerly ran the length of the façade, hardly improve matters.

But step now into the central hall of the palace. At once you are in
a different world.[1] Nowhere does Norman Sicily speak more persuasively of the Orient; nowhere else on all the island is that specifically Islamic talent for creating quiet havens of shade and coolness in
the summer heat so dazzlingly displayed. The ceiling is high and
honeycombed, the three inner walls set with deep niches, roofed in
their turn with those tumbling stalactites so dear to Saracen archi-
tects. All around, zig-zagging in and out of the niches, runs a frieze
of marble and multi-coloured mosaic, broadening out in the centre of
the back wall into three medallions in which, against a background of
exquisite decorative arabesques, confronted archers are busy shooting birds out of a tree, while two pairs of peacocks peck dates, with
studied unconcern, from conveniently stunted palms. It takes no
great effort of the imagination to picture the King in this lovely
room, taking his ease with his wise men or his concubines, and
gazing out into his sunlit garden, while from a fountain in the wall
comes the soothing plash of water, trickling down a marble incline
into an ornamental channel and thence to the vivarium outside.

But William never saw the Zisa completed. The finishing
touches were left to his son; and it was William II who was to
sum up what the building meant to him in the second magnificent

[1] Plate 17.

Palermo, the Zisa: interior. The paintings in the foreground illustrate the problems that all restorers of Norman work in Sicily have to face

Palermo, Royal Palace: the so-called *Sala di Ruggero*

Arabic inscription, raised in white stucco round the entrance arch.[1]

Here, as oft as thou shalt wish, shalt thou see the loveliest possession of this Kingdom, the most splendid of the world and of the seas.
The mountains, their peaks flushed with the colour of narcissus . . .
Thou shalt see the great King of his century in his beautiful dwelling-place, a house of joy and splendour which suits him well.
This is the earthly paradise that opens to the view; this King is the *Musta'iz*;[2] this palace the *Aziz*.

Despite the restoration much remains to be done, both to the Zisa itself and to its surroundings, before it can once again live up to this description. The neglect of centuries cannot be repaired overnight, and an air of desolation still lingers over the bleak expanse where once the songbirds sang and the fish leaped lazily in the pools.

From this gentle afternoon of William's reign only one more monument remains—though it too may have been completed after his death. It is a room on the second floor of the royal palace, nowadays irritatingly and misleadingly known as the *Sala di Ruggero*;[3] a small room that could almost have been described as unassuming were it not for the mosaics with which its vault and upper walls are so sumptuously encrusted. Like those of the Zisa—the only other secular mosaics that have come down to us from Norman days[4]— they are decorative rather than devotional; and the emotions they evoke are those of sheer pleasure. Here are scenes of the country-

[1] The central part of this inscription was destroyed when the original high arch was removed and replaced by the lower one which appears, surmounted by a French window, in so many of the older photographs. Now the original proportions have been restored; but the missing words are lost for ever.

[2] *The Glorious One*. The title was used only by William II, hence the dating of the inscription.

[3] Plate 18.

[4] I do not count the few odd traces still clinging to the walls of the *Sala degli Armigeri* in another section of the palace. This hall, forty-five feet high and topped by a stalactite ceiling of considerably greater interest than the mosaic, forms part of the Torre Pisana, and probably served as a guardroom for the Tesoro nearby. It is not normally open to the public, but enthusiasts should have no difficulty in obtaining permission to visit it from the office of the Soprintendenza ai Monumenti on the first floor.

side and the chase, Byzantine in their formal symmetry but Sicilian in their joyful portrayal of palms and orange-trees, and all radiant with a liveliness and humour that is wholly of the west. Here once more are the date-gobbling peacocks and the myopic archers, but now they have been joined by a pair of centaurs and a host of other fauna both probable and improbable, many of them with expressions on their faces that seem almost human—leopards consumed with guilt and suspicion, other peacocks frankly shocked, lions self-conscious, and two burly stags, affronted in both senses of the word, glowering at each other in innocent unawareness of the horrid fate that awaits them in the rear.

We have no documentary evidence to tell us about these mosaics, nothing but their style—and in particular their affinity with those of the Zisa—to help us to date them. No matter. What really counts in this enchanting room, this gorgeous bestiary in blue and green and gold, is the way it speaks to us, like the Zisa but far more loudly and clearly, of the happier and more carefree side of Norman Sicilian life; reminding us how, despite all the intrigues and conspiracies and rebellions that fill so many of these pages, the sun still shone through the forest and men still looked on the world around them, and laughed, and were grateful.

William the Bad ended his reign as he had begun it, leaving all the responsibilities of state to others while he enjoyed all the privileges himself. There is no suggestion that his conscience ever troubled him; not even the appalling earthquake of 4 February 1163 which shook all eastern Sicily, virtually destroying Catania and causing a large section of Messina to crumble into the sea, seems to have worried him unduly. After all, the western end of the island where he lived remained unaffected. In Palermo, the walls of the Palatine Chapel were still further enriched with mosaic and marble;[1] the Zisa rose ever higher; the harem, the library and the game parks were constantly enriched for his pleasure. For him it should have been a happy time.

But it did not last. In March 1166 the King was stricken with a violent dysentery, accompanied by fever. Doctors were summoned,

[1] See p. 75.

among them Archbishop Romuald, who had probably attended the famous medical school at Salerno during his youth and who certainly enjoyed a high reputation as a physician. Later, to explain his lack of success, Romuald was to claim that his royal patient refused to accept many of the medicaments prescribed for him. In any event, after languishing for two months, rallying and relapsing by turns, William died on 7 May 1166, at about three o'clock in the afternoon. He was forty-six years old.

Even Hugo Falcandus, who loathed the late King and who, as we know, never hesitated to adjust historical truth to his own purposes, has to admit that William the Bad was genuinely mourned. The citizens of Palermo, he writes,

dressed themselves in black garments, and remained in this sombre apparel for three days. And throughout that time all the ladies, the noble matrons and especially the Saracen women—to whom the King's death had caused unimaginable grief—paraded day and night in sackcloth about the streets, their hair all undone, while before them went a great multitude of handmaidens, singing sad threnodies to the sound of tambourines till the whole city rang with their lamentations.

Despite energetic demands by the canons of Cefalù—where Roger's two great porphyry sarcophagi still awaited worthy occupants—it was agreed that William should be buried in Palermo; not even with his father in the cathedral, but more privately in the Palatine Chapel. No preparations had been made for an elaborate tomb; the body was laid in a relatively modest receptacle and consigned to the Chapel crypt.[1] Twice since then it has been disturbed. The first time was barely twenty years after the King's death, when it was transferred to its existing sarcophagus—of porphyry, like his father's—and its present position in the sanctuary of Monreale Cathedral. The second was in 1811 when, after a serious fire in the building, the sarcophagus was opened. William's corpse was found to be in a remarkable state of preservation, the pale face still covered with that thick beard that had struck such terror into the hearts of his more timorous subjects.

[1] The place where it rested was rediscovered during the restorations of 1921 and can still be seen today.

He had not been a good king. Despite his formidable appearance, he seems to have had little real confidence in himself. To some extent this was natural. To follow Roger II on the throne of Sicily would have been a daunting enough prospect for anyone; William had received no training for kingship until he was thirty, and if Roger had had a low opinion of his fourth son's capabilities—as there is good reason to believe that he did—he is unlikely to have concealed the fact. It is hardly surprising, then, that William should have tried to conceal his insecurity behind that fearsome exterior, and to pass off his shortcomings as an administrator with elaborate demonstrations of indifference. It may also be more than coincidental that he tended to shy away from those very aspects of statecraft—finance, diplomacy and legislation—that had so fascinated his father. Only where he felt that he could compete with Roger on equal terms could he prove to the world that he too was a Hauteville. Thus he too could build magnificently; and, above all, he could fight. He was a better soldier than his father had ever been, and he knew it. When he was besieged in his own palace, bereft of friends or counsellors, he had revealed himself as what he so often was—a hesitant, frightened man; but once he was in the field, his army behind him, he was transformed. And when the final crisis came, it was his courage and military skill that saved the Kingdom.

This very contrast, however, is typical of him. Throughout his life he remained unsteady and mercurial—a consequence, perhaps, of that same lack of self-reliance that was his most fatal weakness. Long periods of the profoundest lethargy would be interrupted with bursts of frantic, almost hysterical activity. He could be cruel to the point of savagery at one moment, almost unbelievably merciful the next. His attitude to Matthew Bonnellus, hostile and welcoming by turns —to say nothing of his shameful treatment of Henry Aristippus— shows how pathetically easily he could be swayed by his changing moods, or by the counsels of those around him. Lacking any real equilibrium himself, he proved incapable of maintaining all those delicate political balances on which the safety of his realm depended —between himself and his subjects, nobility and bourgeoisie, Christian and Muslim.

And yet—William the Bad? The epithet still rings false. There was nothing evil about him. In no sense was he a wicked man;[1] and, if the above analysis is correct, it would suggest that his reluctance to face up to so many of his political responsibilities was due not only to his natural indolence but also to a genuine conviction that there were others around him better qualified for the task. It might also mean that William, far from being the careless hedonist that Falcandus depicts, was in fact a profoundly unhappy man who saw in every new palace and pleasure merely another temporary refuge for his troubled spirit. Perhaps William the Sad might have been a more accurate description. We shall never know. Of the only two important contemporary chroniclers of his reign, one is accurate but maddeningly sketchy, the other brilliant but hopelessly unreliable. In the absence of any further evidence we can only return a verdict of Not Proven, and leave one of the most enigmatic characters in the history of Norman Sicily to his rest.

[1] There is still a Sicilian popular tradition to the effect that William called in all the gold and silver coinage of the kingdom and replaced it with copper, keeping the proceeds for himself. No contemporary records suggest anything of the kind. Certain measures may well have been taken to restore the economy after 1161, but not even Falcandus accuses the King of deliberately impoverishing his subjects for his own profit.

PART FOUR

SUNSET

14

THE COUNSELLORS OF UNWISDOM

For although both peoples, Apulians and Sicilians, are faithless, unreliable and given to every kind of villainy, yet are the Sicilians more cunning
in dissimulation and in the concealment of their true motives, beguiling
those whom they hate with honeyed words and gentle flattery in order to
do them greater hurt by taking them unawares.

Hugo Falcandus

LEGALLY, there was no problem over the succession. The dying
King had made it clear that he wished the crown to pass to his elder
surviving son, William; and that the younger, Henry, must be
content with the principality of Capua. Since William was still only
twelve years old, his mother Queen Margaret was to act as Regent,
with the continued help of Richard Palmer, Caïd Peter and Matthew
of Ajello. It all seemed straightforward enough.

The three advisers, however, were not so sure. Long minorities
under a woman regent were always dangerous; the prestige of the
Crown had not altogether recovered from the events of 1161; there
might easily be a movement by the aristocracy in favour of the dead
King's illegitimate brother Simon. Young William, after all, had
never been associated with the throne during his father's lifetime; he
had not even been created Duke of Apulia, the traditional title for
the heir apparent. Such were their misgivings that they had even
persuaded Margaret to delay the announcement of her husband's
death while preparations were made for the coronation, and to
proceed with the ceremony as soon as the three-day period of
mourning was over.

They need not have bothered. On the day appointed for his
coronation—which was also the day of his first public appearance—

young William immediately won all hearts. Unlike his father, the boy started off with one supreme advantage: he was quite out-standingly good-looking. When, in Palermo Cathedral, Romuald of Salerno anointed him with the holy oil and laid the Crown of Sicily on his head, and when, later, he rode in state through the city to the Royal Palace, the golden circlet still gleaming on the long fair hair inherited from his Viking forbears, his subjects—whatever their race, creed or political affiliation—could not contain their joy. Fresh-faced but solemn—he was still a few weeks short of his thir-teenth birthday—he seemed to combine the innocence of a child with a gravity beyond his years. Loyalty was suddenly in the air. Even Hugo Falcandus, describing the scene, permits himself one of his rare bursts of charity:

Though always of surpassing beauty, on that day he appeared—by what means I cannot tell—more beautiful than ever before. . . . And so he gained the love and favour of all, to the point where even those whose hatred of his father had been bitter and who had resolved never more to owe any allegiance to his heirs and successors were claiming that the first man to harbour evil designs against him would have passed beyond the bounds of all common humanity. It was enough, they said, that he who was responsible for their ills should have been taken from their midst; an innocent boy should not be blamed for the tyrannies of his father. For truly the child was of such beauty that it would be impossible to allow of an equal, far less of a superior.

On the same day, as a further indication that this was indeed the beginning of a new era for the Kingdom, Queen Margaret declared a general amnesty, opened all the prisons and restored all confiscated lands to their former owners. More significant still, she also abolished redemption money, the most unpopular of all her late husband's impositions, by means of which many cities and towns of the main-land were still being bled white for having dared, five years before, to rise up against him.

It was an auspicious start; but Margaret knew that she would be hard put to maintain her advantage. For one thing, she had grave doubts about her present triumvirate of advisers. She was a strong-willed woman, at thirty-eight still in the prime of life, and they were probably inclined to be overbearing in their attitude towards her, insufficiently mindful of her superior authority; but what made them in the last resort unacceptable was the fact that as former counsellors and nominees of William I they were all irremediably identified with the previous regime. Clearly they would have to go; but who was to take their place?

Among the aristocracy there were countless barons only too eager —and, doubtless, in several cases confidently expecting—to assume the positions of power they had so long coveted; Margaret, however, recoiled at the prospect. Again and again these nobles had shown how shallow their real loyalties were. It was they, and they alone, who had taken up arms against her husband and had held her and her children prisoner; to admit them now to the inner councils of government would lead to a proliferation of feudal estates in Sicily until the island became as unmanageable as Apulia and Campania had always been. This in turn would be bound to sharpen the already smouldering confessional animosities; and the result, sooner or later, would be a *coup* against herself and her son, against which they would have little if any defence. Fortunately since the fall of Matthew Bonnellus the aristocratic party had been without an effective leader and seemed to have lost much of its cohesion. For the time being it constituted no real threat. Margaret could afford to look elsewhere.

There was always the Church—but what a Church it had become. Like so many high ecclesiastics of the Middle Ages, the bishops and archbishops of the Sicilian Kingdom were a worldly lot, more politicians than prelates, many of them never going near their dioceses[1] but remaining permanently at the court in Palermo, endlessly meddling, bickering, squabbling and intriguing against each other. Of them all, by far the ablest and most influential was Richard Palmer—whose absenteeism was such that he was not consecrated Bishop of Syracuse till 1169, fourteen years after his election to the see. He had been largely responsible for the bishops' initiative that had saved William I in 1161 from the hands of the

[1] This practice soon became such a scandal that Pope Alexander III had to pass a decree in 1176 requiring Sicilian bishops who had spent seven years or more at court to return to their posts.

insurgents, as a result of which he had become the late King's closest adviser. He was, however, universally disliked for his arrogance and haughtiness; and his rapid advancement had not endeared him to his colleagues, particularly since he made no secret of the fact that he had his eye firmly fixed on the greatest of all prizes for a Sicilian church-man—the vacant archbishopric of Palermo.

But Richard Palmer was not the only contender. Romuald of Salerno, the present primate, was another obvious possibility; so too was Bishop Tristan of Mazara. Then there was Roger, Archbishop of Reggio, in the description of whom Falcandus finds the top of his form:

Already on the brink of old age, he was tall and so excessively thin that he appeared to be eaten away from the inside. His voice was weak as a whistle. His face—and indeed his whole body—was pale and yet somehow tinged with blackness, making him look more like a corpse than a man; and his external aspect well indicated the charac-ter within. He counted no labour difficult if there were hope of gain therefrom; and he would willingly endure hunger and thirst beyond the limits of human tolerance in order to save money. Never happy at his own table, he was never sad at those of others, and would frequently spend whole days without food, waiting to be invited to dinner.

One of the Archbishop's most frequent hosts was Gentile, the Bishop of Agrigento, felicitously described by Chalandon as a *prélat aventureux et vagabond*, who had originally come to Sicily as an ambassador from King Geza of Hungary and then decided to stay on. Gentile, as Falcandus informs us with some relish, made no secret of his *penchant* for debauchery, and profited by his sumptuous and vaguely orgiastic banquets to start a serious whispering campaign against Palmer with the intention of blocking his candidature. His complaints about the Bishop-elect's foreign origins must have sounded a little strange in the circumstances, but he had rather more success when he persuaded Matthew of Ajello that Palmer was plotting his assassination; Matthew was with difficulty restrained from getting his own knife in first.[1]

[1] Although, as the above paragraphs make clear, pressure of affairs in Palermo normally prevented these clerics from paying any but the most fleeting visits to

One other candidate remained for the coveted archbishopric. At the time he must have seemed something of an outsider, since he could not even boast episcopal rank. He also was an Englishman, whose various orthographical disguises—Ophamilus or Offamiglio to name but two—represent nothing more than desperate Sicilian attempts to deal phonetically with his perfectly ordinary English name, Walter of the Mill. First brought to Sicily as tutor to the royal children, he had been successively appointed Archdeacon of Cefalù, then Dean of Agrigento. Now he was one of the canons of the Palatine Chapel, where he was proving himself even more unscrupulous and ambitious than the compatriot whose career he was working so hard to undermine. Only he, of all the rivals, was to attain his objective. For reasons which we shall presently see, he had to wait for it another three years; but for a quarter of a century after that he was destined to occupy the highest political and ecclesiastical posts in the realm, building the present cathedral and becoming almost certainly the only Englishman in history regularly to sign himself *Emir and Archbishop*. As such, he will play an important—and ultimately disastrous—part in the closing chapters of this story.

The aristocracy, then, was dangerous and of doubtful loyalty; the hierarchy self-seeking and—so far as the personalities of its principal members were concerned—distinctly unattractive. That left only one other significant group—the palace officials and civil servants, headed by the eunuch Caïd Peter and the Grand Protonotary, Matthew of Ajello. Even by eunuch standards, Peter was an uninspiring character; but he too had proved his devotion to the King and his family in 1161, and his administrative efficiency was beyond question. Matthew for his part was at least as able; he had recently completed the herculean task—which no one but he could possibly have

their dioceses, several seem to have tried to make amends by magnificent donations and endowments. Thus Romuald of Salerno is responsible for the superb marble and mosaic ambo in his cathedral (originally founded, it will be remembered, by Robert Guiscard) and Richard Palmer for the glass and mosaics—what is left of them—at Syracuse. The cathedral treasury of Agrigento possesses a very fine Byzantine portable altar, which is certainly of the twelfth century and may well have been a gift from Gentile. Despite his proclivities, however, we cannot alas connect him with the other pride of the Agrigento collection—a handwritten letter from the Devil which is preserved, very properly, in the archives.

accomplished—of recompiling, largely from memory, a comprehensive register of lands and fiefs to replace that which had been
destroyed in the insurrection. Like Richard Palmer, however,
he had one of those dominating characters that Queen Margaret
instinctively mistrusted. He was furthermore obsessed with the idea
of being appointed Emir of Emirs—a rank and title which had remained in abeyance since the death of Maio of Bari—and was
consequently for ever immersed in intrigues of his own, besides
giving himself the airs and graces of a *grand seigneur* and using his
steadily increasing wealth to build a noble church in the city as
George of Antioch and Maio had done before him.[1] Of the pair,
the Queen much preferred Peter. He was not the ideal solution—the
nobles, in particular, hated and despised him—but he seemed
relatively free of personal ambition and was less of an intriguer than
most of his fellows. In any case he would be able to hold the Kingdom together while she found someone more suitable. To the fury of
Matthew and of Richard Palmer, she promoted him over their
heads—thus putting the effective direction of the Sicilian Kingdom,
now one of the richest and most influential powers in Christian
Europe, in the hands of a Muslim eunuch.

But she had also made another decision. To govern the realm as it
needed to be governed and to preserve it for her son, she had to have
someone who was not only firm and capable but disinterested and,
above all, uncommitted. He must also be someone who spoke her
language and whom she found personally sympathetic. In all Sicily,
it appeared, no such paragon existed. Very well, she would look
elsewhere. New situations called for new men to handle them.
Secretly, she wrote a long letter to her cousin[2] Rothrud, Archbishop

---

[1] Though Matthew's church, known as the Magione, was badly damaged
during the second world war, it has been sensitively restored and is well worth a
visit. With its three apses, its blind and interlaced arcading and the lovely
cloister that adjoins it, it provides an excellent example of later Norman-Sicilian
architecture, shorn of all obvious Arabic influences. With the fall of the Norman
Kingdom at the end of the century, the church and neighbouring convent were
given over to the military order of the Teutonic Knights, traces of whose
occupancy are still visible. Most guidebooks, incidentally, give the date of the
original construction as 1150; in fact it was almost certainly begun a good decade
later, and finished during Queen Margaret's regency.

[2] Not her uncle, as Chalandon maintains—see genealogical table on p. 395.

of Rouen, explaining her situation and suggesting that he might send some member of their family out to Palermo to help her. Two names she mentioned in particular: Rothrud's brother Robert of Newburgh or, failing him, another cousin—Stephen du Perche.

That the Queen's anxieties for the future were justified, the next few months were all too clearly to show. On the other hand her confidence, such as it was, in Caïd Peter's abilities proved to have been misplaced. By the middle of the summer Sicily was in chaos. With all the various factions jockeying ever more frenziedly for position, the plots more plentiful, the intrigues still thicker than before, no proper government was possible; and Peter, a civil servant rather than a statesman, was incapable of imposing his will on an unruly and discontented people. To have done so at that time would have needed a man of infinitely greater stature—a Maio of Bari at the least. And even Maio had succumbed in the end.

Typical of those who sought to fish in these troubled waters was the Queen's cousin, Gilbert.[1] Some clue to his character may be seen in the haste with which, on his arrival in Sicily a few years before, he had been placated with the County of Gravina and packed off to Apulia—where, as we have seen, he had later become involved in the conspiracy against Maio. On the late King's death and his cousin's assumption of the Regency he had hurried back to the capital and, with the covert support of Richard Palmer, had soon become the focus of the opposition to Caïd Peter, complaining publicly that Sicily was being run by slaves and eunuchs and constantly pressing Margaret to appoint him her chief minister in Peter's stead. The Queen, with understandable reluctance, had at last offered him a seat on the council, but Gilbert had indignantly refused—in the course of a hideous scene in which, if Falcandus is to be believed, he berated Margaret for having put him on the same level as a slave,

[1] I have not been able to trace Gilbert's relationship with the Queen. Chalandon says that he had arrived from Spain, but gives no references to support this theory; from his name and from subsequent events it seems to me far likelier that he was one of the French side of the family—possibly a son or grandson of a sibling of Margaret of Laigle, the Queen's mother. (See genealogical table, p. 395.) La Lumia accepts him as a Frenchman and even on one occasion refers to him as Stephen's nephew—surely most improbable.

threatened her with a nation-wide revolution, and left her in tears.

But the aristocratic faction had found in the Count of Gravina the mouthpiece they had long been seeking, and as they grew daily more threatening the Queen and Peter recognised that some voice in the council chamber could no longer be denied them. With Gilbert still persisting in his refusal, they therefore nominated one of the army leaders, that same Richard of Mandra who had protected William I with his own body during the 1161 insurrection—whom, in order to give him equal rank with her odious cousin, Margaret now created Count of Molise. This appointment was more than Gilbert could stand. He did his best to conceal his anger; but henceforth he began to plot seriously against the eunuch's life.

It was not long before Peter's agents brought him word of what was going on. At first he merely strengthened his bodyguard; but finally, with Maio's fate constantly at the back of his mind, his nerve failed him. A ship was secretly fitted out in the harbour; and one dark night, taking with him a few fellow-eunuchs and a large quantity of money, Peter slipped back to those shores whence, long ago, he had come. On his return to Tunis he resumed his former name of Ahmed, the religion of his fathers and, ultimately, his original profession; for we later find him commander of Caliph Yusuf's Moroccan fleet, in which capacity he is said to have fought with great distinction against the Christians.[1] After what he had suffered from them in Palermo, this should cause us no surprise; perhaps, as Falcandus maintained, he was ever a Saracen at heart.

Peter's defection came as a blow to Margaret, and also as a severe embarrassment. She vigorously denied allegations that he had absconded with any of the royal treasure, but she could not muffle the triumphant crowings of Gilbert of Gravina. What other conduct could ever have been expected of a Muslim slave, he demanded; had not Peter already once betrayed his country—at Mahdia seven years before? The only wonder was that he had not long ago introduced his Almohad friends into the palace, to make off with the rest of the treasure and, in all probability, with the King as well. Richard of

[1] These details of Peter's subsequent career are given us by Ibn Khaldun (*B.A.S.*, II, pp. 166 and 238). He refers to him as Ahmed es-Sikeli; from the chronological and other details he gives of the flight from Sicily there can be no doubt that Ahmed and Peter are one and the same. (See p. 306.)

Molise, who chanced to be present, could restrain himself no longer and sprang to the defence of his former patron, pointing out that Peter was no slave—he had been formally enfranchised by William I —and that his departure was solely due to the Count of Gravina's notorious intrigues against him. If any man called him traitor, then he—Richard—would be prepared to settle the matter once and for all by single combat.

Somehow the two were separated before any violence was done, but the incident was enough to convince the Queen that her cousin could no longer be permitted to remain in the capital. On the pre-text that Frederick Barbarossa was said to be preparing another expedition to the south, she confirmed Gilbert as Catapan of Apulia and Campania and invited him forthwith to return to the mainland and prepare the army for war. The Count had no delusions as to the real reason for his departure; seeing, however, that in the present state of affairs there was no future for him in Palermo he accepted the charge and, still fuming, took his leave.

With Gilbert of Gravina out of the way, Margaret must have felt some measure of relief; but in other respects the situation was little easier than before. Fortunately she still had one counsellor whom she liked and could trust—Richard of Molise, who had now taken Peter's place as chief minister in the Council. Though Richard had little political experience and was inclined to be intemperate and head-strong, he was completely loyal and, says Falcandus, was greatly feared by all—a useful attribute at such a time. But, he too was powerless to stop the decline. Perhaps because he was held in greater respect than Peter he also failed to draw as much popular criticism on himself, with the result that Margaret found herself increasingly blamed for the state of the realm. Already her popularity—based largely on the amnesty she had declared and by the remission of redemption money, but tinged also with the admiration due to the mother of so beautiful a son—had vanished away. Nowadays, in the street, men were openly grumbling and gossiping about 'the Spanish woman',[1] and even looking nostalgically back to the bad old days of her husband's reign.

---

[1] Just as, six centuries later, Marie Antoinette was to be known as *'l'Autri-chienne'* in the streets of Paris.

And now, at the worst possible moment—which was in itself
typical of him—there arrived in Palermo another of the Queen's
more disreputable relations. Gilbert had been bad enough; the newcomer was more unattractive still. Not only the timing of his arrival
but everything about him seemed inept and tactless—even his birth.
In theory at least, he was Margaret's brother; Falcandus on the other
hand is at pains to point out that it was common knowledge—and
admitted as such even by the gang of Navarrese adventurers whom
the young man had brought with him—that King Garcia had never
accepted him as a son, believing him to be the child of one of his
wife's prodigious collection of lovers. Then there was his name,
Rodrigo, which sounded so barbarous and indeed ridiculous to
Sicilian ears that his sister at once made him change it to Henry.
Finally we have Falcandus's description of his appearance, character
and way of life.

This Henry was short in stature; his beard was extremely thin, his
complexion unpleasantly swarthy. He was imprudent and of poor
conversation, a man who had no interests but dice and gaming, no
wants but a partner to play against and plenty of money to lose; he
would spend wildly, with neither forethought nor consideration.
Having passed some little time in Palermo, during which by his
immoderate spending he had soon squandered the immense sums
given him by the Queen, he announced his intention of crossing to
Apulia; but on his arrival at Messina he at once fell in with many
fellows of the kind he found congenial. Now this city, which is
largely given over to foreigners, predators and pirates, harbours
almost every kind of man within its walls: persons expert in every
villainy, acquainted with every vice, men who esteem nothing illicit
which lies within their power to achieve. Thus he was soon surrounded by thieves, pirates, buffoons, yes-men and criminals of all
descriptions, carousing by day and spending whole nights gambling.
When these things reached the ears of the Queen, she wrote him a
severe reprimand, ordering him to cross the straits without delay.
And so, though hardly able to tear himself away, he took his
comrades' advice and set off for Apulia.

Soon after his arrival in Sicily, Margaret had given up her original
idea of marrying him off to an illegitimate daughter of Roger II,
and had instead bestowed upon him the County of Montescaglioso—
just as she had given Gilbert that of Gravina—with the deliberate

object of keeping him as far as possible from the capital. When at last she received word of his safe arrival in his fief, she may ruefully have reflected that he had already done just about all the damage he could. If so, she was soon to discover that she was wrong; but not before the advent of yet a third member of her family, as different from the other two as it was possible to imagine and distinctly more promising.

When Archbishop Rothrud of Rouen received his cousin Margaret's appeal for help, he acted swiftly. His brother, Robert of Newburgh, seems to have had little inclination to involve himself in Sicilian affairs; but Margaret's other suggestion, young Stephen du Perche, was immediately attracted to the idea. The invitation reached him just in time, as he was on the point of setting out, with a suite of no less than thirty-seven, for the Holy Land. When he left France, this was still his ultimate objective; but he saw no reason not to stop off for a few months in Palermo on his way.

After a short stay in Apulia with Gilbert—who presumably gave him a highly tendentious account of the Sicilian political scene—Stephen arrived in Palermo towards the end of the summer, to an enthusiastic, even effusive, welcome from Queen Margaret. One of the first things that struck the Palermitans about him was his extreme youth. He can have been only in his early twenties at most, while the fact that Falcandus and William of Tyre describe him with the words *puer* and *adolescens*—this in an age when men were often leading armies before they were out of their teens—suggests that he may have been even younger. Such a supposition, on the other hand, raises a new problem. Rothrud II, Count of Perche, whom Margaret referred to as his father, is known to have died in 1143; if Stephen were in fact his son, he could not in September 1166 be less than twenty-two—a little old for boyhood or adolescence. But we also know that soon after Rothrud's death his widow was married again, this time to Robert of Dreux, brother of Louis VII—who, in a letter to his fellow-ruler William II, was later to refer to Stephen as *caro et sanguis noster,* 'our own flesh and blood'. It has therefore been argued that Stephen was not of the family of Perche at all, but a nephew of the French King. If he were, however, why did he not say so and take advantage of the fact, and why is it mentioned by none of the contemporary chroniclers? As Chalandon characteristically puts it, *l'on ne peut pas sortir du domaine de l'hypothèse*; the question must remain unresolved.[1]

Man or boy, Stephen seems to have appeared to the Queen just the person she needed to support her in her tribulations; and she in turn had little difficulty in persuading him, with promises of power, riches and honours for himself and his companions, to postpone his pilgrimage indefinitely and to share with her the government of the realm. From the outset he seemed able and energetic; just as important—and even rarer in Sicily—he proved personally incorruptible. Margaret was delighted with him. In November 1166, scarcely two months after his arrival in Palermo, she appointed him Chancellor.

The news of the appointment, as might have been expected, called forth a storm of protest. It was now over a century since the Normans had invaded the island, thirty-six years since the founding of the Kingdom. The Sicilians were beginning to feel themselves a nation, and to resent seeing more and more of the senior—and most profitable—positions in the land being given to foreign newcomers. Matthew of Ajello, it now appeared, was not the only one in the palace to have had his eye on the Chancellorship. Besides, while the office remained vacant its revenues had been divided among the members of the inner council. Stephen's appointment thus not only blighted their hopes; it reduced their incomes too.

Nor was it the new Chancellor alone who aroused such feelings. He had arrived, it will be remembered, with an entourage of thirty-seven; in the months that followed others came out from France to

---

[1] A genealogical table showing the two possible relationships between Queen Margaret and Stephen du Perche will be found on p. 395. The theory of Stephen's royal parentage was first put forward, by Bréquigny, as long ago as 1780 (*Mémoires de l'Académie des Inscriptions*, vol. XLI). It is strongly contested by La Lumia, while Chalandon, as we have seen, sits firmly on the fence. My own opinion, for what it is worth, is that Stephen was what he purported to be—a younger son of the Count of Perche—and that the phrase of Louis VII must be dismissed as a figure of speech, not too far-fetched in the circumstances. It seems in any case unlikely that he would have been made both Chancellor and Archbishop if he had not been at least in his twenties—hardly more than boyhood for the two highest posts in the kingdom.

join him: and before long the court and many sections of the administration seemed more French than Sicilian. It was perhaps natural that the young man should prefer to surround himself with people he knew, whose native language he understood; but it was natural too that those who suffered by the change should resent it, the more so since many of his friends—especially those who had received Sicilian fiefs—behaved with curious tactlessness, treating the country folk around them as a subject race and everywhere imposing French habits and customs without regard for local susceptibilities.

On the other hand, Stephen was a genuine idealist. He may have lacked sensitivity and finesse, but he sincerely wished to make Sicily a better place and lost no time in instituting the reforms he considered necessary. He turned his attention first to the notaries—thus antagonising Matthew of Ajello, the Protonotary, of one of whose relations he made a public example; then, in rapid succession, he dealt with judges, local officials and castellans, clamping down on injustice wherever he saw it. 'He never,' says Falcandus, 'allowed powerful men to oppress their subjects, nor ever feigned to overlook any injury done to the poor. In such a way his fame quickly spread throughout the Kingdom ... so that men looked on him as a heaven-sent angel of consolation who had brought back the Golden Age.'

Even when we make due allowance for exaggeration, tendentious reporting and the sad scarcity of reliable source material, it is hard to avoid the conclusion that Margaret was initially justified in her decision to bring in an outsider to govern the Kingdom. Reforms were obviously overdue; and in the prevailing atmosphere of discord and mistrust it would have been virtually impossible for any Sicilian—whether by birth or by long-term adoption—to bring them about. Stephen, impartial and uncommitted, was in a position to do so, and because he did not lack moral courage he succeeded. But in the process, however much favour he gained with the masses, it was inevitable that he should have made himself hated by his Sicilian subordinates; and though his preference for Frenchmen around him may have gratuitously provided additional grounds for resentment, his own presence and power in the land would have been more than enough to ensure his lasting unpopularity.

And was this unpopularity so bad a thing? Nothing unites a people like a common enemy, and in a country so torn by factional strife any unifying force, even an oppressive and corrupt tyranny, might have had an ultimately beneficial effect. Stephen was neither oppressive nor corrupt; he was simply disliked. And it is at least arguable that the greatest benefit he conferred on the Kingdom lay not in any of his administrative reforms but in the solidarity he gave to his opponents, reminding them that they were above all Sicilians, and Sicilians with a job to do—to rid their country of foreign intruders.

Just how successfully they did it will be told in a later chapter. Meanwhile there appeared on the horizon another intruder, compared with whom Stephen du Perche and his friends must have seemed petty irritations indeed. Within weeks of their coming to power, news reached Palermo that the Emperor was once again on the march.

15

THE SECOND SCHISM

Quid facis insane   patrie mors, Octaviane!
Cur presumpsisti   tunicam dividere Christi?
Jamjam pulvis eris;   modo vivis, cras morieris.

(Octavian, by what aberration
Do you seek to bring Rome to damnation?
How were you ever enticed
So to sever the tunic of Christ?
You too will be dust by and by;
As you lived, so tomorrow you'll die.)

Britto, a pamphleteer of Rome

WHEN, at the close of the year 1166, Frederick Barbarossa led his immense army southward on the new campaign, he had before him three distinct objectives. First, he intended to liquidate the unofficial Byzantine outpost at Ancona; next, he would march against the Pope in Rome, whom he was resolved to replace on the throne of St Peter by an anti-Pope of his own choosing; finally, as always, there was the Norman Kingdom of Sicily to be smashed. Separate as these three targets were, the reasons which led the Emperor to attack them were closely interrelated; to understand them, however, we must cast a quick retrospective glance at the progress of the imperial-papal duel during the seven years since the death of Pope Adrian—and, in particular, at the melancholy farce which had attended the election of his successor.

It may be remembered how, just before Adrian died, the assembled cardinals of the pro-Sicilian party gathered at Anagni had agreed to elect as the next pope one of their own number—their leader, Cardinal Roland, being the obvious favourite. Since this group

constituted some two-thirds of the electoral college, there was reason
to hope that the election might pass off smoothly enough—as
indeed it might have but for the presence in the pro-imperialist
opposition of Cardinal Octavian of S. Cecilia. This prelate has
already made two brief and faintly ludicrous appearances in our
story—the first when, as a papal emissary to Roger II, he had to be
told by Roger himself of the Pope's death and the consequent expiry
of his own special powers, and the second when, on a similar mission
to Conrad of Hohenstaufen, his behaviour earned him the ridicule
of John of Salisbury.[1] But never in his long and inglorious career
can he have made such an exhibition of himself as on this occasion.[2]

On 5 September 1159, the day after Adrian's body had been laid
to rest in the crypt of St Peter's, about thirty cardinals assembled in
conclave behind the high altar of the basilica;[3] two days later, all but
three of them had cast their votes for Cardinal Roland, who was
therefore declared to have been elected—a declaration, be it noted,
perfectly in accordance with canon law. The scarlet mantle of the
Papacy was brought forward and Roland, after the customary
display of reluctance, bent his head to receive it. Suddenly Octavian
dived at him, snatched the mantle and tried to don it himself. A
scuffle followed, during which he lost it again; but his chaplain
instantly produced another—presumably brought along for just
such an eventuality—which Octavian this time managed to put
on, unfortunately back to front, before anyone could stop him.

There followed a scene of scarcely believable confusion. Wrench-
ing himself free from the furious supporters of Roland who were
trying to tear the mantle forcibly from his back, Octavian—whose
frantic efforts to turn it right way round had resulted only in getting
the fringes tangled round his neck—made a dash for the papal throne,

[1] See pp. 110 and 150n.
[2] I have taken the following account from Gerhoh of Reichensburg (*De Investigatione Antichristi*, i. 53), whose version is not only the fullest but also—in the
opinion of at least one authority (Mann)—'more likely to be impartial than any
of the others'. Impartiality, however, is a rare virtue among historians of the
twelfth century; and it is only fair to add that among writers of more imperialist
sympathies Octavian also has his champions.
[3] By the end there may have been only twenty-nine; according to Arnulf of
Lisieux (*Ep. ad cardinales*, Migne, vol. 201, col. 41) Bishop Imarus of Tusculum, a
renowned epicure, left early because he refused to miss his dinner.

sat in it and proclaimed himself Pope Victor IV.[1] He then charged off through St Peter's until he found a group of minor clergy, whom he ordered to give him their acclamation—which, seeing the doors suddenly burst open and a band of armed cut-throats swarming into the church, they hastily did. Temporarily at least, the opposition was silenced; Roland and his adherents slipped out while they could and took a hasty refuge in St Peter's tower, a fortified corner of the Vatican which was safe in the hands of Cardinal Boso. Meanwhile, with the cut-throats looking on, Octavian was enthroned a little more formally than on the previous occasion and escorted in triumph to the Lateran—having been at some pains, we are told, to adjust his dress before leaving.

However undignified in its execution, the *coup* could now be seen to have been thoroughly and efficiently planned in advance—and on a scale that left no doubt that the Empire must have been actively implicated. Octavian himself had long been known as an imperial sympathiser and his election was immediately recognised by Frederick's two ambassadors in Rome, who at the same time declared a vigorous war on Roland. Once again they opened their coffers, and German gold flowed freely into the purses and pockets of all those Romans—nobles, senators, bourgeoisie or rabble—who would openly proclaim their allegiance to Victor IV. Meanwhile Roland and his faithful cardinals remained blockaded in St Peter's tower.

But almost at once Octavian—or Victor, as we must now call him—saw his support begin to dwindle. The story of his behaviour at the election was by now common knowledge in the city and, we may be sure, had lost nothing in the telling; everywhere, the Romans were turning towards Roland as their lawfully-elected Pope. A mob had formed around St Peter's tower and was now angrily clamouring for his release. After a week he had to be removed to a place of greater security in Trastevere, but they only clamoured the louder. In the street, Victor was hooted at and reviled; lines of doggerel were chanted mockingly at him as he passed. On the night of 16 September he could bear it no longer and fled from Rome; and on the following day the rightful Pontiff was led back into the capital amid general rejoicing.

[1] Strangely, it was the second time this title had been chosen by an anti-Pope. See p. 65.

But Roland knew that he could not stay. The imperial ambassadors were still in Rome, where they still had limitless money to spend. Victor's family, too, the Crescentii, was among the richest and most powerful in the city. Pausing only to assemble an appropriate retinue, on 20 September the Pope travelled south to Ninfa, then a thriving little town under the sway of his friends the Frangipani; and there, in the church of S. Maria Maggiore, he at last received formal consecration as Alexander III[1]. One of his first acts, predictably, was to excommunicate the anti-Pope—who soon afterwards and equally predictably excommunicated him in return. For the second time in thirty years, the Church of Rome was in schism.

The election of his old friend Cardinal Roland to the Papacy had been the last major diplomatic triumph for Maio of Bari; but the fact that it proved an even greater blessing to the Kingdom of Sicily than Maio had ever dreamed was due, paradoxically, to Frederick Barbarossa himself. Had Frederick bowed to the inevitable and accepted Alexander as the rightful Pope he undoubtedly was, there is no reason why the two should not have reached some accommodation; instead, at the Council of Pavia in February 1160, he formally recognised the ludicrous Victor, thereby forcing Alexander—whose claim was soon accepted by all the other rulers of Europe—into even closer alliance with William I and saddling himself with a new series of vain and useless obligations which were to cripple him politically for the best part of twenty years. But for these obligations he would almost certainly have been able to take advantage of the Sicilian crisis of 1161–62 as we know he planned to do;[2] and the Norman Kingdom of Sicily might have ended even sooner and more tragically than it did.

It was that crisis that decided Alexander to take positive action against the Emperor. To be sure, he had excommunicated Frederick

[1] The town of Ninfa was sacked and destroyed in 1382, since when it has lain in ruins. By then, however, it had been acquired by the Caetani family, to whom it still belongs; and since 1922 they have turned the site into one of the loveliest and most romantic gardens in all Italy.

[2] Treaties signed by Frederick with Genoa and Pisa during the early summer of 1162 made his intention clear. In both of them he seems to consider his conquest of Sicily a foregone conclusion.

as early as March 1160—after Pavia he had had little choice—and absolved all imperial subjects from their allegiance; until the end of the following year, however, he had divided his time—apart from one short and unsuccessful attempt to re-establish himself in Rome—between Terracina and Anagni, two papal cities conveniently close to the borders of the Sicilian Kingdom, to which he looked both for his physical protection and for the financial subsidies he so desperately needed. The events of 1161, starting with the Palermo insurrection and ending with the whole of South Italy up in arms against the King, changed all that. The Pope saw that William of Sicily could no longer be relied upon in an emergency; other allies were needed. Leaving Terracina on a Sicilian ship in the last days of 1161, he landed in April near Montpellier.

For the next three and a half years, Alexander was to live in exile in France—mostly at Sens, where Peter Abelard had been crushed by the oratory of St Bernard almost a quarter of a century before—working to form a great European League comprising England, France, Sicily, Hungary, Venice, the Lombard towns and Byzantium, against Frederick Barbarossa. He failed, as he was bound to fail. Long conversations with the kings of England and France resulted in broad measures of agreement, cordial expressions of support and —more important still—further heavy subsidies; but no alliance. Henry II in particular he found impossible to trust. In the early days of the schism he had been a firm friend; as early as 1160 Arnulf of Lisieux had reported that while the King 'received all Alexander's communications with respect, he would not so much as touch Octavian's letters with his hands, but would take hold of them with a piece of stick and throw them behind his back as far as he could'. But in 1163 his difficulties with Thomas Becket had begun, and in the following year his promulgation of the Constitutions of Clarendon—deliberately designed to strengthen his hold over the English Church at the expense of the Pope—had caused a distinct chill in Anglo-Papal relations.

William of Sicily too had made difficulties. Alexander had no firmer friend, Barbarossa no more convinced opponent. William was on excellent terms with England, France, Hungary and the Lombard towns, and would willingly have reached some sort of agreement with Venice. But Byzantium was another matter. In 1158, at the insistence of Pope Adrian, he had made his peace with Manuel Comnenus—and a generous peace at that, considering how soundly he had trounced him only two years before. Even at the time, however, he had known that it could not last; the Byzantines showed no signs of giving up their long-term ambitions in Italy. Subsequent developments had proved him right. Within a year or two Manuel was building up his position again, not only in his old headquarters at Ancona but in all the main towns of Lombardy, to say nothing of Genoa and Pisa; everywhere his agents were busy, encouraging anti-imperial feeling and dispensing subsidies with a generous hand. Insofar as this policy was directed against Barbarossa it was no doubt to be welcomed, but William had had enough experience of the Greeks to know that their presence anywhere west of the Adriatic was, directly or indirectly, a threat to Sicily. Besides, if Manuel's intentions were honourable, why was he still giving shelter to Sicilian rebels? He was no better than Frederick. William replied to the Pope's overtures in the only way he could—that he would never, at any price, voluntarily allow Byzantine troops on his territory.

But Alexander's disappointment at his diplomatic failure must have been forgotten when, early in 1165, he received an invitation from the Roman Senate to return to the city. His rival, the anti-Pope Victor, who had also been forced to spend the last years in exile, had died the year before in pain and poverty at Lucca, where he had been keeping alive on the proceeds of not very successful brigandage and where the local hierarchy would not even allow him burial within the walls. Frederick, stubborn as ever, had immediately given his blessing to the 'election', by his two tame schismatic cardinals, of a successor under the name of Paschal III; but the action had earned him and his anti-Pope nothing but scorn, and it may well have been the ensuing wave of resentment and disgust at the absurdity of the schism and the pig-headedness of the Emperor that had at last brought the Romans to their senses. Besides, the pilgrim trade had dried up. Without a Pope, mediaeval Rome lost its *raison d'être*.

For all that, the homecoming was not an easy one. Frederick did everything he could to prevent it, even hiring pirates to waylay the papal convoy on the high seas. Next he sent another army into Italy, which established the wretched Paschal at Viterbo and ravaged all the Roman Campagna until Gilbert of Gravina, at last justifying his existence, appeared with a Sicilian force and drove it back into Tuscany. But somehow Alexander defeated all these machinations. In order to escape the Pisan, Genoese and Provençal ships that he knew were lying in wait for him he took a roundabout route and landed, in September 1165, at Messina. William I did not come to greet him; by that time he had retired so completely into seclusion that not even the Roman Pontiff himself could bring him out. But he sent orders that his honoured guest should be treated as a 'lord and father', and furnished with all the money and troops he needed; and on 23 November the Pope reached Rome where, escorted by senators, nobles, clergy and people, all bearing olive branches in their hands, he rode in state to the Lateran.

Although at the time of Alexander's visit King William had only a few more months to live, this was not the last instance of his generosity towards the Pope whose closest ally he had never ceased to be. On his death-bed he sent Alexander a further gift of forty thousand florins, the better to continue his struggle against the Emperor.[1] The gesture was not altruistic, nor was it merely a selfish attempt to purchase divine favour in the life to come. It was the dying King's last recognition of political reality; William knew that if Pope Alexander did not emerge victorious from that struggle, the Kingdom of Sicily could not long survive.

Frederick Barbarossa's army crossed the plain of Lombardy early in 1167; then it split into two parts. The smaller was jointly commanded by the Archbishop of Cologne, Rainald of Dassel—who was also imperial Chancellor and the Emperor's right hand—and by another warlike ecclesiastic, Archbishop Christian of Mainz. Their orders were to march down the peninsula towards Rome, enforcing the imperial authority as they went, and to open up a safe road to the city for the anti-Pope Paschal, still sitting nervously in Tuscany. On their way they were to stop at Pisa, there to secure the services

[1] John of Salisbury's letter 145 (to Bartholomew, Bishop of Exeter).

of its fleet for the moment when, later in the year, the whole weight
of the Empire was to be flung against Sicily. Meanwhile Frederick
himself, with the bulk of his army, pressed on across the peninsula
towards Ancona, the nucleus of Byzantine influence in Italy.

Frederick was, if anything, even angrier with the Greek Emperor
than with Pope Alexander. For well over a decade Manuel Comnenus had been stirring up trouble in Venice and Lombardy. His
agents treated Ancona—a city standing squarely within the territory of the Western Empire—as if it were a Byzantine colony. More
irritating still, he had recently tried to take advantage of the papal
schism by putting himself forward as a protector of Alexander. He
seemed to forget that he was himself a schismatic. He would be
reminded—forcibly—of this and of many other things as well once
the German army reached Ancona.

Barbarossa would have been more enraged still had he understood
the full extent of his fellow-Emperor's ambitions; for Manuel had
seen in the schism nothing less than a chance of realising his father's
old dream—the reunion of the Christian Church under the Pope of
Rome in return for that of the Roman Empire under the Emperor
at Constantinople. Frederick's recent behaviour had persuaded him
that the time was now ripe for a direct approach; and some time in
the spring of 1167—possibly at the very moment that the imperial
troops were marching on Ancona—a Byzantine ambassador in the
person of the *sebastos* Jordan, son of Prince Robert of Capua, arrived
in Rome to offer Alexander men and money 'sufficient', as he put it,
'to reduce all Italy to papal obedience' if he would endorse the
scheme.

Manuel was fully aware that at this of all moments the Pope could
not antagonise the King of Sicily; and he had no delusions about the
Sicilian view of his interference in Italian affairs. But even this
problem, he believed, might be soluble. Though he had now been
married for six years to his second wife, the fabulously beautiful
Mary of Antioch, their marriage was still childless; the heir to
the Empire remained his daughter by Bertha-Irene, a girl named
Maria now fifteen years old.[1] Though she was theoretically betrothed

[1] Bertha-Irene had died of a sudden fever in 1060. Manuel had given her a
splendid funeral and had her buried in the church of the Pantocrator; but he
had married Mary within a year.

to Prince Béla of Hungary, he now proposed that she should be given in marriage to young William of Sicily; once the boy found himself heir apparent to the throne of Constantinople, he would see Byzantine ambitions in a very different light. It was a bold and imaginative proposal, and Manuel had had it formally put to the Queen Regent immediately after her husband's death. So far, however, the Sicilians had expressed only a cautious interest, and the Emperor was still awaiting a definite reply.[1]

All this, we must assume, was unknown to Frederick Barbarossa as he marched towards Ancona. But his dislike of the Greeks was already more than enough to give him enthusiasm for the task before him, and as soon as his army had dug itself in the siege of the city began. The inhabitants put up a spirited resistance. Their defences were strong and in good order, and they were determined not to be deprived of an association that was bringing so much wealth to them all. Luck, too, was on their side. First the Emperor was diverted by the appearance further down the coast of a Sicilian force under Gilbert of Gravina; soon after his return he received news which caused him to raise the siege altogether and leave at once for Rome. The Anconans were saved.

The Romans, on the other hand, were as good as lost. On Whit Monday, 29 May, just outside Tusculum, their large but undisciplined army had attacked the Germans and Tusculans under Christian of Mainz, and, though outnumbering them many times over, had been utterly shattered. Out of a total estimated at some thirty thousand, barely a third had escaped. Before the last survivors had left the field, imperial messengers were already speeding to Frederick with the news. Rome itself, they reported, was still holding out, but failing massive reinforcements it could not last long; still less could it hope to resist a new German attack at full strength. When he heard the news, the Emperor was jubilant. With Rome ripe for the plucking, what did Ancona matter? He could deal with the Greeks later.

Although the troops under Archbishop Christian had now been swollen by the local militias of several neighbouring towns, all

[1] For a fuller discussion of this proposal—which, if it had been accepted, would quite possibly have changed the course of history—see J. S. F. Parker, 'The attempted Byzantine Alliance with the Sicilian Norman Kingdom, 1166–1167', *Papers of the British School at Rome*, vol. XXIV, 1955.

eager for revenge after years of Roman arrogance and oppression, Rome itself was still fighting hard. The Emperor's arrival, however, sealed the fate of the Leonine City.[1] A single savage onslaught smashed the gates; the Germans poured in, only to find an unexpected inner fortress—St Peter's basilica itself, ringed with strong-points and hastily-dug trenches. For eight more days, we are told by an eyewitness, Acerbus Morena, it held out against every attack; it was only when the besiegers set fire to the forecourt, destroying first the great portico so carefully restored by Innocent II, then the lovely little mosaic-covered oratory of S. Maria in Turri, and finally hacking down the huge portals of the basilica itself, that the defending garrison surrendered. Never had there been such a desecration of the holiest shrine of Europe. Even in the ninth century, the Saracen pirates had contented themselves with tearing the silver panels from the doors; they had never penetrated the building. This time, according to another contemporary,[2] the invaders left the marble pavements of the nave strewn with dead and dying, the high altar itself stained with blood. And this time the outrage was the work not of infidel barbarians but of the Emperor of western Christendom.

It was on 29 July 1167 that St Peter's fell. On the following day, at that same high altar, the anti-Pope Paschal celebrated Mass and then invested Frederick with the golden circlet of the Roman *Patricius*—a deliberate gesture of defiance to the Senate and People of Rome. Two days later still, he officiated at the imperial coronation of the Empress Beatrice, with her husband—whom Pope Adrian had crowned twelve years previously—standing by. That day marked the summit of Frederick's career. He had brought the Romans to their knees, imposing on them terms which, though moderate enough, should ensure their docility in the future. He had placed his own Pope on the Throne of St Peter. North Italy he had already subdued; and now, with the imperial strength still undiminished and the Pisan ships already moored along the Tiber quays, he was ready to mop up the Kingdom of Sicily. He foresaw no difficulties. The Sicilians were governed—if that was the word—by a woman, a child and, he understood, some Frenchman who was little more than a child himself. Soon they would all three be grovelling before

[1] See p. 181n.   [2] Otto of St Blaise.

The abasement of Frederick Barbarossa before Alexander III—from a fresco
by Spinello Aretino in the Palazzo Pubblico, Siena

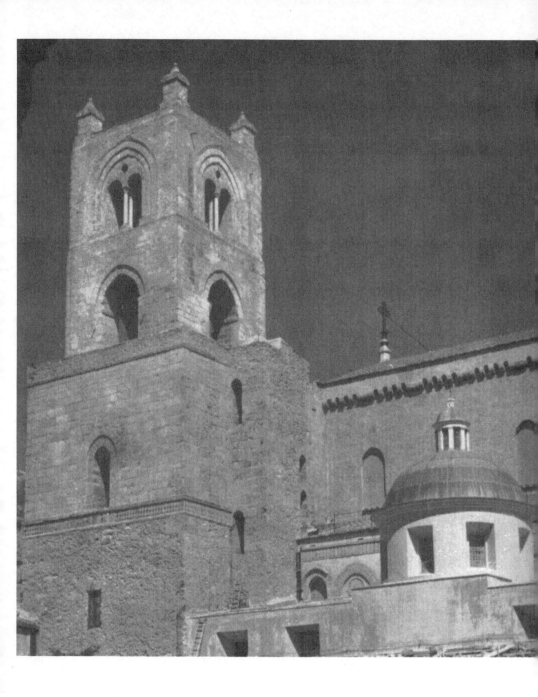

Monreale: the view to the north-west from the cloister

him, and the ambition that had been gnawing away at him for fifteen years would be fulfilled at last.

Poor Frederick—he could not have foreseen the catastrophe that was so soon to overtake him, one that in less than a single week was to destroy his proud army in a way that no earthly foe could ever have matched. On that memorable first of August, the skies had been clear and the sun had blazed down on his triumph. Then, on the second, a huge black cloud suddenly obscured the valley by Monte Mario; heavy rain began to fall, followed immediately by a still and oppressive heat. On the third came pestilence. It struck the imperial camp with a swiftness and a force such as never before was known; and where it struck, more often than not, it killed. Within a matter of days, it was no longer possible to bury all the dead; and the growing piles of corpses, swollen and putrefying in the heat of a Roman August, made their own grim contribution to the sickness and the pervading horror. Frederick, by now in despair, seeing the flower of his army dead or dying around him, had no choice but to strike his camp; and by the second week of August, 'like a tower in flames' as John of Salisbury describes him, he and his silent, spectral procession were dragging themselves back through Tuscany. The plague went with them. Rainald of Dassel, his Chancellor-Archbishop, succumbed on the fourteenth,[1] so, at about the same time, did Frederick of Rotenburg, son of Conrad III and thus the Emperor's first cousin, who had been responsible for the destruction of the doors of St Peter's; so, did Bishop Daniel of Prague, Acerbus Morena the historian and more than two thousand others.

And even now the nightmare was not over. Full reports of the plague had already spread through Lombardy, and the Germans arrived to find town after town closed against them. At last, and with considerable difficulty, they reached the imperial headquarters at Pavia; and there Frederick was forced to halt, watching in impotent despair when, on 1 December, no less than fifteen of the leading cities of the region formed themselves into the greater Lombard League, the foundations of which had been laid at

[1] So convinced were his followers—on what grounds it is hard to say—that Rainald had been a saint, that they boiled his body until there was nothing left but the bones, which they took back as relics to Germany.

Anagni eight years before. It was his crowning humiliation;
such was his Italian subjects' contempt for him that they had not
even bothered to wait until he was back over the Alps before making
their ultimate gesture of defiance. And indeed, when the spring at
last came and the snows began to melt, he saw that even this last lap
of his homeward journey would be a problem; all the mountain
passes were now controlled by his enemies and closed alike to himself and his shattered army. It was secretly, shamefully and in the
guise of a servant that the Emperor of the West finally regained his
native land.

But, it may be asked, while Frederick Barbarossa was tasting his
triumph and his disaster, what had happened to his old enemy the
Pope? Alexander had first taken refuge with his Frangipani
friends in the Cartularia tower near the Colosseum. Serious as the
situation was, he seems to have thought that he might still be able
somehow to maintain himself in the capital; and when two Sicilian
galleys sailed up the Tiber with further massive subsidies from
Queen Margaret, he had actually refused their captains' offer to
carry him away to safety. It was a noble decision but, as he soon saw,
an unwise one. The Romans, fickle as ever, turned against him.
Disguised as a pilgrim, he had embarked in a small boat just as the
Pisans were arriving and slipped down the river to freedom. Landing
at Gaeta, he had then made his way via Terracina to Benevento
—where, ultimately, his loyal cardinals joined him. He had escaped
not a moment too soon. If he had fallen into the Emperor's hands,
it would have been the end of his active pontificate; even if he had
somehow avoided capture, he would probably have perished in the
epidemic which, it need hardly be said, did not confine itself to the
imperial army but raged through Rome until the Tiber was thick
with corpses. The Almighty, perhaps, had been on his side after all.

Such was certainly the view of the papal supporters. God-
fearing men everywhere, and in Germany perhaps most of all, saw
in that dreadful visitation on Barbarossa the hand of the exterminating angel—not only a just retribution for his crimes, but also a
proof of the rightness of Alexander's cause. The Pope's popularity
soared, and with it his prestige. The Lombard cities made him patron

and chief of their new League and even invited him—though he did not accept—to take up residence among them. Meanwhile they founded a new city between Pavia and Asti and named it Alessandria in his honour.

In Rome, the anti-Pope Paschal had meanwhile lost what derisory support he had ever had. No longer did he dare even to set foot outside the melancholy tower of Stephen Theobald, the only place in the city where he felt safe. His health too was failing fast, and everyone knew that he had not long to live. In such circumstances it would have been a simple matter for Alexander to return to the Lateran; but he refused. He had come to hate Rome, and he despised the Romans for their faithlessness and venality. Three times in eight years they had welcomed him to their city; three times, through intimidation or bribery, they had turned against him and driven him into exile. He had no wish to go through it all again. Benevento, Terracina, Anagni—there were plenty of other places from which, as he knew from previous experience, the business of the Papacy could be transacted with efficiency and despatch, free from the intrigues and the ceaseless violence of the Eternal City. He preferred to remain where he was.

It was eleven years before he saw Rome again.

16

THE FAVOURITE'S FALL

... for that land devours its inhabitants.

Peter of Blois, Letter 90

THE exterminating angel that had wrought such havoc and destruction on the army of Frederick Barbarossa must have appeared, in Sicilian eyes, a messenger of deliverance. In the century and a half that had elapsed since the Normans first arrived in the peninsula, South Italy had faced the threat of imperial invasion more times than its inhabitants cared to remember; but never could the danger have loomed more large than in that agonising summer of 1167. Then, suddenly, it was past. Expenses, largely in the form of papal subventions, had admittedly been heavy; but the actual losses—apart from a few stragglers in Gilbert of Gravina's army who had failed to retreat fast enough south of Ancona—had been nil. The Kingdom was safe again—at least from the outside.

In the capital, Stephen du Perche remained at the centre of power, still beloved by the faceless masses but more and more hated by those upon whom, had he but realised it, his survival depended—a hatred which had grown even more bitter after that day in the early autumn when the Queen, while retaining him as her Chancellor, had also had him elected by the complaisant canons of Palermo to the vacant archbishopric of the city. It was an extraordinary step—one in which both Margaret and Stephen demonstrated yet again their strange imperviousness to the sensibilities of those around them. The young man had never been intended for the Church; he had been ordained—by Romuald of Salerno, with one can imagine what reluctance—only a few days before. Richard Palmer in particular had made no secret of his disgust. And it was not only Romuald and Richard who felt the appointment as a personal affront. From the moment Stephen took his seat on the Archbishop's throne in Palermo Cathedral and the choir shattered the sullen silence with the *Te Deum*, the entire ecclesiastical party became his enemy.

Once more, plots against the Chancellor began to proliferate, just as they had proliferated against Maio and Caïd Peter, until Stephen saw that he could now trust no one outside his French entourage. Among the Sicilians, all were now suspect—even the palace eunuchs, even Matthew of Ajello himself, who had made no secret of his hostility ever since the business of the notaries. One day Stephen, hoping to obtain material proof of Matthew's sinister intentions, arranged with a crony, Robert of Bellême, to waylay a messenger travelling between the protonotary and his brother, the Bishop of Catania, and to bring him whatever letters the man was found to be carrying. Robert's ambush failed; the messenger escaped and reported the whole incident to his master, who was understandably furious—so much so that when Robert died shortly afterwards in somewhat sinister circumstances Matthew immediately fell under the suspicion of having had him murdered. This suspicion was increased at the ensuing enquiry, when a certain doctor, known to be a close friend of Matthew's and a fellow-Salernitan to boot, was revealed as having introduced himself into Robert's house with a curious medicament which he described as a simple rose syrup, but which another witness testified to have burnt all the skin off his hand. Though the doctor was found guilty and imprisoned, he never confessed. Nothing was ever proved against Matthew; but his relations with Stephen became worse than ever.

Some time during the summer of 1167, Queen Margaret's wastrel brother Henry of Montescaglioso had returned to Palermo. Once again, the circumstances of his arrival were typical of him. On reaching Apulia the year before, he had allowed himself to be persuaded by a group of discontented vassals that this ostracism to a remote fief was an insult to his royal dignity, and that his proper place was at his sister's side in the capital, in the seat at that time still occupied by Count Richard of Molise. Count Richard, they explained, was nothing but an upstart opportunist who had wormed himself into Margaret's favour—and, most likely, into her bed—in the cold-blooded pursuit of his own ends. Henry's only honourable course was therefore to go to Palermo and demand his dismissal, thus simultaneously vindicating his own and his sister's honour. It was a task in which they would be happy to assist.

When, however, Henry arrived in Sicily a few months later with his followers, both Spanish and Apulian, it was only to discover what everyone else in the Kingdom had known long ago—that Richard had already surrendered his position to Stephen du Perche. Though he probably knew little enough of Stephen, it must have been immediately clear to him that he could not object to a blood relation in the same way as he had objected to a local *parvenu* like the Count of Molise. On the contrary, this new appointment might prove very much to his advantage—if he played his cards right.

The Chancellor, meanwhile, played his own very cleverly indeed. From what he had been told of Henry, it seemed likely that a few promises and a fair measure of flattery would be all that was needed to render him harmless. Once he himself were won over, there would be nothing to fear from his hangers-on. And so it proved. Stephen, whose career throughout his short life shows that he must have possessed considerable charm, exerted it to the full. In next to no time Henry was one of his cousin's most enthusiastic supporters. The Apulian discontents were disgusted to see their former leader riding everywhere at the Chancellor's side, even accompanying him to the baths, and generally behaving as if the city belonged to him. Beaten, they had no course open to them but to return to their lands—which, not long afterwards, they did.

So, for some months, Henry basked; but he was too unstable—or perhaps simply too gullible—to remain quiet for long. The weakness of his character, his conceit and his close kinship with the Regent made him the perfect tool for intriguers and, as the summer wore on, more and more of them began to murmur in his ear how disgraceful it was that the Queen's cousin should rank above her brother, how instead of calling on the Chancellor, Henry should insist that Stephen should call on him—how iniquitous it was, in fact, that Stephen du Perche rather than Henry of Montescaglioso should hold the reins of power in Sicily.

At first, Falcandus tells us, Henry would reply that he had had no practice in the art of government, and that in any case he spoke no French, an indispensable language at the court. He was therefore perfectly content to leave state affairs in the hands of his good friend Stephen, who was after all a wise and prudent man, admirably qualified by his noble birth to occupy his high office. Soon, however, the murmurs took on a new note, with more than a tinge of scorn. How could the Count of Montescaglioso continue on such friendly terms with the Chancellor in view of the latter's notorious relationship with the Queen? Was he publicly pandering to their ignoble and incestuous desires? Or was he still feigning ignorance of what was going on under his nose? Surely he could not be so crass and supine—the words are Falcandus's own—as to be genuinely unaware of what was now the talk of the city?

Whether there was any foundation for these rumours we shall never know. Falcandus speaks elsewhere of how the Queen would be seen 'devouring the Chancellor with her eyes'. Margaret was still under forty and is said to have been beautiful;[1] she had been largely ignored by her late husband, and it would perhaps have been surprising if she had not formed some sort of attachment to a young and handsome man of high birth, intelligence and marked ability who was, incidentally, one of the few people in Sicily whom she could trust. Even if there had been no such attachment, gossip on the subject would have been unavoidable. In any event, Henry was convinced. He became morose; where hitherto he had sought Stephen's company probably a good deal more often than the Chancellor found necessary or agreeable, now he began to avoid him. More ominous still, he took advantage of his free *entrée* into the palace to recount to the King the stories he had heard about his

---

[1] La Lumia describes her as *bella ancora, superba, leggiera*—but gives no references. His beautifully-written book on William II's reign, though now just a century old, remains the standard work for the period; occasionally, however, he allows his romantic imagination to cloud his scholarship.

mother, in an attempt—not very successful, as it turned out—to cause a rift between them.

The Count of Montescaglioso seems to have had no thought of concealing his altered feelings from his benefactors, and Stephen soon saw that—incredible as it might appear—he had overestimated his cousin; Henry was even more unreliable than he had supposed. His faithlessness had, on the other hand, served one useful purpose: it had indicated, more surely than any number of agents' reports could have done, that another conspiracy was in the wind and that the Count was a party to it. A few secret enquiries— and Henry could have been followed by a dozen spies without ever being aware of the fact—were enough to confirm the Chancellor's suspicions. He resolved to strike.

But could he? One of his bitterest enemies among the palace eunuchs, the Great Chamberlain Caïd Richard, had control of the royal guard and could certainly not be relied upon in the event of trouble. Indeed, one of the inevitable results of a successful *coup* by the Chancellor would have to be the arrest and probably the imprisonment of all the senior Muslims of the court, including the baptised Caïds; a step which, in the present circumstances, might easily provoke a general rising among the Islamic population of the capital. If then he were to forestall his enemies with a sudden swoop of his own, he would be well advised to do it elsewhere than in Palermo. Fortunately it had already been agreed that young William should make his first official visit to the mainland in the following year. On the pretext of making the necessary arrangements, it was accordingly announced that the whole court would move for the winter to Messina.

Hugo Falcandus's description of Messina has already been quoted. The second city of Sicily, with a harbour as busy if not busier than that of Palermo itself, it enjoyed, like all great ports, an agreeably *louche* reputation. For Stephen, however, it had one overriding advantage: it was a purely Christian city. Ibn Jubair, visiting it some twenty years later, noted that it seemed 'full to overflowing with the adorers of the Cross' and that 'it was thanks only to the handful of Muslim menials and servants that a traveller from the Islamic lands was not treated like some wild beast'. The population was in fact largely Greek, with a generous admixture of Italians and Lombards; none had ever shown any dissatisfaction with the present regime. Another point in the city's favour was its proximity to the mainland; and Stephen now wrote secretly to his cousin Gilbert, with whom he had been on excellent terms ever since his visit to Gravina the previous year, asking him to hurry to Messina, bringing with him as many soldiers as he safely could without arousing suspicions or causing alarm.

Meanwhile, in court circles, news of the coming move had been received with almost general consternation. Except, we may imagine, for Henry of Montescaglioso, who never understood much of what was going on and probably looked forward to a reunion with his witty Messinan companions, those who planned the Chancellor's overthrow recognised at once how much, in a strange city where they could not rely on any popular support for their action, their strategic position would be weakened. The high ecclesiastics, in particular, were horrified. They knew that they would have to go —anyone who did not would be sure to suffer from the intrigues of the others the moment his back was turned—but they were loath to leave their sumptuous Palermitan palaces in order to pass the winter in rented accommodation which threatened to be both cold and uncomfortable, and to venture their cossetted persons on the rough mountain tracks which, at this time of year, might well be washed away altogether.[1] Here, to be fair, they had a point; the rains that autumn proved the heaviest in living memory. But Stephen was firm. Letters were sent under royal seal to all the local authorities on the route, ordering them to look to the state of the roads throughout the region under their control, widening or levelling them wherever necessary and preparing them in all respects for the passage of the King. A day or two before the date fixed for the departure the skies cleared, and on 15 December[2] William and his family set out in state for Messina, his courtiers and churchmen riding morosely behind.

[1] Until the middle of the last century the road from Palermo to Messina was still so bad that travellers normally went by sea from one city to the other.

[2] Falcandus gives the date as 15 November, but this is probably a copyist's mistake. See Chalandon, II, p. 331n. Romuald of Salerno expressly states that it was around Christmas.

Messina greeted its King with joy, and William settled with his mother into the royal palace—'rising white as a dove,' wrote Ibn Jubair, 'from the water's edge, a building in which a great number of pages and young girls find employment'. Meanwhile Stephen du Perche, well-meaning as always—but conscious too that he might need their support in a crisis—made a genuine effort to endear himself to the local inhabitants, even restoring to them privileges that they had been formerly granted by Roger II but since lost. Try as he might, however, he could not hold their affection for long. Within a month, the arrogance and high-handedness of his entourage had made the French hated throughout the city and alienated even those who, on their arrival, had been the most favourably disposed towards them.

In these circumstances the long-discussed plot against the Chancellor's life which—owing largely to the inanity of the Count of Montescaglioso—had till now remained somehow inchoate and formless, suddenly began to take shape. Though there had never been any shortage of adherents, their numbers were now further increased by certain Calabrian vassals, whom the King's arrival had attracted across the straits; but participation was by no means confined to the noble faction. Several court officials, among them Matthew of Ajello and Caïd Richard, were heavily implicated; while the hierarchy was represented by that old voluptuary Gentile of Agrigento—who only a few weeks before had insisted on swearing his faith to Stephen in an oath of quite unnecessary length and almost baroque pomposity. The whole weakness of the conspiracy, in fact, lay in its size. The agreed plan, which was simply to strike Stephen down on a given morning as he was leaving his palace, needed no very large group to implement it. What it did demand was secrecy; and it was the inability of the conspirators to preserve this one essential that led to their undoing.

The member responsible, it need hardly be recorded, was Henry of Montescaglioso. For some reason we shall never understand, he blurted out full details of the plot to a local judge, who at once passed them on to the Chancellor. Stephen acted with equal swiftness, pausing only to tell the King and his mother what he proposed to do and then summoning, in the Regent's name, an immediate council of the whole court, including all the bishops, nobles and justiciars at that time in Messina. As soon as it was assembled, Gilbert of Gravina was to have his men surround the palace; those of the clerks known to be loyal were discreetly advised to carry daggers or short swords concealed about their persons. The Chancellor himself, when he entered the council chamber, was wearing a coat of mail under his state robes.

As soon as the meeting opened, the Count of Montescaglioso rose to his feet and launched into a passionate if incoherent diatribe, in which pride and self-pity were uneasily combined. He was, he confessed, heavily in debt—a fact which nobody had any difficulty in believing—the revenues of his fief being nowhere near adequate to maintain the scale of living to which he was accustomed and, by his rank, entitled. As uncle to the King, he therefore laid formal claim to the Principality of Taranto—with which Roger II had invested his bastard son Simon but which William I had taken back—or, failing that, all the lands and properties which Simon had formerly possessed in Sicily.

His outburst, for which such a gathering clearly offered neither a suitable time nor place, seems to have been deliberately intended to provoke bad feeling in the chamber. The Chancellor would be certain to refuse; Henry or one of his supporters would protest, as offensively as possible; and the ensuing uproar would provide an ideal opportunity for the assassination. At this point, however, things took a different turn. Scarcely had Henry finished speaking when Gilbert of Gravina leaped up and delivered, before the assembled company, not so much a reply as a blistering indictment of the Count of Montescaglioso, his character and his misdeeds. Had Henry ever comported himself with a minimum of dignity or decency, Gilbert pointed out, he might long ago have been freely offered what he was now demanding with menaces; instead, he had dissipated huge sums in the pursuit of immorality and vice; he had oppressed his feudatories and inflicted unspeakable outrages upon them; he had done his best to poison relations between the King and his mother, suggesting to Margaret that her son was plotting her overthrow while simultaneously vilifying her to William, and all the time insinuating that he himself should be entrusted with the

government of the Kingdom. Let Henry deny it if he dared; both
King and Queen were present to hear him. Finally, thundered the
Count of Gravina, let him confess to them and to the entire assembly
the evil which he had been plotting against the Chancellor for that very
day, thus revealing himself as 'a perturber of the Kingdom, against
the King's majesty contumacious and rebellious; one who, saving
the royal mercy, deserved to lose not only all the lands he already
possessed, but his own miserable life as well'.

Taken utterly by surprise and paralysed with fear, Henry could
only bluster. He was quickly cut short. A witness was called—the
very judge to whom he had confided his plans only a day or two
before, and whose evidence now settled the matter. The Count
relapsed into silence; and when he heard the Chancellor ordering
his arrest and detention in the castle of Reggio he made no objection.

The news spread quickly through Messina, and with it the usual
crop of rumours. In the house only recently vacated by the Count
of Montescaglioso his Spanish henchmen prepared for armed
resistance. But Stephen was ready. Gilbert's men were still stationed
around the palace and at other strategic points in the town; and now
heralds were despatched through all the streets and squares announcing that every Spaniard had twenty-four hours to leave Sicily.
Henry's men, who had not expected to escape so easily, accepted
without hesitation; many Calabrians who had been involved in the
conspiracy also elected to leave while the going was good. Unfortunately, it proved rather less good than they had hoped. Bands
of Greek brigands from Messina pursued the fugitives before they
were able to cross the straits and stripped them of all they possessed
—including, so Falcandus assures us, their clothes; so that the majority of them, left with no protection against the winter snows,
perished miserably in the mountains.

Though several of his advisers recommended the hanging or
mutilation of all concerned in the plot, the Chancellor refused to
listen. He had a natural dislike of violence; moreover, the sheer
numbers of the conspirators argued against any such savage measures.
Only one or two of the ringleaders followed Henry of Montescaglioso into prison; the rest, like the Bishop of Agrigento—who had
been stricken with a convenient indisposition on the very day of

1168] RICHARD OF MOLISE

the *débâcle*—were allowed to slip away. There was only one notable and undeserving sufferer—Richard, Count of Molise. Although he had had good reason to dislike Stephen du Perche, having been supplanted by him in power, he had almost certainly taken no part in the conspiracy; but he was hated by Gilbert of Gravina, who had not forgotten the circumstances of his own dismissal from Palermo some eighteen months before and was determined to have his revenge. He now had the unfortunate Count arraigned on a charge of illegal tenure of his lands; the accusation was upheld on a technicality and the estates in question were confiscated. Richard protested, loudly and with vehemence, against the sentence; and his enemies pounced. That sentence, they crowed, was passed in the name of the King. To question it was, by Sicilian law, tantamount to sacrilege. The poor Count was dragged before an ecclesiastical court composed of such bishops and archbishops as were still in the neighbourhood, found guilty and imprisoned at Taormina.

Bluff, impulsive, not too intelligent, innocent alike of malice or guile, there is something likeable about Richard of Molise—and, in the fetid atmosphere of lies and subterfuge in which he lived and which emerges with such sickening vividness from the pages of Falcandus—something refreshing. Twice, admittedly, he was himself involved in conspiracies; but on the first occasion, the moment he saw his King in danger, he had sprung forward to shield him with his own body; while on the second, as we shall see, he could hardly have behaved otherwise than he did. Never did he deliberately strive for advancement or personal gain; he accepted high office when it came his way, laying it down again when required to do so without complaint or resentment. A sheep among wolves, the only wonder is that he lasted for so long.

When Stephen du Perche returned to Palermo with the King and the Regent towards the end of March 1168, it was to find that he had indeed been too lenient with his adversaries. In particular, he had feigned to overlook the complicity in Count Henry's plot of the two most powerful palace officials, the Grand Protonotary Matthew of Ajello and the Great Chamberlain, Caïd Richard—trusting, presumably, that they would congratulate themselves on a lucky escape and keep well away from sedition in future. He had miscalculated badly. Matthew and Richard knew that the Chancellor could not possibly be ignorant of the part they had played; sooner or later he was bound to strike, and the blow would fall none the less heavily for being deferred. Immediately after Henry's arrest they had therefore hurried back to the capital with the Bishop of Agrigento to plan one more attempt. There, with a population already hostile to Stephen and no Gilbert of Gravina to contend with, their task promised to be easier. By the time the Chancellor returned with the rest of the court, all would be in readiness. He would be given no chance even to discover what had been going on in his absence; they would move too quickly. Within a day or two of his arrival—on Palm Sunday to be precise—he would be dead.

But Stephen was better informed than they thought. After eighteen months in Sicily he had developed a keen nose for plots, and his first action on reaching Palermo was to throw Matthew and several of his accomplices into prison. Fears of a Muslim rising dissuaded him from doing the same to Caïd Richard, whom he placed instead under close surveillance. The Bishop of Agrigento fled hastily to his diocese but, on the arrival of a royal justiciar to arrest him, his flock handed him over with every appearance of relief. He was taken under guard to the fortress of S. Marco d'Alunzio—the first Norman castle ever built on Sicilian soil which, having once been a Hauteville residence, was probably not too uncomfortable—there to be kept in indefinite detention.

Now at last the Chancellor might have been forgiven for believing that all was well, and that he would henceforth be able to resume the normal tasks of government free from the constant necessity of looking over his shoulder or behind the arras. But cut off as he was, by the barriers of language and his own eminence, from the Sicilian population, he seems to have had no idea of the strength of anti-French feeling. Nowhere was this more true than in Messina, where memories of the insults and abuses suffered during the past winter were still fresh and where, after so many encouraging rumours, the news of the failure of Count Henry's plot had been received with gloom and despondency. The Messinans had no need of conspirators or demagogues to rouse them to action; among the Greek majority in particular, the atmosphere was already explosive enough. All it needed was a spark, and that spark was provided, ironically, by the Chancellor-Archbishop's own Master of the Household, a canon of Chartres Cathedral named Odo Quarrel.

Odo had been one of the original party who had arrived in Sicily with Stephen in the autumn of 1166. Though he never seems to have considered making a permanent home for himself in the island, he had promised to remain for two years while his friend found his feet. He sounds, from Falcandus's description, like one of the worst of the lot:

He was neither cultivated nor even prudent in the ordering of civil affairs; but was of such cupidity and greed that he would seize on to any method by which he might extort money; he measured friendship not by virtue or faithfulness but only by the value of the gifts which he hoped to receive.

By Easter 1168 Odo was in Messina preparing for his departure. His time had in theory another six months to run, but the Regent had asked him to leave rather earlier so that he could escort Henry of Montescaglioso back to Spain—she having decided, rather than keeping her brother indefinitely in prison, to send him home with a bribe of a thousand gold pieces in return for a promise never to return to Sicily. Despite exhortations from Palermo, however, Odo's preparations were extremely slow—chiefly, Falcandus maintains, because he had discovered a splendid new way of augmenting his income and was now making a small fortune by levying his own harbour dues on all ships that passed through the straits on their way to Palestine. This practice, as may be imagined, had not endeared him to the people of Messina; and when, one evening, some of his domestics became involved in a tavern brawl with a party of Greeks, what began as a minor disturbance soon developed into a riot. The news was brought to Odo, who immediately summoned the governor of the city[1] and ordered him to arrest all the Greeks

---

[1] In Latin, *stratigotus*. These officials, as their name suggests, were formerly confined to the Greek-speaking areas of the Kingdom; but in later years they crop up elsewhere as well. Their duties are hard to define, since they seem to have varied from place to place. In Messina, a largely Greek city, the *stratigotus* was the highest civil authority.

concerned. The governor protested, then—fearing Odo's influence
in high places—reluctantly agreed; but no sooner did he appear on
the scene and make his purpose known than he was met by a volley
of stones and forced to retire. By nightfall Messina was under mob
rule. Old rumours were reborn, new ones sprang up. Stephen du
Perche, it was whispered, had already married the Regent; he had
killed the young King; he planned to seize the throne; once he had
done so, he would dispossess all Greeks, dividing their property
among the French and Latins; the true purpose of Odo Quarrel's
journey was to fetch the Chancellor's brother from Normandy, so
that he could be married to Roger II's posthumous daughter
Constance, now a child of fourteen.

But by now Odo can have had little thought of returning to
Sicily for any reason whatever—if indeed he ever managed to
leave it alive. He barricaded himself into his house and waited,
terrified, for developments. Meanwhile a crowd of Messinans
hurried to the harbour, commandeered seven galleys and crossed
the straits to Reggio where the Count of Montescaglioso was imprisoned. Once there, they had no difficulty in persuading the local
population to make common cause with them, march on the citadel
and insist on the Count's immediate release. Their arrival took the
local garrison by surprise; outnumbered many times over, it soon
capitulated and handed over its prisoner.

Henry of Montescaglioso had never been renowned for his
intelligence, but he was quick to seize an opportunity. On his return
to Messina, his first thought was to assure himself of Odo Quarrel—
and in particular of the immense treasure which the canon was
known to be taking back with him to France. A notary was called
and instructed to make a complete inventory of all the gold and silver,
jewels and silks in his house and have them stored in a place of
safety; Henry then ordered Odo to be transferred from the royal
palace, where he had hoped to find a safe refuge from the mob, to
the old fortress overlooking the harbour. At this point, however,
the Messinans objected. They still did not altogether trust their
chosen leader—he was, after all, well known in certain sections of the
town—and they suspected, probably with good reason, that he
might at any moment start negotiating with Stephen du Perche,

using his quivering captive as a bargaining counter. Their leaders went straight to Henry and demanded that Odo be surrendered to them for punishment; the Count hesitated, but dared not refuse.

Odo Quarrel was an unattractive character; he was also a stupid one, who by his stupidity brought about not just his own downfall but that of all his recently arrived compatriots in Sicily. But he did not deserve the fate that awaited him. Stripped naked and tied backwards on a donkey, he was led through the streets under a hail of stones. When he reached the gates some citizen, whether deputed for the task or acting on a sudden impulse we do not know, stepped forward and plunged a long Pisan knife into his neck, licking the blade afterwards as a final gesture of hatred and contempt. The mob then fell on its victim, stabbing the lifeless body again and again in its fury, cutting off the head, impaling it on a lance and parading it through the city. Finally they flung it into the public sewer, from which it was later recovered and secretly buried.

Odo's end was but a beginning. The following morning, when dawn broke over Messina, there was not a Frenchman left alive.

Away in Palermo, Stephen du Perche began to see that he was faced no longer with a local uprising, but with a rapidly spreading rebellion. Messengers were now arriving daily at the capital, and the news they brought grew daily more ominous. The rebels had taken Rometta, an important vantage-point commanding the Palermo–Messina road; they had swept down the coast to Taormina, attacking the citadel and releasing Richard of Molise; the Bishop of Cefalù had declared openly in their favour, and where the bishop led, other ecclesiastics would be sure to follow. There were no reports as yet of any further incidents on the mainland, but the recent events at Reggio were a clear enough indication that the fire of revolt could jump the straits whenever necessary.

The Chancellor's first reaction was to mobilise an army and march against Messina. Many of the regular detachments, he knew, might be of doubtful loyalty; but the Lombard colonies round Etna—who had no special love for the Greeks—had offered on their own initiative to put twenty thousand men into the field against them, and with such a nucleus it should be possible to build up a reasonably effective striking force. But there were delays. The fifteen-year-old King, in his first recorded political intervention, counselled postponement of the campaign until the stars should be in a more favourable conjunction—a poor augury for his future statecraft. And now Stephen himself, in the gravest crisis of his short career, hesitated. Should he, as his French friends advocated, remain with the King and the Regent in Palermo where, in an atmosphere now more highly charged than ever, his life was once again in peril? Or should he follow the advice of Ansald, the palace castellan, leave the capital and organise resistance from some distant stronghold, where William and Margaret could later join him?

Had Stephen known that Matthew of Ajello in his prison cell had already arranged for his assassination, it might have helped him to make up his mind. Using Constantine, Ansald's deputy, as his intermediary, Matthew had had no difficulty in making contact with his friends among the domestics of the palace and persuading them to do the deed. His plan, like its two predecessors, was simple; Stephen was to be struck down on a given morning as he entered the building, at a point between the first and second gates where he would have little room to defend himself.

The Chancellor, alerted in time, remained in his house. His non-appearance, however, was an unmistakable sign that the alarm had been given, and warned his enemies that they must act again quickly if they wished to save their own lives. Fortunately for them, Ansald the castellan was ill; confined to his room on an upper floor of the palace, he had left his deputy Constantine in command. The latter at once summoned the sergeants-at-arms and ordered them to go through the city, calling on the whole population to unite in preventing the Chancellor from making a getaway with the royal treasure. Whether Constantine really believed in this last possibility is open to doubt; but his appeal had the desired effect. Ever since the first reports from Messina, excitement in Palermo had been growing; Matthew's agents had fanned it yet higher; Christian and Saracen alike were now avid for the chance of avenging themselves on the foreigners they loathed, while in the stews and alleys of the town bands of ruffians were already preparing for the looting that would surely follow. Now, as the sergeants spread their message, men everywhere snatched up their swords and streamed into the streets. Within the hour the Chancellor's house was under siege.

At the first sign of disturbance Stephen had been joined by a number of his followers. They put up a brave defence, but their task was hopeless. Outside, the crowd was growing larger and more menacing every moment; its numbers had now been swelled, as the defenders saw to their horror, by the archers of the royal guard. Such troops as had remained faithful, fewer in number than the aggressors and probably no better armed, were unable to force their way through to the beleaguered building—which itself, being the official residence of the Archbishop of Palermo, was ill equipped to withstand a siege. It had, however, one advantage—a narrow corridor linking it directly with the cathedral. To Stephen and his companions, desperate now, this corridor represented their one slender chance of escape. Down it they sped, leaving a few knights behind to cover their retreat, thence through the great church to the bell-tower. Here at last was something they could defend; here, at any rate, they would be safe for a little longer.

In the general tumult that had spread through the city it had been an easy matter for Matthew of Ajello and Caïd Richard to escape and to place themselves once more at the head of the rebellion. Now, calling out the royal trumpeters, they had them blow a fanfare outside the archbishop's palace where the mob, unaware of Stephen's flight, was still hammering at the doors. It was a brilliant move. To all who heard it, the sound could mean one thing only—that the King was behind the insurgents. Those who were already in the streets found new enthusiasm and redoubled their efforts; many who had remained in their homes—often through uncertainty as to where their duty lay—hurried out to join them. Meanwhile someone, probably Matthew himself, had remembered the little corridor—seeing it not so much as an escape route for the besieged but as a means of infiltrating the palace from the rear. At once there was a rush to the cathedral. Stephen's men had locked and bolted every entrance, but faggots were brought up and soon the great wooden doors themselves were aflame. The crowd burst in, overwhelmed the few brave swordsmen who tried to turn them back, and, without giving a thought to the bell-tower, poured down the corridor into the palace.

Only when the entire building had been ransacked—and, we may imagine, stripped bare by looters—did it dawn on the mob leaders where Stephen must have gone. Back to the bell-tower they ran; but its winding stair was narrow, its defenders fighting for their lives. The few hot-heads who ventured up soon reappeared, streaming with blood. There was a pause. Some were for burning the whole tower down; others held that a stone building would be better attacked by a siege engine; yet others proposed undermining the foundations. They were still arguing when darkness fell. Enough had happened for one day; it was agreed that, however the tower was to be attacked, the operation was better left till the morrow.

But Matthew of Ajello was growing anxious. The building, he knew, was strong—stronger than most of its would-be assailants seemed to think. Stephen and his friends would have carried provisions with them from the palace; once settled in, they might easily be able to hold out for a week or more—a good deal longer, probably, than the mob's enthusiasm. The King, also, presented a problem. He was showing signs of unexpected spirit. Already he had demanded to be allowed to ride out and face his subjects, calling upon them to lay down their arms and return to their homes; and Matthew, strong as his position was, had had a hard time restraining him. The boy's popularity in the city was as great as ever; once he managed to make his true sympathies known, support for the rebellion would dwindle rapidly.

And so Matthew and his associates decided to offer the Chancellor terms. Emissaries were sent to the tower with their offer. Stephen and all those of his compatriots who wished to accompany him would be taken in Sicilian galleys to Palestine; the rest would be given free passage back to France. As for those Sicilians who had supported him, there would be no reprisals taken against either their persons or their property. Such mercenaries as he had employed would be allowed to continue in service with the King if they so wished; otherwise they might leave the country unhindered. The agreement would be guaranteed by Richard Palmer, Bishop John of Malta,

Romuald of Salerno and Matthew himself. In the circumstances, they could hardly have been more generous. Stephen accepted.

It remained only to get the Chancellor and his friends out of Sicily as soon as possible. A suitable vessel was found, and all that night the loading and provisioning went on until, by the following morning, it was ready to sail. To avoid incident, the party was embarked a little distance from the capital, near the modern suburb of Mondello; but just as the ship was about to weigh anchor, a commotion broke out on the quay. The canons of the cathedral had suddenly remembered that they had failed to obtain from Stephen an instrument of resignation from his archbishopric; without such a document they would be unable to elect his successor. At first Stephen—whose mood by now cannot have been of the best—refused to give it; only when he heard the mutterings of those present and saw their hands tightening on their swords did he understand how they had interpreted his refusal—as a sign that he secretly intended to return to Sicily and seize power once more. Then he relented—probably in genuine horror that anyone should think him willing, in any circumstances, to set foot again in a land which he had sincerely tried to serve and by which he had been so shamefully repaid.

Poor Stephen: he was to do so sooner than he knew. Hardly was his galley out of the harbour than it proved totally unseaworthy. Whether it had been sabotaged or not we shall never know; but by the time it reached Licata, half-way along the south-west coast of the island, it could go no further. The local population was openly hostile; it was only with the utmost reluctance that Stephen was allowed to land at all, and then for a period not exceeding three days. In so short a time repairs were out of the question; it was in another vessel, bought at his own expense from some Genoese merchants he found in the harbour, that he finally reached the Holy Land.

Into the two years since he had left France, Stephen du Perche had packed a lifetime of experience. He had attained the highest ranks, both civil and ecclesiastical, in one of the three greatest kingdoms of Europe, he had risen from layman to metropolitan archbishop, he had won the respect of some, the detestation of many—and, probably, the love of a queen. He had learned much—about power and the abuses of power, about the art of government; about loyalty, friendship and fear. But about Sicily he had learned nothing. He never understood that the nation's strength, if not its very survival, depended upon the maintenance of its unity; and that since it was by nature heterogeneous and fissile, that unity must be imposed from above. Because of this incomprehension, he failed; and the fact that in the end he accidentally and involuntarily united his enemies against him in no way diminishes his failure.

It might be said that he was unlucky, and perhaps he was; unlucky in that he came to Sicily at a moment when the island was more demoralised than it had been at any time since the Normans first landed on its soil; unlucky in his companions, for whose arrogance and boorishness he was inevitably blamed; unlucky, even, in his age and inexperience—for it is all too easy to forget that at the time of his inglorious departure he was still in his early or middle twenties. Yet even at the end Fortune had cast on him one thin, watery smile; if the ship's captain had elected, on setting sail, to head east instead of west, taking the more direct route through the straits rather than the longer one via Trapani, his vessel might have been forced to put in not at Licata but at Messina instead. Had it done so, the Sicilian adventure of Stephen du Perche might have had a different and still unhappier end.

Of the thirty-seven Frenchmen who had accompanied Stephen to Sicily, two only were still alive when the time came to depart. One was a certain Roger, 'learned, industrious and modest', who now makes his first and last appearance in our story. The other was Peter of Blois, one of the foremost scholars of his day. Peter had studied the humanities at Tours, theology at Paris, and law at Bologna; soon after his return to France, he had been selected by Rothrud of Rouen to go to Sicily as tutor—with Walter of the Mill—to the young King. It was a position that was bound to excite the envy of the court, and his enemies had never stopped trying to get rid of him, twice offering him the see of Rossano and once even the archbishopric of Naples; but he had always refused. Despite a highly-developed sense of his own importance, he was neither grasping nor ambitious; and though intellectuals no longer enjoyed the same pre-eminence as in the two previous reigns, learning was still respected in Palermo more than in any other contemporary court of Europe. He had had no desire to leave.

But the events of the summer of 1168 changed all that. When the crisis came, Peter was lucky enough to be ill in bed, under the expert care of Romuald of Salerno; but when, on his recovery, the King explained that the expulsion of all Frenchmen did not apply to him and pleaded with him to remain, Peter showed himself as firmly determined to depart as he had previously been to stay. As he wrote later to his brother, he 'would not be persuaded by gifts, or promises, or rewards'. A Genoese ship was about to leave for France with the last forty of Stephen's friends on board; Peter insisted on taking it; and before long he was congratulating himself on having exchanged the bitter wines of Sicily for the rich and mellow vintages of his native Loire. Three or four years later his old friend Richard Palmer wrote to him suggesting that he might like to revisit his old friends. Peter's reply speaks for itself:

Sicily drags us down by her very air; she drags us down too by the malice of her people, so that to me she seems odious and scarcely habitable. The distempers of her climate render her abominable to me, as does the frequent and poisonous dissemination by whose immense power our people in their heedless simplicity are constantly endangered. Who, I ask, can live in safety in a place where, leaving aside all other afflictions, the very mountains continually vomit infernal flame and fetid sulphur? For there beyond doubt is the gate of hell . . . where men are taken from the earth and descend living into the regions of Satan.

Your people err in the meagreness of their diets; for they live on so much celery and fennel that it constitutes almost all their sustenance; and this generates a humour which putrefies the body and brings it to the extremes of sickness and even death.

To this I would add that, just as it is written in books of science that all island peoples are in general unworthy of trust, so the inhabitants of Sicily are false friends and, in secret, the most abandoned betrayers. . . .

To you in Sicily, most beloved father, I shall not return. England shall cherish me, an old man, as she cherished you, a child.[1] Rather

[1] She did so rather well, and for some forty years. Peter became Archdeacon, first of Bath and then of London, before he died early in the following century.

is it for you to leave that mountainous, monstrous land and return to the sweetness of your native air. . . . Flee, father, from those flammivomitous mountains, and look on the land of Etna with suspicion, lest the infernal regions greet you on your death.

As the ships disappeared over the horizon, bearing first Stephen du Perche and his reluctant fellow-pilgrims and then Peter of Blois with his home-bound compatriots, Queen Margaret must have been near despair. She had staked everything on these Frenchmen, and she had lost. With her son William still only fifteen, her own regency had another three years to run; but her reputation, both political and moral, was ruined. The last sad champion of the departed order, the 'Spanish woman' was now neither feared nor resented; she was simply ignored.

No longer, even, could she choose her own advisers. All three principal factions—the nobles, the Church and the palace—had had enough of her friends and relations, and were resolved that neither she nor they should have any more say in the conduct of affairs. Scarcely had she recovered from the shock of the revolution when she found a self-styled and self-constituted council of *familiares* already in existence—a coalition of the three groups that would have been unthinkable only two years before. The aristocracy was represented by Richard of Molise and Roger of Geraci, the first baron to join the Messinan revolt; from the Church there were Archbishop Romuald, Bishops John of Malta, Richard Palmer of Syracuse, Gentile of Agrigento (now released from prison) and Walter of the Mill; while palace interests were assured by Caïd Richard and, of course, Matthew of Ajello. For a short time this Council also included Henry of Montescaglioso, who had returned from Messina in quite unnecessary pomp with a fleet of twenty-four ships, doubtless taking full credit for the success of the revolution and infuriating everyone by his smugness. But Henry was the one issue on which Margaret and the council found themselves in agreement. The absence of his name from any subsequent documents suggests that he soon accepted his sister's bribes and returned, at long last, to Spain.

One only of the Queen's family now remained to be dealt with; and among the council's first pronouncements was a sentence of banishment on Gilbert of Gravina. He, his wife and his son, Bertrand of Andria, dispossessed of their lands but promised safe conduct from the Kingdom, followed Stephen du Perche to the Holy Land; and Sicily, with an almost audible sign of relief, settled down to govern herself alone once more.

For Margaret, Gilbert's removal must have been the ultimate humiliation. She had had her differences with him in the past, but he had shown himself a good friend to Stephen and, in the last resort, to herself as well. Now that it was his turn to face expulsion, and by a government of which she remained the titular head, she was powerless to help him. Meanwhile the whole Kingdom saw her impotence, and rejoiced. In her anger and frustration, however, Margaret gave continued proof of her total unfitness to govern. After the events of the past few months she might have been expected to have learnt some sort of a lesson. Had she collaborated with the council, she might even have managed to regain some of her lost influence. Instead, she sought to obstruct them at every turn. They had been the enemies of Stephen; for this reason alone, she could never be a friend of theirs. More than ever one suspects that between the Queen and her Chancellor there had existed something more than a working partnership and a family tie.

And still, unbelievably, Margaret seems to have cherished a hope that Stephen might one day return. His departure had left the archbishopric of Palermo once again vacant, and after the usual intrigues the choice of the canons had at last been forcibly directed towards Walter of the Mill.[1] From Margaret's point of view it would not have been a bad appointment. Walter had served as her son's tutor for several years. He was less hidebound than Romuald, less overbearing than Richard Palmer, less disreputable than Gentile and younger, probably, than any of them. But he was not Stephen; and so she turned her face against him, protesting that her cousin was still the rightful archbishop—his renunciation having been extracted only under duress—and sending an appeal to Pope Alexander, persuasively backed with seven hundred ounces of gold, that he should refuse to ratify Walter's election.

[1] The circumstances of his elevation are not recorded. Falcandus, however, refers to Walter as having succeeded to the archbishopric 'less by election than by violent intrusion', so we may fear the worst.

Not content with badgering the Pope, the Queen had also written to the second most respected churchman in Europe—Thomas Becket, Archbishop of Canterbury, now in exile in France. From the very beginning, some five years before, of Thomas's quarrel with King Henry, both protagonists had looked to Sicily for support— the King as a potential intermediary with Pope Alexander, the archbishop as a possible place of refuge for himself or his friends. As time went on, the Sicilians had found their position more and more embarrassing. Emotionally, there had been much sympathy for Becket. Richard Palmer was a regular correspondent of his and Walter of the Mill, another compatriot, seems to have been similarly well-disposed, together with most other members of the hierarchy; while Stephen du Perche, high-minded, religious and suddenly to his surprise a fellow-archbishop, had always championed Becket's cause. On the other hand, as Matthew of Ajello had been quick to point out, King Henry was fighting, just as Roger I and II had fought, to free his country of papal interference in civil affairs; the privileges he was now demanding were in many respects a good deal more modest than those which Sicily had enjoyed for decades. It hardly became the government in Palermo to take a sanctimonious line against him.

It had therefore been agreed to remain as far as possible on the sidelines of the dispute; but Sicily had soon emerged as a favourite centre for all those friends and relations of the exiled archbishop for whom England was no longer safe. Thus, when Stephen and his associates were expelled, the Regent in her despair had felt justified in writing to Becket also, asking him to use whatever influence he could to bring about their return. It was a patently forlorn hope, but Thomas did his best. Soon afterwards we find him replying to Margaret:

Though we have never met[1] . . . we owe you a debt of gratitude; and we render our heartiest thanks for the generosity which you have shown to our fellow-exiles and kinsfolk, those poor ones in Christ, who have fled to your lands from him that persecutes them and

[1] In fact Thomas may have known Margaret's family quite well. The constant companion of his youth, Richer de Laigle, was almost certainly a relation of her mother's.

have there found consolation. . . . So, as the first fruits of our devotion, have we used our good offices with the most Christian King [Louis VII] to second your prayers, as you may know by the requests that he has made to our dear friend the King of Sicily.[1]

In a letter written about the same time to Richard Palmer, Thomas is still more explicit. After similar expressions of thanks, he goes on to say:

There is one other request, which I will whisper in your ear and which I hope you will grant me; and that is that you will do your utmost with the King and Queen to obtain the recall to Sicily of that noble man Stephen, Elect of Palermo; both for reasons which shall at present be nameless and also because by doing so you will earn the lasting gratitude of the King of France and his entire Realm.[2]

We can be perfectly sure that Palmer took no action on this request, which Thomas would probably never have made if he had had a better understanding of the circumstances. Meanwhile Queen Margaret's near-hysterical refusal to accept the political reality of her favourite's expulsion, combined with Stephen's own last-minute reluctance to surrender his see, made the council more determined than ever to have the new archbishop enthroned as quickly as possible. A mission left at once for the papal court to offer Alexander, in return for his early approval, a yet larger sum than that by which Margaret had hoped to pursuade him to refuse. After a seemly interval for consideration the Pope notified his agreement—keeping both bribes. On 28 September, in the presence of the King and court, Walter of the Mill received his consecration in Palermo Cathedral.[3]

After this last reverse, Margaret seems to have lost heart. She made little or no further effort to maintain her authority. Her name continues to figure on the occasional deed or diploma until her son's

[1] Letter 192.
[2] Letter 150.
[3] When he heard the news, Peter of Blois wrote Walter a splendidly two-edged letter of congratulation—worthy of St Bernard himself—begging him to thank Providence for having raised him up to his present glory from the 'contemptible poverty' and the 'dust of destitution' whence he had begun. (Letter 66.) As joint tutors to the young King, one suspects that the two may not have been the very best of friends.

coming of age in 1171; she then retires, probably with considerable relief, into obscurity. Of these twilight years of her life, one monument only remains—the church of S. Maria di Maniace, built on the site of the Byzantine general George Maniakes's victory over the Saracens in 1040.[1] According to legend, Maniakes had already raised a castle there, in whose chapel he had placed a portrait of the Virgin said to have been painted by St Luke himself; and it was the better to house this treasure that Margaret in 1174 endowed a great Byzantine abbey on the same spot.[2] We can only hope that her interest in this new foundation did something to brighten the last lonely decade of her life. She lived on until 1183, when she died at the age of fifty-five.

But she never saw Stephen again. For the end of his story we have to look not in any Sicilian chronicle but in that of William of Tyre, the historian of Outremer. 'The following summer,' he writes:

. . . a certain nobleman, Stephen, Chancellor of the King of Sicily and elected to the Church of Palermo, a young man, handsome and of excellent character, brother of the noble Rothrud, Count of Perche, was expelled from the Kingdom as a result of the intrigues and conspiracies of the Prince of that country; to the great regret of the King, still a child, and of his mother, who had not the strength to put down these troubles. Stephen was hard pressed to escape from the snares of his enemies; but he succeeded, with a small number of persons, and landed in our Kingdom.

A short while after, he was seized with a serious malady, and died. He was buried with honour at Jerusalem, in the chapter-house of the Temple of the Lord.

[1] See *The Normans in the South*, p. 54 n.
[2] The remains of this abbey now form part of the Brontë estate, which was given in 1799 by Ferdinand III of Naples to Lord Nelson and is now the property of Lord Bridport, the descendant of Nelson's niece Charlotte. Of the church itself, the three apses were destroyed in the famous earthquake of 1693, but much of the rest is as Margaret left it—notably the splendid doorway with its fantastically carved capitals and most of the wooden roof. Also preserved is the Virgin's portrait, now on the altar—beside which, incidentally, stands a marble figure which may well represent Queen Margaret herself.

17

THE ENGLISH MARRIAGE

Ora conosce come s'innamora
Lo ciel del giusto rege, ed al sembiante
Del suo fulgor lo fa vedere ancora.

Dante, Paradiso, XX

Now knows he how the righteous king compels
The love of heaven, and the consciousness
Thereof his glorious semblance yet forthtells.

Tr. Bickersteth

QUEEN MARGARET'S relief at laying down the burdens of state
was fully shared by her subjects. Though her regency had lasted only
five years it must have seemed to them like an eternity; and they
looked gratefully and hopefully towards the tall, fair-haired youth
who, some time during the summer of 1171, formally took the
government of Sicily into his hands.

Not that they knew much about him. His beauty, to be sure, was
famous; he had preserved it intact through his adolescence, and the
boy who had seemed like an angel on the day of his coronation now
at eighteen reminded people more of a young god. The rest was
largely rumour. He was said to be a studious lad, who read and
spoke all the languages of his kingdom, including Arabic; mild-
mannered and gentle, given neither to those brooding silences nor
to those sudden outbursts of rage that had rendered his father so
formidable; deeply religious, yet tolerant of faiths other than his own.
Ibn Jubair recounts with approval one of the best-known stories
about him—how, during the 1169 earthquake, he had reassured the
staff of the palace, Muslim and Christian, with the words, 'Let each of
you pray to the God he adores; he who has faith in his God will

feel peace in his heart.' His statecraft and political judgment were still untried, but this was more an advantage than anything else; having heretofore been kept well away from public affairs, he was safe from blame for any of the disasters his mother had brought upon the Kingdom.

If, in the years immediately following William's assumption of power, Sicily had once again fallen victim to the political instability that had so blighted her past history, there is no telling how long her new young ruler would have maintained his people's love. It was his good fortune that there should have now begun, simultaneously with his majority, a period of peace and security which was soon to become identified with his reign. This much-needed *détente* was not of William's making; though he was never himself to lead an army in the field, he had a disastrous predilection for foreign military adventures and ultimately proved more bellicose than either his father or his grandfather before him. But those adventures, costly as they might be in lives and money, scarcely even ruffled the surface of domestic life in his own realm. Thus it was he, both during his lifetime and posthumously, who took the credit for this new tranquillity; thus too, in later years, men looked back on the Indian summer—for such it turned out to be—of the Sicilian Kingdom, thought of their last legitimate Norman King who looked so glorious and who died so young, and gave him in gratitude the name by which he is still known—William the Good.

Nothing bears more persuasive testimony to this change of atmosphere than the fact that, for the first five years of William's majority, the greater part of Sicilian diplomatic activity in Europe was taken up with the relatively pleasant task of finding him a wife. This was not a new issue. Sicily's domestic upheavals never seemed to have much effect on her international reputation, and it had long been evident that when the time came there would be no shortage of prospective brides; indeed there was not a ruler in Europe who would not have been proud to have the young King as a son-in-law. First in the field, as we have seen, had been Manuel Comnenus; since his daughter would probably have brought the whole Empire of the East as her dowry, Queen Margaret and her advisers might well have accepted the proposal on the spot. But they had refused to be hurried,

and the field was still open when, some time in 1168, King Henry II
of England suggested his third and youngest daughter, Joanna.

To all Sicilians of Norman or English origin, such an alliance must
have seemed even more attractive than the Byzantine proposal.
Links between the two kingdoms had been forming ever since
Roger's day. The English scholars, churchmen and administrators
whose names have already appeared in these pages constitute only a
small fraction of the total;[1] and by the 1160s there were few important
Norman families in either country who could not claim members
in both.[2] Henry himself, whose French dominions alone covered
considerably more territory than those of Louis VII, was beyond
question the most powerful king in Europe. Moreover, though
Joanna was still little more than a baby—she had been born in 1165
—he seemed genuinely keen for the match. There was, admittedly,
the problem of Thomas Becket. Had Stephen du Perche remained in
Sicily the obstacle would have been almost insuperable, but once he
was out of the way it no longer seemed quite so serious. He and
Thomas were known to have been on excellent terms, and some of his
own unpopularity may have rubbed off on to his friend. Meanwhile
Matthew of Ajello, now Vice-Chancellor of the Kingdom and at the
height of his power,[3] was a constant champion of Henry's cause. It
was almost certainly on his advice that, early in 1170, Count Robert
of Loritello and Richard Palmer of Syracuse set off to discuss the
whole question with the Pope at Anagni.

It was a curious choice of delegates. Robert, after years of rebellion

---

[1] Apart from Richard Palmer and Walter of the Mill, there were at least two
other English prelates in the Kingdom during William II's reign—Hubert of
Middlesex, Archbishop of Conza in Campania, and Walter's brother Bartholomew who succeeded Gentile as Bishop of Agrigento. This latter see had in
fact listed a certain John of Lincoln among its canons as early as 1127, while the
name of Richard of Hereford appears among those of Palermo in 1158.

[2] In the contemporary *Lai des Deux Amants* by Marie de France, the Princess of
Pitres on the Seine confides to her lover that

> *En Salerne ai une parente,*
> *Riche femme, mut ad grant rente*

to whom she sends him that he may build up his strength before returning to
win her hand by carrying her bodily over a steep mountain.

[3] After Stephen's departure the office of Chancellor had been allowed to lapse
—just as that of Emir of Emirs had lapsed after the death of Maio.

THE ENGLISH MARRIAGE [1170–71

which had on several occasions nearly cost him his life, had been recalled from exile only the year before, when his former fiefs had been restored to him. He was, however, a cousin of the King and his rank gave the mission a status it would otherwise have lacked. The name of Richard Palmer, at one time perhaps Becket's most trusted friend in Sicily, comes as still more of a surprise—just as it did to Thomas himself when he heard it. The archbishop's own explanation for what he considered a betrayal—that King Henry had won Palmer over to his side with the promise of the bishopric of Lincoln[1] —somehow seems hard to accept. Richard had recently and at long last been consecrated at Syracuse, which had been declared a metropolitan see, under the direct authority of the Pope; he had received his *pallium*[2] shortly afterwards. There is no conceivable reason why he should have wished to exchange Syracuse for Lincoln at such a moment, and certainly he never did so. It is much more likely that, as an Anglo-Norman who had settled in Sicily, he favoured the proposed alliance and was simply anxious to smooth its path all he could; as far as the Becket issue was concerned, he probably saw himself more as a mediator than anything else.

Alexander raised no objection to the marriage, and after the news came of Henry's reconciliation with Thomas in the summer of 1170, the last uncertainties must have been swept away. Then, at nightfall on 29 December, came the archbishop's murder. A dark pall hung over England. Henry's continental subjects were placed under an interdict; the King himself was forbidden to enter any church until such time as the Pope saw fit to absolve him. All Europe was horror-stricken; to the Sicilians, little Joanna suddenly seemed a less desirable bride. Negotiations were broken off abruptly and, once again, the hunt for a Queen began.

Three months later, in March 1171, Manuel Comnenus offered William his daughter Maria for the second time. The princess no longer possessed quite the attractions of five years before; in the interim her stepmother had given birth to a son, Alexius, and the succession to the Byzantine throne was again assured. But she was still an Emperor's daughter, her dowry would be worthy of her

---

[1] Confided in a letter to Humbald, Bishop of Ostia, in 1169.
[2] See p. 149n.

Monreale doors by Bonannus of Pisa: Cain and Abel

Monreale, doors by Barisanus of Trani: St Paul

Monreale: Christ walking on the water

Monreale: St Thomas Becket

Monreale: William the Good crowned by Christ

rank and the marriage would, with any luck, put a stop to her father's eternal meddling in Italian affairs.[1] The offer was accepted, and it was agreed that Maria should arrive in Apulia the following spring.

On the appointed day William, accompanied by his twelve-year-old brother Prince Henry of Capua, Walter of the Mill and Matthew of Ajello, was waiting at Taranto to greet his bride. She did not appear. On the next day there was still no sign of her, nor on the next. After a week of waiting, the King decided to make the pilgrimage to Monte Gargano and the cave of the Archangel Michael. That would take him another ten days at least; Maria would surely have arrived by the time he returned. But when on 12 May he was back on the coast at Barletta, it was to learn that there was still no news. Clearly the girl was not coming; the Greeks had deceived him. Angry and humiliated, he started for home. Still worse misfortunes were to come. The royal party had intended to pass through Capua, where young Henry was to be formally invested with his Principality; shortly before they reached the city, the boy came down with a raging fever. He was hurried to Salerno and thence by ship to Sicily; but when William followed a few weeks later, his brother was dead.[2]

Why had Manuel changed his mind at the last moment, incurring the lasting bitterness of Sicily's young King? He never, so far as we know, apologised or explained, and his motives remain a mystery. The most probable answer is that Frederick Barbarossa had begun bidding for Maria's hand on behalf of his own son; but to us the incident of the bride that never was is important for one reason only; it explains the resentment against Constantinople that was to smoulder in William's heart for the rest of his life—a resentment that was to cost both Sicily and Byzantium dear in the years to come.

What made this snub from Constantinople still more galling to the

[1] In the past three years or so Manuel had sent handsome contributions for the rebuilding of Milan, destroyed by Frederick in 1162; poured, as one chronicler put it, 'a river of gold' into Ancona; and married his niece to one of the Frangipani to assure himself of support in Rome.

[2] According to an old tradition, perpetuated by several of the more venerable historians of Sicily, Prince Henry at his death was betrothed to a daughter of King Malcolm of Scotland. There is no truth in this story. King Malcolm IV, who reigned from 1153 to 1165, not only died unmarried and without issue, but was known during his lifetime as the Virgin King.

King of Sicily was the fact that he was already beginning to envisage an important role for himself in the eastern Mediterranean. Though without any personal appetite or aptitude for military activity, he cherished immense political ambitions which soared far beyond the existing boundaries of his realm. The mere thought of how his father had thrown away his North African possessions—almost without a struggle—was enough to rouse his anger; he preferred to look upon himself as a successor to his grandfather Roger and to Robert Guiscard, as a young scion of the Hautevilles whose destiny it was to win for Sicily a new and glorious overseas empire.

For the time being, at least, there could be no question of reconquering the territories along the North African coast. The Almohads were now supreme; thanks to their brilliant admiral Ahmed es-Sikeli (the Sicilian)—our old friend Caïd Peter[1]—they had built up a fleet of their own which, if not the equal of William's, might still prove a dangerous adversary. They were also in a position, if so inclined, to stir up trouble among the Sicilian Muslims, by no means all of whom had forgotten the terrors of recent years. Fortunately the Almohads remained well-disposed towards their northern neighbour; trade was flourishing, and their leader, Abu-Yakub Yusuf, was anxious to keep his hands free for his projected conquest of Spain—an enterprise which was ultimately to lead to his death. William, headstrong as he was, had no wish to make trouble in that quarter.[2]

His expansionist dreams would have to be directed elsewhere; and he was consequently more than a little intrigued to receive, some time during 1173, a letter from Amalric, the Frankish King of Jerusalem. It appeared that the Fatimids of Egypt, incensed by the abolition of their Cairo Caliphate the previous year, had decided to rise in rebellion against their overlord Nur ed-Din, King of Syria, and his local vizier, Saladin. Knowing that the whole question of Christian survival in the Levant depended in the last resort on Muslim disunity, Amalric had undertaken to give the Egyptians all the help he could; he was now canvassing the princes of the West for support.

[1] See p. 256.

[2] It was not until 1181, however, that William was to conclude a formal treaty of peace with the Almohads—which he sealed, according to the historian Abdul-Wahid al-Marrakeshi, by sending Abu-Yakub a ruby the size and shape of a horseshoe.

It was just the kind of opening that William was looking for; an opportunity to make his name in the East, to show the rulers of Outremer—and Manuel Comnenus too, for that matter—that a new Christian leader, and one to be seriously reckoned with, had emerged on the Mediterranean stage.[1] He responded with enthusiasm. Command of the expedition was given to his first cousin Tancred, Count of Lecce, bastard son of Duke Roger of Apulia, now long since forgiven for his part in the *coup* against William I in 1161; and on an appointed day in the last week of July 1174 a massive Sicilian fleet appeared off Alexandria—two hundred ships, if the Arab chroniclers can be believed, carrying a total of thirty thousand men, including fifteen hundred knights; another thirty-six vessels for the horses, forty for stores and provisions, and six for siege materials.

Had King Amalric seen this huge force, he would doubtless have been as impressed as William had hoped. But King Amalric was dead —of dysentery, just a fortnight before the Sicilians' arrival. And his death meant that there was no Frankish contingent from Jerusalem waiting to join forces with them. Nor was this the only unpleasant surprise in store. Saladin had already uncovered the plot against him and had crucified the ringleaders. There would be no revolt after all. Tancred and his men disembarked to find themselves on hostile territory, utterly unsupported. Almost at once the Alexandrians, who had previously retreated within their walls, burst out again, set fire to the Sicilian siege engines and followed up with a night attack that threw the invaders into total confusion. By now Saladin, apprised of the landings by carrier pigeon, was hurrying up from Cairo at the head of an army. He need not have troubled. Long before he arrived Tancred had given the order to re-embark and the Sicilian ships had disappeared over the horizon, leaving behind them three hundred knights whose retreat had been cut off and who, after heroic but hopeless resistence, were taken prisoner.

To give him his due, William had inherited all his grandfather's resilience. He does not seem to have been particularly cast down by the disaster, and showed it by sending, for the next few summers,

[1] Another Arab historian, al-Maqrisi, claims that a Sicilian fleet had already been sent to the Levant in 1169, to assist in the Frankish siege of Damietta. But no other source confirms this, and extracts from one of Saladin's letters quoted by Abu-Shama strongly imply that no Sicilian ships were present on that occasion.

annual raiding parties to harry the Egyptian coast. But none of these operations was of any real political importance; in the Crusader states of the Levant they passed virtually unnoticed. And they certainly did not obscure the plain fact that William II's first foreign adventure had ended in catastrophe.

The murder of Thomas Becket, deeply as it had shocked all Christian consciences, had no lasting effect on Anglo-Papal relations. At Avranches on 21 May 1172, having performed a public penance and given various promises for the future—some of which he actually kept—Henry II received his absolution; thenceforth, with his abrasive archbishop no longer there to complicate matters, his reconciliation with the Pope was complete. Where Alexander led, the states of Europe were quick to follow; and it was not long before Henry found his diplomatic position stronger than at any time in the previous decade.

William of Sicily, having attained his majority, was among the first of his fellow-rulers to re-establish contact, and for the next few years the two Kings maintained a cordial if rather spasmodic correspondence. Curiously, however, neither seems to have liked to resurrect the marriage proposal—not even after the Byzantine fiasco of 1172, when William was once more on the lookout for a wife. When at last the idea was raised again, it came not from William or Henry but from a more august source than either—Pope Alexander himself.

For Alexander was growing uneasy. Sicily was still his most important ally against Frederick Barbarossa, and it was vital for him that this alliance should be maintained. An ill-advised marriage, however, could destroy it overnight. There had already been one bad moment in 1173 when Barbarossa, to everyone's surprise, had offered William one of his own daughters—a proposal which, if accepted, would have delivered up all South Italy to imperial control and left the Papacy surrounded. Fortunately the King had turned it down; but the very thought of such an eventuality and its consequences had been enough to stir the Pope to action. The Sicilian marriage, he had decided, was too important to be left to chance. He himself would have to intervene.

The alacrity with which both Kings responded to Alexander's new overtures makes it even more surprising that they had not reopened the discussions on their own initiative; and early in 1176 three specially accredited Sicilian ambassadors, the Bishops-Elect of Troia and Capaccio and the Royal Justiciar Florian of Camerota, left Palermo to make a formal request on behalf of their sovereign for Joanna's hand. On their way they were joined by Archbishop Rothrud of Rouen, and at Whitsuntide they presented themselves before the King in London. Henry received them warmly. Although for form's sake he had to summon a council of prelates and nobles to consider the question, their unanimous agreement was a foregone conclusion. But before the betrothal could be announced there remained one further—and potentially embarrassing—preliminary; William had sensibly stipulated that he would enter into no formal commitment without some assurance as to the physical attractions of his bride. The ambassadors therefore proceeded to Winchester, where Joanna was living with her mother Eleanor—held captive by the King since her involvement in her sons' rebellion three years before—'to see', in the words of a contemporary chronicler,[1] 'whether she would be pleasing to them'. Fortunately, she was. 'When they looked upon her beauty,' he continues, 'they were delighted beyond measure.' Back to Palermo hurried the Bishop of Troia with an English embassy led by John, Bishop of Norwich, bearing letters signifying the King's consent to the match; his colleagues meanwhile stayed in England until Joanna should be ready to leave.

Though she was still only ten years old, Henry was determined that his daughter should travel in a state appropriate to her rank and the occasion. To the Bishop of Winchester he entrusted the task of engaging a suitable household and preparing her wardrobe, while he himself ordered seven ships to be made ready to carry the party safely across the Channel. In mid-August he held a special court at Winchester where he showered the Sicilian ambassadors with presents of gold and silver, clothes, cups and horses, and formally surrendered

---

[1] Roger of Hoveden, whose authorship of the *Gesta Regis Henrici Secundi*—formerly known by the name of Abbot Benedict of Peterborough—has now been established by Lady Stenton (*English Historical Review*, October 1953.)

Joanna to their care. Then, accompanied also by her uncle, Henry's natural brother Hameline Plantagenet, the Archbishops of Canterbury and Rouen and the Bishop of Evreux, the little princess rode off to Southampton and, on 26 August, set sail for Normandy. Her passage through France was smooth; her eldest brother Henry escorted her as far as Poitiers, where her second brother Richard took over, conducting her safely through his own Duchy of Aquitaine and the tributary County of Toulouse to the port of St Gilles.

At St Gilles Joanna was greeted in King William's name by Richard Palmer and the Archbishop of Capua. Twenty-five of the King's ships were waiting in the harbour; henceforth the princess's safety was in Sicilian hands. But it was the second week in November, and the winter gales had begun in earnest. The news may already have reached the party that, not long before, two other vessels escorting the Bishop of Norwich back from Messina had foundered, with the loss of all the presents William was sending to his prospective father-in-law; in any event it was decided not to risk the open sea at such a time, but to sail along the coast, keeping as close inshore as possible. Even this journey seems to have been uncomfortable enough; six weeks later the fleet was still no further than Naples, and poor Joanna was suffering so severely from sea-sickness that it was decided to remain there over Christmas, giving her a chance to recover her strength—and, perhaps, her looks. She would then complete the journey overland.

Early in the New Year the party was off again, following the coast road through Campania and Calabria, then across the straits to Messina and on to Cefalù; at last, on the night of 2 February 1177, they reached Palermo. William was waiting at the gates to welcome his bride. She was mounted on one of his royal palfreys, and escorted by her husband-to-be to the palace which had been prepared for herself and her household—probably the Zisa—through streets so brightly illuminated that, in the words of the same chronicler, 'it might have been thought that the city itself was on fire, and the stars in the heavens could scarcely be seen for the brilliance of the lights'. Eleven days later, on St Valentine's Eve, they were married and garlanded with flowers; and immediately afterwards Joanna, her long hair flowing down over her shoulders, knelt in the Palatine

Chapel before her countryman Walter of the Mill, now Archbishop of Palermo, as he anointed and crowned her Queen of Sicily.

At the time of her coronation, the young Queen was barely eleven, her husband twenty-three. Yet despite the difference in ages the marriage was, so far as we can tell, an ideally happy one. There was no language problem; Joanna, born in France and educated largely at the abbey of Fontevrault, was by her upbringing far more French than English, and Norman French was still the everyday language of the Sicilian court. Her new subjects, too, took her to their hearts and seemed to identify her, as they had her husband, with those radiant, tranquil years when the Kingdom, finally at peace with the world and with itself, prospered and was happy.

They were quite right to do so; for within a few months of the marriage there occurred in Venice an event which was to put an end to hostilities between William and his most formidable adversary for the rest of the latter's life. On 29 May of the previous year, at Legnano just outside Milan, Frederick Barbarossa had suffered at the hands of the Lombard League the most crushing defeat of his career; and while the Milanese had celebrated their triumph by carving a series of suitable bas-reliefs on the Porta Romana,[1] imperial ambassadors had sought out Pope Alexander at Anagni, negotiating the terms of a treaty that would bring an end to the seventeen-year schism and peace to Italy. At last the broad outlines of the agreement emerged; and it was duly arranged to hold, in July 1177, a great conference in Venice—to be attended by the Pope, representatives of both the League and the King of Sicily, and ultimately, when all their deliberations were concluded, by the Emperor himself.

The two envoys chosen by William were Count Roger of Andria and—fortunately for posterity—Archbishop Romuald of Salerno, who has left us a remarkably detailed account (for him) of all that took place. On the morning of 24 July, he reports, the Pope went early

---

[1] Or fairly suitable. In his book *Italian Sculptors*, quoted by Augustus Hare, C. C. Perkins refers to two carved portraits of Frederick and his Empress, 'one of which is a hideous caricature, the other too grossly obscene for description'. The Porta Romana was demolished in the eighteenth century; but what is left of it—including Frederick's bas-relief—has been incorporated in a reconstruction now to be seen in the Castello museum.

to St Mark's and despatched a delegation of cardinals to the Lido, where, at the church of St Nicholas, Frederick was waiting. There the Emperor solemnly abjured his anti-Pope and made formal acknowledgement of Alexander as rightful pontiff, while the cardinals in return lifted his long excommunication. Now at last he could be admitted to the Republic, to which he was escorted with great pomp by the Doge in person, the Patriarch of Venice and the cardinals. Landing at the Piazzetta, he proceeded on foot between the two high masts from which flew the banners of St Mark, to the front of the great basilica where Alexander, enthroned and in full pontificals, waited to receive him. Romuald goes on:

As he approached the Pope, he was touched by the Holy Spirit; venerating God in Alexander, he flung aside his imperial mantle and prostrated himself at full length on the ground before him. But the Pope, with tears in his eyes, gently raised him up, kissed him and gave him his blessing, while the assembled Germans lifted up their voices in a *Te Deum*. Then, taking him by the right hand, the Pope led him into the church for a further benediction, after which the Emperor retired with his following to the Doge's Palace.[1]

The treaty of Venice marks the culmination of Alexander's pontificate. After all the sufferings and humiliations he had had to endure, through eighteen years of schism and ten of exile, and in the face of the unremitting hostility of one of the most redoubtable figures ever to wear the imperial crown, here at last was his reward. By now well over seventy, he had lived to see the Emperor's recognition not only of himself as legitimate Pope but of all the temporal rights of the Papacy over the city of Rome—those same rights that Frederick had so arrogantly claimed for the Empire at the time of his coronation. The fifteen-year peace that Barbarossa had signed with Sicily meant the end of those fears of imperial encirclement that had in the past

[1] Plate 19. In the atrium of St Mark's, immediately in front of the central doorway, a small lozenge of red and white marble still indicates the place of the Emperor's abasement. 'The Venetian legends say that the Emperor, facing Alexander on this very spot, agreed to apologise to St Peter but not to the Pope, and that Alexander replied sternly: "To Peter *and* the Pope." ' (James Morris, *Venice.*) It is a nice story, but it hardly accords with Romuald's version; and Romuald, as a highly-placed eyewitness, should have known.

so tormented the papal Curia; while the six-year truce concluded with the Lombard League was, it was agreed, only a preliminary to the formal acknowledgement by the Empire of the Lombard cities' independence. It was a triumph—greater far than that which Pope Gregory had scored over Henry IV exactly a century before; but to the faithful who rejoiced with the old Pope at Venice during those sweltering summer days it was also a tribute to the wisdom and firmness with which he had steered the Church through one of the most troubled times of her history.

Even now the troubles were not quite over. It was a further year before first one anti-Pope and then another made their submission to him; even then, the Roman Senate remained so hostile that in the summer of 1179 Alexander left Rome for the last time. He had never liked the city, never trusted its people; to him, all through his life, it had been enemy country. And when, after his death at Civita Castellana on the last day of August 1181, his body was brought back to the Lateran, the Romans proved him right. Not four years before, they had welcomed him back from exile to the sound of trumpets and with hymns of thanksgiving; now, as his funeral cortège entered the city the senseless populace, not content with flinging curses on Alexander's name, threw mud and stones at the bier that carried his corpse, scarcely suffering it to be buried in the basilica.[1]

The thing that struck people most about Alexander's successor, Lucius III, was his immense age. Such little evidence as we have suggests that he had been born in the previous century; if so, he would have already have been in his eighties when he ascended the throne of St Peter. '*Vir grandaevus*' is how William of Tyre describes him, adding—perhaps a trifle bitchily—'*et modice litteratus*'.[2] The Treaty of Venice had absolved him, during his four-year pontificate, from the necessity of paying much attention to Sicilian affairs; and his principal contribution was a Bull, dated 5 February

---

[1] It was, all the same; but the original tomb has, alas, gone and has been replaced by a nasty baroque affair, erected in 1660 by his namesake and enthusiastic admirer, Alexander VII.
[2] 'A very old man, and—up to a point—cultured'.

1183, granting the status of an archbishopric to William II's new foundation—the abbey and cathedral of Monreale.[1]

William had been working on this huge project for the past nine years. In 1174, so runs the legend, the Virgin Mary had appeared to him while he was resting from the hunt in his royal deer-park just outside Palermo, had revealed the location of a hoard of treasure secretly buried there by his father, and had commanded him to unearth it and devote it to some pious purpose. The story doubtless served to justify the astronomical sums of money that the King was to lavish on Monreale in the years to come—just as variants of it have done for so many other expensive foundations over the centuries. William's real motives, however, were more complex. Deeply religious by nature, he was unquestionably sincere in wishing to raise up some mighty edifice to the glory of God; and the hero-worship that he had always felt for his grandfather, the founder of Cefalù and S. Giovanni degli Eremiti and the builder of the Palatine Chapel, must have further strengthened his determination. If the church he was to build served also as a monument to himself, then so much the better.

But the considerations that led him to press on so hurriedly with the work were more political than personal. From the moment he had assumed power he had been aware—and Matthew of Ajello had constantly reminded him—of the growing influence of Walter of the Mill. As Archbishop of Palermo Walter had by now managed to unite nearly all the leading barons and prelates behind him in a reactionary, feudalist party that, if it were allowed to develop unchecked, boded ill for the Kingdom. Even in ecclesiastical affairs he was pursuing a dangerous course. The upheavals of the Regency had given the Sicilian Church the opportunity to assert itself independently not just of the Pope—there was nothing new in that—but of the King as well; and this tendency Walter was doing everything he could to encourage. His power in the land was already second only

[1] There can be no clearer indication of the change that had come about in Sicilian-Papal relations since the days of King Roger. He would never for a moment have tolerated such interference in what he would have considered the domestic affairs of his kingdom. A legend exists to the effect that Pope Lucius actually visited Monreale for its consecration; but this is certainly untrue.

314

to William's own; and William knew that he must curb it while there was still time.

But how could he do so? Only by creating a new archbishopric as near as possible to Palermo, whose incumbent would be equal in rank to Walter himself and could serve as a direct link between Crown and Papacy. This in turn raised another problem: Archbishops were normally elected by the Church hierarchy, and the hierarchy was under Walter's control. Thus it was that William and his Vice-Chancellor decided on a further refinement to their plan. The new foundation must be a Benedictine abbey, run on strictly Cluniac lines, whose abbot would automatically receive archiepiscopal rank and could be consecrated by any other prelate he might choose, subject only to the King's approval.

Such a scheme, it need hardly be said, could not fail to meet with furious and determined opposition from Walter of the Mill. William and Matthew seem to have managed to conceal their plan for the new archbishopric till 1175, but after that they had to fight every step of the way. They might indeed have failed altogether if it had not been for two factors. One was that by a fantastically lucky chance there still stood, in the grounds of the new abbey, the little chapel of Hagia Kyriaka[1] which had been the official see of the Greek Metropolitan of Palermo during the Arab domination. This enabled the champions of Monreale to claim that in establishing the archbishopric there they were merely continuing a venerable tradition. The second factor was the support given to the plan by Pope Alexander, who from 1174 onwards issued a series of Bulls emphasising the exceptional character of the proposed foundation. Against such artillery even Walter was powerless. He was forced to stand by while several churches and parishes were removed from his archdiocese and transferred to that of Monreale; and, in the spring of 1176, having grudgingly agreed to the exemption of its first abbot from his jurisdiction, he watched in impotent fury as a hundred monks from La Cava arrived in Palermo on their way to colonise the new monastery.

---

[1] 'The name does not refer to a saint but characterises the church as the Sunday Church, in contrast to the former cathedral of Palermo which under the Arabs was the Friday Mosque of the town.' (O. Demus, *The Mosaics of Norman Sicily*.)

It was therefore probably as much in the nature of a counter-attack as anything else that in 1179 Walter began his own building programme—a completely new cathedral for Palermo itself. But however rich he was himself, and however unscrupulous his methods of extracting money from others, he could not hope to rival Monreale; and when William announced that he wished this latest royal foundation, rather than Cefalù or Palermo, to be the burial-place of the Hauteville dynasty, it can only have been a further blow to the Archbishop's hopes. Palermo Cathedral, by the time he finished it, must have been a credit to himself and to the city—very unlike the sad travesty we see today; but it could not begin, any more than it can now, to stand comparison with one of the most sumptuously magnificent religious buildings in the world.

Sumptuous and magnificent, certainly; yet from the start it must be admitted that Monreale, considered as a whole, is more impressive than beautiful. It lacks the gem-like perfection of the Palatine Chapel, the Byzantine mystery of the Martorana, the sheer magic that streams down from the great Pantocrator at Cefalù. Its impact is principally due to its size and its splendour. But this impact, like the cathedral itself, is colossal.

As so often in the churches of Norman Sicily, the exterior is unpromising. Except for the eastern apses and the north-west view from the cloister,[1] it has been radically changed since William's day. The long north colonnade was clamped on by the Gagini family in the sixteenth century, the west porch by someone else in the eighteenth. This latter addition in particular need not cause us much distress, since it screens some of that original decoration of interlaced blind arches in reddish lava (Gothic now and ornate, with none of the rounded purity of Cefalù), the full unpleasantness of which can still be experienced by anyone walking along to the east end. This vacuous doodling, especially when contrasted with the simple statement of the south-west tower, illustrates better than any words just how great was the loss to European architecture when Romanesque began to decline.

Before entering the building, it is worth taking a close look at its

[1] Plate 20.

two sets of bronze doors. Those in the north porch are the work of
Barisanus of Trani and date from 1179, while the main doors at the
west end were made by Bonannus of Pisa in 1186.[1] Apart from their
considerable intrinsic beauty, these doors are interesting for two
reasons. First, they are Italian. Throughout the eleventh and early
twelfth centuries, such craftsmanship was virtually a monopoly of
Byzantium; to mention only those shrines which have a place in our
story, the cathedrals of Amalfi and Salerno and the cave at Monte
S. Angelo all possess Byzantine doors of outstanding quality,[2] in all
of which the Greek masters have followed their usual practice of
engraving their designs on the metal and then picking them out with
silver thread—or, occasionally, enamel. By the latter half of the twelfth
century, however, the Italians had not only adopted Byzantine
techniques but were rapidly improving on them and trying their
hand at real bas-reliefs; and the second point of interest about the
Monreale doors is in the opportunity they give us to compare the
progress of the two leading bronzeworkers of their day towards the
evolution of that specifically Italian style that was to reach its apogee
with Ghiberti two centuries later. As is only to be expected, Barisanus,
whose life had been spent in southern Italy where Greek influence
was strongest—and who had already been responsible for the cathedral doors at Ravello as well as those of his home town of Trani—is
the less evolved of the two; his techniques may be western, but
his designs—the hieratic saints, the oriental archers, the descent
into Hell and the deposition from the Cross—are still the designs of
Byzantium. Bonannus, by contrast, though possibly less fine an
artist, is a westerner through and through; his biblical scenes are as
earthy and naturalistic as any twelfth-century religious art can be.

Unlike the outer façade, the interior of the cathedral remains
essentially as it always was—apart from the roof over the nave, which
had to be replaced after a fire in 1811. Most of the obvious features of
the Palatine Chapel are there—the polychrome marble inlays of the
floor and lower walls, the antique cipollino columns, the superb

---

[1] Plate 21.

[2] Those of Monte S. Angelo were the cause of angry demonstrations as
recently as March 1964, when the local inhabitants refused to allow them to be
removed to Athens for the Byzantine Exhibition held later that year. (*The Times*,
4 and 6 March 1964.)

Cosmati work fringing the dado with its line of palmettes, the ambo, the altar-rail, the thrones. And yet the atmosphere is utterly different. It is not simply the difference between a chapel and a cathedral; rather does it stem from the fact that the architecture of Monreale is fundamentally undistinguished. West of the apse, the vast expanses of wall are flat and unarticulated; one longs in vain for a niche or a buttress—anything to break this relentless uniformity. Thus, while the Palatine Chapel throbs, about Monreale there is always something dry and a little lifeless.

It is redeemed by its mosaics; for this building is above all a picture-gallery, and to this function every architectural feature has been subordinated. There they glitter in all their vastness, covering the better part of two acres of wall space. Perhaps by reason of their very quantity, it has been the fashion in recent years to decry these mosaics, to suggest that they are somehow a little crude in comparison with those in the other churches of Norman Sicily. They are nothing of the kind. The gigantic Christ Pantocrator in the central apse—his arms outstretched as if to embrace the entire congregation, his right hand alone more than six feet high—cannot admittedly be classed with his counterpart at Cefalù; few works of art can. He is none the less superb. For the rest, although so immense a work must inevitably show some variations in quality, the general standard both of design and of execution remains astonishingly high.

This fact becomes all the more remarkable when we remember that the entire group was completed in the space of five or six years, and quite possibly less—between 1183 and the end of the decade. The leading authority on the subject, Professor Demus, therefore deduces that the artists were Greeks, since 'only at Byzantium could [William] find an organised workshop able to finish the enormous task in so short a time';[1] and indeed the upper half of the apse, with its Greek inscriptions and the hieratic formalisation of the figures, is Byzantine in its very essence. But where the anecdotal mosaics are concerned the attribution is surprising; for they show a fluidity of expression and invention which is hard to reconcile with the stylised rigidity that still characterised most Greek art of the twelfth century. Look, for example, at the south wall of the transept, and in particular at the

[1] *The Mosaics of Norman Sicily*, p. 148.

three pictures that form the lowest row—the Washing of the Feet, the Agony in the Garden, the Betrayal. The iconography is impeccably Byzantine; but the relaxed attitudes, the swirling draperies, the movement and the rhythm of the drawing have developed as far beyond the styles of the Palatine Chapel or the Martorana as have Bonannus's doors from those of Barisanus. And this development is surely Italian. Christian art as we know it was born on the banks of the Bosphorus, and for nearly a thousand years Constantinople continued to point the way forward—evolving in the process the only idiom that has completely succeeded in translating Christian spiritual values into plastic terms. Then, with the end of the twelfth century, Italy began to take the lead. It is another hundred and fifty years before we find, in the church of the Chora in Constantinople,[1] purely Greek mosaics executed with the dynamism and *panache* of those at Monreale.

Wandering slowly through the cathedral, one might be forgiven for supposing that these endless mosaics tell every Bible story, from Genesis to the Acts of the Apostles, in strip cartoon. So indeed they very nearly do; and the visitor, once he has gazed his fill at the Pantocrator, might easily pass over the figures of the saints below and turn at once to more narrative material. But this would be a pity, for he would be missing one of the few real iconographical surprises Monreale has to offer—the second figure to the right of the central window. There is no problem of identification; in conformity with the usual canons of the time, the name runs down each side of the halo for all to read: SCS. THOMAS CANTUR. Whether or not it bears any physical resemblance to the martyred archbishop we cannot tell; mosaic portraits of saints are seldom known for their fidelity to the originals.[2] It remains, however, the earliest certain representation of

---

[1] Nowadays better known by its Turkish name of Kariye Cami.

[2] Plate 23. It certainly gives no hint of the only one of Thomas's distinguishing characteristics of which we can be absolutely sure—his remarkable height. This was first mentioned by his own chaplain, William Fitzstephen, and again in a fifteenth-century manuscript at Lambeth Palace (306 f. 203) where, under the general heading 'The Longitude of Men Folowynge', Thomas is described as being 'vij fote save a ynche'. The most telling evidence of all, however, is provided by the saint's own vestments, still displayed in the cathedral treasury at Sens. 'On the feast of St Thomas till very recently, they were worn for that

Thomas Becket known to us, dating from less than a generation after his death.[1]

At first sight, this seemingly gratuitous distinction accorded to a saint by the son-in-law of his arch-enemy strikes one as a little strange—and even in rather doubtful taste. We know from other sources, however, that Queen Joanna always held Thomas in particular veneration, and it may well be that she encouraged her husband to commemorate him in this way. What better means, after all, could she have had of making her own personal atonement for her father's conduct? A closer look at Thomas's fellow-saints around the apse lends still more weight to this theory. The first pair, immediately to the left and right of the window, are two early Popes, Clement I and Sylvester, both long-time exiles and defenders of the temporal and spiritual primacy of Rome.[2] Next, opposite Thomas, comes St Peter of Alexandria, another prelate who fought for the Church against temporal encroachment and returned from exile to face martyrdom. Beyond them stand the protomartyrs Stephen and Lawrence, who died for the same cause. Finally, facing the nave, we find two other canonised archbishops—Martin, always a favourite among the Benedictines, and Nicholas of Bari, one of the chief patrons of the Norman Kingdom. The conclusion seems inescapable; the choice of figures for the apse not only symbolises the principles for which Monreale stood from the moment of its foundation; it is also a deliberate tribute to one of those depicted: England's most recent—and already most beloved—saint and martyr.

Above the thrones, on each side of the main eastern arch, stands

one day by the officiating priest. The tallest priest was always selected—and, even then, it was necessary to pin them up.' (Dean Stanley, *Memorials of Canterbury*, 1855.)

[1] A curious little reliquary of Becket in the form of a gold pendant, now in the New York Metropolitan Museum of Art, bears the inscription ISTUD REGINE MARGARETE SICULORUM TRANSMITTIT PRESUL RAINAUDUS BATONIORUS, surrounding the engraved figures of the Queen and a prelate in the act of benediction. Since Margaret died in 1183 this must very slightly antedate the mosaic. But is the prelate Rainaud or Thomas? There is no means of knowing. (*Bulletin of the Metropolitan Museum of Art*, vol. XXIII, pp. 78–9.)

[2] Clement, according to tradition, was martyred under Trajan; Sylvester is credited with having baptised Constantine the Great and having received the legendary Donation.

William himself; on the left receiving his crown at the hands of Christ,[1] on the right offering his church into those of the Virgin. Judged as mosaics they are not particularly good; they cannot be compared with the corresponding pair in the Martorana. But this time there can be no real doubt that the two portraits are as lifelike as the artist could make them. After all we have heard of William's beauty, that round face, fair scrubby beard and slightly vacant expression come as a faint disappointment; for a man only just into his thirties, one had hoped for something more impressive. But perhaps he has been done less than justice.

He was even unluckier in his tomb. Following his plan of making Monreale the St Denis of Sicily, William had interred Queen Margaret there after her death in 1183, shortly afterwards transferring his father's remains from the Palatine Chapel and those of his two brothers Roger and Henry from Palermo Cathedral and the chapel of St Mary Magdalene. But when William himself died in 1189, Walter of the Mill quickly intervened and ordered the sarcophagus brought at once to his own new cathedral, now almost completed. After a long and acrimonious struggle between the two archbishops, the King's body was finally laid to rest in Monreale as he had wished; but the sarcophagus was retained in Palermo and has since disappeared. Its eventual replacement, carved in white marble and donated nearly four hundred years later, in 1575, by Archbishop Lodovico de Torres, is as unsuited to a Norman king as anything that could be imagined, and contrasts sadly with the great porphyry tomb of William the Bad, standing four-square and magnificent on its marble pedestal nearby.[2]

Staggering as Monreale is, there is something gloomy about its grandeur. Perhaps it is the lacklustre quality of the gold, which gives it none of the Martorana's glowing radiance, nor any of the joyous sparkle of the Palatine Chapel. It is too big, too impersonal. After half an hour or so one is grateful to emerge once again into the sunshine.

[1] Plate 24.

[2] The tombs of Margaret and her two sons, set against the north wall of the sanctuary, were refurbished in the last century and are worth only a cursory glance. Of greater interest is the altar of St Louis of France, who died of the plague while crusading in Tunisia in 1270 and whose heart and other internal organs are here preserved.

And, above all, into the cloister. Here at last is the splendour without the gloom. Here, too, is the only touch of Saracen influence to be found at Monreale—the slim, arabising arches, a hundred and four of them, supported by pairs of slender columns, some carved, some inlaid with that same glorious Cosmati-work in marble and mosaic that is such a feature of the interior. In the south-west corner they have been extended to make a fountain, Arabic again, but in a form unique to the cloisters of Norman Sicily.[1] (There is a similar one at Cefalù.) The effect of the whole is that of radiant, yet tranquil beauty—more formal than the exquisite miniature at S. Giovanni degli Eremiti, but a place none the less where life seems good and the brethren of Monreale must have found serenity as well as shade. And this is not all; for the capitals of the columns, each one an individual triumph of design and invention, together constitute a *tour de force* of romanesque stone-carving unequalled in Sicily.[2] Their variation is endless—biblical stories (including a marvellous Annunciation in the north-east corner), scenes of daily life, the harvest, the battlefield and the chase, subjects contemporary and antique, Christian and pagan; even—on the south wall, two pairs of columns along from the fountain—a sacrifice to Mithras. Finally, on the west, the eighth capital from the south end translates into stone what we have already seen in its mosaic form: William the Good, beardless now, presents his new cathedral to the Mother of God. The last and greatest religious foundation of Norman Sicily is offered and accepted.

[1] Plate 25.   [2] Plate 26.

18

AGAINST ANDRONICUS

The King's palaces are strung around the hills that encircle the city, like pearls around the throat of a woman. And in their gardens and courts he takes his ease. How many palaces and buildings, watch-towers and belvederes he has—may they soon be taken from him!—how many monasteries he has endowed with rich lands, how many churches with crosses of gold and silver! . . .

Now, as we hear, the King intends to send his fleet to Constantinople. . . . But Allah, who is glorious and all-powerful, will throw him back in confusion, showing him the iniquity of his way and sending tempests to destroy him. For as Allah wills, so can He perform.

Ibn Jubair

A KINGDOM in the sun, prosperous and peaceful; youth, good looks, and limitless wealth; the love of his subjects and of a beautiful young Queen; with such gifts as these, William II must have appeared to his contemporaries—even to his fellow-princes—as a man upon whom the gods had always smiled. And so, up to a point, they had. Three blessings only they withheld from him: first, a long life; second, a son and heir; third, a modicum of political wisdom. Had he been granted any one of these, his kingdom might have been spared the sadness that lay in store for it. As he lacked all three, Sicily was doomed. And it was William the Good, all unconscious of what he was doing and with the best will in the world, who wrought her destruction.

Frederick Barbarossa had long been turning over in his mind the possibility of a Sicilian marriage alliance. As long ago as 1173, when William was still looking for a suitable bride, the Emperor had proposed one of his daughters; he may not have been altogether surprised, in the circumstances prevailing at the time, when his offer was rejected out of hand. A decade later, however, the situation was very different. The Treaty of Venice had brought about a striking *volte-face* in imperial policy. Frederick, having at last understood that his North Italian enemies could never be overcome by force, had adopted new tactics of friendship, negotiation and compromise; and they had served him well. After the death of Alexander III, relations between the Lombard cities and the Papacy had once again become strained; and the Emperor had had no difficulty in concluding a treaty with the League, signed at Constance in 1183, allowing the cities full liberty to elect their own leaders and enact their own laws, in return for recognising his own overall sovereignty. As a result of these concessions the League lost its cohesion, and Frederick found his position in North Italy stronger than ever. With the Papacy correspondingly weaker, there seemed a possibility that a renewed approach to the Sicilians might have a better reception. Some time during the winter of 1183–84, imperial ambassadors arrived in Palermo with his proposal—nothing less than the marriage of his son and heir, Henry, with Princess Constance of Sicily.

It seems, in retrospect, incredible that William and his advisers should have contemplated the idea for a moment. Constance, the posthumous daughter of Roger II—she was in fact a year younger than her nephew the King—was heiress-presumptive to the realm. If she were to marry Henry and William were to die childless, Sicily would fall into the Emperor's lap, its separate existence at an end. Admittedly, there was plenty of time yet for Joanna to bear children; in 1184 she was still only eighteen, her husband thirty. But life in the twelfth century was even more uncertain than it is today, infant mortality was high, and to take such a risk before the succession was properly assured would be, by any standards, an act of almost criminal folly.[1]

[1] A contemporary chronicler, Robert of Torigni, writes of how he has heard from certain people that Joanna did indeed bear a son, Bohemund, in 1182, and that his father invested him immediately after his baptism with the Duchy of Apulia. If this were true, it might go some way towards explaining William's agreement to the imperial marriage, particularly if the child were still alive at the time. But in that case why is Robert—who, as Abbot of Mont St Michel, was hardly well placed to report on Sicilian affairs—the only chronicler who thought the event worth mentioning? Richard of S. Germano, our best source for this last period of the Kingdom and one of William's own subjects, laments Joanna's barrenness in his very first paragraph.

In Palermo there were plenty of counsellors to suggest as much. Matthew of Ajello in particular, who like most South Italians of his time had been brought up on ghoulish tales of the havoc wrought by successive imperial invasions and who looked upon all Germans as potential despoilers of his homeland, spoke out violently against the proposal; and few Sicilians relished the prospect of surrendering their independence to a distant and in their eyes barbarous Empire that had always been the traditional enemy of their country. Walter of the Mill, however, took the opposite view. His reasons are not altogether clear. One authority, Richard of S. Germano, asserts that he did so purely to spite Matthew—an unworthy motive, perhaps, but one which, knowing the bitterness that existed between them, we cannot quite discount. Chalandon, more charitably inclined, suggests that as an Englishman Walter saw the situation more dispassionately than his fellows and considered imperial domination a lesser evil than the civil war which in his eyes may have been the only alternative.

But was it? Could not Constance have married any other husband, reigned in her own right, then passed the crown in the fullness of time to a legitimate son? Possibly. But whatever may have been the Archbishop's motives, there was a further consideration in William's own mind when he came to make his decision—a single, overriding reason why, for the next few years, he needed to be sure of the goodwill of the Western Empire; and why, in the summer of 1184, to the horrified dismay of the large majority of his subjects, he gave his consent to the betrothal.

He was preparing to march, as Robert Guiscard had marched just a hundred years before, against Byzantium.

On 24 September 1180 Manuel Comnenus had died in Constantinople after a long illness. He was buried in the church of the Pantocrator; next to his tomb was placed the red stone slab on which Christ's body had been embalmed, and which Manuel himself had carried on his shoulders from the harbour when it had arrived from Ephesus some years before. He had not been a good Emperor. Over-ambitious abroad, over-prodigal at home, in his thirty-eight years on the throne he had managed to drain his Empire of almost all its resources, leaving it in a state of economic near-collapse from which it never properly recovered. During his lifetime, by the brilliance of his personality, the splendour of his court and the lavishness of his entertainments, the world had been deceived into thinking that Byzantium was still the force it had always been; after his death, disillusion was swift and cruel.

The successor to the throne was Manuel's only legitimate son Alexius, now eleven years old. He was an unimpressive, unattractive child. According to Nicetas Choniates, who was imperial secretary under Manuel and who has left us one of the most reliable and—with that of Psellus—the most entertaining histories of mediaeval Byzantium, 'this young prince was so puffed up with vanity and pride, so destitute of inner light and ability as to be incapable of the simplest task. . . . He passed his entire life at play or the chase, and contracted several habits of pronounced viciousness.' Meanwhile his mother, Mary of Antioch, governed as Regent in his stead. As the first Latin ever to rule in Constantinople, she started off at a serious disadvantage. Her husband's love of the West and his introduction of western institutions into Byzantine life had always been resented by his subjects; in particular, they had hated seeing the greater part of the Empire's trade falling into the hands of the Italian and Frankish merchants who thronged the business centre of the city. They now feared—and with good reason—still further extensions to these merchants of their trading rights and privileges; and they were more worried still when Mary took as her principal adviser another character of extreme pro-western sympathies— Manuel's nephew, the *protosebastos* Alexius, uncle of the Queen of Jerusalem. Before long it was generally believed that her adviser was also her lover, though from Nicetas's description it is not easy to see what the Empress—whose beauty was famous throughout Christendom—saw in him:

He was accustomed to spend the greater part of the day in bed, keeping the curtains drawn lest he should ever see the sunlight. . . . Whenever the sun appeared he would seek the darkness, just as wild beasts do; also he took much pleasure in rubbing his decaying teeth, putting new ones in the place of those that had fallen out through old age.

As the dissatisfaction grew, various conspiracies began to take shape for Mary's overthrow; notably one by her step-daughter Maria—that same princess whose hand her father had twice offered to William of Sicily. The plot was discovered; with her husband Rainier of Montferrat and her other associates, Maria barely had time to flee to St Sophia and barricade herself in. But the Empress-Regent was not prepared to respect any rights of sanctuary; the imperial guard was despatched with orders to seize the conspirators; and the great church was saved from desecration only through the mediation of the Patriarch himself. This incident deeply shocked the Byzantines, and the subsequent exile of the Patriarch to a monastery for his part in the affair made the regime more unpopular than ever—unnecessarily too, since such was the state of public indignation against her that Mary never dared to punish her step-daughter. Nor, later, did she lift a finger when the people of Constantinople marched *en masse* to the Patriarch's monastery and led him back in triumph to the capital. The whole matter, in fact, could scarcely have been handled worse.

This first *coup* had, none the less, failed; but there followed a threat from another of the Emperor's relatives—a man this time, and one of a very different calibre. Andronicus Comnenus was a unique phenomenon. Nowhere else in the pages of Byzantine history do we find so extraordinary a character; perhaps his cousin Manuel comes closest; but next to him, even Manuel is outshone. And nowhere else, certainly, do we find such a career. The story of Andronicus Comnenus does not read like history at all; it reads like a historical novel that has gone too far.

In 1182, when Andronicus first enters this story, he was already sixty-four years old, but looking nearer forty. Over six feet tall and in magnificent physical condition, he had preserved the good looks, the intellect, the conversational charm and wit, the elegance and the sheer *panache* that, together with the fame of his almost legendary exploits in bed and battlefield, had won him an unrivalled reputation as a Don Juan. The list of his conquests was endless, that of the scandals in which he had been involved very little shorter. Three in particular had roused the Emperor to fury. The first was when Andronicus carried on a flagrant affair with his cousin—and Manuel's niece—the Princess Eudoxia Comnena, effectively answering criticism by pointing out that 'subjects should always follow their master's example, and two pieces from the same factory normally prove equally acceptable'—a clear allusion to the Emperor's relationship with another niece, Eudoxia's sister Theodora, for whom he was well known to cherish an affection that went well beyond the avuncular. Some years later, Andronicus had deserted his military command in Cilicia with the deliberate intention of seducing the lovely Philippa of Antioch. Once again he must have known there would be serious repercussions; Philippa was the sister not only of the reigning prince, Bohemund III, but of Manuel's own wife, the Empress Mary. But this, as far as Andronicus was concerned, merely lent additional spice to the game. Though he was then forty-eight and his quarry just twenty, his serenades beneath her window proved irresistible. Within a few days she had capitulated.

His conquest once made, Andronicus did not remain long to enjoy it. Manuel, outraged, ordered his immediate recall; Prince Bohemund also made it clear that he had no intention of tolerating such a scandal. Possibly, too, the young princess's charms may have proved disappointing. In any case Andronicus left hurriedly for Palestine to put himself at the disposal of King Amalric; and there, at Acre, he met for the first time another of his cousins—Queen Theodora, the twenty-one-year-old widow of Amalric's predecessor on the throne of Jerusalem, Baldwin III. She became the love of his life. Soon afterwards, when Andronicus moved to his new fief of Beirut—recently given him by Amalric as a reward for his services—Theodora joined him. Consanguinity forbade their marriage, but the two lived there together in open sin until Beirut in its turn grew too hot for them.

After a long spell of wandering through the Muslim East they finally settled down at Colonea, just beyond the eastern frontier of the Empire, subsisting happily on such money as they had been able to bring with them, supplemented by the proceeds of a certain amount of mild brigandage; and their idyll was only brought to an end when Theodora and their two small sons were captured by the Duke of Trebizond and sent back to Constantinople. Andronicus, agonised by their loss, hurried back to the capital and immediately gave himself up, flinging himself histrionically at the Emperor's feet and promising anything if only his mistress and his children could be returned to him. Manuel showed his usual generosity. Clearly a *ménage* at once so irregular and so prominent could not be allowed in Constantinople; but Andronicus and Theodora were given a pleasant castle on the Black Sea coast where they might live in honourable exile—and, it was hoped, peaceful retirement.

But it was not to be. Andronicus had always had his eye on the imperial crown and when, after Manuel's death, reports reached him of the growing unrest against the Empress Regent he needed little persuading that his opportunity had come at last. Unlike Mary of Antioch—'the foreigner', as her subjects scornfully called her—he was a true Comnenus. He had energy, determination and ability; more important still at such a moment, his romantic past had lent him a popular appeal unmatched in the Empire. In August 1182 he marched on the capital. The old magic was as strong as ever. In a scene inescapably reminiscent of Napoleon's return from Elba, the troops sent out to block his advance refused to fight; their general, Andronicus Angelus, surrendered and joined him[1]—an example followed soon afterwards by the admiral commanding the imperial fleet in the Bosphorus. As he progressed, the people flocked from their houses to cheer him on his way; soon the road was lined with his supporters. Even before he crossed the straits, rebellion had broken out in Constantinople; and with it exploded all that pent-up hatred of the Latins that the last two years had done so much to increase. What followed was a massacre—the massacre of virtually all the Latins in the city—women, children, the old and infirm, even the sick from the hospitals, as the whole quarter in which they lived was burnt and pillaged. The Protosebastos was found cowering in the palace, too frightened even to try to escape; he was thrown into the dungeons and later, on Andronicus's orders, blinded;[2] the young

---

[1] It was typical of Andronicus Comnenus that he should have had a joke ready when Angelus came over to his colours. 'See,' he is said to have remarked, 'it is just as the Gospel says: "I shall send my *Angel*, who shall prepare the way before thee." ' The Gospel in fact says no such thing; but Andronicus was not a man to quibble over niceties.

[2] Though not before he had recovered his nerve and lodged a formal complaint that his English guards were not allowing him enough sleep.

Emperor and his mother were taken to the imperial villa of the Philopation to await their cousin's pleasure.

Their fate was worse than either of them could have feared. Andronicus's triumph had brought out the other side of his character —a degree of cruelty and brutality that few had even suspected, unredeemed by a shred of compassion, or scruple, or moral sense. Though all-powerful, he was not yet Emperor; and so, methodically and in cold blood, he set about eliminating all those who stood between himself and the throne. Princess Maria and her husband were the first to go; their deaths were sudden and mysterious, but no one doubted poison. Then it was the turn of the Empress herself. Her thirteen-year-old son was forced to sign her death-warrant with his own hand, and she was strangled in her cell. In September 1182 Andronicus was crowned co-Emperor; two months later the boy Alexius met his own death by the bowstring and his body was flung into the Bosphorus.

'Thus,' wrote Nicetas, 'in the imperial garden, all the trees were felled.' Only one more formality remained. For the last three years of his short life, Alexius had been betrothed to Agnes of France, the second daughter of Louis VII by his third wife Alix of Champagne. Owing to their extreme youth—at the time of their engagement Alexius was eleven, Agnes barely ten—the marriage itself had never taken place; but the little princess was already installed at Constantinople, where she had been rebaptised in the more seemly Byzantine name of Anna and was treated with all the respect due to a future Empress. And so indeed she proved. Before 1182 was out the new Emperor, now sixty-four, had married the twelve-year-old princess—and, if at least one modern authority is to be believed— consummated the marriage.[1]

No reign could have begun less auspiciously; yet in many ways Andronicus did more good to the Empire than Manuel had ever done. He attacked all administrative abuses, wherever he found them and in whatever form. The tragedy was that as he gradually eliminated

---

[1] Diehl, *Figures Byzantines,* vol. II, which includes scholarly but highly readable short biographies of both Andronicus and Agnes. What became of Theodora is unknown. She may have died; but she was still relatively young and it is more probable that she was packed off to end her days in a convent.

corruption from the government machine, so he himself grew more and more corrupted by the exercise of his power. Violence and brute force seemed to be his only weapons; his legitimate campaign against the military aristocracy rapidly deteriorated into a succession of blood-baths and indiscriminate slaughter. According to one report,

he left the vines of Brusa weighed down, not with grapes but with the corpses of those whom he had hanged; and he forbade any man to cut them down for burial, for he wished them to dry in the sun and then to sway and flutter as the wind took them, like the scarecrows that are hung in the orchards to frighten the birds.

But it was Andronicus himself who was afraid—both for his own skin and for his Empire. His popularity was gone; the saviour of his country had revealed himself a monster. The air was once again thick with sedition and revolt; conspiracies were springing up, hydra-headed, in the capital and the provinces alike. Traitors were everywhere. Those who fell into the hands of the Emperor were tortured to death—often in his presence and by his own hand—but many others escaped to the West, where they could be sure of a ready welcome for, as Andronicus was well aware, the West had not forgotten the massacre of 1182. He also understood, all too clearly, the implications of the Treaty of Venice. For a long time now, Byzantium had had two principal enemies in Europe: the Western Empire and the Kingdom of Sicily, the Hohenstaufen and the Hauteville, both equally determined to block the Greeks from realising their legitimate claims in South Italy. While these two had remained at loggerheads Constantinople had had no cause for alarm; but now they were friends, and soon they might be allies. In that event, Andronicus had an unpleasant suspicion in which direction they would march; and when, in the autumn of 1184, there was announced at Augsburg the betrothal of Constance of Sicily to Henry of Hohenstaufen, his alarm was not diminished.

Early in January 1185 the Arab traveller Ibn Jubair was in Trapani, having just taken passage on a Genoese ship to return to his native Spain. A day or two before he was due to depart, an order arrived from the government in Palermo: the harbour was closed to all outgoing traffic till further notice. A great war fleet was being made ready. No other vessel might leave until it was safely on its way.

The same order had been simultaneously circulated to all the ports of Sicily—a security embargo on an unprecedented scale. Even within the island, few people seemed to know exactly what was happening. In Trapani, Ibn Jubair reports, everyone had their own idea about the fleet, its size, purpose and destination. Some said it was bound for Alexandria, to avenge the fiasco of 1174; others suspected an attempt on Majorca—a favourite target for Sicilian raiders in recent years. There were also, inevitably, many who maintained that the expedition would be against Constantinople. In the past year hardly a ship had arrived from the East without its quota of blood-curdling reports concerning Andronicus's latest atrocities; and it was now widely rumoured that among the increasing number of Byzantines taking refuge in Sicily was a mysterious youth claiming to be Alexius II, the rightful Emperor. If, as men said, this youth had actually been received by the King and had convinced him of the truth of his story, what was more natural than that William the Good should launch an expedition to re-establish him on his throne?

These last years of William's reign are sadly undocumented. Archbishop Romuald of Salerno had died in 1181; and with his death we lose the last of the great chroniclers of Norman Sicily. We shall therefore never know whether such a claimant did in fact present himself at the court in Palermo. There is nothing inherently improbable in the idea. *Coups d'état* of the kind Andronicus had achieved in Constantinople normally produce a pretender or two; Robert Guiscard had unearthed one to strengthen his hand before his own Byzantine adventure in 1081, and Metropolitan Eustathius of Thessalonica—of whom we shall be hearing more before long— assumes that a pseudo-Alexius was wandering through northern Greece shortly after the time of which Ibn Jubair was writing. But whether the rumour was true or false, we know for a fact that William did not lack encouragement for his enterprise: one of Manuel Comnenus's nephews—maddeningly, also called Alexius— had recently escaped to Sicily and had been received at the Court, since when he had been urgently pressing William to march to Constantinople and overthrow the usurper.

Throughout the winter of 1184–85 the King was at Messina. True to his normal practice, he had no intention of himself participating in the campaign, but he had taken personal charge of preparations. Though he naturally admitted it to no one, his ultimate objective was nothing less than to gain for himself the crown of Byzantium; and he was determined that the force he sent out to attain it should be worthy of such a prize—stronger, both on land and sea, than any other ever to have sailed from Sicilian shores. And so it was. By the time it was ready to start, the fleet—commanded once again by his cousin Tancred of Lecce—is said to have comprised between two and three hundred vessels and to have carried some eighty thousand men, including five thousand knights and a special detachment of mounted archers. This huge land army was placed under the joint leadership of Tancred's brother-in-law Count Richard of Acerra and a certain Baldwin, of whom virtually nothing is known apart from an intriguing passage by Nicetas:

Although of mediocre birth, he was much beloved of the King and was appointed general of the army by virtue of his long experience of military affairs. He liked to compare himself with Alexander the Great, not only because his stomach was covered—as was Alexander's—with so much hair that it seemed to sprout wings, but because he had done even greater deeds and in an even shorter time —and moreover, without bloodshed.

The expedition sailed from Messina on 11 June 1185 and headed straight for Durazzo. Although William's attempt to seal all Sicilian ports had not been entirely successful—Ibn Jubair's Genoese captains had had little difficulty in bribing their way out of Trapani— his security precautions seem to have had some effect; it is hard to see how Andronicus could otherwise have been caught so unprepared. As we know, he had long mistrusted western intentions, and he must have been aware that Durazzo, as his Empire's largest Adriatic port and the starting point from which the main imperial road—the old Roman *Via Egnatia*—ran eastward across Macedonia and Thrace to Constantinople, was the obvious if not the only possible Sicilian bridgehead. Yet he had made little effort either to strengthen the city's fortifications or to provision it for a siege.

When he did at last receive reports of the impending attack he quickly sent one of his most experienced generals, John Branas, to take charge of the situation; but Branas arrived at Durazzo only a day or two before the Sicilian fleet, too late to accomplish anything of value.

When Durazzo had fallen to Norman arms a century before, it had been only after a long and glorious battle, fought heroically on both sides; a battle in which the Byzantine army had been led by the Emperor himself, the Norman by the two outstanding warriors of their age, Robert Guiscard and his son Bohemund; in which the Lombard Sichelgaita had proved herself the equal in courage of both her husband and her stepson; in which the stalwart axe-swinging Englishmen of the Varangian Guard had perished to the last man.[1] This time it was a very different story. Branas, knowing that he had no chance, surrendered without a struggle. By 24 June, less than a fortnight after the fleet had sailed out of Messina, Durazzo had surrendered.

The subsequent march across the Balkan peninsula was swift and uneventful. Not a single attempt was made to block the invaders' progress. On 6 August the entire land force was encamped outside the walls of Thessalonica; on the fifteenth the fleet, having sailed round the Peloponnese, took up its position in the roadstead; and the siege began.

Thessalonica was a thriving and properous city, with fifteen hundred years of history already behind it and a Christian tradition going back to St Paul. As a naval base it dominated the Aegean; as a commercial centre it vied with Constantinople itself, even surpassing it during the annual trade fair in October, when merchants from all over Europe gathered there to do business with their Arab, Jewish and Armenian colleagues from Africa and the Levant.[2] Thanks to this fair the city also boasted a permanent European mercantile community living in its own quarter just inside the walls.

[1] See *The Normans in the South*, pp. 231–3.

[2] The fair has continued, intermittently, until the present day. Thessalonica maintained its predominantly Jewish character throughout Ottoman times and up to the second world war, when its entire Sephardic population of some fifty thousand was deported to Poland, never to return.

Largely composed of Italians, it was to prove of more than a little value to the besiegers during the days that followed.

Yet the principal blame for the disaster that overtook Thessalonica in the summer of 1185 must lie not with any foreigner but with its own military governor, David Comnenus. Although he had strict instructions from the Emperor to attack the enemy at every opportunity and with all his strength,[1] and although—unlike Branas at Durazzo—he had had plenty of time to prepare his defences and lay in provisions, he had done neither. Within days of the beginning of the siege his archers had run out of arrows; soon there were not even any more stones for the catapults. Worse still, it soon became clear that he had failed to check the water cisterns, several of which were found—too late—to be leaking. Yet at no time did David Comnenus betray the slightest sign of shame or discomfiture. Nicetas Choniates, who probably knew him personally, writes:

Weaker than a woman, more timid than a deer, he was content just to look at the enemy, rather than to make any effort to repulse him. If ever the garrison showed itself eager to make a sortie he would forbid it, like a hunter who holds back his hounds. He was never seen to carry arms, or to wear a helmet or cuirass. . . . And while the enemy battering-rams made the walls tremble so that the masonry was crashing everywhere to the ground, he would laugh at the noise and, seeking out the safest corner available, would say to those around him, 'Just listen to the old lady—how noisy she is!' Thus he would refer to the largest of their siege-machines.

Nicetas was not himself at Thessalonica during those dreadful days; his account of them, however, is based on the best possible authority—that of the city's Metropolitan Archbishop, Eustathius. Though a Homeric scholar of repute, Eustathius was no stylist;[2] neither, as a good Greek patriot, did he ever try to conceal his own hatred of the Latins, whom—with good reason in his case—he

[1] Andronicus's orders were 'to see that the city was preserved and, far from being afraid of the Italians, to leap on them, bite them and prick them. Those were his own exact words, though I believe that only he knew precisely what he meant. Those who liked to joke about such things gave them a most unseemly interpretation—which I have no intention of repeating here.' (Nicetas.)

[2] Unless, perhaps, he was too much of one. Even Chalandon, whose own prose style can hardly be described as compulsive, speaks with feeling of what he calls 'l'ennui que cause sa rhétorique ampoulée'.

considered no better than savages. But his *History of the Latin Capture of Thessalonica*, turgid and tendentious as it is, remains the only
eye-witness account we have of the siege and its aftermath. The
story it tells is not a pretty one.

Even had it been adequately prepared and defended, it is unlikely
that Thessalonica could have held out very long against so furious
and many-sided an attack as that which the Sicilians now launched
upon it. The garrison resisted as bravely as its commander permitted, but before long the eastern bastions began to crumble.
Meanwhile, on the western side, a group of German mercenaries
within the city was being bribed to open the gates. On 24 August,
from both sides simultaneously, the Sicilian troops poured into the
second city of the Byzantine Empire.

So huge an army must have contained hundreds of soldiers of
Greek extraction; hundreds more, from Apulia and Calabria as well
as from the island of Sicily itself, must have grown up near Greek
communities, been familiar with their customs and religious traditions, even spoken a few words of their language. It would have
been pleasant to record that these men had exerted a moderating
influence on their less enlightened comrades; but they did nothing
of the kind—or, if they tried, they failed. The Sicilian soldiery gave
itself up to an orgy of savagery and violence unparalleled in Thessalonica since Theodosius the Great had massacred seven thousand of
its citizens in the Hippodrome eight centuries before. It is perhaps
more than coincidental that Eustathius puts the number of Greek
civilian dead on this present occasion at the same figure; but even
the Norman commanders estimated it at five thousand, so he may
not be very far out. And murder was not all; women and children
were seized and violated, houses fired and pillaged, churches desecrated and destroyed. This last series of outrages was surprising.
In the history of Norman Sicily we find very few cases of sacrilege
and profanation, none on such a scale as this. Even the Greeks, for
all their poor opinion of Latin behaviour, were as astonished as
they were horrified. Nicetas admits as much:

These barbarians carried their violence to the very foot of the altars,
in the presence of the holy images. . . . It was thought strange that

336

Monreale: fountain in the cloister

Monreale: capitals in the cloister

they should wish to destroy our icons, using them as fuel for the fires on which they cooked. More criminal still, they would dance upon the altars, before which the angels themselves trembled, and sing profane songs. Then they would piss all over the church, flooding the floors with urine.

Some degree of pillage had been inevitable and expected—the recognised reward to an army after a successful siege, and one which the Greeks would not have hesitated to claim for themselves had the roles been reversed. But these atrocities were something different, and Baldwin took firm measures at once. The city had been entered during the early hours of the morning; by noon he had managed to restore a semblance of order. But then the logistical problems began. Thessalonica was not equipped to cope with a sudden influx of eighty thousand men. Such food as there was tended to disappear down Sicilian gullets, and the local population soon found itself half-starved. The disposal of the dead presented further difficulties. It was several days before the task was completed, and long before that the August heat had done its work. An epidemic ensued which, aggravated by overcrowding—and, Eustathius maintains, the immoderate consumption of new wine—killed off some three thousand of the occupying army and an unknown number of the local inhabitants.

From the start, too, there were serious confessional troubles. The Latins took over many of the local churches for their own use, but this did not stop certain elements of the soldiery from bursting into those that had remained in Greek hands, interrupting the services and howling down the officiating priests. A still more dangerous incident occurred when a group of Sicilians, suddenly startled by the sound of urgent, rhythmic hammering, took it to be a signal for insurrection and rushed to arms. Only just in time was it explained to them that the noise they had heard was simply that of the *semantron*, the wooden plank by which the Orthodox faithful were normally summoned to their devotions.[1]

[1] The beating of the *semantron* is of considerable symbolic significance. The Church represents, as we know, the ark of salvation; and the monk who balances the six-foot plank on his shoulder and raps his tattoo on it with a little wooden hammer is echoing the sound of Noah's tools, summoning the chosen to join

Within a week or so some uneasy kind of *modus vivendi* had been established. Baldwin, conceited as he may have been, showed himself a tactful commander and Eustathius, though technically a prisoner, seems to have done much to prevent unnecessary friction. His flock, for their part, soon began to discover—as peoples under occupation are apt to do—that there was money to be made out of these foreigners who had so little understanding of real prices and values. Before long we find him lamenting the ease with which the ladies of Thessalonica were wont to yield to the Sicilian soldiery. But the atmosphere in and around the city remained explosive, and it must have been a relief to Greek and Sicilian alike when the army drew itself up once more in line of battle and, leaving only a small garrison behind, headed off to the east.

By this time Andronicus had despatched no less than five separate armies to Thessalonica to block the Sicilian advance. Had they been united under a single able commander they might have saved the city; this fragmentation of his forces seems to be yet another indication of the Emperor's growing instability. As it was, all five retreated to the hills to the north of the road whence, apparently hypnotised, they watched the Sicilian advance. Baldwin's vanguard had thus pressed as far as Mosynopolis, nearly half-way to the capital, when there occurred an event that changed the entire situation—completely and, as far as Sicily was concerned, disastrously. The people of the capital rose up against Andronicus Comnenus and murdered him.

In Constantinople as elsewhere, the news from Thessalonica had brought the inhabitants to the verge of panic. Andronicus's reactions were typical of his contradictory nature. On the one hand he took firm action to repair and strengthen the city's defences. The state of the walls was carefully checked, houses built too closely against them were destroyed wherever it was considered that they might provide a means of entry for a besieging army; a fleet of a hundred ships was hastily mobilised and victualled. Though this

him. In Ottoman times, when the ringing of church bells was forbidden, the *semantron* continued in regular use. It is rarely heard nowadays, except on Mount Athos—where it remains the rule—and in a few isolated rural monasteries.

was less than half the size of the Sicilian naval force—now reported to be fast approaching—in the confined waters of the Marmara and the Bosphorus it might still serve its purpose.

But at other moments and in other respects the Emperor seemed totally indifferent to the emergency, drawing back further and further into his private world of pleasure. In the three years since his accession his life had grown steadily more depraved.

He would have liked to emulate Hercules, who lay with all the fifty daughters of Thyestes in a single night;[1] but he was nevertheless obliged to resort to artifice as a means of strengthening his nerves, rubbing himself with a certain balm to increase his vigour. He also ate regularly of a fish known as the *scincus*, which is caught in the river Nile and is not dissimilar to the crocodile; and which, though abhorred by many, is most effective in the quickening of lust.

By now, too, he was developing a persecution mania that led him to new extremes of cruelty. A day on which he ordered no one's death, writes Nicetas, was for him a day wasted; 'men and women lived only in anxiety and sorrow, and even the night afforded no rest, since their sleep was troubled by hideous dreams and by the ghastly phantoms of those whom he had massacred.' Constantinople was living through a reign of terror as fearful as any in its long, dark history—a terror which reached its culmination in September 1185, with the issue of a decree ordering the execution of all prisoners and exiles, together with their entire families, on charges of complicity with the Norman-Sicilian invaders.

Fortunately for the Empire, revolution came just in time to avert the tragedy. The spark was fired when the Emperor's cousin, Isaac Angelus, a normally inoffensive nobleman who had incurred Andronicus's displeasure when a soothsayer had identified him as successor to the throne, leaped on the imperial henchman who had been sent to arrest him and ran him through with his sword. Then, riding at full gallop to St Sophia, he proudly announced to all present what he had done. The news spread; crowds began to

[1] Nicetas nods here. The patriarch concerned was not Thyestes but Thespius. This thirteenth labour of Hercules must surely have been the most arduous of the lot, but its success rate was remarkable: all the girls produced male children, in many cases twins.

collect, among them Isaac's uncle John Ducas and many others who, though they had had no part in the crime, knew that in the present atmosphere of suspicion they would be unable to dissociate themselves from it. Therefore, says Nicetas, 'seeing that they would be taken, and having the image of death graven in their souls, they appealed to all the people to rally to their aid'.

And the people responded. The next morning, having spent the night in a torchlit St Sophia, they ran through the city calling every householder to arms. The prisons were broken open, the prisoners joined forces with their deliverers. Meanwhile, in the great church, Isaac Angelus was proclaimed Emperor.

One of the vergers climbed on a ladder above the High Altar and took down the crown of Constantine to place it on his head. Isaac showed reluctance to accept it—not for reasons of modesty nor because of any indifference towards the imperial diadem but because he feared that so audacious an enterprise might cost him his life. Ducas, on the other hand, stepped forward at once, and taking off his cap presented his own bald head, which shone like the full moon, to receive the crown. But the assembled people cried out loudly that they had suffered too much misery from the grizzled head of Andronicus, and that they would have no more senile or decrepit Emperors, least of all one with a long beard divided in two like a pitchfork.

When the news of the revolution had reached Andronicus on his country estate of Meludion, he had returned to the capital confident in his ability to reassert his control. Going straight to the Great Palace at the mouth of the Golden Horn he had ordered his guard to loose its arrows on the mob, and finding the soldiers slow to obey had seized a bow and begun furiously shooting on his own account. Then, suddenly, he understood. Throwing off his purple buskins, he covered his head with a little pointed bonnet 'such as the barbarians wear'; and hastily embarking his child-wife Agnes-Anna and his favourite concubine Maraptica—'an excellent flautist, with whom he was besottedly in love'—on to a waiting galley, he fled with them up the Bosphorus.

Simultaneously the mob burst into the Great Palace, falling on everything of value that it contained. Twelve hundred pounds of gold bullion alone, and three thousand of silver, were carried off, and jewels and works of art without number. Not even the imperial chapel was spared: icons were stripped from the walls, chalices snatched from the altar. And the most venerable treasure of all—the reliquary containing the letter written by Jesus Christ in his own hand to King Abgar of Edessa[1]—disappeared, never to be seen again.

The Emperor, Agnes-Anna and Maraptica were soon caught. The ladies, who behaved throughout with dignity and courage, were spared; but Andronicus, bound and fettered and with a heavy chain about his neck, was brought before Isaac for punishment. His hand was cut off and he was thrown into prison; then, after several days without food or water, he was blinded in one eye and brought forth on a scrawny camel to face the fury of his erstwhile subjects. They had suffered much from him, but nothing could excuse the brutality they now showed. As Nicetas remarks:

Everything that was lowest and most contemptible in the mob seemed to combine. . . . They beat him, stoned him, goaded him with spikes, pelted him with filth. A woman of the streets poured a bucket of boiling water on his head. . . . Then, dragging him from the camel, they hung him up by his feet. He endured all these torments and many others that I cannot describe, with incredible fortitude, speaking no other word among this demented crowd of his persecutors, but *O Lord, have pity on me; why dost thou trample on a poor reed that is already quite broken?* . . . At last, after much agony, he died, carrying his remaining hand to his mouth; which, in the opinion of some, he did that he might suck the blood that flowed from one of his wounds.

It is tempting to go on about Andronicus Comnenus—a figure, as Eustathius of Thessalonica observed, so full of contradictions that he can with equal justice be extravagantly praised or bitterly condemned; a colossus who possessed every gift save that of moderation, and who died as dramatically as he had lived; a hero and a villain, a preserver and a destroyer, a paragon and a warning. He has his place in this book, however, only in so far as his fortunes affect those of the Kingdom of Sicily; and just as his rise to power gave William II his pretext to march against Byzantium, so his fall was to bring about the Sicilian defeat.

[1] See p. 117.

Isaac Angelus, when at last he accepted the crown, inherited a desperate situation. At Mosynopolis, the invaders' advance column was less than two hundred miles from Constantinople; their fleet, meanwhile, was already in the Marmara, awaiting the army's arrival before launching its attack. Immediately on his accession, he sent Baldwin an offer of peace; when it was refused, he did what Andronicus should have done months before—appointed the ablest of his generals, Alexius Branas, to the overall command of all five armies, sending him the most massive reinforcements the Empire could provide. The effect was instantaneous; the Greeks were infused with new spirit. They saw too their enemy grown overconfident; no longer expecting resistance, the Sicilian soldiers had dropped their guard and relaxed their discipline. Carefully selecting his place and his moment, Branas swooped down upon them, routed them completely and pursued them all the way back to the main camp at Amphipolis.

It was, wrote Nicetas, a visible manifestation of the Divine Power.

Those men who, but a short while before, had threatened to overturn the very mountains, were as astonished as if they had been struck by lightning. The Romans,[1] on the other hand, no longer having any commerce with fear, burned with the desire to fall upon them, just as an eagle falls upon a feeble bird.

At Dimitritza,[2] just outside Amphipolis on the banks of the river Strymon, Baldwin at last consented to discuss peace. Why he did so remains a mystery. The defeat at Mosynopolis had not affected the main body of his army, encamped in good order around him. He

---

[1] The Byzantines always so described themselves, seeing their Empire as the unbroken continuation of that of ancient Rome. The word *Romiós* is still used by their descendants today—on occasion. See Patrick Leigh-Fermor's brilliant essay on the subject in *Roumeli*, London, 1966.

[2] I have had some trouble over Dimitritza. This is the version given by Nicetas Choniates ($\Delta\eta\mu\eta\tau\rho\iota\tau\zeta\alpha$) but there is no trace of any place of such a name along the Strymon. Chalandon calls it Demetiza, then adds in brackets (without giving his authority) the obviously Turkish word Demechissar. If he is right in so doing, it is tempting to see this word as a corruption of Demir-Hisar, i.e. Iron Fort; in which case we must be talking about the modern Greek town of Siderókastron, which today stands just where Dimitritza might have been expected to be.

still held Thessalonica. Though the new Emperor in Constantinople was not senile as his predecessor had been, he was not in his first youth; and his claim to the throne was certainly weaker than that of Andronicus or of the pretender Alexius, who had accompanied the army all the way from Messina and was seldom far from Baldwin's side. But winter was approaching, and the autumn rains in Thrace fall heavy and chill. To an army that had counted on spending Christmas in Constantinople, Mosynopolis had probably proved more demoralising than its strategic importance deserved.

Alternatively, Baldwin may have had a darker purpose. The Greeks certainly claimed that he did. On the pretext that he intended to take advantage of the peace negotiations to catch them in their turn unprepared, they decided to strike first—'awaiting,' Nicetas himself assures us, 'neither the sound of the trumpets nor the orders of their commander'. Baldwin's army was taken unawares. His men resisted as best they could, then turned and fled. Some were cut down as they ran; many more were drowned as they tried to cross the Strymon, now swift and swollen from the rains; yet others, including both the Sicilian generals, Baldwin and Richard of Acerra, were taken prisoner, as was Alexius Comnenus, whom Isaac subsequently blinded for his treachery. Those who escaped found their way back to Thessalonica, where some managed to pick up ships to return them to Sicily. Since, however, the bulk of the Sicilian fleet was still lying off Constantinople waiting for the land army to arrive, the majority were not so lucky. The Thessalonians rose up against them, taking a full and bloody revenge for all that they had suffered three months before. Of the titanic army which had set out so confidently in the summer, it was a poor shadow that now dragged itself back through the icy mountain passes to Durazzo.

Byzantium was saved. Isaac Angelus would, however, have done well to take the Sicilian invasion as a warning. There were other western eyes fixed covetously on his Empire. Only twenty years later Constantinople was to face another attack, ludicrously known to history as the Fourth Crusade. Then too, Norman adventurers would be playing their part, and this time they would be victorious.

For William of Sicily, this destruction of the greatest army he or any of his predecessors had ever sent into the field spelt the end of his Byzantine ambitions. But he was not yet ready to admit himself beaten. His fleet under Tancred of Lecce, after seventeen days' waiting in the Marmara, had returned unscathed; and the following spring he sent it off to Cyprus, where another member of the Comnenus family, Isaac, had seized power and, in defiance of his namesake in Constantinople, had proclaimed himself Emperor. Although this histrionic gesture was to result in the permanent loss of the island to the Byzantine Empire, neither it nor the indecisive and somewhat desultory struggle that followed it need concern us here—except in one particular. It is in Cyprus that we first hear of the fleet's new commander Margaritus of Brindisi, the last great admiral of Norman Sicily, whose brilliance and courage were to do much to restore his country's military reputation and to shed a few last rays of glory over a doomed Kingdom.

The squabble over Cyprus gave Margaritus little opportunity to show his qualities. To appear at his best advantage he needed a greater challenge and a wider conflict. Neither was long in coming. In the autumn of 1187 he was summoned back to Sicily, ordered to refit his ships in haste and then to sail, at the earliest possible date, for Palestine. William had at last forgotten his differences with Byzantium; there were graver matters on hand. On Friday 2 October the Muslim armies under Saladin had retaken Jerusalem. The whole future of Christianity in the Holy Land hung in the balance.

19

THE RESPLENDENT SHADOW

Vos matrone nobiles	Ye noble matrons,
Virgines laudabiles	Most excellent virgins,
Olim delectabiles	Once so full of joy,
Nunc estote flebiles . . .	Now is the time for tears . . .
Iacet regnum desolatum	Desolate lies the Kingdom,
Dissolutum et turbatum,	Torn asunder and in disarray,
Sicque venientibus	Lying open to the enemies
Cunctis patet hostibus	Approaching from all sides;
Est ob hoc dolendum	A cause for weeping
Et plangendum	And for lamentation
Omnibus . . .	By all people . . .
Rex Guilielmus	William the King
Abiit non obiit.	Has departed, not died.
Rex ille magnificus	Glorious he was,
Pacificus	And a bringer of peace,
Cujus vita placuit	Whose life was pleasing
Deo et hominibus.	To God and to men.

Contemporary dirge quoted by Richard of S. Germano

EARLY in August 1185, while his still unvanquished army was battering on against the walls of Thessalonica, William of Sicily had escorted his aunt Constance across the sea to Salerno on the first stage of her bridal journey; and on the 28th of the same month, just four days after those walls had crumbled, Constance was delivered into the care of Frederick Barbarossa's special emissaries, waiting at Rieti. Thence, followed by a retinue of five hundred pack-horses and mules laden with a dowry appropriate to a future Empress who was also the wealthiest heiress in Europe, she travelled by easy stages to Milan.

The marriage was to take place in the ancient capital of Lombardy at the request of the Milanese themselves. To them the bride's name had a special significance; for it was at Constance, only two years previously, that Frederick had recognised the claims of the Lombard cities to self-government. What more fitting gesture could there be to mark the ending of their long struggle than to select the greatest of those cities for the marriage of his son?

Twenty-three years before, the Emperor had sacked Milan and left it a pile of rubble. He now returned to find a proud new city already risen on the ruins of the old. Only the cathedral was not yet rebuilt; fortunately, however, the imperial soldiery had spared the loveliest and most venerable of the city's churches, the fourth-century basilica of S. Ambrogio.[1] Long abandoned as a place of worship, S. Ambrogio had in recent years been doing service as a granary; it was now hastily refurbished and before its high altar, on 27 January 1186, Henry and Constance were declared man and wife. The ceremony was immediately followed by another, in which the couple were both crowned by the Patriarch of Aquileia with the iron crown of Lombardy.

Brides, by their very nature, have always provided a rich field for speculation and gossip—royal or imperial ones most of all. But few have ever caught the imagination of their subjects as Constance did. Not that there was anything particularly romantic about her: she was tall and fair-haired and, according to at least one source,[2] beautiful; but at thirty-one she was also eleven years older than her husband— by the standards of her day, a middle-aged woman. What intrigued people was her power, her wealth, and above all the mysterious seclusion in which she was said to have passed her early life, a seclusion which quickly gave rise to the rumour that she had actually taken the veil in her youth and had left the cloister only when reasons of state gave her no alternative. This theory was to gain more and more credence as the years went by; little more than

[1] S. Ambrogio is still there, and still the most beautiful building in Milan. It was founded by St Ambrose in A.D. 386, and despite a good deal of subsequent reconstruction—notably after the bombing of August 1943—still looks substantially the same as on the day of Constance's marriage. Visitors are implored not to miss the little fifth-century chapel of S. Vittore in Ciel d'Oro, refulgent with contemporary mosaic, tucked away in the south-east corner.

[2] Godfrey of Viterbo.

a century later Dante was even to allow her a place in Paradise—
though admittedly in the lowest heaven—on the strength of it.[1]

But whatever Constance's new subjects thought about the marriage, for the Papacy it spelt disaster. Ever since the days of Robert
Guiscard, when the Normans in the South had first become a force
to be reckoned with, the thought of any alliance—let alone a union—
between its two mighty neighbours had been a recurrent papal
nightmare. Now that the Lombard cities had gained their independence, the danger of encirclement might seem a little less fearsome
than before; but the cities still acknowledged the Emperor as their
suzerain, their relations with Rome were strained, and they might
even serve to increase the potential pressure if they had a mind to do
so. In such an event the Papacy—which even in the days of the Sicilian alliance had often been hard put to hold its own—would be
cracked like a nut.

The aged Pope Lucius was dead.[2] His successor, Urban III,
seeing that there was nothing further to be done, had bowed gracefully to the inevitable and had even sent legates to Milan to represent
him at the ceremony. He had not, however, been told about the

[1] *Sorella fu, e così le fu tolta*
Di capo l'ombra delle sacre bende.
Ma poi che pur al mondo fu rivolta
Contra suo grado e contra buona usanza,
Non fu dal vel del cor già mai disciolta.
Quest' è la luce della gran Costanza
Che del secondo vento di Soave
Generò il terzo e l'ultima possanza.

She too a nun, her brows were forced to part
  With the o'ershadowing coif she held so dear.
Yet, when against her will—and though to thwart
  That will was sin—she found herself re-cast
  Upon the world, she stayed still veiled in heart.
This light is the great Constance: from one blast,
  The second Swabian, did she generate
  The third imperial whirlwind, and the last.
                     (Tr. Bickersteth)
                        Paradiso, iii, 113–2

[2] He died at Verona and was buried in the cathedral. In 1879 a great storm
blew down part of the apse on to his tomb, smashing its sixteenth-century cover
and revealing the original stone, bearing a portrait of the Pope in high relief and
a neat but pointless inscription not worth transcribing here. It has now been built
into the wall of the little chapel to St Agatha.

plans for the coronation, news of which threw him into a fury. To crown a son in his father's lifetime was always a dangerous precedent in papal eyes, since any strengthening of the hereditary principle in the imperial succession could only weaken the Pope's own influence; moreover, the coronation of the Lombard Kings was tradtionally the privilege of the Archbishop of Milan—a post which Urban himself had held before his election to the Papacy and which he had never technically given up.

The Patriarch was excommunicated for his presumption; and from that moment, in the words of a contemporary, Arnold of Lübeck, 'the quarrel between the Emperor and the Pope became open, and great trouble arose in the Church of God'. After Frederick returned to Germany, leaving Italy at the mercy of his son, the situation grew even worse; Henry soon showed that he understood no argument save that of violence. Open warfare soon broke out, the King of Lombardy at one moment even going so far as to cut off the nose of a high-ranking papal official. Ten years after the Treaty of Venice, it seemed as if breaking-point had once again been reached; the Pope's patience was exhausted and the Roman Emperor once again faced the prospect of excommunication.

That he escaped it was due neither to himself nor to Urban, but to Saladin. In mid-October 1187, as the Bull of Excommunication lay on the Pope's table ready for signature, a Genoese mission arrived at the papal court with the news of the fall of Jerusalem. Urban was old and ill, and the shock was more than he could bear. On 20 October, at Ferrara, he died of a broken heart.

As usual, the West reacted to the sad tidings from Outremer with genuine emotion but too late. To most Europeans, the Crusader states of the Levant were remote to the point of unreality—exotic, privileged outposts of Christendom in which austerity alternated with sybaritic luxury, where *douceur* and danger walked hand in hand; magnificent in their way, but somehow more suited to the lays of troubadour romance than to the damp and unheroic struggle that was the common lot at home. Even to the well-informed, Levantine politics were hard to follow, the names largely unpronounceable, the news when it did arrive hopelessly distorted and out of date.

Only when disaster had actually struck did they spring, with exclamations of mingled rage and horror, to their swords.

So it had been forty years before, when news of the fall of Edessa and the fire of St Bernard's oratory had quickened the pulse of the continent and launched the ludicrous fiasco that was the Second Crusade. And so it was now. To any dispassionate observer, European or Levantine, who had followed the march of events for the past fifteen years, the capture of Jerusalem must have seemed inevitable. On the Muslim side there had been the steady rise of Saladin, a leader of genius who had vowed to recover the holy city for his faith; on the Christian, nothing but the sad spectacle of the three remaining Frankish states of Jerusalem, Tripoli and Antioch, all governed by mediocrities and torn apart by internal struggles for power. Jerusalem itself was further burdened, throughout the crucial period of Saladin's ascendancy, by the corresponding decline of its leper King, Baldwin IV. When he came to the throne in 1174 at the age of thirteen, the disease was already upon him; eleven years later he was dead. Not surprisingly, he left no issue. At the one moment when wise and resolute leadership was essential if the kingdom were to be saved, the crown of Jerusalem devolved upon his nephew, a child of eight.

The death of this new infant king, Baldwin V, in the following year might have been considered a blessing in disguise; but the opportunity of finding a true leader was thrown away and the throne passed to his stepfather, Guy of Lusignan, a weak, querulous figure with a record of incapacity which fully merited the scorn in which he was held by most of his compatriots. Jerusalem was thus in a state bordering on civil war when, in May 1187, Saladin declared his long-awaited *jihad* and crossed the Jordan into Frankish territory. Under the miserable Guy, the Christian defeat was assured. On 3 July, he led the largest army his kingdom had ever assembled across the Galilean mountains towards Tiberias, where Saladin was laying siege to the castle. After a long day's march in the most torrid season of the year, they were forced to camp on a waterless plateau; and the next day, exhausted by the heat and half-mad with thirst, beneath a little double-summited hill known as the Horns of Hattin, they were surrounded by the Muslim army and cut to pieces.

It only remained for the Saracens to mop up the isolated Christian fortresses one by one. Tiberias fell on the day after Hattin; Acre followed; Nablus, Jaffa, Sidon and Beirut capitulated in quick succession. Wheeling south, Saladin took Ascalon by storm and received the surrender of Gaza without a struggle. Now he was ready for Jerusalem. The defenders of the Holy City resisted heroically for twelve days; but on 2 October, with the walls already breached by Muslim sappers, they knew that the end was near. Their leader, Balian of Ibelin—King Guy having been taken prisoner after Hattin —went personally to Saladin to discuss terms for surrender.

Saladin, who knew and liked Balian, was neither bloodthirsty nor vindictive; and after some negotiation he agreed that every Christian in Jerusalem should be allowed to redeem himself by payment of the appropriate ransom. Of the twenty thousand poor who had no means of raising the money, seven thousand would be freed on payment of a lump sum by the various Christian authorities. That same day the conqueror led his army into the city; and for the first time in eighty-eight years, on the anniversary of the day on which Mohammed was carried in his sleep from Jerusalem to paradise, his green banners fluttered over the Temple area from which he had been gathered up, and the sacred imprint of his foot was once again exposed to the adoration of the Faithful.

Everywhere, order was preserved. There was no murder, no bloodshed, no looting. Thirteen thousand poor, for whom ransom money could not be raised, remained in the city; but Saladin's brother and lieutenant, al-Adil, asked for a thousand of them as a reward for his services and immediately set them free. Another seven hundred were given to the Patriarch, and five hundred to Balian of Ibelin; then Saladin himself spontaneously liberated all the old, all the husbands whose wives had been ransomed and finally all the widows and children. Few Christians ultimately found their way to slavery. This was not the first time that Saladin had shown that magnanimity for which he would soon be famous through East and West alike;[1] but never before had he done so on

[1] Four years before, when he laid siege to the castle of Kerak during the wedding celebrations of its heir, Humphrey of Toron, to Princess Isabella of Jerusalem, he had carefully enquired which tower contained the bridal chamber and had given orders that it was to be left undisturbed.

such a scale. His restraint was the more remarkable in that he had not forgotten the dreadful story of 1099, when the conquering Franks had marked their entry into the city by slaughtering every Muslim within its walls and burning all the Jews alive in the main synagogue. The Christians, for their part, had not forgotten it either; and they could not fail to be struck by the contrast. Saladin might be their arch-enemy; but he had set them an example of chivalry which was to have an effect on the whole of the Third Crusade—an example which was to remain ever before them in the months to come.

The new Pope, Gregory VIII, lost no time in calling upon Christendom to take the Cross; and of the princes of Europe, William of Sicily was the first to respond. The fall of Jerusalem had shocked and troubled him deeply; he dressed himself in sackcloth and went into retreat for four days. Then he despatched Margaritus to Palestine, himself settling down to compose careful letters to his fellow-rulers, pressing them to devote all their energies and resources to the coming Crusade, as he himself planned to do.

It would be naïve to suppose that William's motives in this were purely idealistic. Pious he was, but not so pious that he could not scent another opportunity of realising his old dream of eastern expansion. After all, there were precedents enough in his own family. In the First Crusade the Guiscard's son Bohemund had carved out for himself the Principality of Antioch; in the Second, his own grandfather Roger had emerged with an enormously enhanced reputation—and incidentally, a good deal richer—without stirring from Palermo. Might he himself not now turn the Third to equally good account? The time had come to take his rightful place among the councils of the West. In his letters to the other kings he was careful to stress the advantages of the sea route to the Levant over the long land journey across the Balkans and the treacherous passes of Anatolia. Henry II in England, Philip Augustus in France and Frederick Barbarossa in Germany were all encouraged to break their journey in Sicily, with promises of additional reinforcements and supplies if they did so.

Diplomatically William was in a strong position. Alone of European monarchs, he had a contingent already in the field. His admiral Margaritus commanded a fleet of only sixty ships and some two hundred knights, but all through 1188 and 1189, when for most of the time he represented virtually the only organised resistance to the Saracens, he kept up a steady patrol of the coast which, thanks largely to his admirable intelligence system, proved effective out of all proportion to its strength. Time and again when Saladin's forces arrived at a port that was still in Christian hands, they found that Margaritus had forestalled them. In July 1188 news of the Admiral's arrival off Tripoli caused Saladin to raise the siege of Krak des Chevaliers and decided him against any attack on the city itself. The Saracens were similarly deflected at Marqab and Latakia, and again at Tyre. It was small wonder that during those two years the dashing young admiral, now popularly known as 'the new Neptune', acquired a legendary reputation throughout Christendom. His renown might have been yet greater and his command infinitely further extended had the Sicilians ever been able to raise the mighty army of which their King had dreamed; but suddenly his hopes of crusading glory were dashed. On 18 November 1189 William II died, aged thirty-six, at Palermo.

Of all the Hauteville rulers of Sicily, William the Good is the most nebulous and the most elusive. We know nothing of the circumstances of his death except that it seems to have been non-violent —Peter of Eboli's manuscript contains a picture of the King, surrounded by his doctors and attendants, dying peacefully in his bed[1] —and about his life, short as it was, we are scarcely better informed. Hardly ever in his thirty-six years do we see him clearly face to face. There is a moment on the day of his coronation, when Falcandus gives us a brief glimpse of him riding through the streets of Palermo in the bright morning of his youth and beauty; another, even more fleeting, at the time of his marriage. For the rest we are thrown back on legend, or inference, or hearsay. It is sometimes hard to remember that he ruled over Sicily for eighteen years and occupied the throne for almost a quarter of a century; we are conscious only of a dim, if faintly resplendent, shadow that passes fleetingly over a few pages of history and is gone.

[1] Plate 27.

Yet William was regretted as few European princes have ever been, and far beyond the confines of his kingdom. Among the Franks of Outremer he had already gained, thanks to Margaritus, the renown he had always longed for, and his death was seen as a further disaster to the Christian cause. In Sicily and South Italy, the grief of his subjects was universal and profound. It was not so much that they feared the future—though many of them did so, and with good reason; the overriding feeling was regret for the past, for the peace and tranquillity that had marked his reign but might not survive it. As the Archbishop of Reggio recalled in his memorial address:

In this land a man might lay down his head under the trees, or under the open sky, knowing himself to be as safe as if he were in his own bed at home; here the forests and the rivers and the sunlit meadows were no less hospitable than the walled cities; and the royal bounty extended over all, ever-generous and inexhaustible.

But he spoke, let it be noted, in the past tense.

The orations and encomiums, the threnodies and the laments, to say nothing of the whole labyrinth of legend that grew up around the name of William the Good and still keeps it fresh eight centuries later in Sicilian folklore, would have been more appropriate to a Charlemagne or an Alfred than to the last and weakest of Roger's legitimate line. If few rulers have achieved so enviable a reputation none, surely, have deserved it less. True, the reorganisation of the government machine after the departure of Stephen du Perche may have allowed rather more scope to the feudal nobility than they had formerly enjoyed; certain of them, men like Robert of Loritello or Tancred of Lecce, were able to find an outlet for their ambitions in the King's service rather than in battling vainly against him. But be that as it may, what really kept the Kingdom's internal peace through William's majority was neither his wisdom nor his statesmanship; rather was it a general revulsion on the part of the potential discontents against the unceasing violence of former years. The history of their land from its beginnings had been an almost uninterrupted saga of rebellion and revolt; and what, men suddenly asked themselves, had any of the rebels ever gained by their activities? How many had escaped death, or mutilation, or a prison cell? Was it not better to accept the Hauteville domination as the political reality it was, and to concentrate instead on amassing the largest possible share of the ever-increasing national wealth? Suddenly, rebellion was no longer in the air; and for this William can take little enough of the credit.

Meanwhile, on the debit side, he has a lot to answer for. His reign did nothing to strengthen his country; instead it marked a return to the most dangerous and irresponsible foreign policy that any state can pursue—that of land-grabbing for its own sake, without consideration for political consequences. The fact that all William's attempts in this direction were ignominious failures, that time and again he emptied the national coffers on enterprises that brought him nothing but defeat and humiliation, can hardly serve as an excuse; nor can it be claimed that he was merely reverting to the policies of Robert Guiscard. Robert was an adventurer whose achievement was to create a dominion out of chaos; William was an anointed sovereign of an influential and prosperous kingdom, with moral duties to his subjects and to his fellow-rulers. One might, perhaps, have had a little more sympathy for him if, like the Guiscard, he had led his troops in person on these escapades; but he never ventured beyond the point of departure. To others would be left the ungrateful task of trying to satisfy their master's ambitions; he himself would withdraw once again to his harem and his pleasure-domes, and await results.[1]

On such a record alone William II must stand condemned; but that is not all. He must also bear the blame for the most disastrous decision of the whole Sicilian epic—his agreement to Constance's marriage. He knew that if he died childless the throne would be hers; and he had been married long enough to understand that

[1] Two of these pleasure-domes have lasted to the present day and are—just—worth a visit. The first and more important is the Cuba. Once set in an ornamental lake within the royal park—its main entrance is half-way up the wall—it later became a cavalry stable for the Neapolitan army and now stands in the middle of a gloomy barracks at No. 94, Corso Calatafimi. Noble but now sadly neglected, its walls defaced with painted goalposts, one finds it hard to believe that this pavilion in its heyday provided the setting for one of Boccaccio's stories (Day 5, No. 6). Not far off, in the garden of Cav. di Napoli at No. 375, stands another, smaller kiosk, the Cubula; and on the east front of the Villa Napoli a line of arcading marks the remnants of yet a third, the Cuba Soprana.

Joanna might well fail to bear him a son. True, he could always put her away and take another wife; but who was to say that his second marriage would be any more fruitful than the first? Meanwhile Constance was the Kingdom; and by giving her to Henry of Hohenstaufen he sealed the death warrant of Norman Sicily.

Handsome is—for monarchs even more than for their subjects— as handsome does. Youth, beauty and piety are not enough, and the record of the last legitimate Hauteville king is not an edifying one. Apart from Monreale—a monument to himself as much as to his God—he can be credited with only one real achievement: the fact that by his promptness in sending help to the Levant at the very start of the Third Crusade he was able, through the brilliance of Margaritus of Brindisi, to save Tripoli and Tyre, temporarily, for the Christian cause. As to the rest, he is revealed as irresponsible, vainglorious and grasping, lacking even the rudiments of statesmanship and quite possibly a coward into the bargain. His sobriquet is thus more misleading even than his father's before him. William the Bad was not so bad; William the Good was far, far worse. And for those who like to see a connection between sanctity in life and incorruptibility in death, this judgment was given a macabre confirmation when, in 1811, their two sarcophagi were opened. In contrast to the body of William the Bad, almost perfectly preserved, of William the Good there remained only a skull, a collection of bones covered with a silken shroud, and a lock of reddish hair.

20

THE THREE KINGS

Behold, an ape is crowned!

Peter of Eboli

SHORTLY before the Princess Constance left the territory of her
future kingdom, her nephew had called a great assembly of his chief
vassals at Troia and made them swear fealty to her as his heir and
eventual successor. But not even William can have been foolish
enough to imagine that her succession would be unopposed. Whatever his own feelings on the subject, the fact remained that to the
immense majority of his people the Western Empire had always been
the most persistent and dangerous of enemies. In South Italy, to
which it had never renounced its claim, few could remember how
often in the past two centuries one Emperor after another had
descended into the peninsula to claim his due; but every town and
village had its stories of the atrocities wrought by the imperial
soldiery. In Sicily, where there had been no such invasions, the
prevailing emotion was not so much fear as contempt—the contempt
of a highly cultivated and intellectually arrogant society for the one
European culture of which it had no experience or understanding.
This attitude seems to have been already prevalent in the days of King
Roger;[1] and forty years later we find Hugo Falcandus writing to Peter,
church treasurer of Palermo, of the terror felt by Sicilian children at
the sound of 'the harsh stridencies of that barbarian tongue'.

This is not to say that Constance was left entirely without supporters. Walter of the Mill, for one, had backed her marriage from

[1] 'All foreigners were more or less welcome in his domain, except men of the
Kingdom of Germany, whom he was unwilling to have among his subjects; for
he distrusted that people and could not endure their barbarous ways.' John of
Salisbury, *Historia Pontificalis*, ch. XXXII. Tr. Chibnall.

the outset, and apart from the anarchy-loving barons on the mainland there were plenty of fatalists who, even if they had originally deplored the idea, now accepted it as an accomplished fact. Nothing, such men reasoned, could now prevent Henry from coming to Sicily to claim his wife's throne; better surely that he should come in peace and friendship than in power and wrath. But in these early days the legitimist party was small; its leader, Walter of the Mill, had only a few months to live; and it was in any case almost immediately overshadowed by two other factions, bitterly opposed to Constance, which had sprung up even before William's death was announced. One of these called for the succession to the throne of Roger, Count of Andria; the other favoured Tancred of Lecce. Both candidates had important qualities to recommend them. Separately and together—they had fought side by side against the imperial forces in 1176 and gained an impressive if ultimately insignificant victory—they could boast outstanding military records. Tancred had commanded the Sicilian fleet in William's two principal foreign expeditions; though both of these had ended in disaster, no blame had attached to him personally. Roger had for his part also won diplomatic distinction as one of the leading negotiators of the Treaty of Venice. He was now Great Chamberlain of the Kingdom, a widely admired and respected figure.

But whereas the Count of Andria's claim to the blood royal was tenuous to say the least,[1] Tancred's was undeniable: he was the illegitimate son of Duke Roger of Apulia by Emma, daughter of Count Achard of Lecce. He was small, and villainously ugly. That arch-polemicist Peter of Eboli, who hated him, hexametrically describes him as an *embrion infelix, et detestabile monstrum* and depicts him, both in verse and in his accompanying illustrations, as a monkey.[2] But like so many small men, Tancred was energetic, able and determined; his youthful disloyalty to William I had been forgotten; and he had recently been appointed Grand Constable and Master Justiciar of Apulia. Above all, he had as his champion Matthew of Ajello. Matthew was by now an old

[1] La Lumia, p. 344, refers to him as the great-grandson of Drogo de Hauteville and thus second cousin to the dead King; but I can find no corroboration and the lineage looks distinctly uncertain.
[2] Plate 28.

man, tormented by gout,[1] who had long contemplated retirement and had even, a dozen years before enrolled himself as a lay
brother in the Basilian monastery of the Saviour at Messina. But his
love of power had proved too strong for him; and he and Walter
of the Mill together, despite their mutual loathing, had continued
to stand as what Richard of S. Germano was later to describe as
'the two firmest columns of the Kingdom'. Now one of those columns was showing signs of collapse; but Matthew remained as
firm as ever. A genuine Sicilian patriot, he never disguised his
revulsion at the Hohenstaufen marriage; and before King William's
body was cold he had flung all his energies, his political expertise
and his considerable financial resources into the campaign to secure
Tancred's succession.

The struggle was hard and bitter. The nobility and their hangers-
on were overwhelmingly in favour of Roger of Andria; the bourgeoisie and populace preferred Tancred. Neither side pulled its
punches and on at least one occasion the rival factions fought it out
in the streets of Palermo. But Matthew knew of certain irregularities
in the Count of Andria's private life, and used his knowledge to
disastrous effect. He also had no difficulty in obtaining support from
Pope Clement III—who, he rightly guessed, would jump at any
chance of preventing the union of his two formidable neighbours.

Thus it was that some time in the first weeks of 1190 Tancred of
Lecce received the crown of Sicily, at the hands of Archbishop
Walter of the Mill who appears to have resigned himself, if only
temporarily, to the inevitable. Tancred's first act was to appoint
Matthew of Ajello Chancellor of the Kingdom—an office that had
lain vacant since the departure of Stephen du Perche. Nothing, he
knew, would give the old man greater pleasure or bind him more
closely to the throne; besides, his support would be still more
necessary in the future. There was desperate fighting ahead for them
all if the Kingdom were to survive.

Strangely enough, the first challenge to the new King's authority
came from neither of the two factions he had just defeated. It revealed,

---

[1] Which Peter of Eboli, in a masterpiece of sustained invective, claims that he
sought to alleviate by bathing his feet in the blood of slaughtered children (Plate
29).

however, another still more ominous rift in the structure of the state —a growing antagonism between the Christian and the Muslim sectors of the population. Hardly had Tancred assumed power when inter-confessional strife broke out in the capital. The trouble seems to have been started by the Christians, who took advantage of the disorder following William's death to attack the Arab quarter of Palermo. In the ensuing affray several Muslims lost their lives; many others, fearing a general massacre, fled to the hills where they managed to take possession of several castles, and where they were gradually joined by increasing numbers of their co-religionists. Before long Tancred saw that he had a full-scale insurrection on his hands.

Tension between the two communities had naturally been heightened by the news of the fall of Jerusalem and the subsequent preparations for the Crusade; but the true causes of the revolt lay deeper in the Sicilian past. For half a century and more the steady immigration of Christians from northern and western Europe, unmatched by any corresponding movements of Greeks or Muslims, had led to the dangerous strengthening of the Latin element at the expense of the others. Intolerance was bound to follow. Ever since the anti-Muslim riots that followed the *coup* against William the Bad in 1161 the situation seems to have been progressively deteriorating. Here is Ibn Jubair, reporting from Palermo at the end of 1184:

The Muslims of this city preserve the remaining evidence of their faith. They keep in repair the greater number of their mosques, and come to prayers at the call of the muezzin. . . . They do not congregate for the Friday service, since the *khutbah*[1] is forbidden. On feast-days only may they recite it with intercessions for the Abbasid Caliphs. They have a *qadi* to whom they refer their law-suits, and a cathedral mosque where, in this holy month [of Ramadan] they assemble under its lamps. . . . But in general these Muslims do not mix with their brethren under infidel patronage, and enjoy no security for their goods, their women, or their children.

In the royal palace itself, although it was almost entirely staffed by Muslims, the actual practice of Islam seems to have been tolerated

---

[1] The sermon delivered on Fridays at the time of the midday prayer.

only when it was conducted in private. Ibn Jubair tells of an interview in Messina with one of the leading eunuchs of the court:

He had first looked about his audience-room, and then, in self-
protection, dismissed those servants about him whom he suspected.
. . . 'You can boldly display your faith in Islam,' he said, '. . . but we
must conceal our faith and, fearful of our lives, must adhere to the
worship of God and the discharge of our religious duties in secret.
We are bound in the possession of an infidel who has placed on our
necks the noose of bondage.'

Apart from the specifically religious issue, the prevailing attitude
of the Sicilian Christians towards their Muslim fellow-subjects by
the end of the century is inescapably reminiscent of that shown by
the British sahibs towards the people of India in the heyday of the
Raj:

Their King, William, . . . has much confidence in Muslims—who all,
or nearly all, concealing their faith, yet hold firm to the Muslim
divine law. He relies on them for his affairs, and the most important
matters, even the supervisor of his kitchen being a Muslim; and he
keeps a band of black Muslim slaves commanded by a leader chosen
from amongst them. His ministers and chamberlains he appoints
from his pages, of whom he has a great number and who are his
public officials and are described as his courtiers. In them shines the
splendour of his realm for the magnificent clothing and fiery horses
they display; and there is none of them but has his retinue, his
servants, and his followers.

Thus, in scarcely more than a generation, the status of the Muslims of Sicily had declined from that of a universally respected,
learned and immensely able sector of the population to the level at
the worst of menials and at the best of privileged purveyors of local
colour. Their women might set the fashions which Christian women
were happy to follow; Ibn Jubair notes with wonder how on Christmas Day 1184 the latter 'all went forth in robes of gold-embroidered
silk, wrapped in elegant cloaks, concealed by coloured veils and shod
with gilt slippers . . . bearing all the adornments of Muslim women,
including jewellery, henna on the fingers and perfumes.' The King
himself might read and write Arabic, and murmur oriental endear-

ments to his Muslim handmaidens and concubines.[1] Yet it was all a
far cry from the ideals of the two Rogers. The betrayal of those
ideals by their successors was probably unwitting, possibly inevitable,
certainly catastrophic. And it was, perhaps, more than fortuitous
that the final breakdown of the confessional interdependence on
which Norman Sicily had been founded should have coincided with
the extinction of the Kingdom itself.

The first year of his reign was a particularly hard one for King
Tancred. The Muslim insurrection grew—one chronicler puts the
numbers involved as high as a hundred thousand—and though he
managed to confine it to the west of the island it was not till the end
of 1190 that order was restored. Meanwhile, on the mainland, his
enemies were gathering fast. The adherents of Roger of Andria, who
included nearly all the principal barons of Apulia and Campania,
had been outraged by Tancred's election, and had no intention of
recognising him as their lawful sovereign. In this they were joined by
the legitimists, who genuinely championed Constance and Henry,
and by the fatalists—this last group by now increasing rapidly as the
news spread of Henry's preparations to march. By spring much of the
peninsula was in open revolt. Roger of Andria had gathered all the
malcontents under his banner; and in May a small German army
under Henry of Kalden crossed the frontier near Rieti and descended
the Adriatic coast into Apulia.

But Tancred too had acted fast. The Muslim insurrection and his
own shaky political position made it unwise for him to leave Sicily,
or even to despatch any substantial body of troops; but he had sent
his wife's brother, Count Richard of Acerra, a large sum of money
with which to raise an army locally and, if need be, abroad. Richard
had risen splendidly to the occasion. That summer he successfully prevented the forces of the Count of Andria and Henry of Kalden from
joining up with the rebels of Campania—where Capua and Aversa
had already declared against Tancred—and held the position until
September when, for reasons unknown, the German army withdrew

[1] 'One of the strangest things told us by Yahya ibn Fityan, the embroiderer,
who embroidered in gold the King's clothes, was that the Frankish Christian
women who came to his palace became Muslims, converted by these handmaidens. All this they kept secret from their King.' (Ibn Jubair.)

once again into imperial territory. He then pursued the demoralised
rebels back into Apulia where, during a swift and triumphant campaign, he ambushed the Count of Andria and took him prisoner.[1]

As 1190 ended it was clear that, thanks in a large measure to his
brother-in-law, Tancred had won the first round. An imperial
expedition sent against him had proved abortive, the rebels both in
Sicily and on the mainland had been forced into submission. His two
principal enemies within the Kingdom were both in their graves—
Roger of Andria, whom he had had executed for his part in the
rebellion, and Walter of the Mill who had died of natural causes
earlier in the year, to be succeeded by his brother Bartholomew as
Archbishop of Palermo.

It would be pleasant to be able to write a friendly word or two
about a compatriot who played so prominent and prolonged a part
in the history of his adopted country. The inescapable fact is, however, that of all the Englishmen whose names have from time to
time appeared in these pages, it was Walter of the Mill who exerted
the most baleful influence on the Kingdom. He was not, so far as
one can tell, a wicked man; but he was the very prototype of those
prelates, vain and ambitious and worldly, who were such a feature of
mediaeval Europe. It is impossible to like him. In his quarter of a
century as Archbishop and chief minister to William II, there is no
evidence of his having taken a single constructive step to improve
the Sicilian position or to advance Sicilian fortunes. When the
crisis arose over Constance's marriage his influence, allied with that
of Matthew of Ajello, could almost certainly have secured William's
rejection of the imperial proposals. Instead, he encouraged his
master to give away the Kingdom. Time-server as he was, he did not
hesitate soon afterwards to lay the crown on Tancred's head; but
even this did not stop him from resuming his intrigues against the
new King within weeks, if not days, of the coronation.

Thus, in the absence of any more attractive achievement, Walter's
chief memorial must be his cathedral of Palermo,[2] where his tomb
may still be seen in the crypt. Though the building is curiously
appropriate to its founder—imposing in a messy sort of way,
pompous, grandiloquent, yet vacuous and fundamentally hypocritical

[1] Plate 28.   [2] Plate 30.

—Walter cannot really be blamed for its present appearance; it has been reworked and restored so often that even the exterior allows us only a few glimpses of the original conception—the east end with its apse decorations uncomfortably reminiscent of Monreale, and the long range of windows along the south wall above the side aisles. Even here, nothing seems particularly distinguished; for the most part, the fourteenth-century work somehow contrives to look like a nineteenth-century *pastiche*. But the crowning desecration, literally and figuratively, on the outside and within, took place in the eighteenth century when the Florentine architect Fernando Fuga clapped on a ludicrous and totally unrelated dome, hacked away the side walls to make fourteen chapels, removed the wooden roof and replaced it with inferior vaulting, then whitewashed the whole thing—the apse mosaics had already been torn down two centuries earlier—and baroqued it up beyond recognition. Today, the kindest thing to do about Palermo Cathedral would be to ignore it—were it not for the royal tombs. But the time to speak of these has not yet come.

Walter of the Mill left one other building in the capital, and a much more satisfying one it is. The church of Santo Spirito, built for the Cistercians a decade or so before the cathedral, has miraculously escaped the attentions of restorers and improvers and retains all the austere, uncluttered purity of Norman architecture at its best.[1] Its fame rests, however, less on its beauty than on its historical associations; for it was outside Santo Spirito, just before the evening service on 31 March 1282, that a sergeant of the Angevin army of occupation insulted a Sicilian woman, was stabbed to death by her husband and so, unwittingly, sparked off that triumphantly successful rebellion by the Sicilians against their overlord Charles of Anjou that was ever afterwards to be known as the Sicilian Vespers. Thus, of the two foundations of an English archbishop, one was destined to witness, with the coronation of Henry and Constance, the most abject betrayal of Sicily by her own people; and the other, a century later, the proudest upsurge of popular patriotism in all her history.

King William's proposals to his fellow-monarchs that they should use Sicily as an assembly-point for their crusading forces had not

[1] Plate 31.

passed altogether unheeded. Frederick Barbarossa, despite what must have been fairly painful recollections of his journey to Palestine more than forty years before, had resolved once again to take the land route—a decision that was shortly to cost him his life; but Philip Augustus had accepted the invitation, and so had the new King of England—Richard I, Cœur de Lion.

In the high summer of 1190 these two Kings and their armies met together at Vézelay—a choice of meeting place that might have seemed to some people another ominous precedent. They were to set off on the journey together less for reasons of companionship than because neither trusted the other an inch; and indeed no pair could have been more unlike. The King of France was still only twenty-five; but he was already a widower and apart from a shock of wild, uncontrollable hair there was nothing youthful about him. His ten years on the throne of France had given him unusual wisdom and experience for one so young, making him permanently suspicious, and teaching him to conceal his thoughts and emotions behind a veil of taciturn moroseness. Never handsome, he had now lost the sight of one eye so that his face looked somehow asymmetrical. He lacked courage on the battlefield and charm in society; he was, in a word, a thoroughly unattractive man and he knew it. But beneath his drab exterior there lay a searching intelligence, coupled with a strong sense of both the moral and political responsibilities of kingship. It was easy to underestimate him. It was also unwise.

Yet whatever his hidden qualities, Philip Augustus cannot have looked upon his fellow-ruler without envy. Richard had succeeded his father Henry II in July 1189, just a year before. At thirty-three, he was now in his prime. Though his health was often poor, his superb physique and volcanic energy gave the impression of a man to whom illness was unknown. His good looks were famous, his powers of leadership no less so, his personal bravery already a legend through two continents. From his mother Eleanor he had inherited the Poitevin love of literature and poetry, and to many people he himself must have seemed like some glittering figure from the troubadour romances he loved so much. Only one element was lacking to complete the picture: however sweetly Richard might sing of the joys and pains of love, he had left no trail of betrayed or broken-hearted damozels behind him. But if his tastes ran in other directions they never appreciably affected that shining reputation, burnished as his breastplate, that remained with him till the day of his death.

Those who knew Richard better, on the other hand, soon became aware of other, less admirable sides to his character. Even more impetuous and hot-tempered than the father he had so hated, he altogether lacked that capacity for sustained administrative effort that had enabled Henry II, for all his faults, to weld England almost single-handed into a nation. His ambition was boundless and, nearly always, destructive. Himself incapable of love, he could be faithless, disloyal, even treacherous, in the pursuit of his ends. No English king had fought harder or more unscrupulously for the throne; none was readier to ignore the responsibilities of kingship for the sake of personal glory. In the nine years of life left to him, the total time he was to spend in England was just two months.

The hills round Vézelay, wrote an eyewitness, were so spread with tents and pavilions that the fields looked like a great and multicoloured city. The two Kings solemnly reaffirmed their crusading vows and sealed a further treaty of alliance; then, followed by their respective armies and a huge multitude of pilgrims, they moved off together to the south. It was only at Lyons, where the collapse of the bridge across the Rhône under the weight of the crowds was interpreted as a bad augury for the future, that French and English parted company; Philip turned south-east towards Genoa, where his navy was awaiting him, while Richard continued down the Rhône valley to meet the English fleet at Marseilles. They had agreed to join forces again at Messina, whence their combined army would sail for the Holy Land.

Philip arrived first, on 14 September, and Richard nine days later. Nothing was more typical of the two men than the manner of their disembarkation:

When the King of France was known to be entering the port of Messina, the natives of every age and sex rushed forth to see so famous a King; but he, content with a single ship, entered the port of the citadel privately, so that those who awaited him along the shore saw this as a proof of his weakness; such a man, they said, was not likely to be the performer of any great matter, shrinking in such fashion from the eye of his fellows. . . .

But when Richard was about to land, the people rushed down in crowds towards the beach; and behold, from a distance the sea seemed cleft with innumerable oars, and the loud voices of the trumpets and the horns sounded clear and shrill over the water. Approaching nearer, the galleys could be seen rowing in order, emblazoned with divers coats of arms, and with pennons and banners innumerable floating from the points of the spears. The beaks of the vessels were painted with the devices of the knights they bore, and glittered with the rays reflected from the shields. The sea was boiling with the multitude of oars, the air trembling with the blasts of the trumpets and the tumultuous shouts of the delighted crowds. The magnificent King, loftier and more splendid than all his train, stood erect on the prow, as one expecting alike to see and be seen. . . . And as the trumpets rang out with discordant yet harmonious sounds, the people whispered together: 'He is indeed worthy of empire; he is rightly made King over peoples and kingdoms; what we heard of him at a distance falls far short of what we now see.'[1]

Not all of Richard's admirers on that memorable day may have been aware that that superb figure had preferred, through fear of seasickness, to take the land route down the peninsula; and that this mighty landfall was in fact the culmination of a sea journey that had brought him only a mile or two across the straits. Fewer still could have guessed that, for all the golden splendour of his arrival, Richard was in a black and dangerous mood. It was not the fact that a few days previously, passing through Mileto, he had been caught in the act of appropriating a hawk from a peasant's cottage and narrowly escaped death at the hands of the owner and his friends; it was not even the discovery, on landing at Messina, that the royal palace in the centre of the city had already been placed at the disposal of the King of France and that he himself had been allotted more modest quarters outside the walls. Neither of these misfortunes can have improved his temper, but this time there was more at stake than a simple matter of *amour-propre*.

The truth was that he bore a deep grudge against Tancred. Though William the Good had died intestate, he seems at some stage to have

---

[1] *Itinerary of Richard I.*

promised his father-in-law Henry an important legacy that included
a twelve-foot golden table, a silken tent big enough to hold two
hundred men, a quantity of gold plate and several additional ships,
fully provisioned, for the Crusade. Now, with both William and
Henry dead, Tancred was refusing to honour the promise. Then
there was Joanna. As he rode south through Italy, Richard had
heard unpleasant stories of how his sister was being treated by the
new King of Sicily; it seemed that Tancred, knowing her to be a
partisan of Constance and fearing her influence in the Kingdom,
was keeping the young Queen under distraint and wrongfully withholding the revenues of the County of Monte S. Angelo which she
had received as part of her marriage settlement. From Salerno her
brother had already sent word to Tancred calling for satisfaction on
both these points and adding, for good measure, a demand that
Joanna should also be presented with the golden throne that was, he
claimed, her traditional right as a Norman queen. The tone of his
letter was threatening, and clearly implied that once in Sicily with his
army and navy he had no intention of continuing his journey until
he had received satisfaction.

How far these complaints were justified it is not easy to say.
Richard's subsequent behaviour suggests that he saw Sicily as a
potential new jewel in his own crown and that he was already on
the lookout for any excuse to make trouble. On the other hand
he was genuinely fond of Joanna, and there seems little doubt
that her freedom had been in some degree restricted. Tancred,
in any case, was seriously alarmed. He had too much on his plate to
risk hostilities in yet another quarter, and his first reaction was to get
his unwelcome guest away from the island as soon as possible. If
this meant making concessions, then concessions there would have
to be.

Richard did not have to wait long for results. Only five days after
his arrival at Messina he was joined there by Joanna herself, now once
more at complete liberty and the richer by one million *taris*, given
her by Tancred in compensation for her other losses. It was a
generous offer; but Richard was not to be bought off so easily.
Coldly rejecting Philip Augustus's well-intended attempts at mediation, on 30 September he set off furiously across the straits to occupy

the inoffensive little town of Bagnara on the Calabrian coast. There, in an abbey founded by Count Roger a century before, he settled Joanna under the protection of a strong garrison. Returning to Messina he then fell on the city's own most venerable religious foundation, the Basilian monastery of the Saviour, magnificently sited on the long promontory across the harbour from the town. The monks were forcibly and unceremoniously evicted; and Richard's army moved into its new barracks.

By this time the 'long-tailed Englishmen,' as the Messinans called them, had made themselves thoroughly unpopular. It was many years since any Sicilian city had been called upon to accommodate a foreign army, and the predominantly Greek population of Messina had already been scandalised by their barbarous conduct. Their free and easy ways with the local women, in particular, were not what might have been expected of men who called themselves pilgrims and bore the Cross of Christ on their shoulders. The occupation of the monastery of the Saviour came as the final outrage, and on 3 October serious rioting broke out. Fearing—with good reason—that the King of England might seize the opportunity of taking possession of their city and even, as many maintained, of the whole island, the Messinans rushed to the gates and bolted them; others barred the harbour entrance. Preliminary attempts by the English to force an entry failed; but no one believed that they could be held in check for long. The sun set that evening on an anxious city.

Early the following day Philip Augustus appeared at Richard's headquarters outside the walls. He was accompanied by Hugh, Duke of Burgundy, the Count of Poitiers and the other leaders of the French army, together with a similarly high-ranking Sicilian delegation—the military governor, Jordan du Pin, several notables of the city including Admiral Margaritus, and the archbishops of Monreale, Reggio and of Messina itself; this last none other than Richard Palmer, transferred from Syracuse some years before. It is unlikely that Palmer's words carried any special weight with the King—who, except in the technical sense, was no more English than any other of those present and scarcely even spoke the language—but the ensuing discussions went surprisingly well. The parties seemed on the point of agreement when suddenly the noise of further tumult was heard.

The death of William the Good, attended by a doctor (Ahmed) and astrologer; the people, nobility and *curia* of Palermo sorrowing below (Peter of Eboli MS.)

Tancred—the Monkey King—rejoices at the sight of his rival, Roger of Andria, in prison (Peter of Eboli MS.)

A crowd of Messinans, gathered outside the building, were shouting imprecations against the English and their King.

Richard seized his sword and ran from the hall; summoning his troops, he gave the order for an immediate attack. This time the Messinans were taken by surprise. The English soldiers burst into the city, ravaging and plundering it as they went. Within hours, 'in less time than it took a priest to say matins,'[1] Messina was in flames; only the area around the royal palace, where Philip was quartered, was left undamaged. Margaritus and his fellow-notables narrowly escaped with their lives, leaving their houses in ruins behind them.

All the gold and silver, and whatsoever precious thing was found, became the property of the victors. They set fire to the enemy's galleys and burnt them to ashes, lest any citizens should escape and recover strength to resist. The victors also carried off their noblest women. And lo! when it was done, the French suddenly beheld the ensigns and standards of King Richard floating above the walls of the city; at which the King of France was so mortified that he con-ceived that hatred against King Richard that lasted all his life.

The author of the *Itinerary of Richard I* goes on to explain how Philip insisted, and Richard finally agreed, that the French banners should be flown alongside the English; he does not mention how the citizens of Messina felt about this new insult to their pride. And there were further humiliations in store for them. Not only did Richard demand hostages as a guarantee of their future good conduct; he also caused to be built, on a hill just outside the city, an immense castle of wood—to which, with typical arrogance, he gave the name Mategrifon, 'curb on the Greeks'. Just whom, the Messin-ans must have asked themselves, was the King of England supposed to be fighting? Did he intend to remain indefinitely in Sicily? It seemed a curious way to conduct a Crusade.

To Philip Augustus, the incident over the flags seemed to confirm his worst suspicions. Within a fortnight of his arrival as an honoured guest, Richard was in undisputed control of the second city of the

---

[1] *Plus tost eurent il pris Meschines*
C'uns prestres n'ad dit ses matines.
            Estoire de la Guerre Sainte

island; and the King of Sicily, though not far distant at Catania, had made not the slightest effort to oppose him. To Catania therefore Philip now despatched his cousin the Duke of Burgundy, charging him to warn Tancred of the gravity of the situation and to offer the support of the French army if Richard were to press his claims any further.

Tancred needed no warning—from the French King or from any-one else. He was well aware of the danger of leaving Messina in Richard's hands. But a new idea was now taking shape in his brain. He had the long-term future to consider, and he knew that in the final reckoning Henry of Hohenstaufen was a greater menace than Richard would ever be. Sooner or later Henry would invade, and when he did he would find plenty of support in Apulia and elsewhere. If Tancred were to resist him successfully he too would need allies; and for this purpose the English would be preferable to the French. Crude and uncivilised they might be—and their King, for all his glamorous reputation, was as bad as any of them; but Richard with his Welf connections—his sister Matilda had married Henry the Lion of Saxony—had no love for the Hohenstaufen. Philip, on the other hand, had been on excellent terms with Frederick Barbarossa; if the Germans were to invade now, while the Crusaders were still in Sicily, French sympathies would be to say the least uncertain. Tancred therefore returned the Duke of Burgundy to his master with suitably lavish presents but not much else, and sent his own most trusted envoy—Richard, the elder son of old Matthew of Ajello—to negotiate direct with the King of England at Messina.

This time the financial inducements offered were more than the King could resist. Tancred could not return to Joanna her county of Monte S. Angelo; its position on his north-east frontier was of too much stategic importance at such a moment. But he was prepared to grant her twenty thousand ounces of gold in compensation, over and above the million *taris* she had already received, while to her brother he offered another twenty thousand in lieu of the lost legacy. It was further agreed that Richard's nephew and heir, the three-year-old Duke Arthur of Brittany, should forthwith be betrothed to one of Tancred's daughters. In return Richard promised to give the King of Sicily full military assistance for as long as he and his men should remain within the Kingdom, and undertook to restore to its rightful owners all the plunder he had taken during the disturbances of the previous month. On 11 November, with due ceremony, the resulting treaty was signed at Messina.

The reaction of Philip Augustus to this sudden *rapprochement* between his two fellow-monarchs can well be imagined. As usual, however, he concealed his resentment. Outwardly his relations with Richard remained cordial. The two of them had plenty to discuss before they set off again. Rules of conduct must be drawn up for soldiers and pilgrims alike; there were endless logistical problems still unsolved; it was vital, too, that they should reach agreement in advance about the distribution of conquests and the division of spoils. On all these matters Richard proved surprisingly amenable; on one point only, unconnected with the Crusade, did he refuse to be moved. It concerned the French King's sister Alice, who had been sent to England more than twenty years before as a bride for one of Henry II's sons. She had been offered to Richard who, predictably, would have nothing to do with her; but instead of returning her to France Henry had kept her at his court, later making her his own mistress and, almost certainly, the mother of his child. Now Henry was dead and Alice, at thirty, was still in England and as far away from marriage as ever.

Philip was in no way concerned for her happiness; he had never lifted a finger to help his other, even more pathetic sister Agnes-Anna of Byzantium, twice widowed in hideous circumstances before she was sixteen. But this treatment of a Princess of France was an insult which he could not allow to pass. He found Richard just as adamant as Henry had been. Not only did he refuse once again, point-blank, to consider marrying Alice himself; he had the effrontery to try to justify his attitude on the grounds of her besmirched reputation. Here indeed was a test of Philip's *sang-froid*; and when Richard went on to inform him that his mother Eleanor was at that very moment on her way to Sicily with another bride, the Princess Berengaria of Navarre, relations between the two monarchs came near breaking point. It was probably more to keep up appearances than for any other reason that Philip accepted Richard's invitation to the great banquet at Mategrifon that was held on

Christmas Day; but he may have been consoled by the reflection that most of the Sicilian notables also present had had a similar struggle with their consciences.

On 3 March 1191 the King of England rode down in state to Catania to call on the King of Sicily. The two reaffirmed their friendship and exchanged presents—five galleys and four horse transports for Richard who, according to at least two authorities, gave Tancred in return a still more precious token of his affection—King Arthur's own sword, Excalibur itself, which had been found, only a few weeks before, lying beside the old King's body at Glastonbury.[1] The meeting over, the two returned together as far as Taormina, where a disgruntled Philip was waiting. A new crisis was narrowly averted when Tancred, for reasons which can only be guessed, showed Richard the letters he had been sent by the King of France the previous October, warning him of English machinations; but by the end of the month the allies were again reconciled and relations seem to have been comparatively cordial all round when, on 30 March, Philip sailed with his army for Palestine.

He had timed his departure well; or, perhaps more likely, it was Eleanor and Berengaria who had timed their arrival. Scarcely had the French fleet disappeared over the horizon when their own convoy dropped anchor in the harbour. It was forty-four years since the old Queen had last seen Sicily, calling on Roger II at Palermo on her journey from the Holy Land. On this second visit she had hoped to witness the marriage of her favourite son to the wife she had chosen for him; but Lent had begun, and a Lenten marriage was out of the question. Despite a recent prohibition of women from going on the Crusade, it was therefore decided that Berengaria should accompany her future husband to the East. Young Queen Joanna, who could obviously not be left in the island, would make a perfect

[1] *Le ray Richard saunz plus à ly a redonez
La meyllur espeye ke unkes fu forgez.
Ço fu Kaliburne, dount Arthur le senez
Sei solait guyer en gueres et en mellez.*

So writes Peter of Langtoft in his curious brand of Yorkshire French, echoing Roger of Hoveden a century earlier. But since the so-called grave of Arthur was discovered only at the beginning of 1191, Excalibur would have needed all its magic properties to reach Sicily by early March.

chaperon for her. Once everything was settled, Eleanor saw no reason to delay any longer. After only three days in Messina, with that energy for which she was famous all over Europe—she was now sixty-nine and had been travelling uninterruptedly for over three months—she left again for England.

The day after bidding her mother goodbye for the last time, Joanna herself set off with Berengaria for the Holy Land. Richard had put at their disposal one of his heavy *dromons*; it was slower than a galley but a good deal more comfortable, and it had plenty of room for the ladies' attendants and their enormous quantities of baggage. He himself remained another week, organising the embarkation of his army and the demolition of Mategrifon. Finally, on 10 April, he too sailed away. The Messinans cannot have been sorry to see the last of him.

But their King did not share their relief. Certainly Sicily might be a happier and more peaceful place without Richard's turbulent presence—but only for as long as Henry of Hohenstaufen delayed his invasion. Had Richard been able to stay a little longer, his help would have been invaluable, perhaps even decisive. He could not be blamed for leaving when he did; his presence was urgently needed in Palestine—where, four years after Hattin, the situation was now desperate—and his crusading oath took precedence over all other commitments. None the less, his departure shattered Tancred's greatest single hope of saving his country from the imperial clutches. Now, when the crisis came, he would have to face it alone. He could not know that that crisis was less than three weeks away.

21

NIGHTFALL

O Singer of Persephone!
In the dim meadows desolate
Dost thou remember Sicily?

Wilde, Theocritus

IF Henry of Hohenstaufen had been able to follow his original
plan of campaign, he would have left Germany in November 1190
and almost certainly arrived in Sicily before the departure of the
English troops. His failure to do so was principally due to a report
that reached him just as he was setting out. On 10 June his father,
Frederick Barbarossa, after a long and arduous journey across Anatolia, had led his army out of the last of the Taurus valleys and on to
the flat coastal plain. The heat was sweltering and the little river
Calycadnus[1] that ran past the town of Seleucia to the sea must have
been a welcome sight. Frederick spurred his horse towards it,
leaving his men to follow. He was never seen alive again. Whether he
dismounted to drink and was swept off his feet by the current,
whether his horse slipped in the mud and threw him, whether the
shock of falling into the icy mountain water was too much for his
tired old body—he was nearing seventy—remains unknown. He
was rescued, but too late. The bulk of his army reached the river to
find their Emperor lying dead on the bank.

His son Henry, with two crowns to claim instead of one, was still
more anxious to leave for the South as soon as possible. Internal
problems following his father's death kept him occupied for some
weeks; fortunately the winter was mild, the Alpine passes still open.

[1] In modern Turkish Seleucia has become Silifke, while the Calycadnus is
now less euphoniously known as the Göksu.

374

By January he and his army were safely across. Then, after a month spent strengthening his position in Lombardy and securing the assistance of a fleet from Pisa, he headed towards Rome where Pope Clement III was expecting him.

But before Henry could reach the city Pope Clement was dead. Hurriedly—for the imperial troops were fast approaching—the Sacred College met in conclave and selected as his successor the Cardinal-deacon of S. Maria in Cosmedin, Hyacinthus Bobo. It seemed, in the circumstances, a curious choice. The new Pope was of illustrious birth—his brother Ursus was founder of the Orsini family—and could boast a long and distinguished ecclesiastical record, having stoutly defended Peter Abelard against St Bernard at Sens more than fifty years before. But he was now eighty-five—hardly, one might have thought, the man to handle the overbearing young Henry during a crisis that threatened the position of the Church almost as much as it did that of the Kingdom of Sicily. There is every indication that he shared this view himself; only the proximity of the German army, together with widespread fears of another schism if there were any delay in the election, at length persuaded him to accept the tiara. A cardinal since 1144, it was only on Holy Saturday, 13 April 1191, that he was ordained priest; on the following day, Easter Sunday, he was enthroned at St Peter's as Pope Celestine III; and on the 15th, as the first formal action of his pontificate, he crowned Henry and Constance Emperor and Empress of the West.

With his experience of half a century in the papal service, no one knew better than Celestine the dangers of allowing the Empire to annex the Kingdom of Sicily. In the circumstances, however, he could hardly insist on an undertaking from the new Emperor to advance no further to the south; and such attempts as he did make to dissuade Henry from pursuing his plans were, as might have been expected, poorly received. On 29 April, just a fortnight after his coronation—*papa prohibente et contradicente* as Richard of S. Germano puts it—Barbarossa's son led his army across the Garigliano and into Sicilian territory.

Within the limits of his possibilities, Tancred was ready for him. The defection of so many of his mainland vassals had prevented him from raising an army capable of defeating the imperial forces in the field; he therefore wisely concentrated on building up his defences in those areas on whose support he could rely—in Sicily itself, in his own territory around the heel of Apulia and, above all, in the larger towns on both sides of the peninsula where the bourgeoisie, republican as they might be, far preferred a King to an Emperor and readily accepted the privileges, charters and indemnities he promised them. Meanwhile he sent Richard of Acerra north, at the head of as large a force as he could muster, to stiffen local resistance.

At first Richard made little progress. He probably knew that any attempt to secure the loyalties of the lands along the northern frontier would be doomed to failure and, like Tancred, focused his energies where he felt they would be most effective. Thus, in the first weeks of the invasion, Henry carried all before him. One town after another opened its gates; more and more of the local barons joined the imperial ranks. From Monte Cassino to Venafro, thence to Teano—nowhere was there a sign of opposition. Even Capua, once the most jealously independent of the cities of Campania, now welcomed the Germans as they approached, its archbishop giving orders for the Hohenstaufen standard to be hoisted on the ramparts. At Aversa, the first Norman fief in all Italy, it was the same story; Salerno, King Roger's mainland capital, did not even await the arrival of the imperial troops before writing to assure Henry of its loyalty—simultaneously inviting Constance to spend the hot summer months in her father's old palace. Only when the Emperor reached Naples was he brought to a halt.

In the half-century during which it had formed part of the Norman Kingdom, Naples had grown and prospered. It was now a rich trading port numbering some forty thousand inhabitants, including an important Jewish community and commercial colonies from Pisa, Amalfi and Ravello. Recently, to encourage their loyalist sympathies, Tancred had accorded to the Neapolitans a whole series of grants and privileges. Richard of Acerra had therefore wisely selected the city as his headquarters. Its defences were in good order—Tancred had had them repaired the year before at his own expense—its granaries and storehouses full. When the Emperor appeared with his army beneath its walls, the citizens were ready for him.

The ensuing siege was not, from their point of view, a particularly arduous one. Thanks to the incessant harrying of the Pisan ships by the Sicilian fleet under Margaritus, Henry never managed properly to control the harbour approaches, and the defenders continued to receive reinforcements and supplies. On the landward side the walls took a heavy battering; the Count of Acerra was wounded and temporarily replaced as commander by Matthew of Ajello's second son Nicholas, now Archbishop of Salerno, who had deliberately left his flock a few weeks previously in protest at their disloyalty. But the defences held firm; and it became clear, as the summer dragged on, that it was the besiegers rather than the besieged who were beginning to feel the strain.

Looking back—as we can now do, for the end is near—over the whole chequered history of the Normans in the South, we might well be forgiven for seeing it as an almost unrelieved saga of treachery and betrayal. Only one of their allies had never let them down: the heat of the southern summer. Again and again it had saved them from successive waves of imperial invaders, from that distant day in 1022 when Henry the Holy had withdrawn in despair from the siege of Troia to now, the best part of two centuries later, when his namesake, seeing his forces decimated by malaria, dysentery and wholesale defections and eventually himself falling seriously ill, recognised that he too must turn his army homeward while there was still time.

It was on 24 August that Henry gave the order to raise the siege of Naples, and within a day or two the imperial host, still impressive but now noticeably smaller and slower than it had been a few weeks before, had trailed off northward over the hills. The Neapolitans watched them go with satisfaction. They knew, however, that to Henry this withdrawal was nothing more than an irritating reverse; it meant delay, but not defeat. He had posted imperial garrisons in all the most important towns and cities and, in order that there should be no possible doubts about his future intentions, had arranged to leave Constance in Salerno till his return.

Here, however, he made a serious mistake. He did not understand the temper of the South, and it obviously never struck him that news of his retreat, combined with fears of Tancred's vengeance at their disloyalty, would, within days of his own departure, reduce the Salernitans to panic. In their frantic search for a scapegoat, a Salernitan mob attacked the palace in which Constance was staying and would probably have killed her had not Tancred's nephew, a certain Elias of Gesualdo, appeared on the scene just in time and taken her into protective custody, sending her on at the earliest opportunity to the King in Messina.

To Tancred the capture of the Empress must have seemed like a godsend. He had been much heartened by the news of Henry's departure, but he knew that the battle was still scarcely joined. Henry might have found the going harder than he had expected, but his army had not been routed—it had not even been opposed in the open field—and much of northern Campania, including Monte Cassino, remained under his control. The first round, though less disastrous than Tancred had feared, could at best be said to have ended in a draw; and prospects for the second were not particularly bright.

Not, at least, until Constance appeared. But now the situation was suddenly altered; the most valuable diplomatic hostage that Tancred could ever have hoped for had fallen into his lap. No longer was he obliged to wait in impotent suspense till Henry should choose to invade his territory again: he was in a position to negotiate. Meanwhile, as a further encouragement to him, Pope Celestine was showing unmistakable signs of friendship. Even while the siege of Naples was still in progress, the Pope had gone behind the Emperor's back and negotiated with Henry the Lion; and four months later, in December, he excommunicated the whole monastery of Monte Cassino as a punishment for having espoused the imperial cause. Monte Cassino still maintained its opposition to Tancred, but there could no longer be any question where the Pope's own sympathies lay.

Sympathy, however, did not mean endorsement. To any pope, too powerful a Sicily was every bit as dangerous as too powerful an Empire. Safety, as always, lay in holding the balance between them. What was required was mediation; and if in the course of that mediation the Pope were to incline towards the Sicilian point of view, he saw no reason why he should not extract concessions in return.

Tancred's popular support was reduced, in particular, by his still shaky legal position; a papal investiture confirming his right to the crown would be of immense value to his cause—if he were prepared to pay for it.

Which of the two took the initiative, and when, is no longer known; but discussions through intermediaries must have been going on during the spring and summer of 1192 for when Tancred, fresh from a successful punitive expedition against his rebellious vassals in the Abruzzi, met the papal envoys at Gravina in June, the main terms of a treaty had already been agreed. They were simple enough in their way, and they obtained for the King the investiture he wanted; but they involved the surrender of all those special rights over the ecclesiastical administration in the island of Sicily that had been secured with such difficulty by Roger I and II and re-negotiated by William the Bad at Benevento in 1156.[1] Henceforth the Sicilian clergy would be entitled, in just the same way as their mainland brethren, to appeal to Rome in cases of supposed injustice. The Pope might send his special envoys to Sicily whenever he liked and not only when the King asked for them. Elections to the hierarchy would no longer be subject to royal approval.

Seeing the Latin Church in Sicily placed, for the first time in its history, under full papal control, Pope Celestine could justifiably congratulate himself on a diplomatic *coup* of some magnitude. It was not often that Popes had got the better of Normans in negotiations of that sort. Tancred, however, had not been disposed to argue. He had his back to the wall. The privileges he had surrendered seemed to belong to a happier and more spacious age; they were a small enough price to pay for legitimacy.

But, though he did not yet know it, he had also lost something else—something far more valuable to him at that moment than any number of ecclesiastical sanctions. Pope Celestine, undeterred by Henry's reception of his last proposals, still cherished the hope that one day, through his mediation, King and Emperor might be reconciled; and he had therefore pressed Tancred as a gesture of goodwill to deliver Constance into his care. Chalandon, with unaccustomed heat, condemns the Pope's advice as *détestable*; it was

[1] See pp. 197-9.

379

certainly ill-conceived, and its effect was disastrous. Tancred, not wishing to antagonise the Pope at such a time, reluctantly complied. The Empress was entrusted to a special escort that included several cardinals, and set off for Rome.

Had she gone by sea, all might have been well; but the land route passed through territory still under Henry's control, and the inevitable happened. When the party reached the frontier at Ceprano it ran into a group of imperial knights. Constance at once placed herself under their protection. The cardinals objected, but were ignored. They returned empty-handed to Rome while the Empress, carefully avoiding the city, hastened back over the Alps to her husband.

Tancred had been robbed of his trump card. He was not to be dealt another.

During the last weeks of 1192 Joanna Plantagenet called at Palermo on her way back from Palestine—accompanied by her sister-in-law Berengaria, now Queen of England since her marriage to Richard at Limassol in Cyprus some eighteen months before. The fact that she chose to do so suggests that, whatever her brother may have pretended, she had not been too badly treated by Tancred after her husband's death; she certainly bore him no grudge, and Tancred and his wife Sibylla gave the two young queens a suitably royal welcome. A week or two later they sailed on again, Berengaria to welcome widowhood in France, Joanna towards a second marriage.[1] She seems to have been delighted with her reception, in a Palermo that must have appeared outwardly unchanged from the days when she and her godlike young husband had reigned over Norman Sicily at its loveliest and most peaceful. One hopes that she understood how fortunate she was to have known it at such a time—or even to have found, on her return, her old realm still in existence at all.

[1] She had had a narrow escape in Palestine when Richard, for reasons more diplomatic than humane, had tried to marry her off to Saladin's brother al-Adil. Her second husband was in fact to prove much more to her taste—Count Raymond VI of Toulouse, whom she was to marry as his fourth wife in 1196. They were happy together, but not for long. Three years later, when still not quite thirty-four, Joanna died in childbirth, having been received on her death-bed into the religious order of Fontevrault—where she lies buried, with her father, mother and brother.

For if, that summer, Henry VI had led a second expedition to the South as he had intended to do, better equipped than its predecessor and provided with adequate naval support, it is unlikely that Tancred, even with the help of Margaritus and his fleet, would have been able to hold out. The long peace that had marked the reign and made the reputation of William the Good was now over; after twenty-five years anarchy had returned; already the mainland had lapsed once again into chaos. Not a road was safe, scarcely a baron could be trusted; in such conditions organised resistance to an invader was well-nigh impossible. But Henry had not marched. The Welfs, transparently supported by Pope Celestine, were making too much trouble for him at home. The best he had been able to do was to send a relatively meagre force under Berthold of Künsberg to hold the situation until conditions became more favourable to his purpose. Norman Sicily was granted a stay of execution.

But it was still fighting for its life. Though Tancred had spent nine months continuously on campaign up and down the peninsula, he had returned to Sicily in the autumn with little to show for his efforts and more convinced than ever that without active help from abroad the days of his Kingdom were numbered. Much of the winter he spent concluding negotiations with the Byzantine Emperor Isaac Angelus, as a result of which he was soon able to announce the betrothal of his elder son Roger—whom he had duly created Duke of Apulia some time before—to the Emperor's daughter Irene.

The wedding was celebrated the following spring, at Brindisi. It served little practical purpose. Isaac could provide the King of Sicily with a daughter-in-law, but he was too busy with his own troubles to furnish anything else. Duke Roger was dead by the end of the year; his young wife was left, disconsolate and alone, in Palermo. Meanwhile King Richard of England, who might otherwise have been ready to help, had been captured by one of Henry's vassals on his return journey from Palestine and was now languishing in a German castle. Sicily's only ally remained Pope Celestine; but the Pope was hamstrung by an openly imperialist Roman Senate, and had no army. He was also eighty-seven.

Tancred fought on alone. Still there was no sign of the Emperor, but even without him the situation was deteriorating; the royalist troops might recapture a few towns and castles here and there, but they could make no real headway. Monte Cassino in particular proved as impregnable as it always had, still shamelessly flying the imperial standard from its tower. Then, in the late summer, Tancred fell ill. He continued as long as he could, but the sickness increased until he was forced to return to Sicily. All winter long he lay in Palermo, growing steadily weaker; and on 20 February 1194 he died.

Now there was no hope left. With Tancred of Lecce Sicily had lost her last effective champion. Of all the Norman kings, he was the most selfless and the most tragic. In happier times he would never have sought the crown; nor, when it was thrust upon him, did he ever have an opportunity to savour the delights of kingship. His four years on the throne were years of unremitting strife—against the Empire above all, but also against his fellow-Sicilians, Christian and Muslim, who were too egotistical or too blind to understand the enormity of the crisis that faced them. Seeing it himself with such terrible clarity, he strove to turn it aside by every means within his power, military and diplomatic, overt and clandestine. Had he lived, he might even have succeeded—though the odds were heavily against him. Dying as he did in early middle age, he is remembered in Sicily—when he is remembered at all—as a mediocrity and a failure, or even as the misshapen ogre of the imperial propagandists. It is an unfair judgment. Tancred lacked, perhaps, the greatness of his proudest forbears; but with his persistence, his courage and—most of all—his political vision, he surely proved himself a not unworthy successor.

To the ever-superstitious subjects of the crumbling Kingdom, the deaths of both King Tancred and his heir within a few weeks of each other seemed yet another sign from heaven that the Hautevilles had run their race and that Henry of Hohenstaufen must now prevail. The fact that Tancred's only other son, William, was still a child and that Sicily, at the time of her greatest trial, was once more to be entrusted to the care of a woman Regent appeared only additional, unnecessary confirmation of the divine will. The dark clouds of defeatism that had long been gathering over the *Regno* now spread to the capital itself as Queen Sibylla, still in the first paralysing numb-ness of her widowhood, took the reins of government into her tired, reluctant hands.

She had no illusions. To her as to her husband, the crown had never been anything but a burden, and she knew as well as anyone that the task before her was impossible. If Tancred with all his energy and courage had ultimately failed to unite his people against the oncoming menace, how could she and her little son hope to succeed? She herself was without political ability or understanding; the one adviser on whom she might have relied, old Matthew of Ajello, had died the previous year. His two sons, Richard and Nicholas, the latter now Archbishop of Salerno, remained loyal and capable enough in their way; but neither could hope to match the experience or prestige of their father. Her third chief adviser was Archbishop Bartholomew of Palermo, brother and successor of Walter of the Mill. She did not trust him, and she was almost certainly right. All she could do was to wait for the blow to fall—and, meanwhile, to try to keep her head.

She did not have long to wait. Henry VI, his domestic problems settled, was now once again directing all his energies towards the conquest of Sicily. He was not in any particular hurry; time was on his side, and there was no point in risking any repetition of the Naples disaster of three years before. Then he had been let down by inadequate naval support; thanks to Margaritus, the Pisan fleet had been rendered useless and the Genoese, arriving only after the imperial retreat had begun, had narrowly escaped total destruction. This time he would be properly prepared. Margaritus would find himself faced not only by Pisans and Genoese, but by fifty fully-equipped galleys from the one source, perhaps, that he least expected —King Richard of England.

It was not really Richard's fault; he had had little choice. On 4 February 1194—less than two and a half weeks before Tancred's death—he had at last obtained his release from captivity; but Henry had made him pay dearly for his freedom. To the original ransom figure of a hundred thousand silver marks he had added another fifty thousand, to be used specifically for the Sicilian expedition, together with the fifty galleys and the services of two hundred knights for not less than a year. As a final piece of gratuitous humiliation, the

Emperor had forced his prisoner to do homage to him for the Kingdom of England itself.

For the moment, however, it was the ships that mattered. Henry expected little serious opposition from Tancred's army—and none at all in Campania where his garrisons, aided by the reinforcements brought in by Berthold of Künsberg, had been steadily extending their authority since Tancred's death. Everything depended on his power at sea. Towards the end of May he crossed the Splügen pass into Italy and spent Whitsun in Milan. A week or two later he was in Genoa and then in Pisa, making sure of his ships and planning every detail of the coming campaign. The dates were fixed; and on 23 August the combined fleets under the overall command of the Steward of the Empire, Markward of Anweiler, appeared in the bay of Naples. They found the city open to them. The Neapolitans, who only three years before had defied the imperial army to do its worst and had soon afterwards triumphantly watched it go limping back to Germany, had this time capitulated even before the enemy had arrived. With Tancred's death, the last remaining shreds of South Italian morale were gone.

Henry did not even bother to stop at Naples. He went straight on to Salerno, where he had an old score to settle. Three years before, the Salernitans had betrayed him. They had made their submission, had offered his wife their hospitality and then, at the first reports of an imperial retreat, had turned against her and delivered her up to her enemies. The Emperor was not the man to let such treachery go unpunished. Fear of his vengeance, rather than courage or feelings of loyalty towards their King, at first led the Salernitans to resist, but they could not do so for long. Their city was taken by storm and given over to merciless pillage. Such of the population as escaped massacre had their property confiscated and were sent into exile. The walls were reduced to rubble; by then there was little left for them to enclose.

If any example was necessary of the treatment to be expected by towns that sought to resist the German advance, Salerno provided it. With two heroic exceptions—Spinazzola and Policoro—which suffered a similar fate, Henry's authority was accepted everywhere without question. His ensuing march through the South was less of a campaign than a triumphal progress; even the cities of Apulia, long the focus of anti-imperial feeling, accepted the inevitable; Siponto, Trani, Barletta, Bari, Giovinazzo and Molfetta, each in turn opened its gates to the conqueror. In Calabria it was the same story. At the end of October Henry VI, now master of the mainland, crossed the straits of Messina. For the first time in well over a century, a hostile invading army was encamped on Sicilian soil.

The navy had arrived several weeks earlier, and the Emperor disembarked to find Messina already an occupied city. So too—despite serious differences between the Pisans and Genoese which were resolved only after a full-scale naval battle fought by their respective fleets—were Catania and Syracuse. Everywhere, the central administration was breaking down; the island was in a state of growing confusion. Once Henry had established his bridgeheads, it was clear that no real opposition could be organised against him. Queen Sibylla did her best; whatever her other faults, she did not lack courage. The boy King and his three small sisters she sent off to comparative safety in the fortress of Caltabellotta,[1] near Sciacca on the south-west coast; then she attempted to rally a last-ditch resistance. It was no use. The citadel overlooking the port was commanded by Margaritus; he too was eager to hold out till the end. But the fatalism that had paralysed the capital had now spread to the garrison. They laid down their arms. Margaritus could not continue the struggle single-handed. While the Queen Regent, seeing that her cause was lost, fled with the Archbishop of Palermo and his brother to join her children at Caltabellotta, he remained to negotiate the final surrender.

Henry, meanwhile, advanced on Palermo. A few miles outside the walls, at Favara, he was received by a group of leading citizens to assure him of the city's submission and future fidelity.[2] In return he issued strict orders, immediately relayed throughout the army, that there should be no pillage or licentiousness. Palermo was his king-

---

[1] A single tower of this castle—where, incidentally, the peace was signed in 1302 that brought to an end the war of the Sicilian Vespers—still rises from a pinnacle above the town, commanding one of the most stunning views in all Sicily. Below, the Chiesa Madre is also worth a visit; it was erected by Count Roger I when he captured Caltabellotta in 1090.

[2] Plate 32.

dom's capital, and was to be treated as such; at all times the strictest discipline was to be maintained. His promise given, he rode through the gates and made his solemn entry into the city.

Thus, on 20 November 1194, the rule of the Hautevilles in Palermo was brought to an end. It had begun nearly a century and a quarter before, when Robert Guiscard, with his brother Roger and his magnificent wife Sichelgaita riding behind him, had led an exhausted but exultant army into the city. They had fought with tenacity and courage—qualities that had been matched in full measure by the defenders; and in the soldierly admiration felt by each side for a worthy adversary was born the mutual respect and understanding that lay at the root of the Norman-Sicilian miracle. The result had been the happiest and most glorious chapter of the island's history. Now that chapter was closed—with the surrender of a demoralised people to an invader whom they feared too much to fight and who felt for them, in return, a contempt which he made little effort to conceal.

On Christmas Day, 1194, the Emperor Henry VI of Hohenstaufen was crowned King of Sicily in Palermo Cathedral. In places of honour before him, to witness his triumph and their own humiliation, sat Sibylla and her children, among them the sad little William III, who after a ten-month reign, was now King no longer. So far, they had been treated well. Instead of attacking Caltabellotta—which he could have quickly subdued—Henry had offered them reasonable, even generous, terms, under which William was to receive not only his father's county of Lecce but also the principality of Taranto. Sibylla had accepted, and had returned with her family to the capital. Now, as she watched the crown of Sicily—that crown that had brought so much misery to her husband, her son and herself during the past five years—slowly lowered on to Henry's head, it is hard to imagine her feeling any emotion but that of profound relief.

If so, however, it was premature—and short-lived. Four days later, the atmosphere suddenly changed. A conspiracy to assassinate the Emperor had, it was claimed, been uncovered in the nick of time. Sibylla, her children and a large number of leading Sicilians who had been summoned to Palermo for the coronation—among them

Margaritus of Brindisi, Archbishop Nicholas of Salerno and his brother Richard, Counts Roger of Avellino and Richard of Acerra, even Princess Irene, the bewildered Byzantine widow of the last Duke of Apulia—were accused of complicity in the plot, and sent off under close guard to captivity in Germany.

How much truth, if any, was there in these charges? Several chroniclers, particularly those writing in Italy such as Richard of S. Germano, categorically deny that there was ever a plot at all; for them the whole story was merely a pretext by which Henry could rid his new kingdom of all undesirable and potentially subversive elements. The idea is not impossible; no one who has followed the course of the Emperor's stormy career can doubt that he would have been fully capable of such conduct had it suited him. But if not out of character with Henry himself, it still runs contrary to the whole policy which we find him pursuing towards his new kingdom. Everywhere except in Salerno—where he had good reason for resentment —we find him in a merciful and conciliatory mood, a phenomenon rare enough, where he was concerned, to be in itself remarkable; and it is unlikely that he would have switched overnight from conciliation to repression without good reason. What is in the highest degree improbable is that, given the unpopularity of the Germans and the Sicilian *penchant* for intrigue, the possibility of a *coup d'état* was never at this time considered. If one was actually planned, several of those arrested would certainly have been involved, or at any rate aware of what was going on. They were lucky in that case to escape a more unpleasant punishment.

Or some of them were. Others proved less fortunate than they had supposed. Two or three years later, following further insurrections in Sicily and on the mainland, many of these prisoners were blinded by order of the Emperor—despite the fact that having been in captivity since 1194 they could have played no part in the more recent disturbances. By then, with the whole Kingdom trembling under a reign of terror more violent than anything known under the Normans, few of its subjects can have cherished any illusions about the disaster that had befallen them.

But the story of Sicily after the Hautevilles are gone has no part in this book. It remains only to record the fate, in so far as we know it, of the last pale representatives of that extraordinary clan that had burst forth so dazzlingly across three continents, only to peter out in less than two centuries with the spectacle of a sad, frightened woman and her children. Sibylla, after five years or so of tolerable captivity with her three daughters in the convent of Hohenburg in Alsace, was eventually released to live out her remaining days in the obscurity she should never have left. Her daughter-in-law Irene, on the other hand, had a very different future awaiting her. In May 1197 she married Henry's brother, Philip of Swabia, and the following year became in her turn Empress of the West.

As for William III himself, his end remains a mystery. According to one theory he too was blinded and castrated in a German prison by order of Henry VI; another story—which does not necessarily contradict the first—relates that he was set free and became a monk. The only fact of which we can be reasonably sure is that, captive or cloistered, he did not long survive. Before the turn of the century he was dead, still hardly out of his boyhood—but the time and place of his death are unrecorded.

And what, finally, of Constance? We have heard nothing of her since her escape from the papal escort and her hasty return to Germany in 1191. She—through no fault of her own—was the cause of her country's suffering, the ultimate justification for her husband's seizure of the Sicilian throne. Theoretically, where Sicily was concerned, she was the true monarch; Henry was merely her consort. Many people must have wondered why, when he invaded the Kingdom for the second time in the summer of 1194, his wife was no longer at his side; or why, on Christmas Day in Palermo, it was Henry alone who knelt at the altar for his coronation.

But there was a reason, and a good one. At the age of forty, and after nearly nine years of marriage, Constance was expecting a child. She did not put off her journey to Sicily on that account; but she travelled more slowly and in her own time, starting out a month or two after her husband and moving by easy stages down the peninsula. Even so, for a woman of her age and in her condition, it was a dangerous undertaking. The days and weeks of being shaken and jolted over the rough tracks of Lombardy and the Marches took their toll; and when she reached the little town of Jesi, not far from Ancona, she felt the pains of childbirth upon her.

Ever since the beginning of her pregnancy, Constance had had one fixed idea. She knew that both her enemies and Henry's, on both sides of the Alps, would do everything they could to discredit the birth, citing her age and the long years of her barrenness to claim that the child she was to bear could not really be hers; and she was determined that on this question at least there should be no possible room for doubt. She therefore had a large tent erected in the market square of Jesi, to which free entrance was allowed to any matron of the town who wished to witness the birth; and on the feast of St Stephen, 26 December, the day after her husband had received the Sicilian crown in Palermo Cathedral, the Empress brought forth her only son. A day or two later she showed herself in public in the same square, proudly suckling the child at her breast. The Hauteville spirit was not quite dead after all.

In the following century it was to appear again, in a new guise but more refulgently than ever, when that son—Frederick—grew to manhood. Though history may remember him as Emperor of the West, he himself never forgot that he was also King of Sicily, the grandson not only of Barbarossa but of Roger II as well. He showed it in the splendour of his court, in his lions and his leopards and his peacocks, in the Italian and Arabic poets he loved, in his classicising architecture and his Apulian hunting-lodges, and above all in that insatiable artistic and intellectual curiosity that was to make him the first of Renaissance princes two hundred years before his time, earning him the appellation of *Stupor Mundi,* the Wonder of the World. He showed it too in 1215, when he brought to Palermo the two huge porphyry sarcophagi that his grandfather had installed seventy years before at Cefalù.

Two other sarcophagi, of similar material but vastly inferior quality, already stood in Walter of the Mill's cathedral. One was that of Roger II, specially prepared for him in the capital when he had been denied burial in his own foundation;[1] the other was that which Constance had had made for her husband after his sudden death at Messina in 1197. This latter receptacle, however, was of poor

[1] See pp. 160–1.

workmanship—closer inspection shows it to have been glued together from fourteen separate parts—and Frederick seems to have thought it unworthy of his father. He therefore transferred Henry's corpse, still overlaid by the long tresses of fair hair cut off by his widow in her grief, to one of those from Cefalù, replacing it with the body of Constance, who had survived her husband by little more than a year; the fourth sarcophagus—that which Roger had originally intended for his own remains—Frederick kept for himself.[1] In it he was duly laid after his death in 1250; but he was not long to retain sole occupancy. In the fourteenth century the tomb was opened to receive two more bodies—those of the feeble-minded Peter II of Aragon and an unknown woman.

Father, daughter, son-in-law, grandson—a natural enough group, one might think, for a family burial. And yet, in those massive sepulchres, silent under their canopies of marble and mosaic, the four lie uneasily together—the architect of the Norman Kingdom and its destroyer, the unwilling cause of the collapse and its ultimate beneficiary. Nor do any of them really belong. Henry, by the time he died at the age of thirty-two, was detested and feared throughout Sicily; Constance was seen—unfairly but understandably—as having betrayed her homeland. Roger, to be sure, was loved; but he belongs at Cefalù, where he had always wished to lie and where the setting is worthy of him. Even Frederick, who was only twenty when he ordered his tomb, would probably have later preferred a different resting-place—in Capua perhaps, or Jerusalem, or, best of all, on some lonely hilltop under the wide Apulian sky. But Frederick's story, superb and tragic as it is, belongs elsewhere; ours is done.

Sixty-four years is a short life for a kingdom; and indeed Sicily might have been saved had William II—his sobriquet is better forgotten—shown himself either sensible or fertile. Instead, to serve the interests of a vain, aggressive ambition, he made a present of it to its oldest and most persistent enemy—an enemy against whom every one of his predecessors from the days of Robert Guiscard onwards had successively fought to defend it. Thus, when the

[1] Such, at least, are the conclusions drawn, after brilliant detective work, by J. Déer. (*The Dynastic Porphyry Tombs of the Norman Period in Sicily.*)

Kingdom fell, it was not even properly defeated; it was thrown away.

And yet, even if Henry VI had never marched to claim his inheritance, it could not have lasted for long. A monarchy so absolute, so centralised, as that created by the two Rogers must depend for its survival on the personality of the monarch; and the decline of the Kingdom only reflects the decline of the Hautevilles themselves. As each generation gave way to the next, it was as though the cold Norman steel were slowly softening, the rich Norman blood growing thinner and more sluggish under the Sicilian sun. At last, with Tancred, saved by his bastardy from the oriental effeteness of the court at Palermo, the old vigour returned. But it was too late. Sicily was lost.

Perhaps, from the start, it carried within itself the seeds of its own destruction. It was too heterogeneous, too eclectic, too cosmopolitan. It failed—indeed, it hardly tried—to develop any national traditions of its own. Patriotism is an overrated and potentially dangerous emotion, but it is indispensable to a nation fighting for its life; and when the crisis came, there was not enough of it to carry the Kingdom through. Norman and Lombard, Greek and Saracen, Italian and Jew —Sicily had proved that for as long as they enjoyed an enlightened and impartial government, they could happily coexist; they could not coalesce.

Yet, if the Kingdom died the victim of its ideals, those ideals were surely worth dying for. Inevitably in the last years, with the slow sickening of the body politic, the status of the religious and racial minorities began to decline. But nations should be judged on their achievements rather than on their lapses, and to the very end Norman Sicily stood forth in Europe—and indeed in the whole bigoted mediaeval world—as an example of tolerance and enlightenment, a lesson in the respect that every man should feel for those whose blood and beliefs happen to differ from his own. Europe, alas, was ungrateful and the Kingdom perished; but not before it had been rewarded by a sunburst of brilliance and beauty that blazes undimmed down the centuries and still speaks its message as clearly as ever. That message is to be read in the Palatine Chapel, when the great Islamic roof seems itself to glow gold with the reflected radiance of Byzantium; in the swell of the five crimson cupolas above the little cloister of St

John of the Hermits; in a little garden outside Castelvetrano, where SS. Trinità di Delia stands lonely and immaculate in the afternoon sun; in the all-embracing Pantocrators of Monreale and Cefalù; and in the swirling Arabic calligraphy of George of Antioch's childhood hymn to the Virgin as it twines mistily round the dome of the Martorana while, far below, Latin fuses with Greek in another, simpler inscription, proud and unadorned: ROGERIOS REX.

GENEALOGICAL TREES

MAPS

APPENDIX: The Norman Monuments of Sicily

BIBLIOGRAPHY

THE HOUSE OF HAUTEVILLE

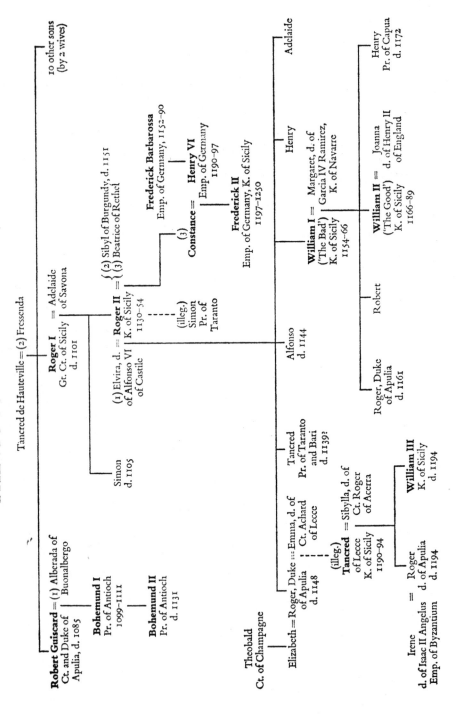

THE HOUSES OF NAVARRE AND PERCHE

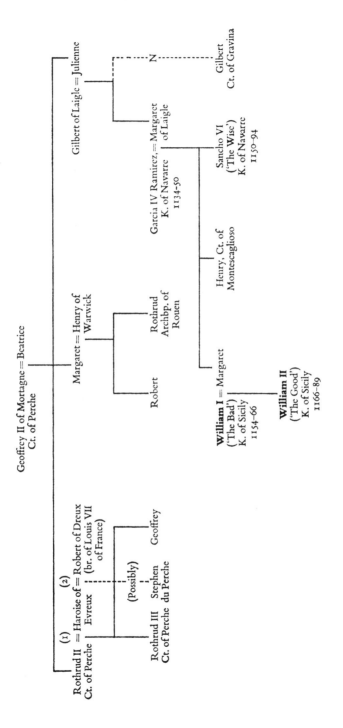

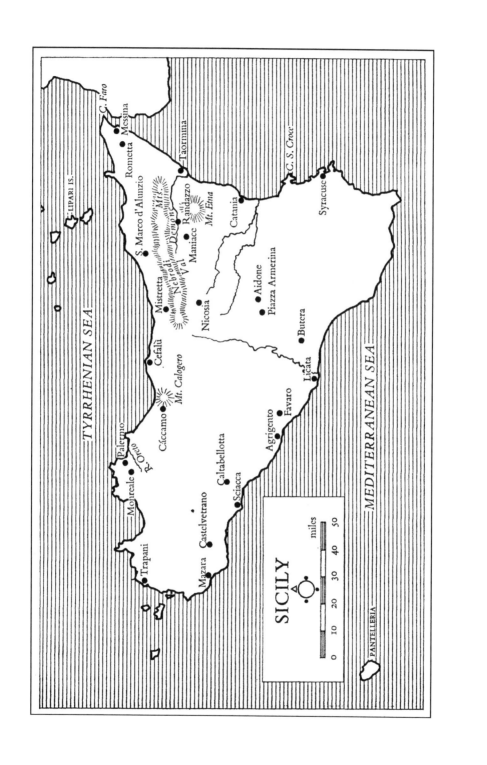

SICILY

TYRRHENIAN SEA

MEDITERRANEAN SEA

LIPARI IS.

C. Faro
Messina
Rometta
S. Marco d'Alunzio
Taormina
Mts.
Nebrodi
Val Demone
Randazzo
Maniace
Mt. Etna
C. S. Croce
Mistretta
Catania
Nicosia
Aidone
Piazza Armerina
Syracuse
Butera
Cefalù
Mt. Calogero
Licata
Palermo
R. Oreto
Cáccamo
Favaro
Agrigento
Monreale
Caltabellotta
Sciacca
Trapani
Mazara
Castelvetrano

miles

0   10   20   30   40   50

PANTELLERIA

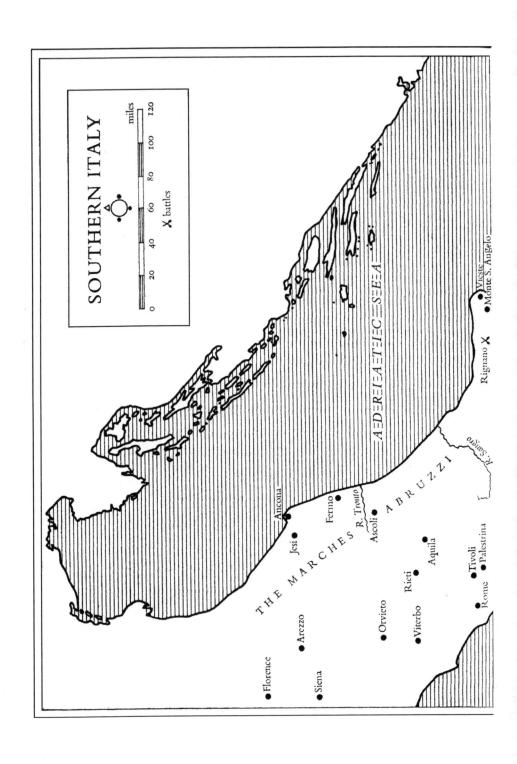

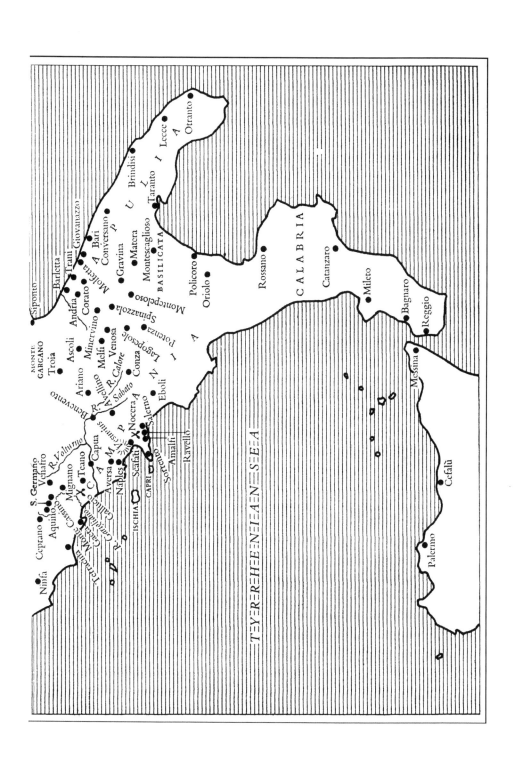

Otranto

Lecce

Brindisi

Taranto

Giovanazzo
Bari
Conversano
Trani
Gravina
Matera
Montescaglioso
BASILICATA
Barletta
Corato
Policoro
Molfetta
Siponto
Andria
Oriolo
Minervino
Spinazzola
Ascoli
Potenza
Montepeloso
Troia
MONTE
GARGANO
Melfi
Venosa
Lagopesole
Ariano
Conza
Benevento
R. Calore
Avellino R. Sabato
Eboli
Noccra
Salerno
S. Germano
Venafro
R. Volturno
Scafati
Amalfi
Mignano
Teano
Capua
Ravello
Aquino
Aversa
Sorrento
Ninfa
Ceprano
Monte Cassino
Cancello
Naples
CAPRI
ISCHIA
Terracina
R. Garigliano

Rossano

CALABRIA

Catanzaro

Mileto

Bagnaro

Reggio

Messina

Cefalù

Palermo

TYRRHENIAN SEA

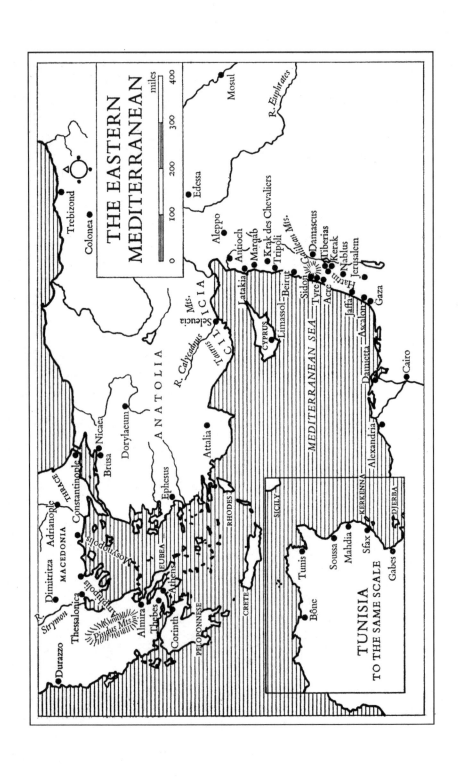

THE EASTERN
MEDITERRANEAN

miles

0   100   200   300   400

TUNISIA
TO THE SAME SCALE

Appendix

THE NORMAN MONUMENTS OF SICILY

A complete list of all the Norman buildings still extant in Sicily is not easy to draw up. Hardly any of them has escaped the attention of restorers or rebuilders at some time or another, often to the point where—as in the outside of the Martorana or the inside of Palermo Cathedral—the original character has been completely lost. I have also ruefully to admit that there remain a few places on the list which I have not visited myself. Usually the invaluable guide-book of the *Touring Club d'Italia* has been able to help me out, but in one or two cases I have had to rely on sketchier and less authoritative accounts. For the sake of completeness, too, I have added four items —identified with a question mark—which may be wholly or partly of Norman origin but can only be classified as doubtful. For the remainder I have adopted the following categories:

   ***The loveliest and best. Worth going to Sicily to see.
   **Memorable.
    *Buildings which have on the whole retained their original appearance and character.
Unstarred—Buildings which have been largely restored or rebuilt. They may be beautiful, but are no longer essentially Norman in feeling.

?AIDONE S. Maria la Cava.

?AIDONE Torre di S. Michele.

ALTARELLO See Palermo.

*ALTAVILLA MÍLICIA S. Michele, known as the Chiesazza. The ruins of a small church built by Robert Guiscard in 1077, about 25 km from Palermo, just off the main coast road to Cefalù. Below it the little *Ponte Saraceno* may go back to the Arab occupation.

*ALTOFONTE Formerly the Parco (see p. 157). The royal palace has gone, but the little chapel behind the *Chiesa Madre* is still standing, though restored.

*BURGIO S. Maria di Rifesi.

*CALTABELLOTTA The *Chiesa Madre* and the castle tower. (See p. 385n.)

*CALTANISSETTA The Badia di S. Spirito was consecrated in 1153; the frescoes are of the fourteenth and fifteenth centuries.

**CASTELVETRANO The little twelfth-century church of the SS. Trinità di Delia is a gem—the perfect fusion of Arab and Byzantine. About two miles outside the town to the west.

CATANIA Of the basically baroque cathedral, only the Norman apses of black lava withstood the earthquakes of 1169 and 1693. The best view of them is from the courtyard of the seminary behind the cathedral (Via Vittorio Emmanuele). Inside, the two Norman chapels, the Cappella della Vergine and the Cappella del Crocifisso, are barely recognisable.

***CEFALÙ CATHEDRAL Though much of the inside is now distressingly baroque, the outside is exquisite and the great apse mosaic the most sublime masterpiece Sicily has to offer. (See pp. 13–15.)

CEFALÙ The Osterio Magno; a few remains of Roger II's palace, on the corner of the Corso Ruggero and the Via G. Amendola.

?ERICE S. Ippolito.

**FORZA D'AGRÒ A few kilometres outside the town, SS. Pietro e Paolo is one of the most important Basilian churches on the island. The inscription over the west door dates it to 1171–72.

*FRAZZANÒ The Basilian abbey of S. Filippo di Fragalà was built by Count Roger I in the late eleventh century.

*GRATTERI S. Giorgio.

ITÁLA S. Pietro.

*MANIACE S. Maria di Maniace. (See p. 300.)

*MAZARA Ruins of Roger I's castle, 1073.

*MAZARA S. Nicolò Regale, or S. Nicolicchio, twelfth century.

*MAZARA Just outside the town to the east is the church of the Madonna dell' Alto or S. Maria delle Giummare, built in 1103 by a daughter of Roger I.

MAZARA In the cathedral, begun by Roger I in 1073, traces of Norman work can still be seen in the apse.

*MESSINA The church of the Annunziata dei Catalani is beautiful, though now so restored as to be virtually rebuilt. Parts of the apse are original.

*MESSINA The Cathedral is aptly described by Christopher Kininmonth as 'a post-war reconstruction of the post-earthquake reconstruction of the Norman original'. Little, if any, of the original

Matthew of Ajello: above, embracing his wives; below,
bathing his feet in the blood of a Muslim child (Peter of
Eboli MS.)

Palermo: the Cathedral from the south

Palermo: the interior of S. Spirito—'the church of the Vespers'

Henry VI receives emissaries from Palermo while Queen Sibylla bewails her
fallen crown. Below: Henry makes his triumphal entry into Palermo.
(Peter of Eboli MS.)

work remains; but it merits inclusion in this list since it is a purely Norman church and a very beautiful one, and tells the visitor as much about Norman-Sicilian architecture as anything on the island. The sculptured slab from Richard Palmer's tomb has, unaccountably, survived almost intact.

?MESSINA La Badiazza.

*MILI S. PIETRO The little church of S. Maria was founded for Basilian monks by Roger I in 1082. Here, too, Roger's bastard son Jordan was buried in 1091. (See *The Normans in the South*, p. 281 n.)

***MONREALE Cathedral and Cloister. (See pp. 316–22.)

*MONREALE The twelfth-century *Castellaccio* stands on the summit of Monte Caputo and commands a sensational view of the Conca d'Oro.

*MONREALE Remains of William II's palace can be seen in the courtyard of the seminary at No. 1, Via Arcivescovado.

***PALERMO In the Royal Palace (the exterior of which, gloomy as it is, merits two stars on its own account) are to be found two of the most stunningly beautiful things in Sicily; the Palatine Chapel and the so-called *Sala di Ruggero*. (See pp. 72–7 and 241–2 respectively.)

***PALERMO S. Maria dell' Ammiraglio, popularly known as the Martorana. (See pp. 93–9.)

**PALERMO S. Giovanni degli Eremiti. (See pp. 88–90.)

**PALERMO S. Spirito, the church of the Vespers. (See p. 363.)

**PALERMO The Royal tombs of Roger II, Henry VI, Constance and Frederick II in the cathedral. (See pp. 389–90.)

*PALERMO S. Giovanni dei Lebbrosi, one of the earliest Norman churches on the island. (See *The Normans in the South*, p. 178 n.)

*PALERMO S. Cataldo. (See p. 216n.)

*PALMERO The Cathedral. (See pp. 362–3.)

*PALERMO SS. Trinità (La Magione). (See p. 254n.)

*PALERMO The Zisa. (See pp. 239–41.)

*PALERMO The Cuba, Cubula and Cuba Soprana. (See p. 354n.)

*PALERMO The Ponte del Ammiraglio. (See pp. 155–6.)

*PALERMO S. Cristina, another foundation of Walter of the Mill.

*PALERMO La Maddalena, a twelfth-century church in the courtyard of the Carabinieri barracks next to the Porta Nuova.

*PALERMO S. Maria della Speranza.

*PALERMO The Castello della Favara, otherwise known as Mare-dolce. (See pp. 156–7.)

PALERMO The Cappella dell' Incoronata behind the Cathedral.

PALERMO In the suburb of Altarello, the Palazzo dell' Uscibene was formerly the royal hunting-lodge of Mimnermo. (See p. 169.)

PALERMO For the sake of completeness, a brief mention should be made of the remains of some Norman work in the tower of the Palazzo Conte Federico. Pedants might also include a house known as the Casa Martorana and one in the Via Protonotaro; but both of these were badly damaged during the last war and hardly anything remains of the mediaeval structure.

*PATERNÒ The Castello was built by Roger I in 1073. It has been much restored but is still worth a visit. Ask at the Municipio for the keys.

PATTI The cathedral is of Norman origin, though there is little enough to show for it now—except the tomb of Roger II's mother Queen Adelaide. (See *The Normans in the South*, p. 289 n.)

*PIAZZA ARMERINA The priory of S. Andrea, a few kilometres outside the town, was founded in 1096 by Simon, Count of Butera, cousin of Roger II. The frescoes are of the fifteenth century. (See p. 234n.)

*S. FRATELLO S. Alfio.

*S. MARCO D'ALUNZIO The church in the Badia Grande di SS. Salvatore was founded in 1176 by Queen Margaret, wife of William I.

*SCIACCA S. Nicolò.

SCIACCA Of the Cathedral, the three apses of the east end are Norman.

SCIACCA S. Maria della Giummare, though today no more than an agreeable hotch-potch, still retains traces of its Norman origins.

SYRACUSE The extraordinary cathedral contains a little Norman work, just as it contains a little of everything else.

TROINA The bell-tower of the Chiesa Matrice.

BIBLIOGRAPHY

NOTES ON THE PRINCIPAL SOURCES

Falco of Benevento

Member of one of the leading families of Benevento, a palace notary and scribe, Falco wrote a retrospective history of his own city and South Italy as a whole between 1102 and 1139. It is of interest not only for its own qualities—it is reliable, methodical, vivid, and contains much of which its author was an eyewitness—but also because it reflects the opinions of a Lombard patriot, for whom the Normans were little better than a bunch of uncivilised brigands. An Italian translation exists and is listed in the bibliography.

Alexander of Telese

Alexander, Abbot of the monastery of S. Salvatore near Telese, wrote his chronicle at the request of Matilda of Alife, half-sister of Roger II. Though ostensibly a biography of Roger, the first part is sketchy in the extreme; we are told nothing about Adelaide's regency and the account becomes interesting only from 1127, with the events leading up to the establishment of the Sicilian Kingdom. From that point until 1136, when Alexander abruptly breaks off, he becomes a valuable source—though allowance must be made for his extreme tendentiousness. For him Roger was divinely appointed to bring peace and order to the South, after meting out just punishment for earlier iniquities. Despite his cloth, the Abbot has little respect for the Pope, and even chides Honorius II for his 'insolence'. There is an Italian translation listed below.

Romuald of Salerno

Romuald Guarna, a member of the old Salernitan nobility, was archbishop of his native city from 1153 until his death in 1181. Throughout this time he played a leading rôle in the political life of the Kingdom, both in Sicily and on the mainland, in domestic and foreign affairs. He was one of the negotiators of the Treaty of Benevento; later he was implicated in the plot against Maio of Bari and was largely responsible for the rescue of William I during the 1161 uprising. Under William II—whose coronation he performed—he represented Sicily at the signing of the Treaty of Venice. His *Chronicon sive Annales*, which begins with the Creation and continues till 1178, is one of the most important sources in existence for the period covered by this book. It would have been more valuable still if Romuald had only been more impartial and less discreet. As it is, he consistently exaggerates his own part in the events he records and minimises that of others. Matters in which he is not directly involved—or those in which he or his friends do not show to particular advantage—he tends to leave out altogether. The work has never been translated into English or French; an Italian translation is listed below.

Hugo Falcandus

Everything, as Chalandon points out, that relates to Falcandus is a mystery; even his name is in doubt. The most distinguished living English scholar of the period, Miss Evelyn Jamison, has cogently argued—in a book listed below—that he is to be identified with Eugenius, a politician and scholar who was appointed Admiral of the Kingdom in 1190. The *Liber de Regno Sicilie* covers only the period from 1154 to 1169. It has little to say of Sicilian foreign policy; but as a picture of the social life and the political intrigues of Palermo during a particularly troubled time, it is a masterpiece. The author needs no more than a couple of lines to transform a name into a character; his eye for the significant detail is unerring. In the art of making his story live, none of the other sources with whom we have had to deal can hold a candle to him—except, perhaps, Amatus of Monte Cassino; but whereas Amatus is a *naif*, Falcandus is a polished and sophisticated man of letters. His great defect is his tendentiousness, and his bitter, almost universal contempt for those around him. For him, every man is a villain; for every action, the worst motives are unfailingly ascribed. Just how accurate he is we have no means of telling; checks are seldom possible, since no other chronicle covers the period in anything like such detail. But he certainly makes splendid reading. It seems almost incredible that a writer who has been compared to Tacitus and Thucydides should never have been translated into English or French; the only version I have been able to find is del Re's Italian one, written in so convoluted a style that Falcandus's elegant Latin is often easier to read.

Peter of Eboli

Peter of Eboli's long poem, the *Carmen de Rebus Siculis,* gives us a detailed account of the last days of the Sicilian Kingdom, from the death of William the Good to the arrival of Henry VI. As with Falcandus, his reliability as a historian is diminished by his hatred—in this case for Tancred of Lecce, his family and his adherents. His facts can all too seldom be checked against other sources, and when they can they are not always found to be accurate. On the other hand he appears to have lived at the court of Henry VI, so that he must have been better placed than most people to see what went on. Here is another work that cries out for a good modern translation; for the moment, none exists. When it appears—as some day it must—we can only hope that it will include reproductions of the delightful and often brilliantly witty drawings with which Peter has embellished his text. Four of them are reproduced in this book.

I. ORIGINAL SOURCES

1. *Collections of Sources*

(The abbreviations used elsewhere in this bibliography and in the footnotes follow each entry in parentheses.)

AMARI, M. *Biblioteca Arabo-Sicula*. Versione Italiana. 2 vols. Turin and Rome, 1880–81. (*B.A.S.*)

Archivio Storico Siciliano. (*A.S.S.*)

BOUQUET, M. *et al. Recueil des historiens des Gaules et de la France*. 23 vols. Paris, 1738–1876. New Series, Paris, 1899– (in progress). (*R.H.F.*)

CARUSO, G. B. *Bibliotheca Historica Regni Siciliae*. 2 vols. Palermo, 1723. (*C.B.H.*)

Corpus Scriptorum Historiae Byzantinae. Bonn, 1828–97. (*C.S.H.B.*)

GRAEVIUS, J. C. *Thesaurus antiquitatum et historiarum Italiae, Neapolis, Siciliae, Sardiniae, Corsicae, Melitae, atque adj. terrarum insularumque*. 10 vols. in 45 fol. Leyden, 1704–25. (Vol. X, which is so called only in the general index, is that specifically relative to Sicily and has 15 parts.) (*G.T.A.*)

GUIZOT, F. *Collection des Mémoires Relatifs à l'Histoire de France*. 29 vols. Paris, 1823–27. (*G.M.H.F.*)

JAFFÉ, P. *Bibliotheca Rerum Germanicarum*. 6 vols. Berlin, 1864–73. (*J.B.R.G.*)

—— *Regesta Pontificum Romanorum ab cond. Eccl. ad a. 1198*. 2nd edn., 2 vols. Leipzig, 1885–88. (*J.R.P.R.*)

Liber Pontificalis, ed. L. Duchesne. 2 vols. Paris, 1886–92. (*L.P.*)

MIGNE, J. P. *Patrologia Latina*. 221 vols. Paris, 1844–55. (*M.P.L.*)

Monumenta Bambergensa, ed. Jaffé. *J.B.R.G.*, vol. V.

Monumenta Germaniae Historica, ed. G. H. Pertz, T. Mommsen *et al.* Hanover, 1826– (in progress). (*M.G.H.*)

Monumenta Gregoriana, ed. Jaffé. *J.B.R.G.*, vol. II.

MURATORI, L. A. *Rerum Italicarum Scriptores*. 25 vols in 28. Milan, 1723–51. New Series, ed. G. Carducci and V. Fiorini. Città di Castello—Bologna, 1900– (in progress). (*R.I.S.*)

RE, G. DEL *Cronisti e Scrittori Sincroni della Dominazione Normanna nel Regno di Puglia e Sicilia*. 2 vols. Naples, 1845, 1868. (*R.C.S.S.*)

Recueil des Historiens des Croisades. Publ. Académie des Inscriptions et Belles Lettres. Paris, 1841–1906. *Historiens Occidentaux,* 5 vols. (*R.H.C.Occ.*) *Historiens Orientaux,* 5 vols. (*R.H.C.Or.*)

STUBBS, W. *Select Charters.* Oxford, 1870. (*S.C.*)

WATTERICH, J. M. *Pontificum Romanorum qui fuerunt inde ab exeunte saeculo IX usque finem saeculi XIII vitae ab aequalibus conscriptae.* 2 vols. Leipzig, 1862. (*W.P.R.*)

2. *Individual Sources*

ABU SHAMA, Shihab ed-Din Abdul-Rahman ibn Ismail, *Book of the Two Gardens.* Extracts, with French tr., in R.*H.C.Or.*, vols IV–V.

AL-EDRISI, Abu Abdullah Mohammed, *Géographie d'Edrisi,* tr. A. Jaubert. 2 vols. Paris, 1836. (Vols V and VI of *Recueil de Voyages et de Mémoires,* published by the Société de Géographie.)

ALEXANDER OF TELESE *Rogerii Regis Siciliae Rerum Gestarum Libri IV.* In R.*C.S.S.*, vol. II (with Italian tr.).

AL-MAQRISI *Histoire d'Egypte.* French tr. by E. Blochet. Paris, 1908.

AL-MARRAKESHI *Histoire des Almohades.* French tr. by E. Fagnan. Algiers, 1893.

AMBROISE *L'Estoire de la Guerre Sainte.* Ed. and tr. into modern French by Gaston Paris. Paris, 1897. English tr. and notes by M. J. Hubert and J. L. La Monte. New York, 1941.

Annales Barenses. In *M.G.H. Scriptores,* vol. V.

Annales Beneventani. In *M.G.H. Scriptores,* vol. III.

Annales Casinenses. In *M.G.H. Scriptores,* vol. XIX.

ANNALISTA SAXO In *M.G.H. Scriptores,* vol. VI.

ANONYMUS VATICANUS *Historia Sicula.* In R.*I.S.*, vol. VIII.

ARNOLD OF LUBECK *Chronica Slavorum.* Ed. Lappenburg. In *M.G.H. Scriptores,* vol. XXI.

ARNULF OF LISIEUX *Letters.* In *M.P.L.*, vol. 201.

—— *Tractatus de Schismate orto post Honorii II Papae decessum.* In *M.P.L.*, vol. 201.

BECKET, ST THOMAS *Epistolae.* In *M.P.L.*, vol. 190. See also in *Materials for the History of Becket,* ed. J. C. Robertson, vols. V–VII. (Rolls Series, 67, 1875–85).

BENEDICT OF PETERBOROUGH *Chronicle of the Reigns of Henry II and Richard I, transcribed by the order of B. of P.* Ed. Stubbs, Rolls Series, vol. 49, London 1867. (Now established as the work of Roger of Hoveden, *q.v.*)

BENJAMIN OF TUDELA *Itinerary.* Tr. with notes by M. N. Adler. London, 1907.

BERNARD OF CLAIRVAUX, ST *Vita Prima* and *Acta.* In *M.P.L.*, vol. 185.

—— *Life and Works.* Ed. J. Mabillon; tr. with notes by S. J. Eales. Vols. I–IV, London, 1889–96.

BERNARD OF CLAIRVAUX *Epistolae*. In *M.P.L.*, vol. 182. English tr. by B. Scott James, London, 1953.

BOSO *Vita Adriani*. (Incorporated in the *Liber Censuum*.) In *L.P.*, vol. II.
—— *Vita Alexandri*. In *L.P.*, vol. II.

CINNAMUS, JOHN Ἐπιτομή. In *C.S.H.B.*, ed. Meineke, with Latin tr.

DANTE. *The Divine Comedy*, translated by G. Bickersteth, Oxford, 1965.

DICETO, RADULPHUS DE *Opera Historica*. In *M.G.H. Scriptores*, vol. XXVII. (Also Rolls Series, 68, i and ii.)

EUSTATHIUS OF THESSALONICA *De Thessalonica a Latinis capta, a. 1185*. Ed. Bekker. In *C.S.H.B.* German tr. by H. Hunger, Vienna, 1955.

FALCANDUS, HUGO *Historia*, or *Liber de Regno Sicilie*, with *Epistola ad Petrum Panormitane Ecclesie Thesauriarium*. Ed. Siragusa, Rome 1897. In *R.C.S.S.*, vol. I with Italian tr.

FALCO OF BENEVENTO *Chronicon*. In *R.C.S.S.*, vol. I, with Italian tr.

GERHOH OF REICHENSBURG. *De Investigatione Antichristi*. In M.G.H., *Libelli de Lite Imperatorum et Pontificum Saeculis XI et XII*. Vol. III. Hanover, 1897.

Gesta Henrici II et Ricardi I. Ed. Liebermann. In *M.G.H. Scriptores*, vol. XXVII.

GODFREY OF VITERBO *Pantheon, Gesta Friderici,* and *Gesta Henrici VI Imperatoris*. Ed. Waitz. In *M.G.H. Scriptores*, vol. XXII.

HELMOLD *Chronica Slavorum*. In *M.G.H. Scriptores*, vol. XXI.

Historia Welforum Weingartensis. Ed. Weiland. In *M.G.H. Scriptores*, vol. XXI.

IBN ABI DINAR *Kitab al-Munis*. Ed. with Italian tr. by M. Amari. In *B.A.S.*

IBN AL-ATHIR *Kamel al Tawarikh*. Ed. with Italian tr. by M. Amari. In *B.A.S.*

IBN JUBAIR *The Travels of Ibn Jubair*. Tr. R. J. C. Broadhurst. London, 1952.

IBN KHALDUN *Kitab al Ibr*. Italian tr. of relevant passages by M. Amari in *B.A.S.*

Ignoti Monachi Cisterciensis S. Mariae de Ferraria Chronica. Ed. Gaudenzi. Società Napoletana di Storia Patria; *Monumenti Storici, Seria Prima, Cronache*. Naples, 1888.

INNOCENT II, POPE *Epistolae*. In *M.P.L.*, vol. 179.

Itinerarium Peregrinorum et Gesta Regis Ricardi. Ed. Stubbs. Rolls Series, 38, i. London, 1864.

JOHN OF HEXHAM *Historia*. In *M.G.H. Scriptores*, vol. XXVII. English tr. by J. Stevenson in *The Church Historians of England*, vol. IV, i. London, 1856.

JOHN OF SALISBURY *Historia Pontificalis*. Ed. with tr. by M. Chibnall. London, 1956.

JOHN OF SALISBURY *Policraticus*. In *M.P.L.*, vol. 199; also ed. with notes by C. C. I. Webb, 2 vols. Oxford, 1909. Partial tr. by J. Dickinson, New York, 1927, and J. B. Pike, Minneapolis, 1938.

—— *Letters*. Ed. with tr. by W. J. Millor, S. J., and H. E. Butler. Vol. I, London, 1955.

Kaiserchronik. In *M.G.H.*, *Deutsche Chroniken*, vol. I.

LANGTOFT, PETER OF. *Chronicle*. Ed. Wright, with English tr. 2 vols. London, 1868.

MORENA, OTTO and ACERBUS *Geschichtswerk des Otto Morena und seiner Fortsetzer über die Taten Friedrichs I in der Lombardei*. Ed. F. Güterbock. In *M.G.H. Scriptores*, New Series, vol. VII.

NICETAS CHONIATES *Historia*. In *C.S.H.B.* French tr. by Cousin in *Histoire de Constantinople*, vol. V. Paris, 1685.

NIGER, RADULPHUS *Chronica Universalis*. In *M.G.H. Scriptores*, vol. XXVII.

ODO OF DEUIL *De Profectione Ludovici VII in Orientem*. Ed. Waquet. Paris, 1949.

ORDERICUS VITALIS *The Ecclesiastical History of England and Normandy*. Tr. with notes by T. Forester. 4 vols. London, 1854.

OTTO OF FREISING *Chronica, sive historia de duabus civitatibus*. In *M.G.H. Scriptores*, vol. XX. English tr. by C. C. Mierow, New York, 1928.

—— *Gesta Friderici Imperatoris, cum continuatione Rahewini*. Ed. Wilmans. In *M.G.H. Scriptores*, vol. XX. English tr. by C. C. Mierow, New York, 1953.

OTTO OF ST BLAISE *Chronica*. In *M.G.H. Scriptores*, in usum scholarum, 1912.

PETER OF BLOIS *Epistolae*. In *M.P.L.*, vol. 207.

PETER THE VENERABLE OF CLUNY *Epistolae*. In *M.P.L.* vol. 189.

PETER THE DEACON *Chronicon Monasterii Casinensis*. Ed. W. Wattenbach. In *M.G.H. Scriptores*, vol. VII of *M.P.L.*, vol. 173.

PETER OF EBOLI *Carmen de Rebus Siculis*. In *R.I.S.*, vol. XXXI, i, 1904.

RADEWIN, RAGEWIN, RAHEWIN See OTTO OF FREISING.

RICHARD FITZNIGEL *Dialogus de Scaccario*. In *S.C.*

RICHARD OF S. GERMANO *Chronicon Regni Siciliae*. In *R.I.S.*, vol. VII.

ROBERT OF TORIGNI *Chronicle*. Ed. Delisle. Société de l'Histoire de Normandie, Rouen, 1873.

ROGER OF HOVEDEN *Annals*. Tr. H. T. Riley. 2 vols. London, 1853. (See also BENEDICT OF PETERBOROUGH)

ROMUALD OF SALERNO *Chronicon*. In *R.I.S.*, vol. VII. Italian tr. in R.C.S.S.

Rouleaux de Cluny ed. Huillard-Bréholles. In *Notices et Extraits des Manuscrits de la Bibliothèque Impériale*, vol. XXI. Paris, 1868.

WIBALD OF STAVELOT *Epistolae*. In *J.B.R.G.* vol. I—*Monumenta Corbeiensia*.

II. MODERN WORKS

AMARI, M. *Epigrafi Arabiche di Sicilia, tradotte e illustrate.* Palermo, 1875–85.

BELOCH, J. *Bevölkerungsgeschichte Italiens,* vol. I. Berlin and Leipzig, 1937.

BERAUD-VILLARS, J. *Les Normands en Méditerranée.* Paris, 1951.

BERNHARDI, W. *Lothar von Supplinburg. (Jahrbücher der Deutschen Geschichte.)* Leipzig, 1879.

——*Konrad III. (Jahrbücher der Deutschen Geschichte.)* 2 vols. Leipzig, 1883.

BERTAUX, E. *L'Art dans l'Italie Méridionale.* Paris, 1903.

—— 'L'Email de St Nicholas de Bari'. In Fondation E. Piot, *Monuments et Mémoires,* pub. by the Académie des Inscriptions, vol. VI, 1899.

BOECKLER, A. *Die Bronzetüren des Bonanus von Pisa und des Barisanus von Trani.* Berlin, 1953.

BIAGI, L. *Palermo.* Istituto Italiano d'Arti Grafiche, Bergamo, 1929.

BLOCH, H. 'The Schism of Anacletus II and the Glanfeuil Forgeries of Peter the Deacon of Monte Cassino', *Traditio,* vol. VIII, 1952. (Fordham University.)

BRANDILEONE, F. *Il Diritto Romano nelle Legge Normanne e Sueve del Regno di Sicilia.* Turin, 1884.

BREQUIGNY, L. DE 'Mémoire sur Etienne, chancelier de Sicile', *Mémoires de l'Académie des Inscriptions,* vol. XLI, Paris, 1780.

BUFFIER, C. *Historie de l'origine du Royaume de Sicile et de Naples, contenant les avantures et les conquestes des princes normands qui l'ont établi.* 2 vols. Paris, 1701.

Cambridge Medieval History 8 vols. Cambridge, 1911–36.

CARAVALE, M. *Il Regno Normanno di Sicilia.* Rome, 1966.

CARINI, I. *Una pergamena sulla fondazione del Duomo di Cefalù.* In *A.S.S.,* New Series, vol. VII, 1883.

CASPAR, E. *Roger II und die Gründung der Normannisch-sicilischen Monarchie.* Innsbruck, 1904.

CERONE, F. *L'Opera politica e militare di Ruggero II in Africa ed in Oriente.* Catania, 1913.

CHALANDON, F. *Jean II Comnène et Manuel I Comnène.* (Vol. II of *Etudes sur l'Empire Byzantin au XIe. et au XIIe. siècles*). 2 vols. Paris, 1912. Republished New York, 1960.

—— *Histoire de la Domination Normande en Italie et en Sicile.* 2 vols. Paris, 1907. Republished New York, 1960.

COHN, W. *Die Geschichte der Normannisch-sicilischen Flotte unter der Regierung Rogers I und Rogers II 1060–1154.* Breslau, 1910.

CONIGLIO, G. *Amalfi e il commercio amalfitano.* Nuova Rivista Storica 28/9, 1944/5.

CURTIS, E. *Roger of Sicily.* New York, 1912.

DEER, J. *The Dynastic Porphyry Tombs of the Norman Period in Sicily,* tr.

G. A. Gillhoff. Dumbarton Oaks Studies No. V, Cambridge, Mass., 1959.

DEER, J. *Der Kaiserornat Friedrichs II.* Berne, 1952.

DEMUS, O. *The Mosaics of Norman Sicily.* London, 1950.

Dictionary of National Biography.

Dictionnaire de Théologie Catholique ed. Vacant and Mangenot. 9 vols in 15. Paris, 1926–50.

Dictionnaire d'Histoire et de Géographie Ecclésiastiques ed. Baudrillart. Paris. (In progress.)

DIEHL, C. *Figures Byzantines.* 2 vols. Paris, 1906–8.

DOUGLAS, D. C. *The Norman Achievement,* London, 1969.

Enciclopedia Italiana.

Encyclopaedia Britannica 11th edn.

Encyclopaedia of Islam London and Leyden, 1913–38. (New edn. now in progress).

EPIFANIO, U. *Ruggero II e Filippo di Al Mahdiah.* In *A.S.S.,* New Series, vol. XXX.

GABRIELI, F. 'Arabi di Sicilia e Arabi di Spagna', *Al-Andalus,* XV, 1950.

—— *Storia e civiltà musulmana.* Naples, 1947.

GALASSO, G. *Il commercio amalfitano nel periodo normanno.* Studi in onore di Riccardo Filangieri, I, Naples, 1959.

GAROFALO, A. *Tabularium Regiae ac Imperialis Capellae Collegiatae Divi Petri in Regio Panormitano Palatio.* Palermo, 1835.

GARUFI, C. A. *Per la storia dei monasteri di Sicilia del tempo normanno. Archivio Storico per la Sicilia,* VI, 1940.

GIBBON, E. *Decline and Fall of the Roman Empire,* ed. J. B. Bury. 7 vols. London, 1896.

GIUNTA, F. *Bizantini e Bizantinismo nella Sicilia Normanna,* Palermo, 1950.

GREGOROVIUS, F. *History of the City of Rome in the Middle Ages,* tr. A. Hamilton. 8 vols in 13. London, 1894–1902.

GREEN, M. A. E. *Lives of the Princesses of England,* vol. I. London, 1849.

HARE, AUGUSTUS. *Cities of Southern Italy and Sicily.* London, 1883.

HARTWIG, O. *Re Guglielmo e il suo grande ammiraglio Majone di Bari.* In *Archivio Storico per le provincie napoletane,* VIII, Naples, 1883.

HASKINS, C. H. *Norman Institutions, 1035–1189.* Harvard Historical Studies, 24. Cambridge, Mass., 1913.

—— 'England and Sicily in the twelfth century', *English Historical Review,* July and October, 1911.

HOLTZMANN, W. *Papst-, Kaiser- und Normannenurkunden aus Unteritalien:* in *Quellen und Forschungen aus italienischen Archiven und Bibliotheken,* 35, 36. Rome, 1955.

HUILLARD-BREHOLLES, J. L. A. *Recherches sur les Monuments et l'Histoire des Normands et de la Maison de Souabe dans l'Italie méridionale.* Paris, 1844.

INVEGES, A. *Annali della Felice Città di Palermo.* 3 vols. Palermo, 1651.

JAMISON, E. 'The Sicilian-Norman Kingdom in the Mind of Anglo-Norman Contemporaries', *British Academy papers*, XXIV, 1938.

—— 'The Norman Administration of Apulia and Capua, especially under Roger II and William I, 1127–66', *Papers of the British School at Rome*, VI, 1913.

—— *Admiral Eugenius of Sicily, his life and work, and the authorship of the Epistola ad Petrum and the Historia Hugonis Falcandi Siculi.* London, 1957. (Reviewed by L. T. White, *q.v.*)

KANTOROWICZ, E. *Frederick the Second*, tr. E. O. Lorimer, London, 1931.

KEHR, K. A. *Die Urkunden der Normannisch-sicilischen Könige.* Innsbruck, 1902.

KEHR, P. *Italia Pontificia,* vol. VIII. Berlin, 1935.

KEHR, P. 'Die Belehnungen der Süditalienischen Normannenfürsten durch die Päpste, 1059–1192', *Abhandlungen der preussischen Akademie der Wissenschaften*, Phil.-hist. Kl., 1934, No. 1.

KELLY, A. *Eleanor of Aquitaine and the Four Kings.* Cambridge, Mass., 1950.

KININMONTH, C. *Sicily.* Travellers' Guides. London, 1965.

KITZINGER, E. *I Mosaici di Monreale,* tr. F. Bonajuto. Palermo, 1960.

KNIGHT, H. GALLY *The Normans in Sicily.* London, 1838.

KRÖNIG, W. *Il Duomo di Monreale e l'Architettura Normanna in Sicilia.* Palermo, 1965.

LA LUMIA, I. *Storia della Sicilia sotto Guglielmo il Buono.* Florence, 1867.

—— *Studi di Storia Siciliana.* 2 vols. Palermo, 1870.

LAMMA, P. *Comneni e Staufer. Ricerche sui Rapporti fra Bisanzio e l'Occidente nel Secolo XII.* Rome, 1955.

LOPEZ, R. S. See SETTON, K. M.

MACK SMITH, D. *Medieval Sicily.* (Vol. II of *A History of Sicily.*) London, 1968.

MANN, H. K. *The Lives of the Popes in the Middle Ages.* Vols. 6–12. London, 1910–15.

MARONGIU, A. 'A Model State in the Middle Ages: the Norman and Swabian Kingdom of Sicily', *Comparative Studies in Society and History*, vol. VI, 1963–4. (See also STRAYER, J. R.)

—— 'Lo Spirito della Monarchia Normanna di Sicilia nell' allocuzione di Ruggero II ai suoi grandi', *Archivio Storico Siciliano*, Ser. 3–4, 1950–51.

MENAGER, L. R. *Amiratus—Αμηρᾶς—L'Emirat et les origines de l'Amirauté (XIe.–XIIe. s.).* Paris, 1960.

MASSON, G. *The Companion Guide to Rome.* London, 1965.

MEO, A. DI *Annali Critico-Diplomatici del Regno di Napoli della Mezzana Età.* 12 vols. Naples, 1795–1819.

MICHAUD, J. F. *Histoire des Croisades.* 10 vols in 5. Brussels, 1841.

MONNERET DE VILLARD, U. *Le Pitture Musulmane al Soffitto della Cappella Palatina di Palermo.* Rome, 1950.

MONTI, G. M. *L'Espansione Mediterranea del Mezzogiorno d'Italia e della Sicilia.* Bologna, 1942.

—— *L'Italia e le Crociate in Terra Santa.* Naples, 1940.

MOR, C. G. 'Roger II et les assemblées du royaume normand dans l'Italie méridionale', *Revue Historique de Droit Français et Etranger.* Sér. 4, 36, 1958.

MUNZ, P. *Frederick Barbarossa, A Study in Medieval Politics.* London, 1969.

NATALE, F. *Avviamento allo studio del medio evo siciliano.* Pub. by the Istituto di Storia Medioevale e Moderna dell' Università di Messina, fasc. 2. Florence, 1959.

New Catholic Encyclopaedia. Washington, 1967.

NIESE, H. *Die Gesetzgebung der normannischen Dynastie im 'Regnum Siciliae'.* Halle, 1910.

OSTROGORSKY, G. *History of the Byzantine State,* tr. J. M. Hussey. Oxford, 1956.

PALMAROCCHI, R. *L'Abbazia di Montecassino e la Conquista Normanna.* Rome, 1913.

PARKER, J. S. F. 'The attempted Byzantine alliance with the Sicilian Norman Kingdom, 1166–7', in *Essays Presented to Miss E. Jamison. Papers of the British School at Rome,* XXIV, 1955.

PEPE, G. *I Normanni in Italia Meridionale, 1166–1194.* Bari, 1964.

PIETRAGANZILI, R. S. DI 'Gli osteri di Cefalù', *Sicilia Artistica ed Archeologica,* Palermo, July 1887.

—— 'La Leggenda della tempesta e il voto del Re Ruggero per la costruzione del Duomo di Cefalù', *Sicilia Artistica ed Archeologica,* Palermo, June–July, 1888.

PIRRO, R. *Sicilia Sacra.* In *G.T.A.,* vol. X, ii, iii.

PONTIERI, E. *Tra i Normanni nell' Italia Meridionale.* Revised edn., Naples, 1964.

PROLOGO, A. DI G. *Le Carte chi si conservano nello Archivio del Capitolo Metropolitano della Città di Trani (Dal IX secolo fino all' anno 1266).* Barletta, 1877.

RASSOW, P. *Zum byzantinisch-normannischen Krieg 1147–9: Mitteilungen des österreichischen Instituts für Geschichtsforschung,* 62, 1954.

RENAN, E. *Vingt Jours en Sicile.* In *Mélanges d'Histoire et de Voyages.* Paris, 1878.

RUNCIMAN, S. *History of the Crusades.* 3 vols. Cambridge, 1954.

SCHRAMM, P. E. *Herrschaftszeichen und Staatssymbolik: Beiträge zu ihrer Geschichte vom 3. bis zum 16. Jahrhundert.* 3 vols. Stuttgart, 1954.

SETTON, K. M. (editor-in-chief) *A History of the Crusades.* See in particular sections by R. S. Lopez and H. Wieruszowski. 2nd edn. by University of Wisconsin Press, vols. I and II, 1969.

SIRAGUSA, G. B. *Il Regno di Guglielmo I in Sicilia.* 2nd edn. Palermo, 1929.

STEFANO, A. DE *La Cultura in Sicilia nel periodo normanno.* 1932.

STEFANO, G. DI *Monumenti della Sicilia normanna.* Palermo, 1955.

STRAYER, J. R. Comment on A. Marongiù's article 'A Model State in the Middle Ages' (*q.v.*). *Comparative Studies in Society and History*, vol. VI, 1963–64.

TESTA, F. *De Vita, et rebus gestis Gulielmi II Siciliae Regis libri quatuor.* With Italian tr. by S. Sinesio. Monreale, 1769.

TOECHE, T. *Kaiser Heinrich VI. (Jahrbücher der deutschen Geschichte.)* Leipzig, 1867.

TOSTI, L. *Storia della Badia di Monte-Cassino.* 3 vols. Naples, 1842.

TOURING CLUB ITALIANO. *Sicilia.* (Regional Guide.) Milan, 1953.

VACANDARD, E. *Vie de St Bernard, Abbé de Clairvaux.* 2 vols. Paris, 1895.

VALENTI, F. *Il Palazzo Reale Normanno.* Bolletino d'Arte, IV, 1924–25.

VASILIEV, A. A. *History of the Byzantine Empire, 324–1453.* Oxford, 1952.

WHITE, L. T. *Latin Monasticism in Norman Sicily.* Pub. 31 (Monograph 13), Medieval Academy of America. Cambridge, Mass., 1938.

—— Review of *Admiral Eugenius of Sicily* by E. Jamison (*q.v.*). *American Historical Review*, 63, 1957–58.

WIERUSZOWSKI, H. 'Roger II of Sicily, Rex-Tyrannus, in twelfth-century political thought', *Speculum*, 38, 1963. See also SETTON, K. M.

WILLIAMS, W. *St Bernard of Clairvaux.* Manchester, 1953.

INDEX

Falcandus, Hugo—*cont.*
  256–9, 261, 279, 284–5, 287, 297, 352,
  356, 406
Falco of Benevento, 17, 22–3, 28–9, 41,
  58–9, 65n., 66, 69, 71, 86, 405
Farfa, 56, 61
Fatimids, 163, 306
Favara, 156–7, 169, 224, 385, 404
Ferrara, 348
Flochberg, 150
Florence, 43
Florian of Camerota, Royal Justiciar, 309
Fontevrault, 311, 380n.
Forza d'Agrò, 402
Frangipani, Cencius, 109–10
Frangipani, family, 17, 26–7, 111, 119,
  266, 274, 305n.
Frazzanò, 402
Frederick I, Barbarossa, Western Em-
  peror, 127, 151; character and appear-
  ance, 173–4; 1st Italian campaign and
  coronation, 175, 177–83, 185–6, 188–9,
  196–7, 199; relations with Papacy,
  202–7; 2nd Italian campaign, 206–9;
  attitude during papal schism, 266–9; 3rd
  Italian campaign, 263, 269–74, 276;
  submits to Pope at Venice, 311–13;
  marries son Henry to Constance of
  Sicily, 323–4, 345–6, 348; on Third
  Crusade, 351, 364; death, 374; other
  references, 305, 308, 370, 389
Frederick II of Hohenstaufen, Western
  Emperor, 104, 161, 389–90
Frederick of Rotenburg, **273**
Fuga, Fernando, 363
al-Furriani, Abu al-Hassan, 210–11
al-Furriani, Omar, 210, 211n.

Gabes, 154
Gaeta, 274
Galluccio, 67–8, 87, 107
Garcia IV Ramirez, King of Navarre, 169,
  258
Garibaldi, 156n.
Garigliano, river, 44, 68, 162, 196, 375
Gaza, 350
Genoa, Genoese, 25–7, 30–1, 33, 37, 52,
  266n., 268–9, 365, 383–5
Gentile, Bishop of Agrigento, 252, 253n.,
  282, 284–6, 296–7
Geoffrey, Count of Montescaglioso, 200
George of Antioch, 11, 93–7, 130–2, 145,
  153, 155–7, 174, 201n., 392

Gerard of Bologna, Cardinal. *See* Lucius
  II, Pope
Gerhoh of Reichensburg, 264
Geza II, King of Hungary, 252
Gilbert, Count of Gravina, 217, 235,
  255–9, 269, 271, 276, 281, 283–6,
  296–7
Giovinazzo, 187, 385
Godfrey, Bishop of Langres, 128–9, 153
Godfrey of Viterbo, 151n.
Gratteri, 402
Gravina, 255, 379
Greek community, 90–3, 162, 172, 239
Gregory the Great, St, 103, 111
Gregory VII, Pope, 27, 111–12, 147, 178,
  205, 313
Gregory VIII, Pope, 351
Gregory, Cardinal (anti-Pope Victor IV),
  62, 65
Grimoald, Prince of Bari, 17, 19, 40
Grosseto, 43
Guido of Castello, Cardinal. *See* Celestine
  II, Pope
Guido of S. Pudenziana, Cardinal, 177
Guiscard, Robert. *See* Robert Guiscard
Guy of Lusignan, King of Jerusalem,
  349–50

Hadrian IV, Pope. *See* Adrian IV
Hadrian, Roman Emperor, 106
Harding, Stephen, 6
Hassan, Prince of Mahdia, 154–5
Hattin, Horns of, 349–50, 373
Hauteville. *See under Christian names*
Havelberg, **Bishop of, 40**
Helena, Roman Empress, 174
Helmold, 179n.
Henry II, 'the Holy', Western Emperor,
  151, 377
Henry III, Western Emperor, 48, 54
Henry IV, Western Emperor, 178, 205,
  313
Henry V, Western Emperor, 178
Henry VI, Western Emperor, 161, 305,
  324, 331, 346, 348, 355, 357, 361, 363,
  370, 373, 374–91
Henry I, King of England, 8, 16, 100, 170
Henry II, King of England, 141, 148, 170,
  267, 298, 303–4, 308–9, 351, 364–5, 367,
  371
Henry, Prince, son of Henry II of Eng-
  land, 310
Henry, Prince of Capua, 249, 305, 321

Robert Guiscard, Duke of Apulia—*cont.*
16, 22, 27–8, 39, 45–6, 53–4, 68, 72, 89,
111–13, 145–7, 187, 196, 230, 253n.,
325, 332, 334, 354, 386, 401
Robert of Bellême, 277
Robert of Bova, 225
Robert of Dreux, 259
Robert, Count of Loritello, 186–7, 194,
196, 202–3, 217, 235–6, 303–4, 353
Robert, Archbishop of Messina, 219,
227–8
Robert of Newburgh, 255, 259
Robert of Selby, 52–3, 108–9, 110, 146,
148, 170
Robert of Torigni, 324n.
Roger I de Hauteville, Great Count of
Sicily, 3–4, 12, 22, 72, 90–1, 125, 149,
158–9, 161–2, 200, 230, 234n., 298, 368,
379, 385n., 386, 402–4
Roger II de Hauteville, King of Sicily,
coronation, 3; background, 4–5; in
papal schism, 5, 9–10; consolidates on
mainland, 11; founds Cefalù, 11–15;
revolt of 1132, 16–24; of 1133, 28–30;
of 1134, 30–4; of 1135, 35–9; invests
sons, 40; during Lothair's invasion of
1137, 41–5, 47–55; pacification of
Regno 1137–9, 58–72; rebuilds Royal
Palace, 72–3; founds Palatine Chapel,
73–5; Assizes of Ariano, 81–6; reconciliation with Rome, 86–9; founds
S. Giovanni degli Eremiti, 88–90;
attitude to Greek community, 90–2;
portrait in Martorana, 97–9; character,
83, 98–9, 104–5, 163; administration,
99–100; patron of art and learning,
100–5; relations with papacy, 107–12;
with the two Empires, 113–16; attitude
to Second Crusade, 117–18, 121, 124–6;
attacks Greece, 129–33; meeting with
Louis VII and Eleanor, 140; bid for
hegemony in West, 143–8; makes son
William co-ruler, 148–9; North African
conquests, 153–4; treatment of Philip
of Mahdia, 157–60; death, 156, 160;
burial, 15, 160; summing-up, 161–3;
other references, 137, 139, 150, 151,
168, 169, 171, 187, 197–8, 210, 234,
244, 264, 282–3, 298, 314, 351, 356, 372,
379, 389–92, 405
Roger, Duke of Apulia, son of Roger II,
17, 36, 40, 59, 67–9, 81, 86–8, 89n., 107,
110, 148, 169, 224, 307, 357

Roger, son of William I, 191, 223, 226–7,
229, 321
Roger, Duke of Apulia, son of Tancred of
Lecce, 381
Roger, Count of Acerra, 217
Roger, Count of Andria, 311, 357–8,
361–2
Roger, Count of Ariano, 112
Roger, Count of Avellino, 387
Roger, Count of Geraci, 296
Roger of Hoveden, 309, 372n.
Roger of Plenco, 29–30
Roger, Archbishop of Reggio, 252
Roland of Siena, papal chancellor, 197,
205, 208–9, 263–6. *See also* Alexander
III, Pope
Rometta, 289
Romuald, Archbishop of Salerno, 71, 98,
110n., 140n., 153, 156–8, 160, 167, 198,
227–8, 236, 239, 243, 250, 252, 253n.,
276–7, 281n., 293, 295–7, 311–12, 332,
405
Rossano, 92, 294
Rothrud II, Count of Perche, 259
Rothrud, Archbishop of Rouen, 254–5,
259, 294, 309–10
Royal Palace, Palermo, 72–7, 220, 224–5,
228–9, 240–2, 250, 403

Sabato, river, 5
S. Agnese fuori le Mura, Rome, 26, 149n.
S. Andrea priory, Piazza Armerina, 234n.,
404
St Andrew's monastery, Rome, 111
S. Cataldo, Palermo, 94, 216n., 221n., 401
S. Fratello, 404
S. Germano, 67, 189
St Gilles, 310
S. Giorgio in Kemonia, Palermo, 90
S. Giovanni degli Eremiti, Palermo, 73,
88–90, 92, 216n., 322, 392, 403
S. Giovanni dei Lebbrosi, Palermo, 403
St John Lateran, Rome, 86, 106, 177
S. Marco d'Alunzio, 286, 404
St Mark's, Venice, 312
S. Maria del Ammiraglio, Palermo. *See*
Martorana
S. Maria di Maniace, 92, 300, 402
S. Maria del Patirion, Rossano, 92
S. Maria in Trastevere, Rome, 106
S. Maria in Turri, Rome, 272
St Nicholas, Bari, 46, 98n., 187, 195
S. Nicola of Filocastro, Calabria, 88

St Peter's, Rome, 26, 43, 64, 119, 151, 176, 178, 181, 208, 264–5, 272–3
S. Quirico, 178
S. Salvatore, Messina, 92, 358, 368
S. Spirito, Palermo, 363, 403
SS. Trinità di Delia, Castelvetrano, 216n., 392, 402
Sala di Ruggero, Royal Palace, Palermo, 228n., 241–2, 403
Saladin, Sultan, 306–7, 344, 348–52
Salerno, 17, 19, 22–4, 30, 35, 37, 51–3, 58–62, 68, 71, 87–8, 108, 151, 187, 198–9, 235–7, 243, 305, 317, 345, 376–8, 284–7
Sangro, river, 67
Saracen troops, 28–9, 52, 58
Sardinia, 25
Sarno, river, 22–3
Saviour, monastery of the (S. Salvatore), Messina, 92, 358, 368
Saxon Annalist, 46, 48
Scafati, 22
Sciacca, 385, 404
Sclavo, Roger, 234–5
Segesta, 12–13
Seleucia (Silifke), 374
Senate, Roman, 107, 110, 141, 176–7, 179–82, 209, 268, 272, 313, 381
Sens, 176, 267, 319n., 375
Sergius VII, Duke of Naples, 11, 33, 36–8, 40–1, 54, 58–9
Sfax, 155, 210–11, 213
Sibyl of Burgundy, Queen of Sicily, 149
Sibylla of Acerra, Queen of Sicily, 380, 382–3, 385–6, 388
Sichelgaita of Salerno, Duchess of Apulia, 36, 334, 386
Sicilian Vespers, 363, 385
Sidon, 350
Simon, Count of Butera, 234n., 404
Simon, Duke of Dalmatia, 46
Simon, Count of Policastro, 192
Simon, Prince of Taranto, 224–5, 227, 231, 249, 283
Simon, Royal Seneschal, 200, 216
Siponto, 46, 59, 385
Sorrento, 51
Soussa, 154
Speyer, 41, 123
Spinazzola, 384
Splügen pass, 384
Spoleto, 186
Stephen, King of England, 121

Stephen du Perche, 255, 259–62, 276–300, 303, 353, 358
Stephen, Admiral, 200–1, 216, 218
Strymon, river, 342–3
Suger, Abbot of St Denis, 121, 150–1, 153
Sutri, 178, 182, 188
Sylvester, Count of Marsico, 221, 237, 239
Syracuse, 4, 101, 133, 162, 235, 251, 253n., 304, 385, 404

Tancred, Prince of Bari, 17, 40, 89n., 148, 169
Tancred of Conversano, 17, 19. 24, 27–9, 32
Tancred, Count of Lecce, later King of Sicily, 200, 224–5, 231, 234–5, 307, 333, 344, 353, 357–9, 361–2, 366–7, 370, 372–3, 375–84, 391
Taormina, 285, 289, 372
Taranto, 224, 235–6, 283, 305, 386
Taverna, 236
Teano, 376
Termini Imerese, 222n.
Terracina, 231, 267, 274–5
Thebes, 130–1, 174
Theobald, Count of Champagne, 88, 121
Theodora, Queen of Jerusalem, 328–9, 330n.
Theodora Comnena, Byzantine Princess, 115, 137, 328
Theodosius the Great, Byzantine Emperor, 336
Theodwine of Porto, Cardinal, 144
Thessalonica, 134, 137, 334–8, 343, 345
Tiber, river, 26–7, 65, 182, 184, 274
Tiberias, 136, 349
at-Tigani, 211n., 212
Tiraz, 132, 203, 225
Tivoli, 151, 183, 188
Toledo, 104
Torcello, 15
Tortona, 177–8, 206
Trani, 10, 29, 46, 50, 70–1, 187–8, 195, 317, 385
Trapani, 331–3
Tripoli, County of, 119, 349, 352, 355
Tripoli, Libya, 125, 153, 162, 211, 213
Tristan, Bishop of Mazara, 228, 252
Troia, 10, 30, 46, 66–7, 69–72, 356, 377
Troina, 404
Tronto, river, 87, 162
Tunis, 153–4, 256
Tusculum, 140, 188, 271